D1492017

# BLOOMSBURY GUIDES TO ENGLISH LITERATURE

## Victorian Literature

The Bloomsbury Guides to English Literature

General Editor: Marion Wynne-Davies

# BLOOMSBURY GUIDES TO ENGLISH LITERATURE

## Victorian Literature

*From 1830 to 1900*
Edited by Jane Thomas

BLOOMSBURY

This edition published in 1994 by
Bloomsbury Publishing Plc
2 Soho Square, London W1V 6HB

This hardback edition produced
exclusively for The Folio Society

The moral right of the authors has been asserted.

Copyright © Bloomsbury Publishing Plc 1994

A copy of the CIP entry for this book is available from the British Library.

ISBN 0 7475 2051 8

Typeset by Hewer Text Composition Services, Edinburgh
Printed in England by Clays Ltd, St Ives plc

# Contents

# Acknowledgements

*General Editor*

Marion Wynne-Davies, Keele University

*Editor*

Jane Thomas

*Originator*

Christopher Gillie

*Authors of Essays*

Jane Thomas
Ian Clarke
Gail Cunningham
Linda R. Williams

*Contributors to Entries*

Jennifer Birkett (French literature) University of Birmingham
Claire Buck (19th-century literature) University of North London
Kathryn Burlinson (19th-century literature) Southampton University
Catherine Byron (Irish literature) Loughborough College of Art and Design
Gail Cunningham (19th-century prose) Kingston University
Alex Hughes (French literature) University of Birmingham
William Humphreys Jones (19th-century prose)
John O'Brien (French literature) University of Liverpool
Andrew Michael Roberts (19th-century prose) University of Dundee
Valerie Pedlar (Context of literature) University of Liverpool
Louise Robbins (French literature) King's College, London
Mercer Simpson (Welsh literature)
Ailbhe Smyth (Irish literature) Women's Education, Research and Resource Centre, University College, Dublin
Jane Thomas (Victorian literature) University of Hull
Linda R. Williams (Victorian poetry) Southampton University
Marion Wynne Davies (19th-century literature) Keele University

*Editorial*

*Editorial Director* Kathy Rooney
*Project Editor* Tracey Smith

# General Editor's Preface

The Bloomsbury guides to English Literature derive directly from the *Bloomsbury Guide to English Literature* (1989), and are intended for those readers who wish to look at a specific period or genre, rather than at the wide-ranging material offered in the original text. As such, the guides include material from the larger and earlier work, but they have been updated and supplemented in order to answer the requirements of their particular fields. Each individual editor has selected, edited and authored as the need arose. The acknowledgements appropriate for the individual volumes have been made in the respective editors' prefaces. As general editor I should like to thank all those who have been involved in the project, from its initial conception through to the innovative and scholarly volumes presented in this series.

Marion Wynne-Davies

# Editor's Note

*Cross References*

A liberal use of cross references has been made. In both the essays and the reference entries, names, titles and topics are frequently marked with an arrow (▷) to guide the reader to the appropriate entry in the reference section for a more detailed explanation. Cross-reference arrows appear both in the text and at the end of entries.

*Dates*

Dates after the names of people indicate their life spans, except when they follow the names of monarchs, when they show the length of the reign.

# Editor's Preface

The *Bloomsbury Guide to Victorian Literature* aims to provide a guide to, and a survey of, the literature produced during one of the most dynamic, agitated and reformatory periods in British history. The seventy years which form the substance of this study witnessed unprecedented developments in technology, industry, science and democracy, and its literature provides, amongst other things, a unique record of the effect of these changes on the lives and the consciousnesses of those most affected by them. It was an age in which sensibility gave way to protest and, eventually, despair; in which subjectivity was displaced by ethics, didacticism and finally decadence; and in which the relationship between man, woman and nature was polarized as never before.

Theorized, cultivated and indulged, the imagination now had to earn its keep. Thomas Carlyle's father regarded fiction and poetry as 'not only idle, but *false and criminal*', and Carlyle himself rejected what he saw as the philosophical aloofness, idealism and impracticality of Coleridge, Byron and Shelley, and brought the debate about art round to a question of 'utility'. The function of literature was 'to understand and record what is *true*'. Its purpose was not the ventilation of private passions but of recognizable and remedial public ills. At the same time art itself underwent a process of democratization – moving out of the hands of the aristocracy and firmly into the hands of the middle classes and particularly into the hands of middle-class women. The literary form most able to reflect the common ownership of art was not poetry but the novel, and it is the novel that dominates this period.

Although writers like Carlyle and John Stuart Mill appeared to catch and pin down the 'spirit of the age', they were more concerned with drawing up its blueprint. As Richard Stein suggests in *Victoria's Year*, their aim was to survey and classify the new, the unknown and the threatening in order to prevent it from destroying the orderly and the known. They did not describe the concerns of the age so much as produce them, and throughout the period there were counter-forces at work: from Emily Brontë's *Wuthering Heights* through Tennyson's *In Memoriam* to Wilde's *The Importance of Being Earnest* and the later novels of Henry James. These forces were to reach their apotheosis in the 'art for art's sake' movement of the 1890s, which in turn led into the revolt against mimesis that was characteristic of modernist aesthetics.

No map can hope to chart the territory in all its complexity and diversity. The purpose of this book is to indicate the 'dominant' features and, if space allows, to draw attention to others which may be of interest to the enthusiast and which may in time become equally prominent landmarks. In editing this book I have sought to do justice to the impressive contribution made by women writers to the literature of the period. For this I have drawn on the work of Claire Buck, who edited *The Bloomsbury Guide to Women's Literature*, and Angela Leighton who own guide to Victorian women poets, *Writing Against the Heart*, is an invaluable source of information on the subject. I have also been concerned to show that so called 'minor' writers, and the sub-genres in which they wrote, are an essential and illuminating part of the 19th-century literary scene. My thanks are due to Ian Clarke, author of *Edwardian Drama: A Critical Study*, for his scholary revisionist essay on Victorian drama which reveals how plays such as John Walker's industrial melodrama *The Factory Lad* (1832) can be read as necessary and revealing precursors of the Social Problem novels, and to Linda R. Williams and Gail Cunningham for their essays on Victorian poetry and the novel respectively. I am grateful to those who supplied scholary assistance with the production of this book, in particular Neil Sinyard, John Thieme and John Osborne. I should also like to thank Angela Leighton, Marion Wynne-Davies and Tracey Smith for their advice and encouragement. There are others whose support was of a more practical nature, and to whom I am equally grateful. These include Julie and Richard Gee and Tim and Pauline Huxley King, who diverted and looked after my children while I was otherwise engaged.

This book is for John Osborne, Rhiannon and Aeronwy.

Jane Thomas, University of Hull

# Essay section

# Introduction: The construction of 'Victorianism'

*Jane Thomas*

*University of Hull*

> Young, fair, trusted, beloved, new to business and to life, the sovereign of England commences a reign, that in the course of nature will last beyond the generations who hailed in the Reform Bill – the charter of new liberties – the transition to a new stage of British Culture.

So wrote ▷ Edward Bulwer-Lytton in the ▷ *Westminster Review* in 1840, less than three years after the eighteen-year-old Princess Alexandrina Victoria had been informed of the death of her uncle, ▷ William IV, in the early hours of 20th June, 1837. The accession of Queen ▷ Victoria was seen by many to mark a new stage in the history of the British nation, and the literature produced from the mid-1830s to the turn of the century has been indelibly stamped with her name. The term 'Victorian' functions as a convenient and historically bounded division of the cultural past, signifying the period between the decline of ▷ Romanticism and the beginnings of the cultural renaissance known as modernism. However, an examination of the literature of this period reveals the haziness of these boundaries. Lines of descent can be traced from the concerns of the major Romantics through the poetry of the ▷ 'Spasmodics', ▷ Tennyson, the ▷ Brontës, the ▷ Brownings, the ▷ Pre-Raphaelites, the ▷ sensation novels of ▷ Mary Braddon, ▷ Mrs Henry Wood and ▷ Rhoda Broughton, right up to the later novels of ▷ Thomas Hardy. Likewise, the modernist concern with narrative experiment can be detected in novels such as Emily Brontë's ▷ *Wuthering Heights* and Hardy's *The Well-Beloved* which appeared half a century later. At the same time the commonly agreed concerns of Victorianism predate Victoria and persist until World War I.

The adjective 'Victorian', denoting a variety of styles, manners and cultural forms 'typical' of a period which spans almost a century, was coined in 1875, and yet as countless critics have revealed, it is impossible to draw an objective and clear literary and cultural picture of an age that changed so rapidly that traditional certainties and ways of knowing were constantly under threat. The choice of the monarch's name as a means of labelling the period is significant. As literary historian Richard Stein has indicated it signifies an attempt to reduce a confusing and unstable world to a known and identifiable regularity (*Victoria's Year*). This essay seeks to chart that process whilst at the same time examining some of the ways in which Victorian literature of the period resists annexation.

In the early years of the 19th century, the British monarchy had seemed less than stable. By 1811, George III was acknowledged to be insane and his son became regent. For the next nine years he reigned as sovereign *de facto*, acceding to the throne on the death of his father in 1820. George IV, whose reign as king lasted less than ten years, systematically deprived the crown of any moral influence or credibility through his indolence, deviousness and profligate behaviour. He was succeeded by his brother, William IV, who died seven years later. Despite fathering ten illegitimate children by the Irish comedienne Dorothea Jordan, William was unable to produce a legitimate heir to the throne. His two daughters by Princess Adelaide of Saxe-Meningen died in infancy. His niece Princess Alexandrina Victoria, who was next in line for the throne, signified a distinct break with tradition – a new and auspicious beginning. Not only did the nation identify with her, it also elevated her into a monumental symbol of its own perceived greatness. The name Alexandrina was dropped in favour of the more anglicized and suitably exalted Victoria – instantly recognizable by her subjects as a shout of triumph. Victoria is derived from the noun 'victory', signifying supremacy or superiority.

Much was made of Victoria's youth, beauty, innocence and femininity, all of which contrasted strongly with her predecessors. England was enthralled, regarding her as a type of elder sister called upon to sacrifice her youth and desires in order to mother her recently orphaned family. Her situation began to resemble a best-selling sentimental novel of the time. On her death in 1901 ▷ Henry James wrote, 'We all feel a bit motherless today.'

As Victoria matured, married and established her own not inconsiderable empire of nine children she became increasingly a symbol of Britain's own development. Britain's energies became focused on consolidation, expansion and economic advance. It gained in confidence, in direction, in size and in complacency. By 1851, as Victoria entered a comfortable middle age, Britain was at the height of its wealth, power and influence. T. Frederick Ball, a contemporary historian, wrote in 1886 of Victoria's ability to inspire 'a loving loyalty that seemed to thrill all classes of the community'. The politician Daniel O'Connell (known in Ireland as 'The Liberator') is quoted as having made a thunderous declaration that, if it was necessary, he could get '500,000 brave Irishmen to defend the life, the honour, and the person of the beloved young lady by whom England's throne is now filled'. On a visit to Leeds Victoria reputedly felt as though she was entering a foreign country, so limited was her knowledge of the conditions of the industrial north of England. Nevertheless a quarter of a million people came to pay their respects to her and ▷ *The Times* reported, somewhat smugly, in 1858:

> this democratic and strong-minded race, who spin and weave and forge under thick canopies of smoke – who know and care little about lords or squires or rectors, are capable, as we see, of the deepest and most heartfelt attachment to the Crown and the illustrious person who now wears it.

Not only was England consolidating its identity at home, it was also continuing to establish its presence abroad (▷ Imperialism). Hong Kong was acquired for the nation in 1839, to be swiftly followed by New Zealand (1840), Natal and

Basutoland (1843, 1868) and, most importantly Sind (1843), the Punjab (1849) and Oudh (1856). In 1877 Victoria was proclaimed Empress of India and the middle classes could congratulate themselves not so much on the extent of the British Empire, but on the philanthropy of the English who were prepared to extend their civilizing influence to the more 'backward' nations. England under Victoria gained a perception of itself as an imperial power whose successful and often violent colonization of large parts of the globe was divinely inspired. In 1883 the historian J.R. Seeley attributed the expansion of the British Empire to 'the God who is revealed in history'. In addition, Britain had become a leading industrial nation. The ▷ Great Exhibition of 1851, initiated by Prince ▷ Albert, was, as critic David Morse has suggested, 'the moment when England definitively proclaimed and demonstrated her superiority over the rest of the world' (*High Victorian Culture*). It was also the moment when the sovereign, and the class whose interests and achievements were celebrated in the vast glass and iron conservatory, bonded together in a new and informal way. Queen Victoria visited the Crystal Palace on over forty occasions, joining with the patriotic middle classes, who also paid repeated visits, to 'positively wallow in the image of national greatness that the exhibition represented'. By 1875 the process of identification between sovereign and subjects was so complete that they were proud to adopt the self-referential adjective 'Victorian'. The Jubilee celebrations of 1887 and 1897 were an occasion to congratulate the Queen on her extended occupation of the English throne and for the English nation to congratulate itself on its achievements, as the then Poet Laureate Alfred Tennyson proclaimed in his official tribute 'On the Jubilee of Queen Victoria':

> Fifty years of ever-broadening Commerce!
> Fifty years of ever-brightening Science!
> Fifty years of ever-widening Empire!

The term 'Victorian' became associated with confidence, direction, progress and identity, and as such functioned as a comforting amulet to ward off everything that threatened to undermine the security of the middle classes. In reality, the period of Victoria's reign was characterized by change and instability: the threat of revolution; the discrediting of old traditions; the usurpation of a God who could always be relied upon to sanction the deeds and words of the philanthropic and paternalistic, by an indifferent and mechanical natural process; the loosening of the chains of matrimony and the empowerment of women and the working classes: what ▷ Thomas Carlyle referred to as 'a boundless grinding collision of the New with the Old' (▷ 'Signs of the Times', 1829). In the very year of Victoria's accession to the throne Carlyle published his ▷ *French Revolution* (1837), with its dire warning to the upper classes that unless they provided a model of responsibility and sound leadership England would soon have a revolution of its own. In *Chartism* (1840) he drew attention to the pressures on the working classes of poverty, the ▷ Corn Laws, the ▷ Poor Law Amendment Act of 1834, *laissez-faire* economic policies and the cash nexus which, in his view, had resulted in the ▷ Chartist Movement, itself a potential catalyst for the 'English Revolution'. George Richardson Porter, a social critic of the time, warned his readers against undue complacency and optimism when surveying the nation's industrial advances:

> It must be owned that our multiple abodes of want, of wretchedness, and of crime – our town populations huddled together in ill-ventilated and undrained courts and cellars – our numerous workhouses filled to overflowing with the children of want – and our prisons (scarcely less numerous) overloaded with the votaries of crimes, do indeed but too sadly and too strongly attest that all is not as it should be with us as regards this most important branch of human progress.
>
> (J.H. Buckley, *The Victorian Temper*)

▷ Disraeli regarded England as essentially two nations, 'Rich and Poor' (▷ *Sybil*), and, like Carlyle, looked towards an enlightened aristocracy to provide the leadership and direction the nation so badly needed. ▷ Dickens lamented in the ▷ *Quarterly Review* for June 1839: 'The one half of mankind lives without knowledge of how the other half dies.' He believed that middle-class complacency and indifference to the plight of the poor was the result of ignorance, but this explanation wasn't sufficient for ▷ Mrs Gaskell's John Barton (▷ *Mary Barton*), who was to be driven to murder by bereavement and frustration at the attitudes of those in charge:

> 'Don't think to come over me with the old tale, that the rich know nothing of the trials of the poor. I say, if they don't know, they ought to know. We are their slaves as long as we can work; we pile up their fortunes with the sweat of our brows; and yet we are to live as separate as if we were in two worlds; ay, as separate as Dives and Lazarus.'

Despite Mrs Gaskell's best endeavours, John Barton's anarchic and revengeful voice echoes in the reader's mind long after the concilatory cooing of Jem and Mary's infant son in their Canadian haven. Tennyson's patriotic Jubilee poem seeks to dispel the nation's anxieties concerning the present time by elevating Victoria as a symbol of unity and a guiding light and, in a somewhat unsubtle play on the origins of the Queen's name, transforming her into an image of triumph over peril and lurking threat:

> Are there spectres moving in the darkness?
> Trust the Hand of Light will lead her people,
> Till the thunders pass, the spectres vanish,
> And the Light is Victor, and the darkness
> Dawns into the Jubilee of the Ages.

However, the narrator of ▷ 'Locksley Hall' exposes the schizophrenia that underlies England's bellicose nationalism. In the midst of his self-indulgent rhetoric concerning the unworthiness of women he is valedictory on the subject of the docile, democratic masses: 'Slowly comes a hungry people, as a lion creeping nigher,/Glares at one that nods and winks behind a slowly-dying fire.' The fire, whose light and heat keep the sleeper safe from the spectres of the night, is going out. The amulet is in danger of losing its charm and its owner 'nods and winks' in a gesture of concilation perhaps, or maybe as prelude to a slumber from which he may never wake. Unhappy love destroys the narrator's optimism and peace of mind but his plight is an index of a larger social malaise. For him the 'Mother-Age' is neither comforting nor secure, but wracked by an unavoidable and violent storm. Although the upheavals are incomprehensible, Tennyson's narrator confronts them with a reckless and slightly hysterical cry which registers a sense of things spiralling out of control, 'Forward, forward let us range, /Let the great world spin forever down the ringing grooves of change.' The sentiment is repeated in a more measured tone in ▷ 'The Lotos-Eaters' where the captain counsels courage to his crew helpless on a wild and stormy sea for 'This mounting wave will roll us shoreward soon'.

The foundations of society were already badly shaken before Victoria came to the throne. As early as 1831 ▷ Macaulay urged the House of Commons to 'Reform, that you may preserve, or else persist in a hopeless struggle against the spirit of the age'. In his essay of the same title, ▷ John Stuart Mill defines the 'Spirit of the Age' as one of transition 'in which worldly power must cease to be monopolized by the landed gentry'. The balance of power was shifting from the aristocracy to the middle classes and the weight of their economic prosperity fell heavily upon those whose labour helped produce it and who as yet had no parliamentary voice. Social commentators, politicians and intellectuals recognized the need for widespread changes in the status quo, a need that was emphasized by government reports of the 1830s and 1840s and by the Chartist Movement of 1837–48. Chartism, activated in the year of Victoria's accession to the throne, was largely working class in orientation and campaigned for democratic rights and improved wages and working conditions by means of mass demonstrations and, at times, mob violence. The reforms in ▷ education and the ▷ Reform Bills which enfranchised men in the industrial middle class in 1832, the urban working class in 1867 and the agricultural labourers in 1884 were designed to relieve the pressure of an increasingly militant proletariat. Much as she hated upheaval, Victoria was influenced by Carlyle's warning concerning an impending 'English Revolution' and alarmed at the sea of 'nasty faces' screaming for reform that swarmed around her carriage as she drove to open Parliament in 1867: her first state appearance since she was widowed in December 1861. In supporting the Reform Bill of 1867 Victoria sincerely believed that enfranchisement would make the nation even more favourable to a benevolent monarch. She recognized the potential of the monarchy to provide a point of stability, an icon for a society riven with tensions, carried along breathlessly in the wake of rapid industrial development and discovering the explosive potential of the unprecedented power of steam for the first time.

The situation in France was still unsettled enough for the British to take note. It seemed to dramatize in violent and shocking form the shifts in the balance of power that had been apparent in their own country for some time. Victoria and Albert were 'bourgeois' enough for the rising middle classes to claim them as their own, although, as Victoria's biographer Elizabeth Longford has shown, Albert's popularity waxed and waned throughout the period (*Victoria I*). Nevertheless Albert, the initiator of the Great Exhibition, was the driving force behind the distancing of the monarchy from the aristocracy. For Victoria, the aristocracy symbolized everything that was despicable and profligate, and she held them responsible for the wayward behaviour of Edward the Prince of Wales. Having wooed and won the middle classes she was keen to exercise her influence over the industrial working classes, or the 'lower classes' as she preferred to call them, and eclipse their differences and dissatisfactions with the regal splendour of her presence. However, there were those among Victoria's subjects who reacted strongly against the elevation of the monarchy as a panacea for all ills. In the course of her reign Victoria experienced no less than six attempts on her life. Empty and inadequate gestures though these were, they were sufficient indication that for some the monarchy was a false idol it was their duty to overthrow.

There were iconoclasts among the more moderate of her subjects also. As Richard Stein has indicated, 'Victorian society was forever subject to tensions which militated against complete spontaneity and singleness of purpose' (*Victoria's Year*), and the literature of the period, annexed by the term 'Victorian' by 1876, is riven with these tensions. Whilst Victoria's poets, novelists and social commentators are quick to defend the status quo – preferring modification to revolution – anarchy persistently haunts the margins of their texts, disrupting the stasis implied by the ubiquitous 'happy ending'. Elizabeth Gaskell's alarm at the centrality assumed by the revengeful figure of John Barton in her novel *Mary Barton* is indicated by her attempts to distract the reader with the reconciliation of Mary and Jem, and the even more unlikely understanding reached between the remorseful Barton and his victim's father. It is significant that Mary and Jem can find peace, prosperity and happiness not in England but in Canada. Charles Dickens, having raised the spectre of working class unrest and dramatized the gulf between employer and employee, undermines and demonizes supporters of the growing ▷ trade union movement: they are a 'slack bridge' between masters and men. He leaves himself with no alternative but to wallow in sentiment and homespun wisdom with his moderate, decent, working-class hero Stephen Blackpool, who gazes weakly at the stars from the bottom of his disused mineshaft, to utter with his dying breath the immortal words 'aw a muddle' (▷ *Hard Times*).

In 1830–33 ▷ Charles Lyell published his *Principles of Geology*. The disasters he catalogued, including the wholesale extermination of species, as necessary antecedents to the earth's present state of repose, had a tremendous effect on his readers. For ▷ Charles Darwin the book 'altered the whole tone of one's mind'. In ▷ *In Memoriam, A.H.H.* (1850) Tennyson's narrator is unable to sustain the heady optimism embraced by the speaker of 'Locksley Hall'. Scientific knowledge brings not wisdom but despair as the individual self is threatened with extermination in the cause of the progress of the species. The strength of much of Tennyson's poetry lies in its insistent gesture towards the dissenting individual who refuses to be blinkered by the happy lie. *In Memoriam* is one of the most powerful poems of doubt and despair to be written during the period of Victoria's reign. It acknowledges the undermining of a concept of self predicated upon the notion of a beneficent and greater 'other' whether that 'other' be God, or perhaps, by implication, Monarch. Faced with the impact of science on religious belief, Tennyson's narrator mistrusts the very ground beneath him.

> I falter where I firmly trod,
>   And falling with my weight of cares
>   Upon the great world's altar-stairs
> That slope thro' darkness up to God,
>
> I stretch lame hands of faith, and grope,
>   And gather dust and chaff, and call
>   To what I feel is Lord of all,
> And faintly trust the larger hope.

God's abdication was brought a stage nearer by the publication of Darwin's *The Origin of Species* (1859) and its vigorous defence by ▷ Thomas Henry Huxley against Bishop Wilberforce the following year. Huxley's attack was directed not only against the bishop's attempts to 'smash Darwin' but also against the innate and threatened conservatism of those members of the Church who sought 'to discredit and crush humble seekers after truth'. The post-Darwinian world was in many ways profoundly pessimistic, and the writers of the period were torn between their conviction that the purpose of art was to educate and guide the newly enfranchised and newly literate classes beneath them, and their desire to use their talents to expose what was damnably wrong with the system.

Thomas Hardy has been accused of replacing a benevolent all-seeing God with a blind, mechanical and unreasoning 'It'. It was a charge that Hardy himself resolutely denied. He regarded his novels not as manifestos of pessimism but evidence of his own practical meliorist philosophy:

> What are my books but one plea against 'man's inhumanity to man' – to woman – and to the lower animals? ... Whatever may be the inherent good or evil of life, it is certain that men make it much worse than it need be. When we have got rid of a thousand remediable ills, it will be time enough to determine whether the ill that is irremediable outweighs the good.
>
> (▷ William Archer, *Real Conversations*)

One of the thousand 'remediable ills' that is held up for analysis in Hardy's novels is the economic, social and sexual repression of women. It isn't 'Fate' that dogs Hardy's heroines to their graves, or into the arms of unsuitable mates, it is their economic dependence on men, their lack of social and political power and their adaptation, in the interests of survival, to the forms of feminity favoured not by Nature but by society. These forms are epitomized by ▷ Coventry Patmore's ▷ 'Angel in the House' or ▷ Ruskin's 'queen' of the domestic garden: 'the centre of order, the balm of distress, and the mirror of beauty' (*Sesame and Lilies*, 1865). Once again Queen Victoria, with her selfless and very public devotion to Albert and her children, her apparent preference for the philanthropic rather than the more practical duties of state, which she preferred to leave to her husband, and her repugnance for the 'mad, wicked folly of Women's Rights', provided a model of domestic virtue which the middle-class woman was encouraged to imitate. However, by 1860 this model was already up for reconstruction. In 1866 John Stuart Mill presented an unsuccessful petition to Parliament which demanded the inclusion of women in what was to become the 1867 Reform Bill. Many women throughout the period challenged the Victorian feminine ideal and the ▷ Women's Movement of the second half of the 19th century was perhaps the most anarchic of all, for it threatened the very foundations of the domestic haven the Victorians constructed as a retreat from the vicissitudes of everyday life. Maria G. Grey writing in the ▷ *Fortnightly Review* in 1879 points to the ▷ 'Woman Question' as an issue which was to create tensions every bit as great as theories of the evolution of human beings and the democratization of the working classes:

> Among the questions agitating men's minds in this age of transition between the old world of thought and faith and custom, so rapidly disappearing, and the new world scarcely yet visible in its rudiments beneath the tide of change and destruction, there are none that go deeper to the very roots of our social life than those touching the relations between the sexes, and the position assigned to women in the family and in the State. For centuries those relations had been considered fixed as the law of nature itself and too sacred to be touched by profane hands; but, of late years, they have shared the fate of other revered institutions and have become open questions, to be tried as freely as any others in the ruthless crucible of doubt and analysis.

Thomas Hardy, for one, had no doubts about the revolutionary potential of the ▷ women's suffrage movement. In 1906, five years after Victoria's death, he wrote to Millicent Garrett Fawcett, a leading women's suffragist, outlining the reasons behind his support for the cause:

> I have long been in favour of [it] ... because I think the tendency of the woman's vote will be to break up the present pernicious conventions in respect of manners, customs, religion, illegitimacy, the stereotyped household (that it must be the unit of society), the father of a woman's child (that it is anybody's business but the woman's own, except in cases of disease or insanity), sport (that so-called educated men should be encouraged to harass, kill for pleasure feeble creatures by mean stratagems), slaughter

houses (that they should be dark dens of cruelty) & other matters which I got into hot water for touching on many years ago.

During the last two decades of the century a reaction was setting in against the cosy certainties associated with the term 'Victorian'. Faith and pride in the Machine Age in the early decades of the century had its counterpart not only in the choleric finger-wagging of Carlyle or the unctuous reasoning of Dickens, but also in the nostalgia for a bygone, simpler pre-industrial age. The ▷ medievalism of Carlyle's ▷ *Past and Present*, Tennyson's ▷ *Idylls of the King* and the work of the Pre-Raphaelite Brotherhood reached its peak in the ▷ utopianism of ▷ William Morris. For Morris art and literature had a purely ornamental and practical function. Its purpose was to improve the existing environment and to compensate for the destruction by creeping industrialization of natural beauty and to replace the ugly utility of mass-produced goods with the lasting aesthetic pleasure of the hand-made artefact. From 1883 onwards Morris was studying and then preaching revolutionary ▷ Marxism. At the same time adherents of the ▷ Aesthetic Movement sought to rise above rather than justify what they regarded as an increasingly sordid and vulgar middle-class value system. Writers like ▷ George Moore and ▷ Oscar Wilde welcomed the ridicule heaped upon them by satirists like ▷ George Du Maurier in ▷ *Punch* because it confirmed their deviation from the norm. Art was seen as an escape from rather than a means of airing intellectual conflict.

If the early years of the 19th century and the accession to the throne of England of a youthful queen encouraged a spirit of ardour and optimism, the closing decade, presided over by a fretful, dour and increasingly reclusive octagenarian, prompted a feeling of pessimism and a sense of apocalypse. Victorian England had already 'fallen prey' to the radicals, socialists and suffragettes, and conservative opinion turned its attentions to the changes threatening the British Empire. Victoria's status was elevated from Queen to Empress as she reached the height of her popularity. The façade of middle-class complacency at home gave way to jingoism: fervent support of England's imperial policy in Europe epitomized in ▷ John Davidson's 'Song for the Twenty-fourth of May':

> Sea-room, land-room, ours, my masters, ours,
> Hand in hand with destiny, and first among the Powers!
> Our boasted Ocean Empire, sirs, we boast of it again,
> Our Monarch, and our Rulers, and our Women, and our Men!

However, even the most jingoistic writers – ▷ Kipling, William Henley (1849–1903), William Watson (1858–1935) and Henry Newbolt (1862–1938) – have been reassessed by present-day critics in such a way that the tensions and schisms in their work have become apparent.

The ▷ Decadents reacted against the optimism, buoyancy and smugness of 'Victorianism' with a languid weariness and despair. Arthur Symons's 'The Pause' (1897) picks up and develops into a dirge for the dying century the bass note of regret and confusion that surfaces periodically in the more conventional literature of the period:

> Trouble has come upon us like a sudden cloud,
> A sudden summer cloud with thunder in its wings.
> There is an end for us of old familiar things
> Now that this desolating voice has spoken aloud.

The Decadents opposed 'Victorian' manliness with effeminacy, earnestness with flippancy, philanthropy with self-indulgence and moral uprightness with sexual delinquency. Anarchy no longer merely haunts the borders of their texts, it takes a central role as the marginalized working-class Chartist of the ▷ Social Problem novels gives way to the amoral aesthete, the criminally insane decadent and the 'unnatural' aristocratic foreigner epitomized by ▷ Oscar Wilde's Dorian Gray, ▷ Robert Louis Stevenson's Mr Hyde and ▷ Bram Stoker's Dracula. However, in defining themselves against 'Victorianism', the '*fin de siècle*' writers were guilty of reducing the complexities of the literature and sensibility that had preceded theirs to a simplified set of clichés. It was this 'Victorianism', floated over the cracks and fissures of Victorian society and culture like a self-levelling compound, that persisted into the 20th century as 'a shield for the conservative and a target for the modernist' (J.H. Buckley, *The Victorian Temper*).

Until relatively recently, the construction of the canon of Victorian literature has sought to determine the meaning of texts in advance by relating them to a monolithic conception of 'Victorianism' designed to resolve rather than problematize its tensions. This has resulted in the exclusion of certain groups of people from representation and the devaluing of genres perceived as aberrant or peripheral to the concerns of the age. This is clearly the case with Victorian drama, dismissed as early as 1894 by one of the period's leading dramatists, ▷ Henry Arthur Jones, as 'A Slough of Despond in the well-tilled field of English Literature'. Jones was referring specifically to ▷ melodrama, which was the dominant genre of the age, and his opinion of the form has remained largely unchallenged. However, as Ian Clarke suggests in his essay 'Drama 1837–1901' (see page 13), the rejection of a large percentage of 19th-century drama as of little worth amounts to literary critical prejudice and trivializes one of the dominant forms of popular cultural entertainment. He argues for a reglossing of the term 'melodrama' to transform it from a pejorative into a purely descriptive term. Far from functioning as mere escapist entertainment, he argues, early domestic melodrama 'offered to newly urbanized working-class audiences valid images, however indirect, of their own alienated and disempowering experience as wage slaves'. Domestic melodrama also served to highlight gender inequities by showing women, and particularly working-class women, in a hostile world 'under almost constant threat of male violence'. In this way early Victorian melodrama can be seen to dramatize for a popular audience the concerns which were to animate the middle-class novel.

The novel was indisputably the dominant literary form of the age but yet again its sheer diversity is commonly overlooked by critics in their devotion to the rise of ▷ realism. Whilst ample attention has been paid to major realists such as Dickens, ▷ Thackeray, ▷ Eliot, the Brontës, Hardy and Henry James the sensationalist writings of Mrs Braddon, Mrs Wood and Rhoda Broughton are commonly grouped together under the heading 'minor novelists'. As Gail Cunningham points out in her essay on 'The Victorian Novel' (see page 27), the single most popular novelist of the 1890s was neither Hardy nor Thackeray nor even Henry James but ▷ Marie Corelli, whose *The Sorrows of Satan* (1895) outsold any previous English novel. Throughout the Victorian period the novel was subject to a form of ▷ censorship designed to isolate the predominantly female readership from exposure to sexual corruption. Novels which failed the test risked being blacklisted by the ▷ circulating libraries, which could ruin a writer's reputation overnight. Sexuality had to be handled delicately or not at all. The ▷ sensation novels of the 1860s, with their thinly disguised eroticism and stimulating if incredible plots, were written in reaction to the morally upright and sternly prosaic atmosphere of middle-class drawing rooms. They proved so popular that their authors (who were predominantly female) were comfortably able to support themselves, their husbands and families on the proceeds. Even the ▷ historical novel and ▷ romance were regarded as subversive by Ruskin, who counselled parents to keep them from their daughters for even 'the best romance becomes dangerous, if, by its excitement, it renders the ordinary course of life uninteresting, and increases the morbid thirst for useless acquaintance with scenes in which we shall never be called upon to act' (*Sesame and Lillies*). However, as Gail Cunningham demonstrates, it was the ▷ 'New Woman' fiction of the 1890s that most effectively undermined the shrine of womanhood.

Linda Williams (see page 43) locates the strength of Victorian poetry in its acknowledgement of crisis: in particular the crisis of the relationship between the self and the material world. The poetry of the period can be seen to challenge the received wisdom of the middle classes that industrial development and technological and scientific advance served only to illustrate the supremacy of man. The myth of personal and national stability is consistently fractured by the work of Tennyson, ▷ Clough, ▷ Arnold, Anne Brontë and Hardy. At the same time women poets such as ▷ Elizabeth Barrett Browning and Emily Brontë were concerned to forge entirely new conceptions of the female self distinctly at odds with the 'Angel in the House'. As the century drew to a close the impulse toward consolidation and complacency was violently checked by the bloody and frequently blasphemous verse of ▷ Swinburne and others of the ▷ 'Fleshly School of Poetry' while the despair and bleakness of much of ▷ Hopkins and Hardy anticipates the apocalypse of World War I.

As we prepare to exit from our own calamitous century, the government and the popular media fondly invoke the 'Golden Age' of the Victorian period. However as this essay and those that follow demonstrate, we should regard the previous century not as the antithesis to our own but as its precursor. The Victorians are moderns, their conflicts are ours, and they deserve better of us than to be reduced to crass political slogans and television costume drama.

# Drama in the Nineteenth Century: 1837–1901   2

*Ian Clarke*

*Loughborough University*

The drama of the 19th century has often been taken to represent a fallow period in literary and theatrical history. According to this view, between the Restoration dramatists of the late 16th and early 17th centuries there is nothing much of interest (apart from slight blips in the 18th century with John Gay, Richard Sheridan and Oliver Goldsmith) until the very end of the 19th century and the arrival of ▷ Oscar Wilde and ▷ George Bernard Shaw. The influential *Pelican Guide to English Literature* offers a typical example of this view of 19th-century drama and theatre: 'The theatrical world was rather a shabby one, dependent largely on poor and economical translations of bad plays . . . Only with the discovery of anti-Victorian zest by Oscar Wilde and by Shaw, under the influence of Butler and a partially understood Ibsen, does the drama recover a measure of linguistic vitality and social function.'[1] The dismissal of 19th-century drama as unworthy of consideration is compounded by the fact that its dominant genre was ▷ melodrama and that, according to a canonical literary view, this genre itself is of little worth. Thus M. H. Abrams in *A Glossary of Literary Terms* clearly establishes a hierarchy of genres that effectively sidelines much 19th-century drama: 'The 19th century in England produced few notable tragedies but many melodramas.' Abrams, as does the essay in the *Pelican Guide*, underpins the argument by subscribing to a literary critical concept of value which cannot accommodate the structures and forms of melodrama: 'The protagonists are pure as the driven snow and antagonists luridly evil, while credibility of both character and action is sacrificed for violent effect, in a drama contrived according to an emotional opportunism.'[2] This view is, however, a distortion and misrepresentation of the actuality of 19th-century stage melodrama; it amounts to an uninformed literary critical prejudice.

Nor is it difficult to find this sort of point of view repeated in specifically theatrical dictionaries and companions. The following examples are taken from two of the most accessible and widely available of such works:

> an extravagant drama making full use of all the possibilities inherent in music, lighting, and stage machinery for the artificial heightening of emotion) . . . drama of an unusually sensational type . . .
>
> naive popular entertainment . . .
>
> [a] diversion (sometimes with pretensions to social significance) . . .
>
> [plays] whose elements were highly coloured and larger than life – the noble outlaw, the wronged maiden, the cold-blooded villain . . .
>
> [melodrama indicates] everything that fed the popular appetite for horror and mystery, violence and double-dealing, but always with virtue triumphant . . .[3]

Again the generalizations misrepresent the actuality. In effect, these reference works are not descriptive of actual cultural forms and history; rather, these theatrical dictionaries codify what is fundamentally a *literary critical* prejudice.

The consignment of 100 years of dramatic writing and theatrical history to the dustbin obscures the sheer amount of theatrical activity and writing that took place in the 19th century. Evidence of the amount and indeed the growth of theatrical activity can easily be found in the handlists of plays appended to the individual volumes of Allardyce Nicoll's *A History of English Drama 1660–1900*.[4] The handlist for the period 1800 to 1850 runs to 395 pages, and for the period 1850 to 1900 to 617 pages.[5]

The growth in dramatic writing was matched, particularly in the second half of the century, by the building of new theatres and the rebuilding and extensive refurbishment of existing ones in provincial towns and cities as well as in London. Technological innovation was constantly put to use in theatres often dedicated to presenting the visually spectacular. Oil lighting began to be replaced by gas soon after the start of the century, and by its end many theatres had replaced or supplemented gas with electricity. The impulses of antiquarianism and literalism resulted in sets that accurately recreated settings for which scenic artists of reputation and merit painted huge backcloths to give the effect of three-dimensionality in a two-dimensional medium. The demand for lavish and often violent spectacle grew throughout the period. Consequently, stage machinery as well as lighting effects became increasingly ingenious and technically complex. By the turn of century the stage adaptation (1899) of Lew Wallace's novel *Ben Hur* staged the chariot race with real horses, and the sporting melodrama *The Whip* (1909) represented not just the running of the Derby but also a train crash.[6] The developing film industry capitalized on the demand for spectacle, and film's ability to present even more elaborate (and seemingly more realistic) spectacles heralded the demise of spectacular stage melodrama in the early years of the 20th century.

Throughout the whole of the 19th century the theatre represented one of the dominant forms of popular cultural entertainment. However, in the latter half of the century, actual legislation, campaigns for further legislative reform, and more general shifts in attitudes and perceptions pressured for a drama that was to have a higher cultural standing and for a mainstream theatre that was to acquire a greater social respectability. While at one level these developments represented a desire on the part of theatre managers, actors and dramatists to be taken and to take themselves more seriously, it also determined theatre-going as a class-defined social activity. From the 1860s onwards the fabric of auditoria (in the more expensive parts at least) of major provincial theatres as well as those of London's West End was designed as part of a social event, providing entertainment for a middle-class audience. The social status of the upper echelons of the acting profession rose throughout the latter half of the century to the extent that in 1895 ▷ Henry Irving was made the first actor knight for services to the theatre. This new-found conventional social respectability determined not just the tone of theatregoing but also the concept of the function of theatre and the nature of the drama it presented.

There was a similar rise in the status of the dramatist. If, in the earlier part of the century, the actor was not generally accepted into polite society, so the dramatist was often viewed as a hack churning out unfortunate adaptations of continental European dramas and farces. By the end of the century, however, a dramatist could, partly as a result of the protection provided by recent copyright legislation, view her/his profession as serious and, indeed, potentially lucrative. In the 1890s dramatists such as ▷ Henry Arthur Jones and ▷ Arthur Wing Pinero issued well-produced editions of their plays to coincide with their premieres. George Bernard Shaw, on the other hand, published his plays when there was, in some cases, little or no chance of their production on the public stage. Both enterprises indicate a reading audience for play texts. The issuing of plays by reputable publishing houses meant that the drama could stand in their lists alongside volumes of novels, poetry, and essays. A point reiterated by Jones in his collected essays, *The Renascence of the English Drama* (1895), was that if the drama were to have any intellectual respectability, dramatists had to be seen as persons of letters and that their product could bear comparison with other literary forms. The intellectual respectability of the drama was further enhanced by the seriousness with which it was taken by late-19th-century commentators and critics such as ▷ George Moore, ▷ William Archer, ▷ Henry James, A.B. Walkley, ▷ J.T. Grein, and Shaw.

According to that classist point of view that links cultural and class formations so as to validate the former by the latter, the social problem drama of the end of the century (despite its indebtedness to earlier drama) is often still viewed as a huge advance on the supposedly unfortunate popular cultural melodramatic forms of the earlier part of the century. Nevertheless, seminal works – Michael R. Booth's *English Melodrama*, and Peter Brooks's *The Melodramatic Imagination* – have done much to shift the critical ground so that the term melodrama, and more importantly its adjectival form, can be used descriptively rather than pejoratively.[7] The re-evaluation of melodrama has also been greatly assisted by the relatively recent emergence of theatre studies and cultural studies as distinct disciplines. Melodrama and the melodramatic can now be considered as an important and, indeed, central cultural form of the 19th century.

The first play in English specifically to identify itself as a melodrama (although in the French form *mélodrame*) was Thomas Holcroft's *A Tale of Mystery* (1802), an adaptation from the French of Guilbert de Pixérécourt's *Coelina, ou l'Enfant de mystère* (1800). The ▷ Gothic elements of *A Tale of Mystery* – the creation of a sense of impending, foreboding doom; settings which included 'A Gothic Hall in the House of [the suitably foreign-sounding] Bonamo' and 'Wild mountainous country . . . with pines and massy rocks' – were to become a mainstay of early English melodrama. Such elements would become even more elaborate and spectacular to include ruined castles, dungeons, ghosts, violent storms. A feature of *A Tale of Mystery* which would remain throughout the century is its use of music – 'Violent distracted music', 'Music of Terror', 'Music to express disorder' are specifically notated, along with many other precisely discriminated types of music, in the stage directions. Music underscores the action and emotional mood, and signifies character function. The use of music in part derives from French and German dramatic antecedents, and from current English theatrical practice. Often viewed as a regrettable consequence of the monopoly of the two patent theatres (Covent Garden and Drury Lane) on the so-called legitimate drama and the legal requirement for the so-called illegitimate drama to contain a certain number of songs and pieces of musical accompaniment, the function of music in melodrama should rather be seen as central and indispensable to the creative signifying practices of the genre. A modern analogy in a popular cultural form is the use of music and song in the soundtrack of a feature film.

The exoticism of Gothic melodrama dominated in the first two decades of the 19th century, but domestic melodrama with native English settings emerged towards the end of the 1820s and became increasingly prevalent. Even in other forms of melodrama – nautical, military, temperance, criminal – domestic elements are crucial. Domestic melodrama offered a construction of domestic ideology in its ideal form so as to provide judgemental systems encoding for the spectator approbation and disapprobation of characters, incidents, and situations. Thus those characters who uphold and protect the domestic ideal are to be approved of; those who threaten it are instantly figured as villains. This places at the centre of the drama the nuclear family, and occasionally the extended family, with its attendant bonds and obligations. Within this arena the dramatic impetus derives from negotiations and intersections of class and gender, wealth and justice, and, above all, power. Far from being escapist entertainment, in the earlier part of the 19th century domestic melodrama offered to newly urbanized working-class audiences valid images, however indirect, of their own alienated and disempowered experience as wage slaves.

In this context, a key figure in the melodrama became the hard-hearted, foreclosing landlord. His activities in turning families out of their homes into the street were represented unequivocally as violating the domestic ideal. The pathos created by the presence of lachrymose children and infirm old folk confirms his behaviour as all the more heinous. The conflict between the sanctity of the family unit and the landlord's actions is brought into direct play in Douglas Jerrold's *Black-Ey'd Susan* (1829) where Doggrass, who intends to evict black-eyed Susan of the title along with the aged and dying Dame Hatley, is not only Susan's landlord but her uncle. By unwaveringly demanding his arrears of rent he jettisons his familial obligations towards, as Susan reminds him, his 'brother's orphan child'. The contradiction between the familial relationship and the relationship between landlord and tenant is made explicit in the following exchange:

> *Susan.* Uncle, the old woman is sick – I fear dangerously. Her spirit, weakened by late misfortune, flickers like a dying light – your sudden appearance might make all dark. Uncle – landlord! would you have murder on your soul?
> *Doggrass.* Murder?
> *Susan.* Yes; though such may not be the common word, hearts are daily crushed, spirits broken – whilst he who slays, destroys in safety.

Susan, whose character function of heroine earns her the support of the audience, leaves no doubt as to how the landlord's behaviour should be judged. Incidents centring on the attempted eviction form only a small part of the varied action of *Black-Ey'd Susan*; such incidents and associated issues are, however, much more dominant in the main action of Jerrold's *The Rent-Day* (1832). The problem of absentee landlords feeding their pleasures with the rents from their tenants is described thus: 'If the landlord lose at gaming, his tenants must suffer for't. The Squire plays a low card – issue a distress warrant! He throws deuce-ace – turn a family into the fields! 'Tis only awkward to lose hundreds on a card; but very rascally to be behind-hand with one's rent!' This speech is followed by advice given to the steward to pass on to the landlord:

> When you write back to the Squire, you can tell him, by way of postscript, if he must feed the gaming-table, not to let it be with money, wrung, like blood, from the wretched. Just tell him, whilst he shuffles the cards, to remember the aching hearts of his distressed tenants. And when he rattles the dice, let him stop and think of the bailiff and tax-gatherer, knocking at the cottage doors of the poor.

The ethical and emotional structuring of melodrama creates patterns of sympathy for the oppressed rather than the oppressor and might thus be described as populist. It is the disempowered – whether by wealth, class, gender, lack of access to legal redress – who form the endorsed moral and ideological centre. Yet, in the speeches above from *Black-Ey'd Susan* and *The Rent-Day*, one can hear that the populism is capable of a significant radical edge.

The radicalism potentially strikes deep. A landlord in demanding his rent and in distraining and evicting if it is not received breaks no law. Yet the ethical structures of domestic melodrama condemn him. Melodrama, therefore, sets up a system of values which come into direct conflict with the actuality of the British legal system, and offers a direct challenge to the laws relating to landlord and tenant as well as those laws which protect the ownership of property. It can be argued that the radical thrust is emolliated by narratives which suggest that it is wicked individuals administrating the system rather than the system itself that is wrong. Thus in *The Rent-Day* the problems of absentee landlords and landlord/tenant relationships are resolved when Squire Grantley reforms, makes reparation and promises to be a good landlord in the future. However, an equally valid counter-argument is that narrative closures of that order are not universal, nor do they negate the articulation of radical sentiment earlier in individual plays. The repeated endorsement in play after play of melodrama's own ethical position in relation to landlords and tenants has a cumulative effect in the ideological work the drama does, and must suggest that the expression of populist radicalism spoke powerfully to the everyday experience and imaginative needs of the audiences.

The populist class consciousness of domestic melodrama sites the central focus of the class inequity in the figure of the wealthy landowner or squire.

More often than not the squire not only has unfair advantages in terms of the power that wealth and class give him, but he is repeatedly an oppressor in gender terms. In ▷ J.B. Buckstone's *Luke the Labourer* (1826), for instance, Luke may be the primary villain enacting vengeful plots against conventionally worthy Farmer Wakefield, but the Squire is a subsidiary villain who plans to abduct and take by force the virtue of Wakefield's daughter, Clara. The analogy within the nautical setting of *Black-Ey'd Susan* is the attempted rape of Susan by a naval officer. The character function of the squire figure also allows for further attacks on the administration of the legal system, for it is he who often represents justice locally. The Squire in *Luke the Labourer* is not only a potential kidnapper and rapist, he is also the local Justice of the Peace. His wrongful imprisonment of the woebegone comic man, Bobby Trott, elicits the following response from the comic woman, Jenny: 'I wish I were a queen or an emperor, for his sake: I'd see whether a Squire should not go in the cage as well as a poor man, when he deserved it'; but the Squire's escape to London where he will evade punishment offers evidence of significant corruption in the judicial system. Very different ideological work is being done here than that erroneous view of melodrama which assumes that there is 'an exact demonstration of poetic justice, in which earthly rewards and punishments are distributed in proportion to the deserts of the characters'.[8]

Even more unrelenting in its attack on corruption in the judiciary is John Walker's industrial melodrama *The Factory Lad* (1832). Squire Westwood, the factory owner, dismisses most of his workforce after introducing steam-driven machinery, and is immediately figured in the play as the equivalent of the foreclosing landlord. It is also he who makes explicit whose interests the legal and judicial systems are designed to protect:

> I must be on the alert, and keep my doors well fastened, and have, too, an armed force to welcome these desperadoes, if they should dare to violate the laws well framed to subject them to obedience ... What have I to fear or dread? Is England's proud aristocracy to tremble when brawling fools mouth and question? No; the hangman shall be their answer.

Later in the play this exchange between the aptly named Justice Bias and Rushton, the incendiarist who destroys the factory and steam machinery, articulates the populist perception of the inequity of the law:

> *Bias.* The law is open to you, is it not?
> *Rushton.* No; I am poor.
> *Bias.* And what of that? The law is made alike for rich and poor.
> *Rushton.* Is it? Why, then, does it so often lock the poor man in jail, while the rich one goes free?

*The Factory Lad* is remarkable for the strength of its radical sentiment and has continued to be performed seriously for its content by theatre groups and companies with left-wing political sympathies.

The construction of gender, both male and female, is enormously varied and complex in 19th-century melodrama and is beyond the scope of the present essay. However, some account of the character function of the heroine – whether as wife or daughter – in domestic melodrama is necessary. In the wake of the second women's liberation movement, the passivity of so many heroine characters is to many modern readers/spectators not only excessive but also extremely irritating. Such a reaction is understandable, but fails to do justice to the ideological work that is being done by showing women in a hostile world under almost constant threat of male violence. The violence is often specifically sexual. Already mentioned are the attempted rapes in *Black-Ey'd Susan* and *Luke the Labourer* of Susan (wife) and Clara (daughter) by upper-class characters. In *The Rent-Day* similar unwanted attentions are paid to Rachel Heywood (wife) by Silver Jack, one of the criminal characters. The most common resolution of these threats derives from the typological pattern that isolated and vulnerable women are in need of male protection. Thus Susan is saved in the nick of time by her husband, and Clara by the unintended intervention of the comic man, Bobby Trott. Rachel, on the other hand, defends herself by tricking the attacker, she then protects herself by threatening to kill her assailant with a woodcutter's bill, and eventually makes her escape. The narrative develops when she overhears a plot to rob and possibly murder the Squire, whom she goes to warn. The drama consequently utilizes the narrative expectation that squires are seducers; when she is discovered in the Squire's rooms it is immediately assumed by her husband (on the prompting of the criminals) that the assignation was a sexual one. This leads to pathos-filled scenes where she is expelled by her husband from the family home and denied access to her children. It may be unwise to extrapolate from the narrative that Rachel is being punished for an 'unfeminine' lack of passivity but the implication may remain.

Notwithstanding, the narrative developments involving Rachel indicate the centrality of the heroine character, especially in her roles of wife and mother, to the construction of domestic ideology in its ideal form; moreover, that her virtue, in conventional terms, is essential to that construction and often carries its burden. The working-class woman, further disempowered by gender and physical strength, is represented as having the consciousness of her own virtue as her only power. The articulation of this is capable, however, of development into a powerful rhetoric instrumental in the judgemental systems of the drama; thus Susan in *Black-Ey'd Susan* berates Doggrass for his suggestion that she may not be faithful to her absent husband:

Sir, scorn has no word – contempt no voice to speak my loathing of your insinuations. Take, sir, all that is here; satisfy your avarice – but dare not indulge your malice at the cost of one, who has now nothing left her in her misery but the sweet consciousness of virtue.

Rachel's similar berating of Silver Jack can stand as axiomatic of the ethical structure of a melodramatic genre that places domestic ideology, and the

heroine's vulnerability and virtue at its centre: 'He who would destroy a
happy fireside, is vile and infamous; but he who insults its wretchedness, is
base indeed.'

It would be wrong to assume that dramatic forms developed throughout the
19th century in clearly defined progressive movements; during the whole period
aspects of the drama would appear and re-appear, would go through negotiations
and re-negotiations, would re-present significant modulations of conventions
and signifying practices. Nevertheless, in the 1860s a number of dramas seem
to abandon the populist radicalism of the earlier domestic melodrama in favour
of the endorsement of an increasingly bourgeois ideological stance. ▷ Tom
Taylor's *The Ticket-of-Leave Man* (1863) is a case in point. The first act shows
the heroine, May Edwards, in a hostile environment. Alone and friendless she
busks with her guitar from table to table in the Bellevue Tea Gardens. Her
presence causes a commotion for which she requires male assistance from the
hero figure, and there are also linguistic pointers to the idea that her activity is
akin to prostitution. By the second act, however, she has been able by her own
efforts to set herself up in lower-middle-class domestic comfort in a rented room
that is 'humbly but neatly furnished', decorated with flowers, and complete
with canary. The ideological work done by the representation of isolated or
independent women under threat which they are not in a position to counter
has been replaced by the ideological imperative of the mid-19th-century concept
of self-help. It is probably no coincidence that ▷ Samuel Smiles's *Self-Help*
(1859) was published some four years before *The Ticket-of-Leave Man*. In the
play the character Gibson, whose wife has employed May, makes explicit in
conversation with May the ways in which approbation is apportioned: 'You've
showed that you deserve her [Mrs Gibson's] kindness. For fifty people ready
to help there's not one worth helping – that's my conclusion. I was telling my
wife so this morning, and she insisted that I should come and satisfy myself that
she had helped one person at any rate who was able and willing to help herself.'
Similarly, the radical critique of the legal and penal system is now abandoned.
Robert Brierly, the wrongfully imprisoned hero, is not utilized to offer such
a critique; rather, his imprisonment is offered as reformative. It rescues him
from bad company, cures him of his incipient dipsomania, and provides him
with skills which will be useful to him in future life. The play, in its treatment
of the social prejudice against ex-convicts, is often claimed to be a forerunner
of the sort of social problem drama represented by John Galsworthy's *Justice*
(1910). But Brierly earns his reparation not by challenging social prejudice but
by thwarting the criminal plans of the villains.

The 1860s also witnessed a growth of the representation of increasingly
mundane ▷ realism on stage. Thus in *The Ticket-of-Leave Man* there is a
moment of playful metatheatricality; in a scene set in Gibson's bill-broking
office, one of the characters looks about her at the stage set and specifically
draws the audience's attention to the dressing of the stage: 'I did *so* want to
see an office – a real one, you know. I've seen 'em set on the stage often but
they ain't a bit like the real thing.' Plays by ▷ T.W. Robertson such as *Caste*
(1867) and *Society* (1865) staged under the Bancroft management also brought

into prominence domestic realism so that they were termed 'cup-and-saucer' and 'milk-and-water' comedies on account of their representation of everyday realism. Robertson's, in comparison to other drama indicates the range of visual pleasures that the 19th-century stage afforded: from large-scale antiquarian literalism; to the spectacle of the chariot race or train crash; to the interest in the everyday.

Other notable plays during this part of the 19th century were adaptations from novels by women writers, including ▷ Mary Braddon's ▷ *Lady Audley's Secret* and ▷ Ellen Wood's ▷ *East Lynne*. ▷ C.H. Hazlewood's stage adaptation (1863) of *Lady Audley's Secret* places the villainess centre stage. She is explicitly excoriated by the wronged husband. Yet the play also articulates the fact that the husband, George Talboys, was inadequate as a provider and insouciant in respect of his marital responsibilities. He leaves her in England while he goes to find his fortune in India. An unresolved point is whether he wrote to her during his period abroad. Believing herself to be abandoned, the question for Lady Audley is one of survival in a society which is represented as offering a worthwhile position for women only in relation to men. Thus Lady Audley publishes a false notice of her death in a newspaper and under an assumed name schemes to gain the affections and hand of the wealthy Sir Michael Audley. In the altercation with her erstwhile husband, Lady Audley defends herself as follows:

> I tell you, not one letter reached my hands; I thought myself deserted, and determined to make reprisals on you; I changed my name; I entered the family of a gentleman as governess to his daughters; became the patient drudge for a miserable stipend, that I might carry my point – that point was to gain Sir Michael Audley's affections; I did so, I devoted all my energies, all my cunning, to that end! and now I have gained the summit of my ambition, do you think I will be cast down by you, George Talboys? No, I will conquer you or I will die!

In conventional terms, Lady Audley, despite her justification of her behaviour and her husband's explicit admission of his failure to fulfil his marital responsibilities, is punished for her actions. Indeed, this particular stage adaptation suggests that her madness at the end of the play is a result/cause of her 'unnatural' (for a woman that is) villainy. And yet, the popularity of this narrative in its various stage adaptations suggests that, despite the overall conventional moral frame, Lady Audley's behaviour in overcoming her disadvantages possibly offered for women spectators the fantasy of a ▷ utopian resolution.

The stage adaptations of *East Lynne* were many.[9] The one by T.A. Palmer (1874) contains the famous, but often misquoted lines: 'Oh, Willie, my child dead, dead! and he never knew me, never called me mother.' Although conventionally moralistic in its treatment of the fate of the unfaithful wife, this version of *East Lynne* shows the protagonist, Lady Isabel, in a variety of roles which implicitly raise questions about the economic as well as moral position of women in society. Thus she first appears as the single woman economically dependent on her extended family; she then makes a marriage more for financial security than love, and becomes the economically dependent wife; believing her husband to be unfaithful, she leaves the family home and her children, and decamps with the villain of the piece. As a ▷ fallen woman she suffers the usual fate of the fictional kept mistress, and is discarded by her lover. Echoing interest surrounding recent divorce legislation (▷ marriage and divorce), the play next offers Lady Isabel as divorcee. Facial disfigurement in a railway accident enables her to re-enter unrecognized the previous marital home as governess to her own children. She takes on the character function of saintly sinner/penitent; she atones and earns some reparation by maternal self-sacrifice in caring incognito for her dying child, tormented by the fact that she cannot claim the role of mother. Her ultimate expiation is through her own death brought on by her weakened state and the exertions of nursing her son.

Contemporary typological constructions of women on the stage, some of which figure in *East Lynne*, took a severe jolt with the stormy appearance of ▷ Ibsen in the English theatre, as did the range of material considered acceptable for the stage. ▷ *A Doll's House* was staged in 1889 and ▷ *Hedda Gabler* and ▷ *Ghosts* in 1891. It was the last play which particularly outraged the critics. Clement Scott in the *Daily Telegraph* was unstinting in his vituperation: it was for him 'an open drain; a loathsome sore unbandaged; a dirty act done publicly; a lazar-house with all its doors and windows open'. Now justly notorious, Scott was more vociferous than others, but his sense of outrage was shared by many. The shock waves were out of all proportion to the number of people who might have been 'contaminated' by exposure to Ibsen's play. The Royalty Theatre, where it played for one night under the auspices of the Independent Theatre Society, had a capacity of only 657. Ibsen's plays, though, with their open discussion of subjects hitherto taboo in the 19th-century English theatre and with their questioning of the traditional (and therefore supposedly natural) role of women, pricked deep-rooted late-19th-century anxieties of a general social and political disintegration.

In the 1890s Ibsen's work was presented by minority theatre ventures; it could not be accommodated to or by the commercial theatre at that time. But the commercial theatre necessarily felt the reverberations of Ibsen's intrusion on to the English stage. Shaw noted that a theatre manager 'must be very careful not to produce a play which will seem insipid and old-fashioned to playgoers who have seen *The Wild Duck*, even though they might have hissed it'.[10] The two English commercial dramatists who seemed to take up the challenge offered to contemporary dramatic writing were Henry Arthur Jones and Arthur Wing Pinero. Jones had established his career writing strong melodramas such as *Saints and Sinners* (1884) and *The Silver King* (1882); Pinero his by writing a series of farces, including *The Magistrate* (1885) and *Dandy Dick* (1887). In 1893 Pinero produced a serious problem play, *The Second Mrs Tanqueray*. The chronology of the appearance of this play, following closely on Ibsen's turbulent entry on to the English stage, is, like Shaw's remark, misleading as well as instructive. *The Second Mrs Tanqueray*, in its examination of the double standard of morality and the unfairness with which a woman with a past like Paula Tanqueray is treated by society, superficially seems to offer a compassionate treatment of weighty moral and social issues. The debt to Ibsen is, however, more apparent than real. The play shows not a direct Ibsenite influence (both Pinero and Jones were adamant in disclaimers of such influence), but reflects an extension of tone and subject matter to which Ibsen's presence contributed. *The Second Mrs Tanqueray*, like many other dramas of the period, is a compromise between the outspokenness of Ibsen, which audiences found objectionable, and the conventional realistic play to which they were accustomed.

*The Second Mrs Tanqueray* examines the misalliance between Aubrey Tanqueray, upper middle class and stolidly respectable, and Paula, who has previously had several liaisons in the *demi-monde* of Europe. Tanqueray may openly articulate a condemnation of the double standard of morality, but he also articulates the idea, endorsed by what the audience actually see of Paula's behaviour, that she is somehow irrevocably damaged by her previous irregular sexual behaviour:

> There's hardly a subject you broach on which poor Paula hasn't some strange, out-of-the-way thought to give utterance to; some curious, warped notion. They are not mere worldly thoughts – unless, good God! they belong to the little hellish world which our blackguardism has created: no, her ideas have too little calculation in them to be called worldly. But it makes it the more dreadful that such thoughts should be ready, spontaneous; that expressing them has become a perfectly natural process; that her words, acts even, have almost lost their proper significance for her, and seem beyond her control. Ah, the pain of listening to it all from the woman one loves, the woman one hoped to make happy and contented, who is really and truly a good woman, as it were, maimed!

The marriage inevitably ends in disaster. Yet the inevitability arises not from the psychological mismatch of husband and wife, nor from society's hostility to the misalliance, but from a coincidence in the plot introduced by Pinero in the last act. Tanqueray's daughter returns from Paris intending to be married to a man who turns out to be a former lover of Paula. Paula's suicide ends the play and resolves the problem. Pinero's use of techniques derived in part from French models (▷ French influence) of the well-made play mediates the experience of a universe dedicated to the preservation of dominant social and moral codes and the punishment of women who have transgressed them. Similarly, in Jones's *Mrs Dane's Defence* (1900), the attempt of the eponymous woman with a past to re-enter society is foiled by an apparently chance discovery in a topographical dictionary which exposes her true identity and past indiscretion. The aesthetic of the well-made play is in essence a function of this ideological imperative. What such plays offer is a passing flirtation with the daring and the mildly risqué, but one which is safely contained by an action that provides resolutions endorsing the validity of the orthodoxies supposedly under serious discussion. Ultimately, the society drama of Jones and Pinero requires the double standard as a kingpin in its endorsement of what is a more extensive conservative ideology and sexual politics.

Other plays raise different problems to be resolved. Pinero's *The Notorious Mrs Ebbsmith* (1895) posits whether a woman of socialist and feminist beliefs can put them into practice by openly keeping house with Lucas Cleeve, a politician of some public prominence; Jones's *The Case of Rebellious Susan* (1894) asks whether a woman can openly repay her husband's infidelity in its own kind and remain in society. Mrs Ebbsmith's unconventional beliefs are rendered invalid when what is represented as her 'natural femininity' reasserts itself and she becomes a theatrically more familiar figure – the ▷ fallen woman. Her transformation in the last act to penitent fallen woman intending to retire to a life of contemplation and prayer in the north of England is not just a sign that she now recognizes the error of her ways, but allows Cleeve to return to his promising political career. In *The Case of Rebellious Susan*, Susan Harabin abandons her rebellion and returns to a patently less than perfect marriage. Jones may well have claimed that 'My comedy isn't a comedy at all. It's a tragedy dressed up as comedy', but any apparent cynicism in the idea that her rebellion can be bought off by what the Bond Street Jewellers supply and her wealthy husband can afford is subsumed by the sense of relief that not just social mores but the very fabric of society have been preserved.

The plays of Oscar Wilde, particularly ▷ *Lady Windermere's Fan* (1892), *A Woman of No Importance* (1893), and *An Ideal Husband* (1895), have, in their settings, thematic concerns and resolutions, clear affinities with the conventions of the social dramas of Jones and Pinero. Where Wilde's plays are acknowledged to differ is in the epigrammatic wit of their dialogue. The relationship between the plays' wit and their conventional theatricality creates a challenging juxtaposition. Wilde's epigrams, in their paradoxical style, logic and subject matter, undermine and subvert the assumed social hierarchies and ethical orthodoxies which are constructed in the settings and conventions of late-Victorian society drama. Similarly, his lack of concern to conceal the improbabilities and coincidences of his plotting strategies has the effect of exposing the conservative ideologies supported by the narratives of Jones and Pinero's plays: indeed, it is the very sophistication of their implementation of such strategies that tends to obscure the ideological work being done there. Wilde is often acknowledged as a satirist of social mores and a moral critic. Yet, in ▷ *The Importance of Being Earnest* (1895) the famous scene where Lady Bracknell interviews Jack Worthing to test his eligibility as a suitor is not just a display of English eccentricity or a comedic parody of theatrical convention; more importantly it also exposes the heart of the power base of the class Lady Bracknell represents. The thematic concern of contemporary society drama, the threat of misalliance, is revealed through Lady Bracknell as an issue of political as well as social and moral consequence:

To be born, or at any rate bred, in a hand-bag, whether it has handles or not, seems to me to display a contempt for the ordinary decencies of family life that reminds one of the worst excesses of the French Revolution. And I presume you know what that unfortunate movement led to?

The political implications, which remain unstated in the work of Jones and Pinero, are here made explicit. The underlying anxiety is not of an undefined disintegration of social and moral values but is one specifically of class conflict and insurrection, of those things that, as Lady Bracknell acknowledges, might 'prove a serious danger to the upper classes . . . and lead to acts of violence in Grosvenor Square'.

The denouement of *The Importance of Being Earnest*, in keeping with the play's genre, re-establishes the previously disrupted social order: Jack really is Earnest and is of acceptable social position – his mother a Lady, his father a general. Yet the play equally suggests that this social settlement is as arbitrary and as absurd as when he was the foundling Jack Worthing and descended from hand luggage.

The society drama of the last decade of the 19th century set the stage for what would become the mainstream of English commercial theatre for at least the next 60 years. It implicitly proposed that subjects worthy or interesting enough for dramatic treatment were only to be found among members of the upper classes, and that the most appropriate way of mediating that experience would be through the conventions of realist staging. It also proposed that what would be most interesting about people from the upper classes would be their peccadilloes, most frequently their sexual peccadilloes.

The dramatist whose career begins in the 19th century but who takes English drama through to what is identifiably a 20th-century style is paradoxically Shaw. The paradox lies in the fact that, unlike progressive dramatists of the first decade of the new century such as John Galsworthy (1867–1933) and Harley Granville Barker (1877–1946) who eschewed what they considered to be outworn dramatic and theatrical conventions, Shaw was flamboyant in his declaration of indebtedness to earlier stage traditions: 'My stories are the old stories; my characters are the familiar harlequin and columbine, clown and pantaloon . . . my stage tricks and suspenses and thrills and jests are the ones in vogue when I was a boy.'[11] Thus, despite the labelling of some of his work in his first volume of published plays as 'unpleasant' ($\triangleright$ *Plays Pleasant and Unpleasant*), *Widowers' Houses* (1892) and *Mrs Warren's Profession* (1902) owe as much to domestic melodrama and romantic comedy, and the commonplace representation of the woman with a past as they do to Ibsen. Others of Shaw's plays are equally identifiable in their adaptation of the conventions of 19th-century commercial theatre: *The Devil's Disciple* (1899), melodrama as practised at the Adelphi; *Caesar and Cleopatra* (1907), large-scale historical drama; $\triangleright$ *Candida* (1900), domestic drama; $\triangleright$ *Arms and the Man* (1894), military melodrama; *Man and Superman* (1904), romantic comedy; *You Never Can Tell* (1899), farcical comedy. For traditional literary history Shaw's plays represent one of the moments where English drama once again gains recognition. The overriding irony is that Shaw's unashamed indebtedness to the vitality of 19th-century theatrical tradition represents an indication of what the canonical literary tradition has missed out on.

*Notes*

1  G.D. Klingopulus, 'The Literary Scene', in *The Pelican Guide to English Literature*, Volume 6, *From Dickens to Hardy*, revised edition (Harmondsworth, Middlesex: Penguin, 1969), p116.

2  M.H. Abrams, *A Glossary of Literary Terms* (New York: Holt, Rinehart and Winston, 1957), p98.

3  John Russell Taylor, *A Dictionary of the Theatre*, revised edition (Harmondsworth, Middlesex: Penguin, 1970), p183; Phyllis Hartnoll (ed.), *The Concise Oxford Companion to the Theatre* (Oxford: Oxford University Press, 1972), p347.

4  Allardyce Nicoll, *A History of English Drama 1660–1900*, 6 vols (Cambridge: Cambridge University Press, 1952–9).

5  By way of comparison the equivalent handlist in the volume covering 1750 to 1800 is only 176 pages long.

6  Dates refer to plays' first UK performances; it should be noted that in the case of Shaw's work the date of first performance often does not coincide with date of publication.

7  Michael R. Booth, *English Melodrama* (London: Herbert Jenkins, 1965); Peter Brooks, *The Melodramatic Imagination: Balzac, Henry James, Melodrama, and the Mode of Excess* (New Haven: Yale University Press, 1976).

8  Abrams, p98; or as another dictionary has it: there is 'a happy ending in which the villain gets all he [*sic*] richly deserves', Ivor H. Evans, *Brewer's Dictionary of Phrase and Fable*, revised edition (London: Cassell, 1981), p727.

9  At least nine different adaptations were presented on the English stage between 1866 and 1899.

10  George Bernard Shaw, *Our Theatre in the Nineties*, 3 vols (London: Constable, 1932), I, p165.

11  George Bernard Shaw, 'Preface' to *Three Plays for Puritans*, in *The Bodley Head Bernard Shaw: Collected Plays and their Prefaces*, edited by Dan H. Laurence, 7 vols (London: Bodley Head, 1970–4), II, pp46–7.

# The Victorian Novel    3

*Gail Cunningham*

*Kingston University*

## Background: Authors, readers and publishers

It is a commonplace of modern criticism that the 19th century – or perhaps more specifically the Victorian age – was dominated by the novel. 'Fiction' is the word which sits naturally, in literary terms, with 'Victorian', in the same way that poetry does with ▷ 'Romantic' or drama with 'Restoration'. It is not only that the century produced a consistent stream of indisputably major practitioners of the form (a conservative listing of whom would need to include ▷ Charles Dickens, ▷ William Thackeray, ▷ Charlotte and Emily Brontë, ▷ George Eliot, ▷ Thomas Hardy and ▷ Henry James, a total difficult to match for a single genre in any other century); more significant, perhaps, is the strength in depth, immense range and variety of interest to be found amongst novelists of less settled reputation. Fiction in the 19th century could and did address every topic, enter every dispute, reflect every ideal of an age perceived by those who lived through it to be one of unprecedentedly rapid change. 'Novels are in the hands of us all; from the Prime Minister down to the last appointed scullery-maid,' wrote ▷ Anthony Trollope in 1870. And of the novels they could have chosen from (an estimated 40,000 titles published in the course of the 19th century), an extraordinarily large number have remained in the common currency of popular rather than scholarly reading habits.

The reasons for this enduring popularity are naturally difficult to pin down; and one immediate answer – that such writers as the Brontës and Dickens are still widely read because they are said to have written good novels – must be considered. But this explanation begs the more interesting question of what exactly is a 'good' novel. Shakespeare and William Wordsworth, for example, both major influences on most 19th-century writers, are not read by the general public to the same extent or for the same reasons as Victorian novelists of considerably lesser claims. There is of course a sense in which the novel is more approachable than drama or poetry. It addresses itself directly to 'life', without the intervening artistic medium of verse or dramatic form, in a way which other literary genres do not. It tells stories, reworks the mundane material of everyday life into something significant, and (most 19th-century readers would add) it teaches moral lessons. More interestingly, perhaps, it could be argued that the 19th-century novel is the first art form to deal explicitly and realistically with issues which speak directly to some of the central concerns of 20th-century consciousness.

The novels of this period sprang from a society undergoing a more massive upheaval under the influence of industrialization than in any previous era. Not only was the population shifting irrevocably from an agricultural to an urban base, with all the profound changes in social, working and family patterns that this entailed; there were also the dramatic visible changes resulting from technological invention which altered people's perceptions and their world. The railway boom of the 1840s (▷ travel and transport) did not merely affect the landscape; its more profound repercussions lay in revolutionizing expectations of speed, mobility and permanence. When in ▷ *Dombey and Son* (1847–8) Dickens describes 'the first great shock of the earthquake' which the building of the railway brings, he is expressing a now familiar paradox inherent in such change: 'from the very core of all this dire disorder, [the railway] trailed smoothly away, upon its mighty course of civilization and improvement'. The chaotic but humane little community of Staggs's Gardens has been 'cut up root and branch' to make way for the 'crowds of people and mountains of goods' to be shifted by the railway: the individual and the idiosyncratic have been sacrificed to the corporate and the homogeneous. ▷ Thomas Carlyle's famous definition of this period as 'the Mechanical Age' focused the anxieties of many contemporaries about the relationship of the individual to society. 'Men are grown mechanical in head and in heart, as well as in hand,' wrote Carlyle, and the development and preservation of individuality within a society dominated by various kinds of mechanistic systems (moral, social, political, economic, even historical) formed a major theme of fiction throughout the century.

However, whereas Carlyle's mechanized individual is tacitly assumed to be a man, the novel of this period belongs in certain crucial respects to women. Not only were women the major consumers of fiction, forming as they did the majority of the readership throughout the century; they were also, to a degree never seen previously, producers as well. Women novelists take equal status with men both as generally acknowledged 'great writers' (fifty per cent of our earlier listing of major novelists were women) and also as part of the huge array of novel writers who produced everything from minor masterpieces to worthless pot-boilers. Throughout the period, writers like ▷ Charlotte Yonge, ▷ Elizabeth Gaskell, ▷ Harriet Martineau, ▷ Ouida and ▷ Margaret Oliphant were producing novels ranging from serious social comment to wild ▷ sensationalism. And in the 1890s the single most popular novelist (though very far from the best) was another woman, ▷ Marie Corelli, whose *The Sorrows of Satan* (1895) sold more copies than any previous English novel. The subject matter of fiction, moreover, fell characteristically into a woman's sphere: even in novels whose thematic interests lie primarily elsewhere, the standard plot and setting were almost invariably domestic and family-orientated, with courtship and marriage providing a major part of the narrative thrust. As George Eliot pointed out, the novel form, more than any other, offered opportunities to women in a society which elsewhere constrained their every activity: 'No restrictions can shut women out from the materials of fiction, and there is no species of art which is so free from rigid requirements.' The 19th-century novel was the first art form in which women could take equal status with men.

For George Eliot, though, as for many others, the unusually dominant role of women as both producers and consumers of fiction was not an unequivocally good thing. Her comments are taken from an essay entitled ▷ 'Silly Novels by Lady Novelists', in which she draws attention to the self-gratifying and unreal stereotypes which the lady novelists offer to an uncritical female readership. In other respects, too, this female orientation had an unfortunate influence on the sphere of the English novel. The popular picture of the Victorian *pater familias* reading out suitable material to his devoted family was not far from the truth and was felt by many practising novelists to be a major restriction on their art. Dickens's Miss Podsnap in ▷ *Our Mutual Friend* (1864–5), the archetypal 'young person', placed a crippling constraint on the material thought proper for inclusion in the novel: 'The question about everything was, would it bring a blush into the cheek of the young person? And the inconvenience of the young person was, that, according to Mr Podsnap, she seemed liable to burst into blushes when there was no need at all.' As Thackeray lamented in his preface to ▷ *Pendennis* (1848–50): 'Since the author of "Tom Jones" was buried, no writer of fiction among us has been permitted to depict to his utmost power a MAN'; Henry Fielding (1707–54) was at liberty to portray a lovable male libertine, whereas Thackeray and his contemporaries looked constantly over their shoulders for the blushes of the young person and the pursed lips of that mythical guardian of morality, Mrs Grundy. This provided a field of tacit warfare throughout the century: where Trollope recorded complacently that 'no girl has risen from the reading of my pages less modest than she was before', other novelists, such as the popular ▷ feminist writer of the 1890s ▷ Mona Caird, chafed furiously against such artificial restraints: 'Mrs Grundy in black silk, with a sceptre in her hand, on the throne of the Ages, surrounded by an angel-choir of Young Persons! Is this to be the end of our democracy?'

Thus for a large part of the 19th century the English novel was significantly limited by the necessity to conform to a moral code which aimed to protect a predominantly female readership from exposure to sexual corruption. Extreme circumspection was required in the depiction of any sort of sexual contact, whether in or outside marriage, often with ludicrous results. Jane Eyre's unusually frank accounts of her feelings for Mr Rochester (which included the confession that she had sat on his knee prior to marrying him) brought accusations of coarseness from several critics. The scene in Hardy's ▷ *Tess of the D'Urbervilles* (1891) in which Angel Clare carries the milkmaids across a flooded lane had to be altered to expunge the image of a man lifting a personable young lady in his arms: in the serialized version, Clare had to be equipped with a wheelbarrow. And in broader terms, too, the novel upheld middle-class morality in matters of sexual conduct. Women were to be pure, and morally superior to men; a marriage was for life; sex was unmentionable. Where a novel depicted deviation from these values, the appropriate moral lesson had to be firmly underlined, so that the ▷ 'fallen woman' who features in so much fiction of the period was invariably seen to be punished. ▷ Mrs Henry Wood's melodramatic and best-selling tale of adultery, ▷ *East Lynne* (1861), rammed home these lessons with almost sadistic relish, warning potential adulteresses that their fate 'will be found far worse than death' and proving the point with

a story of startlingly ingenious retributive suffering. More commonly, the fallen
woman was brought to a dramatic death (like Lady Dedlock in ▷ *Bleak House*)
or banished (like ▷ *David Copperfield*'s Little Em'ly). Even in a work which
pleaded for the moral rights of the fallen woman, such as Elizabeth Gaskell's
▷ *Ruth* (1853), the sinner had to be removed from society by the end of
the novel.

This circumspection had a more profound and potentially damaging effect
on the portrayal of women in the 19th-century novel than it did on the
representation of men. Thackeray was to some extent right to envy Fielding
his Tom Jones, but he might have done better to regret his own inability to
portray a Moll Flanders. Ironically, it was Thackeray himself who in ▷ *Vanity
Fair* (1847–8) encapsulated the Victorian double vision of women which
was seen by many 19th-century commentators to characterize contemporary
attitudes. In Amelia Sedley he satirizes the good woman of conventional
ideals, destructively doting and cloyingly sentimental, passive, long-suffering
and ultimately parasitical; in Becky Sharp he portrays a woman of wit and
initiative, who uses her sexuality and intelligence to exploit a society richly
deserving her machinations, but who must finally be condemned as a neglectful
mother, adulteress and, possibly, a murderer. Charlotte Brontë's ▷ *Shirley*
(1849) explicitly attacks this male polarizing of supposed female attributes:
'Men are often under an illusion about women: they do not read them in a
true light: they misapprehend them, both for good and evil: their good woman
is a queer thing, half doll, half angel; their bad woman always a fiend.' The
bad woman, as we have seen, was habitually disposed of by death; but it was
the good woman, half doll, half angel, who forms the common 20th-century
conception of the typical Victorian heroine. Dickens's Agnes Wickfield, who in
David Copperfield's image of her is 'forever pointing upward', is a typical role
model for the sort of female perfection which is morally impeccable, spiritually
uplifting and a well-earned reward for the world-weary hero. It was an ideal
whose falsity was under constant attack throughout the period and which was
largely discredited by the end of the century: in ▷ Havelock Ellis's phrase,
the stereotyped woman was 'a cross between an angel and an idiot'.

How, then, did what now appears such a patently distorted view of women
retain such a hold in fictional conventions? We must not dismiss out of hand
the notion that Victorian portrayals of women are more reflective of their
repression in reality than we would care to believe. ▷ George Gissing argued
that women actually were intellectually and developmentally feebler than men,
when in typically gloomy mood he stated that 'more than half the misery of
life is due to the ignorance and childishness of women. The average woman
pretty closely resemble ... the average male *idiot*.' In a society which, for
the greater part of the century, denied women access to higher education
and the professions, encased them physically in whalebone and voluminous
skirts, and imbued them with the notion that their highest function was to
serve and inspire men, it is little wonder that the conformist woman of the
time should appear to modern eyes an unacceptably compliant creature – or, as
Edmund Carpenter (1844–1929) more waspishly expressed it, 'a bundle of weak

and flabby sentiments, combined with a wholly undeveloped brain'. However, there is ample evidence from both the numerous examples of independent and rebellious women of 19th-century history, and from the many original and individualized heroines of fiction, that the conventional ideal was not the whole reality. More pervasively influential on characterization, as well as on the form and content of novels, were the actual conditions under which most of them were published.

At the beginning of the 19th century, the majority of novels were published in three, or sometimes four, volumes and the ▷ 'triple decker' retained its popularity until almost the end of the Victorian period. The standard cost of each volume of the novel was half a guinea, a stiff enough price for most middle-class readers and beyond the means of the working class. However, for a subscription of one guinea a year, readers could borrow a volume at a time from one of the ▷ circulating libraries, by far the most influential of which was ▷ Charles Mudie's, opened in 1842. Mudie exercised an influence over the Victorian novel which amounted to a form of ▷ censorship, for he prided himself upon selecting his stock according to its suitability for family consumption. Just as Mudie's moral approval of an author, which could translate into mass buying of copies from the publisher and advance orders for future works, could launch a career in fiction, so his refusal to stock a novel of dubious morality could spell financial disaster. Few novelists could afford the risk of offending the circulating libraries and thus a form of guilty self-censorship constrained the creative freedom of most writers.

Alternatives to publication in three-volume form were initiated by the revival of the monthly serialization of Dickens's ▷ *Pickwick Papers* in 1836. Novels published in this manner were issued as slim volumes appearing at the beginning of each month, continuing as a rule for nineteen numbers. Clearly this form of publication deeply influenced the structure of works in a way largely obscured by their subsequent appearance in a single volume. Writers who wished their readers to continue buying their work over a long period had to end each issue with some form of cliff-hanging incentive to purchase the next volume, and needed also to ensure the memorability of characters whose last appearance could have occurred several months earlier. This may in part account for what is now sometimes taken to be a melodramatic form of plotting and exaggeration in characterization on the part of such habitual practitioners of the monthly serial as Dickens or Thackeray. On the other hand, publication in parts did allow a writer to adjust his or her work in response to readers' preferences: a popular character could boost sales (as Sam Weller did for *Pickwick*) and a narrative red herring could be expeditiously abandoned. As single volume serialization gradually gave way to part publication in family and literary magazines, the questions of sales and censorship moved from the author's to the editor's domain. Hardy was one of the prime sufferers from editorial restraint in his initial serial publication of novels, and frequently had to wait for one-volume publication before he was able to present his work in the form intended. Both Dickens and Thackeray had experience of the business from both ends, the first as editorial instigator of the family weeklies ▷ *Household Words* and ▷ *All the Year Round*, the second as editor of the prestigious ▷ *Cornhill*. Amongst major Victorian novelists, only the Brontës never published in any sort of serial form.

## Development through the century

Given the wealth and variety of 19th-century fiction, as well as the inevitable historical shifts in critical judgements, it is hardly surprising to find widely diverging assessments of how the novel developed over the period. ▷ George Saintsbury's *A History of Nineteenth-century Literature*, first published in 1896, gives almost as much space Maria Edgeworth (1767–1849) as to Jane Austen (1775–1817) and George Eliot, and treats Walter Scott (1771–1832) more fully than Dickens: Hardy receives no mention at all. F.R. Leavis's immensely influential *The Great Tradition* (1948) opens with the characteristically combative statement that 'The great English novelists are Jane Austen, George Eliot, Henry James and Joseph Conrad'; Charlotte Brontë is noted as having 'permanent interest of a minor kind', Dickens as being a 'great entertainer' who lacks 'sustained seriousness'. While few modern critics would wish to eliminate from the canon these four writers, contemporary interest in the 19th-century novel ranges far beyond his vaguely defined but insistently urged criterion of 'significant creative achievement'. Individual writers and sub-genres of the novels which would have been relegated to areas of minor interest by many mid-20th-century critics now attract serious study, and the reputations of many well-known novelists have notably shifted. Of those most highly regarded in the 19th century itself, Scott and ▷ George Meredith have suffered the most serious depression in critical interest; neither is now much read by the general public or widely taught on literature degrees. Dickens, on the other hand, has been reclaimed from the realm of mere entertainer and praised as an incisive social critic of profound symbolic significance. And Hardy, ignored by Saintsbury and patronizingly dismissed by Leavis, now commands as wide a critical industry on both sides of the Atlantic as any 19th-century novelist.

There is no simple way of subdividing the mass of fictional material published during the period, nor, despite Leavis's claim for a great tradition, is there any single line of development which can easily be traced. Conventionally, the pre-Victorian period, where the major figures are Scott and Jane Austen, is seen as having a separate identity, which then gives way to the explosion of talent in the first decades of Victoria's reign, with the emergence of Dickens, Thackeray and the Brontës. The mid-Victorian novel can be seen as dominated by the later Dickens and George Eliot, and the late 19th century by Hardy. These periods will be dealt with separately in conjunction with the major authors within them. However, to identify the major practitioners of the form during the period is very far from finding a consistent train of development. While there is a sense in which James's novels can be seen as a more self-consciously artistic development of Jane Austen's fictional mode, there is no obvious way in which Hardy may be said to emerge from the same tradition. Charlotte Brontë, notoriously, found little to admire in Jane Austen, and Hardy recorded that he was unable to finish reading ▷ *Wuthering Heights* (1847). Arguably, the 19th century saw the emergence in the novel of a privileging of ▷ 'realism', both in the presentation of psychological depth of characterization and in the depiction of humankind's inevitable inter-relation with the newly perceived complexities of social and historical contexts. There is also a clear change, in the Victorian period at least, in the material thought permissible for inclusion in the novel. The tyranny of the circulating libraries and the family magazines was gradually eroded to allow greater frankness in the fictional portrayal of sexuality. By the 1890s outspokenness on questions of sexual behaviour – particularly in women – had become to some extent fashionable, and a host of popular novels which examined such questions in an overtly polemical manner enjoyed a brief vogue. Even so, the violently antagonistic reception of Hardy's ▷ *Jude the Obscure* (1895), which saw the novel reviled in the press and burnt by a bishop, showed how severely limited this increased tolerance could be.

More importantly, an attempt to treat 19th-century fiction as a smoothly developing series of 'great writers' severely distorts the picture of the novel as it would have been viewed by both readers and authors during the period itself. It ignores too much of what was seriously offered and received by contemporary writers and readers, and which is now the subject of increasing critical interest, both as reflections of the 19th-century consciousness and as significant and legitimate variations on the novel form. Late 20th-century taste is perhaps more open to the claims of ▷ romance and fantasy, more sympathetically interested in the overt wrestling with ideas, than was the case when Leavis made high moral seriousness and mastery of form his main criteria of excellence. Minor novelists, and the sub-genres in which they frequently wrote, are an essential and illuminating part of the 19th-century fictional scene.

## Sub-genres of the novel

During the early decades of the 19th century most popular fiction grew out of the traditions of romance and Romanticism. The two terms are of course closely linked, but should not be equated. A romance, in David Masson's phrase of 1859, was 'a fictitious narrative . . . the interest of which turns upon marvellous and uncommon incidents', and the debate between romance and realism formed a continuous part of 19th-century thinking about the theory of fiction. The influence of the Romantic movement was most apparent in the late-18th-century Gothic novel, a form not lacking in marvellous and uncommon incidents, but which also played on the Romantic interest in the supernatural and in the dark and untapped areas of the human psyche. Jane Austen, writing novels of pragmatic realism during the height of the Romantic period, mercilessly satirized the implausibility of the Gothic through the credulous Catherine of *Northanger Abbey* (1818), and neatly pinned down the possible self-indulgence of the romantic sensibility in *Persuasion*'s Captain Brandon. Thomas Love Peacock's spoof Gothic novel, *Nightmare Abbey* (1818), also lampooned the form as well as parodying the romantic excesses of some of that movement's major poets. But the Gothic was still kept vividly alive in Mary Shelley's *Frankenstein* (1817), published in the same year as Peacock's parody, and reappears, subtly transformed, in the works of Charlotte and Emily Brontë. It could also be argued that the ▷ historical novel, first popularized by Scott, and continued less successfully in the works of, for example, ▷ Harrison Ainsworth, owed much to the Romantic and Gothic preoccupation with the past.

In many ways, though, it was romance rather than Romanticism which informed the main sub-genres of the first three decades of the 19th century. Writers of popular fiction were concerned to entertain their readers with dramatic incidents and to draw them imaginatively into worlds remote from their own. The historical novel could obviously offer limitless scope here, in terms both of high drama and (often ponderously academic) period detail. Where Ainsworth's novels catered to the contemporary taste for luridly reconstructed English history, one of the other popular practitioners of the form, ▷ Edward Bulwer-Lytton, mainly remembered now for *The Last Days of Pompeii* (1834), took the wider sweep of Western historical movements as his subject. His historical romances tend to focus on the closing of eras, and may thus be seen as signifying contemporary unease in the face of change and instability. But his writings are too clogged with the fruits of meticulous historical research, and too stilted in the rendering of dialogue, to have lasted well. However, forms of the historical novel continued to be practised throughout the century by major as well as minor writers. George Eliot ventured into historical fiction, not wholly successfully, in ▷ *Romola*, and it is a fact often overlooked by modern readers that large numbers of major Victorian novels are 'historical' in the sense of being set some thirty to forty years before their date of publication.

The historical novel could be both an escape from and a comment on the profound changes which were perceived to be occurring in the contemporary social order. Of less obvious relevance were the other popular sub-genres of the early 19th century, the ▷ Newgate novel and the 'silver-fork' school (▷ Fashionable Novel). The Newgate novel played on morbid tastes for violence and death in ways which relate it to some extent to the Gothic, and in romanticizing its criminals it removed such socially disruptive elements safely into the realm of fantasy. The silver-fork school, on the other hand, displayed the sort of high society life to which increasingly prosperous members of the middle class might hope to aspire and which they could certainly be expected to envy. Novels of this class paraded details of the food, fashions and furniture of the rich and well-bred before a readership which could now begin to dream of emulating such manners. Writers of silver-fork fiction included ▷ Benjamin Disraeli in his early novel *Vivian Grey* (1826), and the now largely forgotten Theodore Hook (1788–1841) and ▷ Catherine Gore. Both Dickens and Thackeray capture and to some degree satirize the mood of envious interest amongst the socially mobile on which these novels played, Thackeray in his portrayal of the *nouveaux riches* Osborne and Sedley families in *Vanity Fair*, Dickens, for example, in his parody 'The Lady Flabella' in ▷ *Nicholas Nickleby* or with the Veneerings in ▷ *Our Mutual Friend*. Interestingly, both the Newgate and silver-fork forms have modern counterparts in popular fiction in what have been neatly designated the 'bodice-ripping' school of historical fiction (in which sex replaces death as the focus) and the 'sex-and-shopping' novel which caters for the emulative dreams of the upwardly mobile.

Of more immediate social relevance, however, as well as in general possessing more lasting literary merit, were the novels which addressed the 'condition of England' question. These works, also known as ▷ 'social problem' novels, arose out of the social and political upheavals which followed the ▷ Reform Bill of 1832. The 1830s and 1840s marked the beginnings of a conscious effort both by Parliament and by social commentators to address the problems caused by the rapid industrialization of the preceding decades. The first Factory Act and the ▷ Poor Law Amendment Act of 1834 reflected the stirrings of governmental conscience and, from the other side, the rise of ▷ Chartism marked the beginnings of concerted working-class demands for reform. The economic depression of the 1840s produced deprivation amongst the industrial workers of the north on a scale which could not be ignored, and Chartist riots and marches on Westminster made poverty and disaffection visibly threatening to the comparatively untouched middle-class southerner. It was Carlyle who first drew attention to the social effects of the industrial revolution in his essay 'Signs of the Times' (1829) and who, in coining the phrase 'condition of England question' in *Chartism* (1839), provided a focus for what to many novelists of the early Victorian period seemed to be the central matter for fiction. Writers like Elizabeth Gaskell, Disraeli, ▷ Charles Kingsley and the Dickens of ▷ *Hard Times* (1854), addressed themselves directly to the question and produced novels which dealt realistically and sympathetically with the problems of the industrialized working class.

Probably the major strength of the social problem novel lay in its educational rather than its polemical function. Written by and for the middle classes, these novels laid out with passionate clarity the plight of a section of the community of which most readers, for geographical and social reasons, were simply ignorant. The new cities of the north of England, where industrial workers were herded into hastily erected housing built round smoke-belching factories, were uncharted territory for large parts of the novel-reading public, and the divisive effects of such developments were repeatedly stressed by novelists. In giving his 'condition of England' novel ▷ *Sybil* (1845) the sub-title 'The Two Nations', Disraeli encapsulated his perception of a country tragically and dangerously split between rich and poor, and Elizabeth Gaskell's ▷ *North and South* (1854–5) explores the differences in values and living conditions between the two halves of the country. The vividly realistic descriptions of working-class life provided by many social problem novels were as educative to contemporary readers as to later social historians, and the pressing issues of Chartism, ▷ trade unions, strikes and master-worker relations receive sensitive if rarely revolutionary treatment in such novels as Gaskell's ▷ *Mary Barton* (1848), Kingsley's ▷ *Alton Locke* (1850) and Disraeli's *Sybil*. Dickens's *Hard Times*, the only one of his novels to be set exclusively in the north of England, contrasts the mechanistic, and as he sees them, inhuman principles of ▷ Utilitarian philosophy with the personal and warm-hearted values of imaginative sympathy, and his handling of the question of solidarity amongst the factory hands is symptomatic of the ambivalence apparently inherent in the genre. His working-class protagonist, Stephen Blackpool, is a saintly victim, his union leader a blustering agitator and the men good-hearted innocents temporarily swayed into an unworthy form of protest against a system portrayed as patently wrong. Blackpool's repeated lament in the face of baffingly obvious injustice, "Tis all a muddle', sums up the helplessness of worker and novelist alike in the face of the enormity of the problem.

Indeed, the one major criticism of the genre, levelled by contemporaries as well as by modern critics, was that it proffered inadequate and often sentimental solutions to questions of great social and political complexity. As Thackeray put it, 'At the conclusion of these tales ... there somehow arrives a misty reconciliation between the poor and the rich; a prophecy is uttered of better times for the one, and better manners in the other ... and the characters make their bow, grinning, in a group, as they do at the end of a drama when the curtain falls.' This is largely true of the novels mentioned: the symbolic handshake between master and man at the end of *North and South*, Mary Barton's escape to Canada with her newly wed husband, or Stephen Blackpool's martyrdom in the cause of truth and understanding, all substitute reconciliation at a personal level for long-term political solutions. Hovever, there is no reason to expect novelists to be in possession of answers which escaped legislators, whereas in articulating and making imaginatively immediate the social problems of the time, writers of the 'condition of England' novels not only provided a valuable information service but also produced works of significant realism and insight.

The social condition of a newly industrialized Britian was a preoccupation of novelists mainly during the 1840s and 1850s. During the same period the spiritual condition of the country also became of pressing concern and novels dealing with religious questions formed another recognizable sub-genre which retained its currency to the end of the century. In some sense all 19th-century novels are 'religious' in so far as they are the product of a society in which Christian observance was the norm amongst the middle classes, and thus the moral and spiritual values of Christianity are necessarily either implicit in or deliberately explored by all writers of fiction. However, the crisis of faith which arose in the middle decades of the 19th century predictably gave rise to works which set out to discuss the problems explicitly, in much the same way in which the condition of England novel articulated social and political questions. The three main influences on religious thought during this time were the ▷ Oxford Movement of the 1830s and 1840s, which sought to restore High Church ideals within the Church of England, and culminated in ▷ John Newman's defection to Roman ▷ Catholicism in 1845; the new German biblical criticism, first made accessible to English readers with the publication of George Eliot's translation of Strauss's *Leben Jesu* in 1846; and of course the impact of ▷ Charles Darwin's *On the Origin of Species* (1859). Spiritual crises and ecclesiastical quarrellings form the subject of such novels as J.A. Froude's *The Nemesis of Faith* (1849), Disraeli's *Lothair* (1870) and ▷ Mrs Humphry Ward's *Robert Elsmere* (1883), as well as being the basis of Trollope's ▷ Barsetshire novels and Margaret Oliphant's imitations of them, ▷ *The Chronicles of Carlingford*.

Nineteenth-century consumers of fiction were thus very much more receptive to the exposition of ideas in fiction than are most modern readers, who tend to resent being preached at under the guise of fiction. Problem novels, or 'novels with a purpose', tackled issues of all kinds throughout the period. Again, the main beneficiaries of this discursive tendency were probably women, whose problems, lumped under the catch-all phrase ▷ 'the woman question', were repeatedly examined. The fallen woman was, as mentioned above, a particularly popular subject, featuring as a dreadful warning in works such as *East Lynne* or as a repentant Magdalen figure in *Ruth*. Charlotte Yonge's *The Clever Woman of the Family* (1865) cautions young women against the temptations of the intellect as memorably as Mrs Henry Wood does against the lure of the flesh. And by the last decade of the century there had arisen a distinct class of novel, the ▷ 'New Woman fiction', which dealt with the current feminist questions of sex, marriage and work. Grant Allen's *succès de scandale*, ▷ *The Woman Who Did* (1895), marked the culmination of the genre, with its hyperbolic attack on the institution of marriage (a 'temple' where 'pitiable victims languish and die in . . . sickening vaults'). Nor was the problem novel exclusively the province of minor writers: almost all major novelists of the period deal with these ideas in some form or other, and in the 1890s, for example, ▷ George Gissing's ▷ *The Odd Women* (1893), Meredith's *Lord Ormont and his Aminta* (1894) and Hardy's *Jude the Obscure* (1895) were all taken by contemporary readers to be variations of the New Woman novel.

There is, then, continuous interaction in terms of themes, issues and genres, between different writers, and between recognizable sub-groups of the novel and what is now regarded as mainstream fiction. The novelists of the period should be viewed within the artistic as well as the social and political context in which they worked.

## The mid-19th century: Dickens, Thackeray, the Brontës

In the early Victorian novel the depiction of society generally expands unrecognizably from Jane Austen's 'little bit of ivory' (a term she used to describe the self-imposed restrictions of her range) to a consciously panoramic perspective in which the individual is likely to be embattled and forlorn. The figure of the innocent child, often lonely and neglected, becomes a powerful symbol of society's guilt; the education and growth from childhood show the process of adjustment within a largely hostile social structure. While the Romantic movement discovered and articulated the moral potency of the child, it was the Victorian novel which produced the first sustained portrayals of children in literature.

Of the major novelists of the period, William Makepeace Thackeray (1811–63) is probably least directly concerned with children, though his best novel, *Vanity Fair* (1847–8), does make use of significant incidents from the childhood of his protagonists in order to account for their subsequent development. Though often astute and original in his perception of his characters' psychology, his main strengths as a writer lay in his sharp eye for the particular kinds of human weakness thrown up by a newly complex society and his ability, in *Vanity Fair* at least, to bind all levels of the social structure into a comprehensive vision of moral and spiritual inadequacy. When Charlotte Brontë described him as 'the first social regenerator of the day', she was responding to qualities which were abundantly present in his early work but which faded notably in his later career. *Vanity Fair*, 'A Novel without a Hero', depicts English society in the years surrounding Waterloo as itself a battleground where money and social standing are the criteria for success and where individuals rise and fall according to their skill in playing social games which are as amoral and arbitrary as the values of the Stock Exchange which determine the fortunes of the Osborne and Sedley families on which the novel centres. Though Thackeray focuses his interest on the newly emerging middle classes, his picture of society extends upwards into the metropolitan aristocracy and the landed gentry, and downwards to the working classes and ▷ Bohemia. What binds them all is the struggle for money and reputation in a cut-throat world where the clever can 'live well on nothing a year' and the weak go to the wall. It is a mark of Thackeray's originality that the character who most successfully exploits the possibilities of his social struggle is a woman, the intelligent and cynical Becky Sharp, whom as we have seen, for all her manifest faults, he can never bring himself thoroughly to condemn. The novel leaves a moral question mark over all its characters and in so doing forces its readers to engage actively in the process of questioning and judgement in a way calculated both to challenge and disturb.

Charles Dickens (1812–70), Thackeray's more successful rival for the affections of the novel-reading public, rarely leaves such moral openness, but develops more consistently towards a bleak view of society in which monolithic institutions (money and commerce in *Dombey and Son*, the law in *Bleak House*, the civil service in ▷ *Little Dorrit*) are potentially crushing to the strongly realized goodness of individuals. It was Dickens more than any other Victorian novelist who exploited the possibilities of the child as symbol of innocence amidst corruption, and this is one major factor which has led to accusations of sentimentality in his works. A catalogue of his maltreated but morally reformative children – Oliver Twist, David Copperfield, Paul and Florence Dombey, Jo the crossing sweeper, Little Nell, Sissy Jupe, Little Dorrit (amongst many others) – suggests a preoccupation with the innocence of childhood which could add weight to such an accusation, and it is largely true that Dickens's children are exempt from the barbs of humorous exposure with which he mercilessly illuminates the grotesque flaws in most of his characters' compositions. But his best portrayals of childhood – those in which the child ceases to be a simple symbolic force – uniquely capture the guilts and fears as well as the pathetic helplessness of juvenile innocence.

Modern mainline humanist criticism tends to base its praise for Dickens on a perception of the development in his later novels of a thematically coherent critique of his society which works through imagery and symbolism rather than through the creation of psychologically convincing characters. One can point, for example, to the recurrent images of imprisonment in *Little Dorrit* (1855–7) or to the sustained exploration of legal ramifications in *Bleak House* (1852–3). His world is so richly animated, his descriptive powers so invigoratingly original, as to invest the inanimate objects of his world with a vitality and significance often assumed to compensate for the lack of realism in the people who inhabit it. His women are prime targets for criticism here, since it is generally female characters who, for obvious reasons, carry the sometimes crippling weight of his moral approval. Dickens, while anatomizing the evils of his society with unique imaginative power, had a characteristically Victorian belief in the possibility of unsullied goodness and it is generally the heroines of his novels who provide examples of its morally regenerative force. Sissy Jupe in *Hard Times* (1854) works a change in the harshly Utilitarian Gradgrind household 'by mere love and gratitude' and it is her 'wisdom of the Heart' which effectively counteracts the mechanistic values that the novel attacks. Her passive goodness and sweetly self-sacrificing nature exemplify the qualities often taken to be regrettably typical of Dickens's portrayal of women. However, it could also be argued that the 20th century's automatic suspicion of pure virtue blinds the modern reader to more subtle qualities in Dickens's heroines. His skill in depicting the psychological results of guilt and repression, often noted in his male characters, is present also in his portrayal of many of the women. There is a great deal more to such characters as Florence Dombey, Esther Summerson or Little Dorrit than is usually perceived by an eye habitually prejudiced against the stereotype of the good woman.

Whatever may be reclaimed for Dickens's reputation in the portrayal of women, though, he can never hope to rival the Brontës in this area. ▷ Anne Brontë (1820–49), less talented and original than her sisters, still writes movingly and perceptively about the loneliness of the governess in ▷ *Agnes Grey* (1847), and adds new dimensions to the depiction of marital misery in ▷ *The Tenant of Wildfell Hall* (1848). Emily Brontë's only novel, *Wuthering Heights*, is generally recognized to transcend normal moral and spiritual expectations. Though Charlotte Brontë (1816–55) felt it necessary in her Preface to apologize for what she felt 'must appear a rude and strange production', the novel is meticulously planned and structured. Its strangeness derives partly from its unaccustomed settings, more perhaps from its extremities of violence and passion, and the central portrayal in Cathy and Heathcliff of a relationship which cannot be assimilated into any conventional framework or concept of character. That Emily Brontë (1818–48) was aware of the difficulties of this structure is shown by the care with which she draws her readers into the story through narrators of familiar social and psychological backgrounds; as their limitations are exposed, so their conventional judgements are progressively rejected and the reader is invited to accept an entirely unfamiliar scheme of values. At the end of the novel, Lockwood's inability to imagine 'unquiet slumbers for the sleepers in that quiet earth' seems more a reflection of his own limitations than an assurance that the grave will provide a final peace for the spirits of Cathy and Heathcliff.

However, the radical nature of Emily Brontë's vision makes her less influenced by social realities. Her main characters, in being largely outside convention, make no direct comment upon it. Charlotte Brontë, on the other hand, in working more within the bounds of recognizable society, produces original depictions of women which are overtly hostile to contemporary ideals. The autobiographical elements in her work create repeated images of women struggling against a world whose expectations they are unable and indeed unwilling to fulfil. Jane Eyre, 'poor, plain and little', and Lucy Snowe, wracked with the pain of unrequited love, obviously call upon Charlotte Brontë's own experiences. Her heroines all struggle in a world whose standards of female behaviour are alien to their own, and their achievements are wrenched painfully from the creation of a personal morality which is frequently at odds with the conventions of their society. Though Lucy Snowe in ▷ *Villette* (1853), who in the novel's slightly ambiguous ending is shown as independent mistress of her own school, may seem the most obvious candidate for modern feminist approval, it is really Jane Eyre who is the more impressive figure. Jane's impassioned cry 'I will be myself' summarizes the novel's sustained plea for a morality in which the heroine has the right and indeed the duty to realize her individuality independent of expectations from more familiar moral systems. Both Charlotte and Emily Brontë participate in the Romantics' championing of the unique individual, the first within, the second largely outside, contemporary social realities. The poetic intensity of their writing, together with the patent influences of the Gothic and Byronic traditions, make their works the most striking inheritors of Romanticism in the fiction of the period.

### The mid-Victorian period: George Eliot

It is gratifying to reflect that arguably the first intellectual amongst major English novelists was a woman. In an age when female ▷ education was largely limited to the acquisition of 'accomplishments', George Eliot (1819–80) could read French, Italian, German, Latin and Greek. Deeply involved in and influenced by the philosophical and scientific movements of the time, she lost her religious faith in early womanhood but retained a profound sense of moral imperatives in a secular context. In common with many of her contemporaries, her interests focused on history and on modern attempts to arrive at systematic descriptions of social, religious and intellectual evolution. Her novels continually show her interest in the relationship between individual and historical change: as the individual is the product of social and historical forces, so society is formed and changed by the apparently inconsiderable lives of the individuals who composed it. Dorothea, who sets out at the beginning of ▷ *Middlemarch* (1871–2) in the view of the narrator as 'a modern Saint Theresa', may be defeated in her youthful objectives of effecting visible or dramatic change in her society but is convincingly displayed at the end as having an effect 'incalculably diffusive' on 'the growing good of the world'. The portrayal of the individual within a complex network of social and historical relationships forms a major part of George Eliot's fictional vision.

The past, and the extent to which her characters are determined by forces contained within it, form a continual theme in her fiction. 'Our deeds determine us, as much as we determine our deeds,' she wrote in ▷ *Adam Bede* (1859), and her novels repeatedly display what in *Middlemarch* she described as 'the slow preparation of effects from one life on another'. Seeing her characters as largely determined by a meticulously charted individual past, and a socially and historically realized present, she nevertheless insists upon the stern exercise of personal responsibility in moral decision-making. Her characters, or more particularly her narrators, are among the first in English fiction to be consistently portrayed in the process of rigorous *thought*, whether about personal choices or larger intellectual systems. However, George Eliot as narrator remains firmly in control of both her structures and her readers' responses. When in *Middlemarch* she comments on the unknowable significance of future developments in individual lives – 'destiny stands by sarcastic with our *dramatis personae* folded in her hand' – she could have legitimately substituted herself for destiny. George Eliot's authorial voice, omniscient, magisterial and tolerant, constantly controls our reactions and to some extent raises her readers to a level close to her own lofty overview. When Virginia Woolf (1882–1941) described *Middlemarch* as 'one of the few English novels written for grown-up people', she was deftly defining the degree to which George Eliot's fiction makes demands of serious moral response in a readership which could previously have rested happily within the safe bounds of entertaining diversion.

## Hardy and the late 19th century

Some contemporary reviewers of Thomas Hardy's early, anonymously published, work speculated that it might be by George Eliot. Presumably they were misled by the superficial similarities in the portrayal of rural communities and perhaps by Hardy's youthful pretensions to a command of contemporary intellectual issues, imperfectly assimilated. Indeed, an inability to judge his readers' tolerance of progressive moral and intellectual views was a continuing, and to modern eyes endearing, quality of Hardy's fiction, deriving as it did from his unusual combination of a countryman's pragmatism with a self-educated intellectualism. As the creator of the semi-fictional world of ▷ Wessex, Hardy (1840–1928) became the most significant regional novelist of the age and, with his unrivalled knowledge of the local customs and accents of his native land, was in a better position than any other writer to chart the changes in agricultural communities under the various dramatic shocks of 19th-century change. Hardy has, moreover, an eye for nature which is at once entirely unsentimental and supremely observant. When in ▷ *A Pair of Blue Eyes* (1873) Henry Knight clings desperately to a cliff with a fatal drop beneath him, Hardy notes that his torments are increased by the fact that rain driven against such an obstacle moves upwards not down: and, metaphorically staring death in the face, Knight's eyes actually meet the fossilized gaze of a trilobite embedded for millions of years in the rock before him. The vulnerable human in his extremity meets the indifferent but infinitely varied forces of nature, yet has contact over a gap of several million years with a fellow creature who has similarly suffered the pangs of life and death.

Such an incident is typical of the way in which Hardy's immense imaginative range and habitual preoccupation with the ironies of time are given solidity by observation of the precisely natural. It is also characteristic in that Knight's eventual rescue is effected by an incident at once stimulating and shocking to Victorian sexual tastes. The novel's heroine, Elfride, strips herself of all her undergarments in order to make a rope and, clad merely in a 'diaphanous exterior robe', hauls him to safety. Throughout his career Hardy found himself embroiled in battles against the prudish sensibilities of his readership and as his later novels began to engage more directly with contemporary questions of sexual morality, he was drawn, apparently protestingly, into fervent debates about women, sex and marriage. His views of the human condition, though, are more comprehensively tragic than would be suggested by confining him to immediate social criticism. Frequently accused of being irredeemably pessimistic, he described himself as a meliorist who portrayed the worst in order to point towards the better. But, despite the sharpness of their social criticism, there is little in his last novels – in *Tess of the D'Urbervilles* (1891) or *Jude the Obscure* (1895) – to suggest that possible future change could effectively alleviate their essentially tragic vision.

Hardy was in many senses the last of the great Victorian novelists. During the final years of the century it was his reputation, together with the more warily expressed admiration for Meredith, which dominated English fiction. Amongst other novelists, though, the debate about the relationship between romance and realism continued to be waged, with Gissing and ▷ Moore as the prime realists vying with the exotic romances of, for example, ▷ Robert Louis Stevenson and ▷ H. Rider Haggard. The vitality of the novel form was undiminished both in its challenge to social and moral convention and in its sheer inventiveness in entertainment. In literary terms, though, it was Henry James, with his infinitely sophisticated narrative and Joseph Conrad's modernism, which pointed the way forwards into 20th-century developments of the novel as a form of art.

# Victorian poetry: 1830–1900

*Linda Williams*
*Southampton University*

*'Dusty answers': Loss and nostalgia in Victorian poetry*

> *Ah, what a dusty answer gets the soul*
> *When hot for certainties in this our life!*
> *(Modern Love; George Meredith, 1862)*

Poetry since 1830 has been written largely in a state of shock. From the shock of electricity to the 'shock of the new', currents of difficulty and doubt animate poetic history, fuelled by a crisis of faith and the instability of living in a rapidly growing and urbanizing society within which values were becoming increasingly unstable. This feeling of uncertainty is indulged by the Victorians through the notion that there was once a time, well into the past, when certainty existed. In ▷ Tennyson's words, Victorian poetry is permeated with 'the quiet sense of something lost' (▷ *In Memoriam A.H.H.*).

Tennyson's long elegy, *In Memoriam A.H.H.* (1850), is perhaps the most famous poem of loss to be penned in the 19th century. Written almost as therapy over a long period, what is being mourned is not simply Arthur Hallam, the poet's greatest friend; rather his death is a pretext for an extended meditation on absence. What is lost is also a fixed personal identity, certainty of perception and judgement, and the idea of a benign or controlling divinity. ▷ Matthew Arnold's elegiac lyric ▷ *Dover Beach* (1867) sketches out this sense of loss:

> *The Sea of Faith*
> *Was once, too, at the full, and round earth's shore*
> *Lay like the folds of a bright girdle furled.*
> *But now I only hear*
> *Its melancholy, long, withdrawing roar . . .*

Reading Tennyson's intense lament alongside the passive melancholy of Arnold gives us two perspectives on how this loss, which is of course nothing new, is characterized in a particularly Victorian way. For Tennyson, trust in God must come despite the abysmal fact that,

> *Nature, red in tooth and claw*
> *With ravine, shrieked against his creed*
> *(In Memoriam A.H.H.)*

So if *Dover Beach* is an elegy, who or what has died?

In many ways the most interesting poetry of the period since 1830 can be called 'death of God' poetry, after ▷ Nietzsche's famous proclamation

that 'God is dead'. In *Easter Day, Naples* 1849 ▷ Arthur Clough writes,
'Ah! "some" did well to "doubt"!', in the midst of a text which repeats an
▷ atheist incantation:

> *Christ is not risen, no,*
> *He lies and moulders low;*
> *Christ is not risen.*
>
> *Ashes to ashes, dust to dust;*
> *As of the unjust, also of the just –*
> *Christ is not risen.*

Such a strong statement runs contrary to our cherished notion that the
Victorians were a nation of devout church-goers, even if read in the context
of the subsequent poem by Clough, 'Easter Day II' which affirms the opposite
view. Despite the explosion in church-building which took place up to the
1850s, the Religious Census of 1851 showed that a large proportion of the
population did not go to church. This feeling reaches a virulent pitch later in
the century with ▷ James Thomson's *The City of Dreadful Night* (1874), a poem
which, in its compulsive repetition, is structured like a nightmare. *City* may be
the nearest thing in English poetry to Rimbaud's *Une Saison en enfer* (1873),
although its invectives against God bring it closer to Lautréamont (1846–70):

> *The vilest thing must be less than Thou*
> *From whom it had its being, God and Lord!*
> *. . . I vow*
>
> *That not for all Thy power furled and unfurled, (. . .)*
> *Would I assume the ignominious guilt*
> *Of having made such men in such a world.*
> *(The City of Dreadful Night)*

Thomson's God is alive and actively malicious, but the God who withdraws
with Arnold's Sea of Faith is conspicuous only by his absence. Tennyson wrote
to fill the absences – 'if there was a blank space I would put in a poem' – and one
such absence has been created by God's departure. *In Memoriam* thus confronts
these absences as the grieving self confronts the Victorian 'Unreal city':

> *He is not here; but far away*
> *The noise of life begins again,*
> *And ghastly through the drizzling rain*
> *On the bald street breaks the blank day.*

As with Tennyson's ▷ *Maud* (1855), *In Memoriam* shows a self so disrupted
and infiltrated that it cannot affirm ▷ Robert Browning's much quoted phrase,
'God's in his heaven – / All's right with the world' (*Pippa Passes*). This is
turned inward, for if God does not exist, man cannot exist in his image,

and so the self's solidity and its possibilities of self-conscious meaningful action are undermined. Two quotations, the first from *In Memoriam* (LIV), the second from the remarkable poem by John Clare (1793–1864), 'I Am' (1864), illustrate this:

> ... *but what am I?*
> *An infant crying in the night:*
>  *An infant crying for the light:*
> *And with no language but a cry.*

> *I am – yet what I am none cares or knows,*
>  *My friends forsake me like a memory lost;*
> *I am the self-consumer of my woes,*
>  *They rise and vanish in oblivious host.*

His 'not being here' renders the urbanized, brave new world of the mid-19th century, the world of cholera and of the Crimean war, all the more ghastly, bald and blank, a world which it seemed, for the most part, God had never visited at all.

In the wake of this appalling possibility, fragments of memory – *In Memoriam* is certainly a fragmented text – are shored up poetically against present fear and ruin,

> ... *when the sensuous frame*
> *Is racked with pangs that conquer trust;*
> *And Time, a maniac scattering dust,*
> *And Life, a fury slinging flame.*
>      (*In Memoriam A.H.H.*)

The sense that history and technology were advancing out of all rational and moral control was acutely felt by poets, characterized by feelings of alienation from home. 'A wanderer is man from his birth' writes Arnold in 'The Future' (1852), and feelings of loss serve to fill the gap between the self and its long-gone place of safety. In Clare's 'I Am' the world is a 'vast shipwreck', and the 'nothingness of scorn and noise', the 'living sea of waking dreams' renders his loved ones even 'stranger than the rest'. ▷ Anne Brontë laments to herself, 'Sad wanderer, weep those blissful times / That never may return!' ('The Bluebell'; 1840). We could turn to countless verses where this sentiment is repeated, culminating in ▷ Thomas Hardy's double vision of loss and dread right at the end of the century. An image is set up across a wide range of Victorian poems of a lost cherished past – an idyllic pre-industrial England, the innocence of childhood, a place where unproblematic faith was possible. But working in tandem with melancholic lament is the Victorian passion for more positive and elaborate retrospection.

The Victorians had a great talent for nostalgia. This means that their interpretation of the past was double-edged, countering present loss with rosily remembered bygone times. In the face of uncompromising industrial expansion and unprecedented urban squalor a sumptuous pseudo-medieval (▷ medievalism) world was erected, a counter-image of ▷ Gothic grandeur activated by the prose celebrations of ▷ John Ruskin and ▷ Thomas Carlyle. The latter looked to the Middle Ages as a point of pre-industrial authenticity where 'Antique devoutness, Antique veracity and heroism' were possible (▷ *Past and Present*, 1843); the former's celebration of the Gothic had a profound influence upon the architectural practice of the second half of the 19th century. ▷ William Morris's championing of the Arts and Crafts Movement was vehemently anti-capitalist in favouring individual production and handiwork over the mass production of advanced technology. All these were impassioned moral responses to the feeling of contemporary spiritual alienation.

For ▷ Elizabeth Barrett Browning, however, poetic nostalgia was tantamount to escapism; shirking the task of producing poetry which engaged with the moment, the nostalgic poet failed to discern 'character or glory in his times, /And trundle(d) back his soul five hundred years' (▷ *Aurora Leigh*). This poetic 'trundling-back' survives in the shadowy Arthurian world of, for example, Tennyson's ▷ *Idylls of the King* (1859–72) and the archaic images of the ▷ Pre-Raphaelite movement. Pieced into an evocative picture of traditional England, legend-spinning countered the squalid present by concentrating on a supposedly more authentic yesterday. This sentimental evocation of a mythical past acted, then, rather like what Sigmund Freud (1856–1939) calls a 'Family Romance', only on a national scale; just as an individual might pretend he or she has more glorious and romantic origins than are in fact the case, so national culture is built upon the wishful creation of images of glorious and graceful past times. By positively forging a myth of the English idyll –

> *Oh, to be in England*
> *Now that April's there*
> ('Home Thoughts From Abroad'; Robert Browning, 1845)

– or of childhood, or of God in His Heaven – personal and national stability is consolidated rather than threatened. By forging an idyllic cultural memory (a sanitized past) which acts as a kind of screen memory, blocking off far more disturbing passages of individual or national history (the dirty materiality of the real past) Victorian verse contributed to glueing together a fracturing present. In the place of what ▷ Chartist poet Gerald Massey (1828–1907) called the 'looming future', a blooming past is constructed.

One way of reading Victorian nostalgia is to assume that the strength of retrospection in a text is an index of the depth of crisis felt at the moment at which it was written. We do find frequent points where crisis is overtly acknowledged; loss in the present is as important a stated element in Victorian verse as the creation of the past. So it is wise to be as suspicious as possible when confronting these images, asking, as Anne Brontë does, why certain things have been remembered and valorized and not others:

> *Sweet memory, ever smile on me;*
> *Nature's chief beauties spring from thee.*

In other words, one remembers what one desires to remember:

> *Is childhood then so all divine?*
> *Or, memory, is the glory thine*
> *That haloes thus the past?*
> ('Memory'; 1846)

What is activated in poetic remembering is, then, highly selective, evading the squalid activity of the past.

*Anchors of desire: Other voices in the 'double-breasted Age'*

> *There cast my anchors of desire*
> *Deep in Unknown eternity,*
> *Nor ever let my spirit tire*
> *With looking for What is to Be.*
> ('Anticipation', ▷ Emily Brontë; 1845)

In her suspicious reading of the tricks of memory Anne Brontë comes close to the cynicism of Gerald Massey, whose concern is to scrutinize the 'real present' and the social contexts of idyllic images. In the ironically titled 'All's Right with the World', he shows what occurs when the 'silken-folded mask' of sweet image-making slips,

> *. . . lo, Hell welters at our very feet!*
> *The Poor are murdered body and soul, the Rich*
> *In Pleasure's chalice melt their pearl of life!*
> *Ay, all goes right, and merrily, with the world.*
> ('All's Right with the World')

Perhaps this 'silken-folded mask' is the tapestry woven by Tennyson's ▷ *The Lady of Shalott* (1832), which contains scenes of the world she cannot see first hand but only as images in her mirror. Massey's verse asks suspicious questions about who has the power to write and myth-make, and who is excluded from the process of remembering – who says what the mirror reflects? More positively, we might look for other images beneath the mask, and listen to other poetic voices.

The canon has often concealed the tears in the 'silken-folded mask' of bourgeois writing. The poetry of the 19th century is, however, extraordinarily heterogeneous. Whilst modernists were able to dismiss Victorian verse as immobile and monolithic, the terms used to discuss it could be much simpler than those which are required to do justice to its plurality and diversity. In this section I wish to point to the cracks in the idea of a Victorian poetic monolith by showing the points at which different voices call from inside the marbling.

The variety of metrical and stanzaic forms in 19th-century writing confesses both technical restlessness and openness to development – Clough's verse in parts anticipates *vers libre*, Browning and Tennyson experimented widely with metre, and as we shall see ▷ Gerard Manley Hopkins developed rhythmic forms which anticipate modernism. Voices other than that of bourgeois Victorian propriety speak in the dialect poetry of ▷ William Barnes, Thomas Hardy, and even Tennyson, in texts such as Thomas Hood's 'The Song of the Shirt' (1843) (the lament of a labouring woman – 'Would that its tone could reach the rich!'), and in the bizarre sexual delirium of ▷ Algernon Swinburne and some writers of the *fin de siècle*. The ▷ Nonsense verse of ▷ Edward Lear and ▷ Lewis Carroll plays with images from the Victorian unconscious, parodying normality to the point of absurdity, the effect of which is hilarious, provocative and disturbing. Carroll's 'The White Knight's Song' from *Through the Looking Glass* (1872), gives a world of capitalism-turned-upside-down by listing a series of utterly absurd ways of making money, a stream of words which 'trickled through my head, / Like water through a sieve'. The lament of manifest loss in Lear's 'The Dong with the Luminous Nose' (1871) parodies the grander losses of Tennyson and Arnold; 'Dong' is a melancholy pastiche, telling the story of the lost Jumbly Girl in the grandiose tones of the mock-epic:

> But when the sun was low in the West,
>   The Dong arose and said; –
> – 'What little sense I once possessed
>   Has quite gone out of my head!' –
> And since that day he wanders still
> By lake and forest, marsh and hill,
> Singing – 'O somewhere, in valley or plain
> 'Might I find my Jumbly Girl again!
> 'For ever I'll seek by lake and shore
> 'Till I find my Jumbly Girl once more!'

Crucially, too, the mask slips when women take up their pens, especially when they are concerned in their writing, as was Elizabeth Barrett Browning, to inscribe literary history with visions which could not be countenanced by masculine masks. Her desire to 'catch / Upon the burning lava of a song / The full-veined, heaving, double-breasted Age' (*Aurora Leigh*) strongly contrasts with much Victorian poetry's listless return to any age but its own. Her adamant belief that poetry be relevant to its times and contemporary in its material builds up in *Aurora Leigh* into a plea for living verse, since dead images kill poems: 'death inherits death'.

The outstanding texts of this period are, not uncommonly, ways into fear, confrontations of, in Hardy's late-Victorian phrase, 'the growing gloom'. With the revolutionary year of 1848, a turbulent one for much of mainland Europe, vague uncertainties were turned into a radical sense of possibility. This was the year in which Clough published his remarkable *The Bothie of Tober-Na-Vuolich*, which interrogates class and sexual difference through the difficult problem of marriage across class barriers; in the face of a socially volatile moment, Clough asserted the necessity that poetry relate to and guide people in their urban experience. Cultural history registered the shocking dissolution of the solitary and integrated self posited by western rationality. In the British Museum Library ▷ Karl Marx was researching *Das Kapital*; 1848 had seen the publication of his and Engels's *Communist Manifesto*. It is helpful to read Victorian verse in relation to other forms of contemporary writing. Such poetry gathered itself together in the intellectual climate which also produced ▷ Charles Darwin's *On the Origin of Species* in 1859, and since the poets under discussion here never saw themselves as writing in splendid isolation from the intellectual revolutions precipitated by these texts, it would be unwise to treat poetic history as generated by a dynamic solely internal to itself.

In the ▷ 'Hungry Forties' many of the young writers which modernism cast as Victorian dinosaurs were only just beginning to reach wide audiences and capitalize most effectively on their poetic energies. The fact that the romantic paradigm was no longer applicable to an acutely altered Britain gradually became a cause for celebration rather than lament. Against a fetishized past, poets countered with a strong vision of the present, even those whose work in other places both celebrates and laments what is in truth a pastiche of medieval England. Tennyson, for instance, also makes use of images of the past to displace ▷ 'the woman question' into a space where it can be imaginatively explored. In 1847 he first published ▷ *The Princess*, that extraordinary engagement with 'the woman question' which gives us an image, albeit set up only to be undermined, of strong women of formidable intellect. The certainties of sexual difference are challenged not only by the very existence of a militantly feminist educational institution, but by the humour of the transvestite episode in which the heroes dress as women to infiltrate the enemy camp. Central to *The Princess* is the separatist University, which is both credible and credited only within a context radically different from Tennyson's own, hence his deployment of a vague medieval setting, further displaced by a variety of narrative layers. *The Princess* questions the notion that poetry springs from a singular, unified voice; it is 'A Medley', the construction of many voices, male and female, which together forge 'a sevenfold story'.

In 1855 (during the Crimean War), Tennyson published an even stranger long poem which engaged with the contemporary issues of mental aberration, sexual difference, and the war itself. This was *Maud*, subtitled 'A Monodrama', a self-undermining word since the 'one' who speaks this long complex poem is an extremely fragmented personality; he isn't 'one' – he isn't 'mono' – he speaks with many voices. The drama of the narrative is thus importantly also an effect of the dialogue between his own selves. For the speaker of *Maud* is 'Sick of a nameless fear'; disordered in his senses, he seems to speak from many positions at once. He is precipitated into paranoia, and the synaesthesia of the famous 'Come into the garden, Maud' passage, by an erotically intangible heroine who had 'fled on the roses and lain in the lilies of life'. Arnold's phrase 'the dialogue of the mind with itself' takes shape in this mad 'hero' who becomes a figure of the introspective poet, fleeing the foul fiend of horror or doubt: 'I will bury myself in myself' (*Maud*, Part II, l 75). Tennyson wrote of his character, 'I took a man constitutionally diseased and dipt him into the circumstances of the time and took him out on fire'. Along with Tennyson's more narcotic lyrics, *Maud* shows how a poetry which explored the loss of the rational self could be articulated behind the Laureate mask, even as the mask of civic poetry was held anxiously in place. But *Maud* is also in part a comment upon the circumstances of the time, of modern and mental alienation: its landscape a metaphor for psychiatric derangement, as it was to become in such later poems as Thomson's *City* and T.S. Eliot's *The Waste Land* (1922).

*Aurora Leigh* had a readership as enormous as *The Princess* and *Maud*, and in content deals with the questions of gender and women's power which the Tennyson texts, as well as Clough's *Bothie*, all probe from different angles. Even Queen ▷ Victoria read *Aurora Leigh*. Indeed, when the queen was faced with the task of choosing a new Poet Laureate in 1850, Elizabeth Barrett (as she then was) was a prime candidate. Stepping into Wordsworth's shoes was indeed regarded as an awesome task for any of the young poets who were penning their most interesting work at this time. Whilst no woman has ever become the Poet Laureate, in the middle of a century characterized by such acute patriarchal oppression a woman was seriously considered for the position. She was, indeed, far more popular then than her husband-to-be, Robert Browning, appropriate to an age when women wrote poetry prolifically and were highly regarded by their contemporaries, and feminist criticism recently has shown her to be a literary figure worthy of stronger recognition than she has received since her death. *Aurora Leigh* explores the boundaries between biography and fiction, identifying poetic work as a unique space for making out a woman's relationship to language and creativity. As a feminist interrogation of female friendship and sexual relations it is courageous, 'life-blood' 'wrung . . . / On every leaf . . .' (*Aurora Leigh*, Bk 5, ll. 356–7). As an exploration of how literature creates the self, it deserves its place in a tradition of poets' own critical theories. As a long narrative poem it was indeed hugely popular, fulfilling its own prescription that poetry should not flinch from history, and should partly be the space where women can begin to write their own histories, the story behind the mask. Matthew Arnold wrote that, 'Poetry is at bottom a criticism of life', and Barrett Browning's verse exemplifies this, constructively engaging with rather than retreating from her 'double-breasted Age'. As Cora Kaplan points out in her 1978 introduction to the poem, *Aurora Leigh* is a ▷ feminist bridge between two other overtly political publications, *Casa Guidi Windows* (1851) and *Poems Before Congress* (1860), forming a triptych which perhaps offers the strongest poetic analysis in English of the immediately post-1848 European situation.

As feminist criticism has shown, no mythical past could offer 19th-century women a positive image of themselves, so they set to writing it in their own way. The work of ▷ Christina Rossetti presents an intriguing exception. Her 'criticism of life' is uniquely strong in its strange combination of morbidity, painful self-denial and simplicity. Rossetti is undoubtedly ruthlessly hard on herself: much of her work is charged with absence and denial, a will to oblivion and silence, which is repeatedly invoked in a style so sparse it seems to be actively wishing to negate itself. Indeed, the word 'silence' itself is often repeated. Her 'almost Paradise' is a return to absolute equilibrium and desirelessness. In 'Rest' (1862) she calls the earth to

> *Lie close around her; leave no room for mirth*
> *With its harsh laughter, nor for sound of sighs.*
> *She hath no questions, she hath no replies,*
> *Hushed in and curtained with a blessed dearth*
> *Of all that irked her from the hour of birth;*
> *With stillness that is almost Paradise.*

The voice of this poem can only afford to desire the absence of pain; for Rossetti positivity isn't full energy but simply the negation of the negative. Plenitude is, perhaps, asking too much. Is this an instance of woman learning to desire her lot, internalizing the Victorian charge that she 'suffer and be still'?

But when colours and positively charged desires giddily burst into this near-silence, that which 'irked her from the hour of her birth' is quite positively broken open and challenged. Rossetti's sparse verse soars to an unnatural high when suddenly rich detail emerges, the mixture of spartan naïve form with Pre-Raphaelite decorativeness invoking a strange intoxication of deprivation and excess. The rich erotic language of ▷ *Goblin Market* (1862) pressed into a strict ▷ ballad form, or the exultation of 'A Birthday' (1862), are both good examples of this:

> *Raise me a dais of silk and down;*
>   *Hang it with vair and purple dyes;*
> *Carve it in doves and pomegranates,*
>   *And peacocks with a hundred eyes;*
> *Work it in gold and silver grapes,*
>   *In leaves and silver fleurs-de-lys;*
> *Because the birthday of my life*
> *Is come, my love is come to me.*

In its privations Rossetti's poetry has a simple beauty, but when it brims over with rich images its singularity and strength are striking.

A more overtly positive woman's poetic voice in the earlier Victorian period is that of ▷ Emily Brontë. Hers is 'No coward soul . . ., / No trembler in the world's storm-troubled sphere' ('No Coward Soul is Mine'; 1846). The quotation which forms the epigraph to this section is typical of her immediate positivity; she would be a poet of the present moment, evoking earth-bound epiphanies which celebrate the material world rather than striving for the transcendental. Significantly, her 'anchor of desire' is cast forward into 'What is to Be' rather than nostalgically backwards. Across her corpus a theory of human freedom is constructed which needs to be read in the context of her position as a woman writer. In 'The Old Stoic' (1841) she desires only 'a chainless soul', not a heavenly transformation – 'Leave me the heart that now I bear, / And give me liberty'. Freedom is more important than heaven, a sentiment which echoes Catherine Earnshaw's dream in chapter nine of ▷ *Wuthering Heights* (1847):

> *Give we the hills our equal prayer,*
> *Earth's breezy hills and heaven's blue sea;*
> *We ask for nothing further here*
> *But our own hearts and liberty.*
> ('And like myself lone, wholly lone'; 1841)

Unlike the more passive mysticism of Rossetti, Brontë is anything but stoical, and her poetry's affirmation of the earth forms a strong critique of organized religion's promise of better things to come:

> *Let others seek its beams divine*
> *In cell and cloister drear*
> *But I have found a fairer shrine*
> *A happier worship here;*
>
> *By dismal rites they win their bliss,*
> *By pennance, fasts and fear –*
> *I have one rite – a gentle kiss;*
> *One pennance – tender tears.*

## *Flesh and the* fin de siècle

Sexuality haunts Victorian poetry as an anxious desire, a force both attractive and repulsive, like the prostitute figure 'Jenny' (1870) in ▷ Dante Gabriel Rossetti's poem of that name. The strict a/a/b/b rhyming scheme of 'Jenny' causes her name to assonate ironically with 'guinea'; she is a fallen goddess, whose access to the 'vile text' of sexual knowledge makes her the object of simultaneous desire and denigration. Jenny's image is distorted by what men desire of her:

> *Yet, Jenny, looking long at you,*
> *The woman almost fades from view,*
> *A cipher of man's changeless sum*
> *Of lust, past, present, and to come,*
> *Is left. A riddle that one shrinks*
> *To challenge from the scornful sphinx.*

From ▷ Coventry Patmore's eulogies to the safe delights of married love in *The Angel in the House* (1858), to ▷ George Meredith's bitter sonnet sequence about estrangement and divorce, *Modern Love* (1862), the Victorians were covertly obsessed with the question of sex. Ahead of Nietzsche's proclamation about God, Meredith declares 'the death of love' and digs its grave with his text (*Modern Love*, (i)).

Through the Victorians' treatment of or silence regarding sexuality we can discover much about what was considered the proper subject matter for poetry. In this section I want to talk briefly about how those norms and rules of propriety gradually broke down as the century closed and as writing itself opened. Tennyson's institutionalization as Poet Laureate caused him to consolidate gradually the shifting selves and voices of his earlier verse, and by the latter decades of the 19th century he had become quite firmly the spokesman of decorum over degeneracy. By the time of 'Locksley Hall Sixty Years After' (1886), subterranean rumbles were shifting the ground beneath Tennyson's feet, causing him to castigate vehemently the author's part in inviting a new dark age in which 'Chaos, Cosmos' are interchangeable, and freedom is only 'free to slay herself':

> *Authors – essayist, atheist, novelist, realist, rhymster, play your part,*
> *Paint the moral shame of nature with the living hues of Art. (. . .)*

> *Feed the budding rose of boyhood with the drainage of your sewer;*
> *Send the drain into the fountain lest the stream should issue pure.*

> *Set the maiden fancies wallowing in the troughs of Zolaism, –*
> *Forward, forward, ay and backward, downward into the abysm.*

> *Do your best to charm the worst, to lower the rising race of men;*
> *Have we risen from out the beast, then back into the beast again?*

The force with which this sewer imagery is impressed upon us is arguably as blatant and shocking as the kind of literature it would repress; Tennyson is calling for a public health drive to counter poetic corruption as the notorious Contagious Diseases Acts of the 1860s sought to control prostitution. In its utter physical disgust this text reveals much about the bourgeois obsession with cleanliness ('next to Godliness') which psychoanalysis was beginning to encounter in its most extreme and mentally destructive forms: as Tennyson penned these words, Freud was working toward the publication, with Joseph Breuer (1842–1925), of *Studies on Hysteria* (1895), one of the founding texts of psychoanalysis. But however eloquently this poem speaks of Tennyson's own preoccupations, it is its role as a critical prescription which interests us here. For at stake in this is both the notion that 'dirty writing' messes up a literary tradition in the process of purifying itself, and also that such poetic 'foul passions' can have a profound effect on the moral welfare of the nation.

The ▷ decadent writings of the later 19th century perversely took such a stance gloriously to heart, actually affirming these powers in an indulgence of the flesh as sin. The period of the 1860s and 1870s, the High Victorian period, was a period of consolidation both politically and poetically, and writing was generally on a grander, surer scale, although this consolidation uneasily co-existed with other tendencies. In the late 1880s and early 1890s Tennyson, Browning and Arnold died, and the emphases of poetry shifted. The artists of what W.B. Yeats (1865–1939) called the 'Tragic Generation' – ▷ Oscar Wilde, ▷ Ernest Dowson, Lionel Johnson (1867–1902), ▷ Aubrey Beardsley and ▷ Arthur Symons (1865–1943) – developed an extreme form of aestheticism, strongly influenced by ▷ Walter Pater's notorious epilogue to *Studies in the History of the Renaissance* (1873). This group of bohemian poets formed ▷ The Rhymers Club in the 1890s, and published their work in a body of journals which reflected their priorities: chiefly ▷ *The Yellow Book* and *The Savoy*. As the century became more ▷ utilitarian, adamantly scientific and technologically precise, poetry turned from the prescription of social relevance and made a virtue of the notion that it was brazenly gratuitous. Perversity, superficiality and hedonism were prioritized over the socially useful, profoundly spiritual and serious. ▷ Nineties poetry in particular embraced the idea of poetry as estranged from the real world. The earlier notion of poetry as 'a weapon of strife in the social conflict', or Arnold's celebration of the moral worth of poetry, were reversed by ▷ aesthetic doctrine – as Wilde wrote, 'The man who could call a spade a spade should be compelled to use one'. Such a shift is, however, most significant in its challenging of the rules of poetic subject matter rather than in any formal innovations which decadent poets enacted. Their work is characteristically sinful rather than amoral, evil rather than atheist. Working within the structures of conventional morality *fin de siècle* writers were anti-Victorian Victorians in that they prioritized beauty over goodness, the aesthetic rather than the ethical, the body over the spirit.

This latter emphasis is what the poet, novelist and dramatist ▷ Robert Buchanan had called (in an essay on D.G. Rossetti) ▷ 'the Fleshly School of Poetry'. In the 1860s this 'school' was opened by Algernon Swinburne under the influence of the Marquis de Sade (1740–1814) and ▷ Charles Baudelaire, and bore its own bizarre progeny in the 1880s and 1890s. Certainly, the earlier obsessions of the Pre-Raphaelites had played an important role in the *fin de siècle*'s spectacular materialization of certain lurid themes, particularly in the movement's representation of *femmes fatales* like Jenny or Swinburne's Dolores. Dante Gabriel Rossetti's verse often adorns his paintings of women so that the woman becomes a fusion of verbal description and detailed visual representation on a gigantic scale.

The painting/sonnet 'Astarte Syriaca' (1877) exemplifies this, representing a woman who combines Venus and Astarte, an embodiment of an ineffable higher knowledge and thus also, an image of Victorian woman worship. Rossetti's power to frame women within a certain range of images could, perhaps, be read alongside Browning's ▷ 'My Last Duchess' (1842), the speaker of which gains power over the Duchess in the painted image of her. Together Jenny and Astarte Syriaca – woman as essentially 'Amulet, talisman, and oracle' – offer the double version of sexual fear and desire with which I began. Christina Rossetti's work supplements this masculine vision, stepping back even further than Browning from the female canvas and sharply disrupting her brother's images of essential femininity.

A more outrageous manifestation of textual fleshiness came, however, with the explosion of Algernon Swinburne on to the relatively conservative poetic scene in the mid-1860s. Swinburne is known about now more for his dissolute lifestyle and sexual excesses. His bloodstained poetry is perhaps best known for its insistence on the themes of lust and violence, not all of which even the most crusading 20th-century writers on sexuality have thought to legitimize. As *enfant terrible* to High Victorian complacency, his early Dionysian work had an intoxicating effect on his young contemporaries.

The initial impact of Swinburne's poetry stemmed in part from his technical innovation, chiefly an obsessive use of alliteration. As he became a more established literary figure his technique was conservatively consolidated. Intoxicated incantations became simply rhythmically tedious, as Swinburne's outrageous and often blasphemous themes were battered into conventional iambic shapes just as the bodies of his subjects are, 'Trodden as grapes in the wine-press of lust' ('Laus Veneris'; l 191; 1866). Thus, whilst bloodblotches are symptoms that his figures have been 'trampled' by desire, the purple effect of his writing contained in regular, conservative form signalled for later generations Swinburne's ultimate lack of poetic dynamism.

This late-Victorian prioritization of the body and the beautiful over moral and social worth may have been rebellious, challenging the moralizations of earlier politically engaged poets, but it certainly wasn't revolutionary; it may have broken the rules but it certainly didn't change the structure within which the rules worked. As well as working within a moral economy which still held matter and spirit to be diametrically opposed, the poets discussed so far were also working within a textual economy which held form and content to be separate dimensions of poetry. This, then, brings us on to another important aspect of late-Victorian writing, and in particular the poetry of those key transitional figures who were beginning to question the rules which dictated how a poem was written, just as the 'fleshly school' was questioning what a poem was written about.

## The fruits of unbelief: Movements toward modernism

Much of the writing discussed so far is, in its versification and syntax at least, familiar – formally it conforms to what the reader is used to. Victorian poetry of this stylistically conventional type in part has trained our readerly sensibilities. This familiarity, however, breaks down in the more difficult verse of Robert Browning and Gerard Manley Hopkins, whose work looks forward to the formal obscurities and syntactical abnormalities of modernism.

Browning's verse is often convoluted and digressive. Ezra Pound found *Sordello* (1840) unreadable, and ▷ Jane Welsh Carlyle read the whole of it without discerning whether Sordello was a book, a man or a city. Browning is concerned to show how his verse is constructed, to leave in the traces of the psychological process he went through in writing it, to lay bare the association of ideas which lead to the final full stop. He foregrounds 'The grand Perhaps' ('Bishop Blougram's Apology', l 190 from ▷ *Men and Women*;

1855) – the doubts and equivocations of writing and modernity – to such an extent that it takes on some kind of positive identity. In the words of 'Bishop Blougram's Apology', Browning's question concerns the uses of doubt and difficulty, 'how can we guard our unbelief, Make it bear fruit to us?' Thus he overtly shows the reader the 'perhapses' of poetry writing itself, the process he goes through in trying to get from 'a' to 'b' of a narrative; the fruit that this bears is a highly unusual and difficult type of poetry. He constantly interrupts himself, leaving trails of dots for us to follow as thoughts tail off and into other thoughts. The traces of the process of a poem's construction are left on show as evidence of how it is produced, but because we are used to these traces and half thoughts being edited out, his poems are difficult reading. What aims to be a realistic representation of the flow of mental processes reads as stilted, stuttering parenthesis. In an effort to mimic the patterns of common speech Browning's verse frequently slips from self to self without formal signal:

> *Ay, because the sea's the street there; 't is arched by . . . what you call*
> *. . . Shylock's bridge with houses on it, where they keep the carnival:*
> *I was never out of England – it's as if I saw it all.*
>
> ('A Toccata of Galuppi's', *Men and Women*)

So one modernist effect of reading Browning is that he causes us to confront the process through which relevant information is usually selected or omitted, through which different textual registers are signalled. In its obscurity Browning's verse takes on the otherwise thematic problem of a dissolving subject and turns it into a question of form and syntax.

Gerard Manley Hopkins is a Victorian poet in the sense that he wrote mainly from 1875 to 1889 but his work was not published until 1918. There is a certain historical appropriateness to this delay, since his difficulty, and his interest in the Metaphysical poets, is akin to the modernists who turned to the English Renaissance as part of 'the direct current of English poetry' (T.S. Eliot). 'Difficulty' becomes the catch-word of early 20th-century writing, a strategy for marking a distinction between modern writing and the 19th-century values of the reader-friendly text. Hopkins's contorted versification, syntactic twists, and dictive and rhythmic experimentation have confounded easy readings. His 'grand Perhaps' came at the point at which he started to 'doubt Tennyson', opening up another important emphasis of poetic modernism – its concern is to move away from the preciousness of 19th-century poetic diction to something more immediate, to the rhythms of common speech. It is paradoxical, then, that readers had become used to the strict versification of the Victorians, and to a specifically poetic vocabulary and range of images, and it is this faculty which has alienated them from modernism's attempt to deploy the language and images of the everyday. Hopkins's case is highlighted by his innovative rhythmic form – ▷ sprung rhythm – which was designed to bring into his verse the energies of ordinary speech. The syllabic stresses in his lines are syncopated, as they might be in a conversation. In 1877 he wrote to ▷ Robert Bridges,

*Why do I employ sprung rhythm at all? Because it is the nearest to the rhythm of prose, that is the native and natural rhythm of speech, the least forced, the most rhetorical and emphatic of all possible rhythms, combining, as it seems to me, opposite and one wd.* (sic) *have thought, incompatible excellences, markedness of rhythm – that is rhythm's self – and naturalness of expression . . .*

(21 August 1877)

His use of sprung rhythm is, however, one of the aspects of Hopkins's poetry which was considered most difficult, since difficulty is an indication of unfamiliarity.

In Hopkins's meticulous and characteristically Victorian visual powers, especially regarding the natural world, he prefigures D.H. Lawrence (1885–1930); he is not a poet of generalization, repeating tiny detail rather than broadly gesturing. But like his later imitator, Dylan Thomas (1914–53), words unroll and suggest each other uncontrollably:

> *. . . now, barbarous in beauty, the stooks rise*
> *Around; up above, what wind-walks! what lovely behaviour*
> *Of silk-sack clouds! has wilder, wilful-wavier*
> *Meal-drift moulded ever and melted across skies?*
> ('Hurrahing in Harvest', 1877)

There is an (arguably unchristian) exuberance, a vision of excess, in Hopkins's verse, and in his philosophy of 'instresses' and 'inscapes' his Jesuitism becomes almost pantheistic. In touching the inscape of a thing – an image, or complex of images, a natural object or experience – poetry claims access to a vision of that thing's essential existence. This existence is communicated to the individual through an energetic pulse or channel – the 'instress' – which is opened between object and perceiver, if she or he is 'ready'. For Hopkins, poetry exceeds meaning; it is in his impulse to commune with the 'isness' of things, to allow material language to touch the thing itself through a poetic experience of epiphany, that Hopkins's modernity lies.

Hopkins's temptation to visit the dark night of the soul (particularly in the 'sonnets of desolation' of 1884–5) brings his later poems of despair close in their painful intensity to Thomas Hardy's bleakest work. Like Hopkins, Hardy is also a poet known for his use of common language and diction, and is quite literally a *fin de siècle* poet in his uniquely pessimistic and Schopenhauerian stance on passing from the old century into the new. Hardy's hopelessness looks forward and backward; a poem such as 'The Darkling Thrush' (1900) is both a poem of loss and a poem of dread, 'greeting' the 20th century from a pivotal point which also implicitly glances backwards:

> *So little cause for carolings*
> *Of such ecstatic sound*
> *Was written on terrestrial things*
> *Afar or high around,*

> *That I could think there trembled through*
> *His happy good-night air*
> *Some blessed Hope, whereof he knew*
> *And I was unaware.*

Hardy, then, writes at the end point of a process and a century in which the self is gradually and systematically estranged from the familiar. Time is no longer simply the dimension of loss, but also that which brings the 'darkening dankness / The yawning blankness' ('The Going') of the future ever closer. His foreboding about what Yeats called (in 'Coole Park and Ballylee, 1931') the 'darkening flood' indeed prefigures much of late Yeats's feelings about the 20th century.

# Reference section

### Adam Bede (1859)

A novel by ▷ George Eliot. Set in a village
in the Midlands, the events take place at the
beginning of the 19th century. Adam Bede
is the village carpenter, a young man of stern
morals and great strength of character, who
is in love with Hetty Sorrel, the vain and
frivolous niece of a farmer, Martin Poyser.
She is seduced and abandoned by the village
squire Arthur Donnithorne and Adam is
powerless to intervene. Heartbroken, Hetty
finally agrees to marry Adam but, finding
herself pregnant, she absconds in search
of her lover. Adam is comforted by Dinah
Morris, a young and beautiful Methodist
preacher. Unsuccessful in her search for
Donnithorne, Hetty is finally arrested,
charged with the murder of her child and
convicted. Aided by Dinah, Hetty faces her
final ordeal, but her sentence is commuted to
transportation. Adam and Dinah eventually
marry. Contemporary reviewers praised the
novel for its characterization, and for its
portrayal of English rural life.

▷ Regional Novel; 'Fallen Woman, The'.

### Adams, Sarah Flower (1805–48)

Poet, journalist and author of the hymn
'Nearer My God to Thee'. A close friend
of poet Percy Bysshe Shelley (1792–1822),
Adams continued to follow the ideals of
▷ Romanticism in direct contrast to the new
sociological aesthetic espoused by writers
such as ▷ Thomas Carlyle and ▷ Charles
Dickens. She is linked with the influential but
eccentric and eventually discredited school of
poets satirized by ▷ William Aytoun as the
▷ 'Spasmodics'. She is chiefly remembered
for *Vivia Perpetua* (1841), a dramatic poem
about the life and death of an early Christian
martyr. An early champion of women's rights,
she insisted on a 'no housekeeping' pact with
her husband and, at the age of eighteen, broke
the record for the ascent of Ben Lomond by a
woman.

▷ Women's Movement.

### Adventures of Harry Richmond, The (1871)

A novel by ▷ George Meredith.

### Adventures of Philip, The (1862)

The last completed novel by ▷ William
Makepeace Thackeray, illustrated by him
and published serially in ▷ *The Cornhill
Magazine* during 1861 and 1862. Reiterating
many of the themes of earlier novels such
as ▷ *Pendennis* and ▷ *The Newcomes* it is
generally regarded as evidence of its author's
failing talent.

▷ Reviews and periodicals.

### Aestheticism

A movement of the late 19th century,
influenced by the ▷ Pre-Raphaelites and
▷ John Ruskin, its immediate inspiration
was the writings of the Oxford don ▷ Walter
Pater. His two most influential books were
*Studies in the History of the Renaissance* (1873)
and ▷ *Marius the Epicurean* (1885). These
show him as a ritualistic moralist, laying
emphasis on the value of ecstatic experience.
Apart from Pater and his predecessors, the
aesthetes owed much to the current French
doctrine of '*L'art pour l'art*' (Art for Art's sake)
but they retained, if sometimes not obviously,
a typically English concern with moral
values and issues. The outstanding aesthete
was ▷ Oscar Wilde, and a characteristic
aesthetic product was his novel ▷ *The Picture
of Dorian Gray* (1891). As the movement
lacked a programme, writers of very different
character were influenced by it: the naturalist
novelist ▷ George Moore; the poet Lionel
Johnson (1867–1902), a Catholic convert;
▷ Swinburne, a main channel for the
art for art's sake doctrine; the poet W.B.
Yeats (1865–1939), the Celtic revivalist. A
characteristic aestheticist periodical was the
▷ *Yellow Book* (1894–7), so called because
French novels, conventionally considered
'daring', were printed on yellow paper. Its
main illustrator was ▷ Aubrey Beardsley,
whose line drawings were notorious for their
sensuality. The excesses and affectations
of the movement's adherents were much
ridiculed in ▷ *Punch*.

▷ Allingham, William; French Influence
on Victorian Literature; Decadents.
**Bib:** Aldington, R. (ed.), *The Religion of
Beauty: Selections from the Aesthetes*.

### Agnes Grey (1847)

A semi-autobiographical novel by ▷ Anne
Brontë which first appeared under the
▷ pseudonym Acton Bell. Agnes is a rector's
daughter who joins the household of the
Bloomfield family to work as a ▷ governess.
The vivid portrayal of the spoilt children
owes much to Brontë's experience with the
Ingham family, for whom she worked in
1839. Similarly, the portrait of Rosalie, the
flirtatious daughter of the Murray family,
draws on Brontë's experience working for the
Robinsons (1841–5). The novel departs from
autobiography in its later chapters, as the
gentle and modest Agnes is united with the

kind curate, Mr Weston, by whom she has three children.

## Agnosticism

The term was invented by biologist ▷ Thomas Huxley, also a champion of ▷ Charles Darwin's theory of evolution, at a meeting of the Metaphysical Society in London in 1869. It describes the state which is neither belief nor disbelief (▷ atheism) with regard to religious faith, and the word derives from the Greek *gnosis*, meaning knowledge. In Huxley's own words, 'It came into my head as suggestively antithetical to the "Gnostic" of church history who professed to know so much about the very things of which I was ignorant.' Huxley used the term to describe applying reason 'as far as it can take you' and then frankly recognizing the limits of your knowledge. In this he was influenced by the 18th-century philosopher David Hume (1711–76), who was the subject of a sympathetic appraisal published by Huxley. The principle of agnosticism was subsequently developed by the mathematician and scientific philosopher W.K. Clifford in his essay 'The Ethics of Belief' (1876), and explored by 19th-century literary critic and historian of thought ▷ Sir Leslie Stephen in *An Agnostic's Apology and Other Essays* (1893). Agnosticism which, when applied to fundamental Christian beliefs, often led to sceptical conclusions, was widespread among writers between 1850 and 1914.
▷ Religious groups.
**Bib:** Huxley, T.H., 'Agnosticism' and 'Agnosticism and Christianity' in *Collected Essays*, vol. 5; Stephen, L., *History of English Thought in the 18th Century*; Armstrong, R.A., *Agnosticism and Theism in the 19th Century*.

## Aguilar, Grace (1816–47)

Aguilar was born in Hackney, London, the eldest child of Spanish-Jewish parents. She is chiefly remembered today as a sentimental novelist and prose writer, although she was also a poet. She never married, and after her father's death she wrote for a profession, publishing several works on Judaism. *The Spirit of Judaism* (1842) was a controversial attack on the formalities of institutionalized religion, while *Women of Israel* (1845) and *The Jewish Faith* (1846) express a concern with the position of women within the faith. Her first novel, *Home Influence* (1847), was the only one to be published in her lifetime. Other novels include *The Mother's Recompense* (1851) and ▷ *Woman's Friendship* (1853).
▷ Jews in Victorian literature.

## Aikin, Lucy (1781–1864)

Poet, critic and historian. She was born in Warrington, the daughter of John Aikin, writer and physician, who educated her at home. She became fluent in French, Italian and Latin and was well-read in history and biography. She was also acquainted with the writings of her aunt, Anna Letitia Barbauld (1743–1824). In 1801 she edited an anthology, *Poetry for Children*, which was several times reprinted. *Epistles on Women*, a moral and didactic work, appeared in 1810, and *Lorimer*, a novel of sensibility, in 1814. Three historical works followed: *Memoirs of the Court of Queen Elizabeth* (1818); *Memoirs of the Court of James I* (1822); *Memoirs of the Court of Charles I* (1833). Her ventures into biography include a *Life of Addison* (1843), and memoirs of her father and aunt. She was well known in literary circles and respected for her scholarship. A staunch ▷ Unitarian, she was also a ▷ feminist who protested against the dominant perception of woman's role in society.
▷ Women's Movement.
**Bib:** Le Breton, P.H. (ed.), *Memoirs, Miscellanies and Letters of the Late Lucy Aikin*.

## Ainsworth, William Harrison (1805–82)

Novelist. His best novels are historical: *Jack Shepherd* (1839), *The Tower of London* (1840), *Guy Fawkes* (1841), *Old St Paul's* (1841), *Windsor Castle* (1843). He tended to idealize the heroic criminal, *eg* highway-man Dick Turpin in *Rookwood* (1834) and Jack Shepherd; this was a literary fashion in the 1830s and 1840s and censured by ▷ Thackeray in his early reviews under the designation 'The ▷ Newgate School of novelists'.
He edited *Bentley's Magazine* 1840–2, *Ainsworth's Magazine* 1842–53 and *New Monthly Magazine* from 1853.
▷ Historical novel.
**Bib:** Ellis, S.M., *W.H. Ainsworth and his Friends*; Worth, G.J., *William Harrison Ainsworth*.

## Albert of Saxe-Coburg-Gotha (1819–61)

Husband (with the title of Prince Consort) of Queen ▷ Victoria. They were cousins. The Queen was devoted to him and the marriage was of considerable political importance; Albert did much to shape the Queen's ideas of her political duties as a constitutional monarch who could not interfere directly in politics but could nonetheless exert great personal influence. ▷ The Great Exhibition of 1851 was organized on his suggestion.

Unfortunately, his foreign origin caused his influence to be regarded with considerable suspicion in Britain. His death was a cause of immense grief to the Queen; it led to her retirement from public appearances between 1861 and the Jubilee of her reign in 1887.

### Alexander, Mrs (Annie Hector, née French) (1825–1902)

Novelist, born in Dublin, who published over forty-five novels, most of which revolve around young heroines seeking to reconcile love and financial security.

They include: *Look Before You Leap* (1865), *Which Shall it Be* (1866), *The Wooing O't* (1873), *Her Dearest Foe* (1876), *The Freres* (1882), *The Admiral's Ward* (1883). *Kitty Costello* (1904) is partly autobiographical. Because of her husband's ill health and relatively early death (in 1875), she supported herself and her family by her writing.

### *Alice's Adventures in Wonderland*
▷ Carroll, Lewis.

### Allen, Charles Grant Blairfindie (1848–99)

Novelist, born in Canada, brought up there and in the USA and educated at Oxford. He is best-known for ▷ *The Woman Who Did* (1895), a ▷ New Woman novel in which the protagonist is opposed to marriage on principle, lives with the man she loves, but is left alone with a child after his death and meets a tragic end. In the 1870s he taught philosophy at the Government College in Jamaica, an experience which helped to promote his interest in questions of emancipation, a theme of many of his novels. A number of these are set abroad, such as *In all Shades* (1886) set in Jamaica and *The Tents of Shem* (1891), an adventure story set in Algeria. He was influenced by the evolutionary theories of ▷ Herbert Spencer. His first novel was a satire, entitled *Philistia* (1884), and he wrote in a range of genres, including the ▷ detective story (*An African Millionaire*, 1897).

### Allingham, William (1824–89)

Poet, born in County Donegal, Ireland where he worked as a customs officer. He moved to Lymington in 1863 and became friends with ▷ Tennyson. Between 1874 and 1879 he edited ▷ *Fraser's Magazine*. In 1850 he published *Poems* which contains his best-known poem 'The Fairies' and the long poem 'The Music-Master', an idyll of young love set in an Irish village. Several volumes of poetry followed including *Day and Night Songs* (1854) and a verse novel of Irish life entitled *Laurence Bloomfield: or Rich and Poor* (1864), which is a plea for land reform and contains a moving account of the eviction of the population of a whole hamlet. His poetry was frequently illustrated by ▷ Dante Gabriel Rossetti, Arthur Hughes and Millais (1829–1896). His early poems are gathered together in the six-volume *Collected Poems* (1888–93) which contains some of his best work including 'The Dirty Old Man', 'George Levison, or, The School-fellows', 'The Wayside Well' and 'Wayconnell Tower'. A contemporary of George MacDonald and friends with ▷ Thomas Carlyle, Rossetti and Leigh Hunt (1784–1859), his *Diary* (1907) is an invaluable record of Victorian ▷ Aesthetic life. In 1874 he married Helen Paterson, a talented water colourist and illustrator of books such as ▷ Hardy's ▷ *Far from the Madding Crowd*.
▷ Irish Literature.

**Bib:** Husni, S.A, *William Allingham: An Annotated Bibliography*; Warner, A.J., *William Allingham: An Introduction*.

### *All the Year Round*

A periodical published by ▷ Charles Dickens from 1859, in succession to ▷ *Household Words*, until his death in 1870. Novels which appeared in it in instalments included Dickens's own ▷ *A Tale of Two Cities* and ▷ *Great Expectations*.

### *Alton Locke: Tailor and Poet* (1850)

A novel by ▷ Charles Kingsley reflecting the social and political turbulence of the ▷ 'Hungry Forties' and one of the ▷ 'Social Problem' novels. Alton Locke, a shopkeeper's son, experiences the horrors of sweated labour during his apprenticeship as a tailor. Convinced of the need for social reform he joins the ▷ Chartist movement. His talent for poetry brings him into contact with Eleanor Staunton, her cousin Lillian, and Saunders Mackaye, a Scottish bookseller modelled loosely on ▷ Thomas Carlyle. At the request of Lillian and her wealthy father, Alton allows his revolutionary verse to be rendered innocuous before publication, thereby earning him the contempt of his Chartist comrades. Responding to their taunts he undertakes a mission that provokes a riot and earns him three years in prison. During that time his beloved Lillian marries someone else and it is Eleanor who nurses him back from typhus while explaining her own views on reform and the role of Christianity. Disillusioned

by demagogy and violence, Alton becomes a
Christian Socialist and dies on his way to the
USA. Deeply flawed as a novel, *Alton Locke*
did draw attention to the wretchedness of the
lives of working people, suggesting Christian
Socialism as a non-violent means of achieving
reform. Its themes are echoed by ▷ Barratt
Browning's ▷ *Aurora Leigh*.

### *Amazing Marriage, The* (1895)
A novel by ▷ George Meredith.

### Amazons
A race of female warriors occuring in ancient
Greek legend, and said by the 5th-century
historian Herodotus to live in Scythia, north
of the Black Sea. The word is often used to
describe aggressive women, women who are
hostile to men or women in positions of power
traditionally held by men. In the late 19th
century the figure of the Amazon was chosen
by feminists to represent women in their
struggle for the vote and as an antidote to
the ▷ 'Angel in the House'. She featured in
novels, poetry and ▷ utopian fiction such as
Elizabeth Burgoyne Corbett's *New Amazonia*:
*A Foretaste of the Future* (1889), which is set
in the year 2472 and describes a utopian
community established in Ireland, with a grant
of £50 million, by 'surplus women' shipped
there by the British Government. In the
course of 600 years the women have grown
two feet taller than the men and their waists,
unrestricted by the corset, have 'thickened'
to twenty-six inches. However, the success
of Amazonia is predicated upon eugenics
and 'compulsory self-extinction' of the old,
deformed and rebellious. In 1888 ▷ Thomas
Hardy used the word 'Amazon' to describe a
handsome 'interesting' female smoker he met
while dining at the house of ▷ Walter Pater.
   ▷ Women's Movement.

### *Amos Barton, The Sad Fortunes of the Rev.* (1857)
The first of the three tales composing
▷ *Scenes of Clerical Life* (1858) by ▷ George
Eliot.
   ▷ Short story.

### Andersen, Hans Christian (1805–75)
Danish author, known in Britain almost entirely
for ▷ fairy tales of his own composition,
such as 'The Tinder Box', and 'The Princess
and the Pea'. They began to appear in
Denmark in 1835 and were first translated
into English in 1846. Their poetic quality has
been much imitated by English writers, *eg*
▷ Oscar Wilde.
   ▷ Children's literature.

### 'Andrea Del Sarto' (1855)
A dramatic monologue by ▷ Robert
Browning published in ▷ *Men and Women*
(1855) in which the painter admits and
laments his devotion to his wife Lucrezia at
the expense of his art. It was written shortly
after his marriage to ▷ Elizabeth Barrett.

### 'Angel in the House, The'
A term which has come to exemplify the
Victorian middle-class ideal of submissive
womanhood, used originally by ▷ Coventry
Patmore in his domestic epic *The Angel in
the House* (1854–62). The Victorian feminine
ideal embodied purity and selflessness, strong
moral and religious principles, coupled with
a willingness to submit to the will of men.
Woman's realm was the home, viewed as
a sanctuary from the harsh public world of
capitalist competition. The 'Angel in the
House' provided spiritual succour as well
as domestic comforts for the middle-class
male, and cherished her maternal role.
In Victorian literature, characters such as
▷ Dickens's Agnes Wickfield in ▷ *David
Copperfield* represent such an ideal, but as the
19th century progressed a number of writers
challenged the stereotype. Well-known texts
such as ▷ Charlotte Brontë's ▷ *Jane Eyre*,
▷ Elizabeth Barrett Browning's ▷ *Aurora
Leigh* and George Eliot's ▷ *Middlemarch* and
▷ *The Mill on the Floss* all present anti-angelic
heroines straining to be released from
conventional domestic roles. The Angel in the
House was nevertheless an extremely powerful
idea, and the emphasis on English women's
moral and spiritual superiority was crucial in
the construction of national identity. In her
famous work on women writers, *A Room of
One's Own* (1929), Virginia Woolf (1882–1941)
cites the import of the Angel in the House
as a central impediment to early 20th-century
women's attempts to write professionally.
   ▷ Feminism; 'Woman Question, The';
Imperialism; Taylor, Jane and Ann.
**Bib:** Poovey, M., *Uneven Developments: The
Ideological Work of Gender in Mid-Victorian
Britain.*

### Anglo-Welsh Literature
Historically a victim of English imperialism,
Wales has been an occupied country since
the Norman period (11th century) and has
suffered from the suppression of its cultural
heritage as a Celtic nation. In addition, Wales
has undergone the systematic erosion of
its language, further weakened by Victorian
government policy. A report on the state
of Welsh education conducted by three

English education ministers for the House of Commons (1846) contained a stinging indictment of the Welsh language, religion and national character, which was reprinted in full as a Blue Book. The commission concluded that 'The Welsh language distorts the truth, favours fraud and abets perjury' and was 'a disastrous barrier to all moral improvement and popular progress in Wales'. The commissioners suppressed the Welsh language as ruthlessly as the ancient languages of India were swept aside a decade earlier, beginning in schools with 'The Welsh Not' regime which prohibited Welsh-language conversation. A piece of wood or slate with the letters 'WN' cut into it was hung round the neck of the last pupil caught speaking Welsh in class – whoever was left wearing it at the end of the school day would be punished.

From the early 19th century, as industrialism increased, the population movement into the south Wales valleys not only drained the rural areas of the west and north of Wales but also brought in labouring or technological expertise for pit-sinking, blast furnace, canal, tramroad, railway and docks construction. English-speaking immigrants in the south Wales valleys accounted for at least 40 per cent of the population, swamping the native Welsh speakers. The subsequent foundation of county schools from 1895 onwards provided secondary education in the medium of English. It was these socio-economic pressures that helped to create the 'first flowering' of Anglo-Welsh literature, as many young provincial writers departed for London to find publishers who encouraged them to adapt their work for the metropolitan market. Thus the Victorian period represents a crossroads in the development of Welsh literature which was stranded between the marginalization of indigenous culture and the hiatus in the growth of the Anglo-Welsh tradition. Poet, critic and translator Anthony Conran regards the poetry of Victorian Wales as unexciting and complacent, subject to a peculiar kind of provincialism, naivete and pompousness. At the same time he detects a tendency to sentimentalize Wales as if Victorian Welsh poets were apologizing for their Welshness.

William Thomas (1832–78), who wrote under the ▷ pseudonym 'Islwyn', was deeply influenced by English poetry but other Welsh writers such as Alun (1797–1840), managed to preserve a purity in their work. Alun's lyrics were written in the style of traditional free-metre poetry sung to a harp. Eben Fardd's (1802–63) composition 'Jerusalem Destroyed' is a melodramatic indictment of the destruction of Wales whereas John 'Ceiriog' Hughes (1832–87) accepts the changes as inevitable. The University College of Wales, founded in the late 19th century and instrumental in the mass exodus of educated young people to share in the massive prosperity of England, also helped to initiate a more responsible attitude to the past and to culture in general. Poets like John Morris-Jones (1864–1929) and T.Gwynn Jones (1871–1949) managed to combine the best of their Welsh heritage with the new European traditions to produce a poetry that addressed itself directly to contemporary social problems.

The cross-fertilization of Welsh and English poetic traditions is perhaps best illustrated in the work of the English poet ▷ Gerard Manley Hopkins who resided for three years at St Beuno's seminary in north Wales. During this period he learnt Welsh and assimilated *cynghanedd* (an internal rhyme scheme with alliteration in a fixed metrical pattern) into his poetry in the form of ▷ 'sprung rhythm'. Hopkins, in turn, transmitted Welsh metric to the 20th-century poet Dylan Thomas (1914–53), who could not speak Welsh.

The most famous Anglo-Welsh poet of the Victorian period was Sir Lewis Morris (1833–1907) who, during the height of his fame in the last twenty years of the 19th century, was second only to ▷ Tennyson in public acclaim and was expected to succeed him as Poet Laureate. Morris's sixth volume of poems *Songs Unsung* (1883) was highly praised by ▷ Gladstone, and *The Epic of Hades* (1877), enthusiastically reviewed by fellow poet Oliver Wendell Holmes and *The Times*, had sold 40,000 copies by 1896. Although Morris's social class and education insulated him from the Welsh-speaking community of his home town, Carmarthen, he developed a keen interest in his Welsh ancestry and in Welsh traditions in his later years. He moved to Sherborne in Dorset at the age of seventeen before entering Jesus College, Oxford in 1851, where he took a double first, and went on to practise as a conveyancing counsel in London. Morris published his first three series of poems *Songs of Two Worlds* (1871, 1874, 1875) anonymously. A combination of graphic social comment and metrical virtuosity tempered with vague moralizing and naive anecdotalism, his poetry was extremely well-received. His ▷ dramatic monologue *Gwen* (1879) has much in common with his great friend Tennyson's ▷ *Maud*. Other volumes include

*Songs of Britain* (1887), *Songs Without Notes* (1894) and *Idylls and Lyrics* (1896).
▷ Imperialism; Pfeiffer, Emily.
**Bib:** Garlick, R., *An Introduction to Anglo-Welsh Literature*; Stephens, M. (ed.), *The Oxford Companion to the Literature of Wales*; Adams, S. and Hughes, G.R., *Essays in Welsh and Anglo-Welsh Literature*; Conran, A., *The Cost of Strangeness*; Mathias, R., *Anglo-Welsh Literature*; Curtis, T (ed.), *Wales: the Imagined Nation*.

## Angria

An imaginary kingdom created by Branwell and ▷ Charlotte Brontë in 1834, matched by ▷ Emily and ▷ Anne Brontë's imaginary world, ▷ Gondal. The inspiration for Angria and Gondal came from a box of wooden soldiers given to Branwell by his father in 1826. All four children took part in the creation of a narrative that became known as the 'Glass Town Confederacy'. Charlotte and Branwell went on to develop their Angrian tales, while Emily and Anne broke away to create Gondal. Charlotte's Angrian stories of 1837–9, 'Mina Laury', 'Henry Hastings' and 'Caroline Vernon', anticipate the themes of her mature novels.
**Bib:** Ratchford, F., *The Brontës' Web of Childhood*.

## Anthology

A collection of short works in verse or prose, or selected passages from longer works, by various authors. Some anthologies lay claim to authority as representing the best written in a given period, *eg* the *Oxford Books (of Sixteenth Century Verse*, etc.) and others are standard examples of taste at the time of compiling, *eg* Palgrave's *The Golden Treasury of the Best Songs and Lyrical Poems in the English Language* (1861). Others have had an important influence on taste, or on later literary development.

## Anti-industrialism

A tradition of writing identified initially by Raymond Williams (1921–87) in *Culture and Society 1780–1950* (1958). 19th-century observers, the foremost of whom was ▷ Thomas Carlyle, identified a number of threats to what they saw as constructive social living brought by expanding industrialism. The pressures of the industrial system were blamed for obliging people to work in a mechanical unison and consequently altering their sense of themselves and their employer's sense of them as human beings. The emphasis it brought on material production and material

acquisition changed the conditions of life and sapped the individual's powers of resistance. Other protesters against the 'Mechanical Age' included ▷ Charles Dickens in his novel ▷ *Hard Times* (1854), ▷ John Ruskin in *Unto this Last* (1860) and *Munera Pulveris* (1872) and ▷ William Morris in *A Dream of John Ball* (1886–7) and *News From Nowhere* (1890).
▷ Utopian literature.

## 'Apollodorus'

▷ Pseudonym of ▷ George Gilfillan, an ebullient Scottish reviewer and champion of the ▷ 'Spasmodic' school of poets.

## *Apologia Pro Vita Sua* (1864)

Originally entitled *Apologia Pro Vita Sua: Being a Reply to a Pamphlet Entitled: 'What Then Does Dr Newman Mean?'* this spiritual autobiography of ▷ John Henry Newman was published in seven parts with an appendix between 21 April and 2 June 1864. It began as a reply to the militantly Protestant ▷ Charles Kingsley with whom Newman had publicly quarrelled, but by the time of its publication in book form (1865) it had developed as an explanation or vindication of Newman's spiritual development, and helped to reduce anti-Catholic feeling. An example of the Victorian's enormous interest in ▷ autobiography and the confessional mode of writing it encouraged, Newman's *Apologia* is also a primary historical source for the ▷ Oxford Movement.
▷ Catholicism (Roman) in Victorian literature.

## *Arabian Nights Entertainments*

Also known as *The Thousand and One Nights*, this collection of stories is supposed to have been told by Scheherazade in order to save herself and others from the wrath of King Shahryar who, in revenge for the unfaithfulness of his first wife, vows to marry and kill a new wife each day. The stories originate from many countries and were transmitted orally and developed over a number of centuries. They were probably gathered together by an Egyptian storyteller around the 15th century, and they became well known and popular in Europe in the 18th century. English translations were made by Edward Lane in 1840 and, with greater literary merit, by ▷ Sir Richard Burton in 1885–8. Burton's translation was published openly, but privately, in sixteen volumes, with exhaustive ethnological footnotes and essays on pornography, ▷ homosexuality and the sexual education of women. It constituted a daring

challenge to the sexual repressiveness of
the period.

### Archer, William (1856–1924)
Journalist and drama critic, born in Scotland.
He joined forces with ▷ George Bernard
Shaw in his championship of ▷ Henrik
Ibsen and helped to improve the standard
of British drama at the end of the 19th
century and influence its development. His
translation of *Quicksands, or, The Pillars of
Society*, was performed in London in 1880
and introduced Ibsen to the English audience.
Later translations included *A Doll's House*
(1899), *Ibsen's Prose Dramas* (1890–1), *Peer
Gynt* (1892), *The Master Builder* (1893), and
the *Collected Works* (1906–12).
   ▷ Essay, Drama 1887–1901.

### Arms and the Man (1894)
An early play by ▷ George Bernard Shaw
with the theme that the glamour of war and of
military heroism is essentially a civilian fiction.
The hero, Bluntschli, is a Swiss mercenary
soldier and unheroic 'anti-hero', a figure to
become common in 20th-century literature,
but, with his ironic intelligence, was a type
special to Shaw. It was the first of Shaw's
plays to be publicly performed.

### Arnold, Matthew (1822–88)
Poet, critic and educationalist, son of
▷ Thomas Arnold. Most of Arnold's verse
was published by the time he was forty-five:
*The Strayed Reveller* (1849); ▷ *Empedocles on
Etna* (1852); *Poems* (1853); *Poems, Second Series*
(1855); *Merope, a Tragedy* (1858); *New Poems*
(1867). From these volumes, the best-known
poems today are *The Forsaken Merman* (1849),
*Sohrab and Rustum* (1853), a narrative in
epic style; ▷ *The Scholar Gypsy* (1853),
*Thyrsis* (1867) and the famous short lyric,
▷ 'Dover Beach' (1867 – perhaps written
much earlier). His poetry is elegiac, meditative
and melancholy; preoccupied with spiritual
alienation and the loss of religious faith.

As Arnold began to abandon poetry writing,
his essay and prose writing career took off;
as a critic, he was strongly influential on
early 20th-century thought, and was a crucial
figure in the development of English studies
as a discipline in its own right. Mediated by
the works of T.S. Eliot (1888–1965), I.A.
Richards (1893–1979), Lionel Trilling, F.R.
Leavis (1895–1978) and the literary critical
review *Scrutiny* (published between 1932 and
1953), his cultural criticism forms a lynch-pin
of traditional English criticism. This influence
does not come from his studies of individual

writers but from his studies of contemporary
culture and of the relationship, actual and
potential, of literature to industrial civilization.
His best known critical works are ▷ *Essays in
Criticism*, First and Second Series, 1865 and
1888; *On Translating Homer*, 1861; and *Culture
and Anarchy*, 1869.

Arnold's work as an inspector of schools
and educationist was related to his most
serious critical preoccupations, and the two
worlds meet in such a work as ▷ *Culture and
Anarchy*. His educational theories and absolute
valuing of culture were pitted against the
▷ Utilitarianism of his historical moment.
Arnold posited a system of humane education
under the headship of an ideal, liberal state,
as the means of ensuring the triumph of
culture over social and spiritual anarchy.
   ▷ German influence on English literature.
Bib: Trilling, L., *Matthew Arnold*; Jump, J.D.,
*Matthew Arnold*; Brown, E.K., *Arnold: a Study
in Conflict*; Tinker, C.B. and Lowry, H.F., *The
Poetry of Arnold*; Honan, P., *Matthew Arnold: a
Life*; Carroll, J., *The Cultural Theory of Matthew
Arnold*; Baldick, C., *The Social Mission of
English Criticism*.

### Arnold, Thomas (1795–1842)
Influential Broad Church liberal ▷ Protestant,
headmaster of ▷ Rugby School, and an
important figure in the development of the
▷ public school system and its values. The
father of ▷ Matthew Arnold, he became
professor of Modern History at Oxford
University in 1841. Famously characterized
in ▷ Thomas Hughes's *Tom Brown's
Schooldays* (1857).
   ▷ Education.

### Arts and Crafts Movement, The
An English aesthetic movement, belonging
to the last thirty years of the 19th century,
founded to combat the effects of growing
industrialization on art and culture.

The ▷ Industrial Revolution led to the
mass production of decorative art leading
to what many regarded as a deterioration
in the standards of craftsmanship, and a
vulgarization of style and public taste. In
1861 the poet and designer ▷ William
Morris established a firm of manufacturers
and interior decorators, which included
the architect Philip Webb (1831–1915)
and the painters Ford Madox Brown
(1821–93), Edward Burne-Jones (1833–98)
and occasionally ▷ Dante Gabriel Rossetti,
who clung to the principles of medieval
craftsmanship. They specialised in hand-
crafted artefacts including metalwork,

jewellery, wallpaper, textiles, furniture and books. The group also numbered among its members the mathematician Charles J. Faulkner and the engineer Peter Paul Marshall.

A generation of artists and designers, deeply influenced by Morris and the art critic ▷ John Ruskin, became the leading lights of the Arts and Crafts Movement: people like the architect and designer Arthur Mackmurdo (1851–1942), the painter, draughtsman, designer and author of children's books Walter Crane (1854–1915), the art critic Lewis Day (1845–1910), the designers Selwyn Image (1849–1930) and Herbert Horne (1864–1916), the architect C. F. Annesley Voysey (1857–1941), and Charles R. Ashbee (1863–1942), writer and silversmith.

The popularity of the movement was established by the 1880s and the Century Guild, an organization for craftsmen, was established by Mackmurdo in 1882. Its object was 'to render all branches of art the sphere no longer of the tradesman, but of the artist'. The Arts and Crafts Exhibition Society was founded in 1888 and actively supported by Crane and Day. The same year saw the establishment of the Guild and School of Handicraft and the National Association for the Advancement of Art and its Application to Industry.

The Arts and Crafts movement was controversial in a number of ways. In addition to reviving the art of hand printing, the movement sought to dissolve the distinction between the fine and the decorative arts. Another and perhaps deeper controversy concerned the practicality, in a mass urban and industrialized society, of the work produced by the movement. It was also viewed by many as intellectually elitist and retrogressive: looking backwards to the medieval past rather than forwards to the future.

The movement gained even wider appeal in the 1890s both in Britain and abroad, becoming more experimental and prolific. Its aims, ideals and styles found an outlet in the Art Nouveau Movement: an ornamental style of art that flourished between 1890 and 1910.

▷ Medievalism; Pre-Raphaelite Movement; Anti-Industrialism; Gothic Revival.
**Bib:** Madsen, S. Tschudi, *The Sources of Art Nouveau*; Pevsner, N., *High Victorian Design*.

### *Atalanta in Calydon* (1865)

A verse drama by the poet ▷ Algernon Swinburne, structured like a Greek tragedy and re-telling the Greek myth of Meleager.

Promised at his birth strength and good fortune by the Fates, Meleager is also warned that his life will only last as long as a stick burning in the fire. His mother Althaea removes the stick from the fire, extinguishes it and hides it. A great hunt is organized to kill a monstrous Calydonian boar sent by the goddess Artemis to punish King Oenus (Meleager's father) for his lack of reverence to her. Atalanta, the virgin huntress and one of Artemis' favourites, is one of the participants in the hunt and, when the boar is killed, the besotted Meleager grants her all the spoils. When his uncles object Meleager kills them. In revenge for the death of her brothers Althaea burns the stick that measures her son's life and kills him. In the poem Swinburne demonstrates his concern with family tensions and his impatience with orthodox religion. Several of the lyrics from the drama achieved fame outside their original context and *Atalanta in Calydon* is generally admired for its metrical versatility and emotional power.

### Atheism

Disbelief in God which, in the Middle Ages and the 16th and 17th centuries, was equivalent to a denial of conscience – an attitude shown in the play *The Atheist's Tragedy* (1611) by Cyril Tourneur. Dramatist Christopher Marlowe (1564–93) was charged with it 1593. Atheism at this time was different from the systematic belief that man's reason suffices for his welfare, a belief which grew in the 18th century and emerged in the French Revolution. It influenced such English intellectuals as William Godwin (1756–1836) and through him the poet P.B. Shelley (1792–1822), whose atheism caused him to be expelled from Oxford.

The development of atheism in the 19th century was influenced by the 17th-century rationalist Benedict de Spinoza whose ideas informed the thought of G.W.F. Hegel, an early 19th-century idealist, who claimed that 'there is no God without a world, just as there is no world without a God'. Hegel's ideas were reappraised by his followers after his death, particularly by Ludwig Feuerbach, an anti-Christian German philosopher who concluded, in 1839, that the aim of the modern age should be to humanize God, thereby transforming theology into anthropology. ▷ Karl Marx developed the atheism of Feuerbach in the mid-1840s, accusing religion of being 'the opium of the people' and responsible for the exploitation and alienation of individuals in society. Towards the end of the 19th century ▷ Friedrich Nietzsche evolved his thesis concerning the 'will to power' and openly demanded that God should 'die' in order to facilitate the rise of the superman.

The atheism of ▷ Utilitarians such as James Mill (1773–1836) and his son ▷ John Stuart Mill was essentially 18th century in its origins. As practical men they saw religion as unnecessary in their scheme for human betterment. The scientific ideas of the Victorian period, especially those of ▷ Charles Darwin and ▷ Thomas Huxley, were more productive of ▷ agnosticism than of atheism. A synonym for atheist is 'freethinker'.

▷ Agnosticism; Eliot, George; Hardy, Thomas; Tennyson, Alfred.

## Athenaeum, The

Founded in 1828, it was one of the most enlightened periodicals of the 19th century. It was honest and independent in literary criticism, and a leader of the movement to spread ▷ education among the working classes. In 1831 it reduced its price by half in order to reach this wider public, and in consequence increased its circulation six times. It was also very progressive in social reform. In 1921 it was incorporated in the *Nation and Athenaeum*, which in turn was merged in 1931 with the socialist weekly, *The New Statesman*.

▷ Reviews and Periodicals.

## Aurora Leigh (1857)

One of ▷ Elizabeth Barrett Browning's most important works, and a key text for Victorian debates about the ▷ 'Woman Question'. Described by its author as a 'novel in verse', this 11,000-line poem is a semi-autobiographical account of the development of a female poet, exploring both the nature of sexual difference and the role of the woman writer.

Aurora is brought up in Italy until she is seventeen, then sent to England to live with an aunt. Educating herself in secret, she refuses a marriage proposal at twenty from her cousin Romney, who wishes her to abandon writing in favour of social reform. Alone and penniless on the death of her aunt, she establishes a reputation as a poet in London. Here she becomes involved with Lady Waldemar, who is in love with Romney and wishes to use Aurora to prevent him from marrying Marian Earle, a poor sempstress. Marian absconds to the continent before the marriage can take place, and Aurora finds her

there with an illegitimate child, the product of a rape. The two women live happily together in Italy for some time until Aurora meets up with the now blinded and politically disillusioned Romney who acknowledges the importance of her work and whom she marries.

Although the narrative is indebted to other 19th-century texts such as ▷ Elizabeth Gaskell's ▷ Ruth and ▷ Charlotte Brontë's ▷ *Jane Eyre*, as well as to Madame de Staël's (1766–1817) *Corinne ou L'Italie* (1807), it is important for its discussion of art, politics, poetic tradition and women's writing. *Aurora Leigh* contains the fullest exposition of issues surrounding female creativity in Victorian literature, despite its elitist political stance and demonstrable fear of the working class. In the year of its publication it ran to three editions and remained enormously popular, achieving seventeen editions by 1882. However, some Victorian parents refused to allow their daughters to read it, fearful of the model of female independence and autonomy it presented. In its themes it echoes ▷ Kingsley's ▷ *Alton Locke*.

*Aurora Leigh* was republished by The Women's Press in 1978.

▷ Women's Movement.

## Autobiography

The word came into English at the very end of the 18th century. In the 19th and 20th centuries the writing of the story of one's own life became a common literary activity: however, the practice already had an ancient history. The English autobiography first manifested itself in the form of the spiritual confession, having as its basic model the *Confessions* of St Augustine of Hippo (345–430), who describes his conversion to Christianity, and John Bunyan's (1628–88) *Grace Abounding to the Chief of Sinners* (1666). It is characteristic of such works that they contain detailed accounts of the emotional life, but little factual description of events.

The memoir, on the other hand, was of French derivation, and originated largely in the 17th century, owing much to the practice of extensive letter-writing which developed at that time, eg the letters of Madame de Sévigné (1626–96) or the historian Edward Gibbon's (1737–94) fragmentary *Memoirs* (pub. 1796). The objective memoir and the subjective confession came together in the *Confessions* of the the French-Swiss Jean Jacques Rousseau (1712–98), published after his death, and this is the most prevalent form of the outstanding English autobiographies of the 19th century. The varieties of this form are extensive: they may be a record of emotional struggles and experiences, eg *The Confessions of an English Opium Eater* (1822) by Thomas de Quincey (1785–1859) or ▷ *Sartor Resartus* by ▷ Thomas Carlyle. They may be essentially a history of the growth of ideas, convictions, and the strengthening of vocation, in the life of the writer, eg ▷ John Stuart Mill's *Autobiography* (1873); ▷ Beatrice Webb's *My Apprenticeship* (1926) or ▷ John Henry Newman's ▷ *Apologia Pro Vita Sua* (1864). An autobiographical element becomes prominent in works which are not strictly autobiographies from the early 19th century on, eg Wordsworth's (1770–1850) *Prelude, or Growth of a Poet's Mind* (first version 1805).

It may be said that from 1800 on it becomes the instinct of writers of many kinds to use autobiographical material, or to adopt from time to time an autobiographical standpoint. This is particularly the case in the autobiographical novel, beginning with the novels of ▷ Charlotte Brontë (▷ *Jane Eyre*, 1847, and ▷ *Villette*, 1853), and ▷ Charles Dickens's ▷ *David Copperfield* (1849–50). This method of writing a novel really came into its own, however, with ▷ Samuel Butler's ▷ *The Way of All Flesh* (1903). The anti-feminist writer ▷ Eliza Lynn Linton chose to portray her life using a male protagonist in ▷ *The Autobiography of Christopher Kirkland* (1885) thereby enjoying a certain freedom to write about events which would have been denied her had she published it under her own name. ▷ Charles Darwin and ▷ Thomas Huxley both wrote autobiographies.

### Autobiography of Christopher Kirkland, The (1885)

The autobiography of ▷ Eliza Lynn Linton, anti-feminist journalist and author of the sensational essay ▷ 'The Girl of the Period' (1868). Although the book accurately and frankly records Linton's life, it is written from the perspective of a male. One reason for this may have been that a male persona enabled Linton to write more freely about her own close female companions without attracting speculation or scandal (especially since she had explicitly condemned ▷ lesbianism in *The Rebel of the Family*, 1880). The book was not a commercial success.

▷ Pseudonyms.

### Awkward Age, The (1899)

A novel by ▷ Henry James. Nanda Brookenham is a young girl brought up in a smart but corrupt section of London society; her mother and her mother's circle are willing to carry on immoral intrigues so long as respectable appearances are scrupulously protected. Nanda is in love with Vanderbank, who, as she learns later, is her mother's lover, and she feels some affection for Mitchett, a young man of less charm than Vanderbank, but with an attractive simplicity of heart. Unlike the other members of her mother's circle, she is free and candid in her feelings and open in her conduct; this alarms Vanderbank and inhibits him from declaring his love for her. Her elderly friend, Mr Longdon, an admirer of her dead grandmother, gives Nanda a dowry to attract Vanderbank, but this only increases the latter's fastidious reluctance to declare himself. Meanwhile, the Duchess, Mrs Brookenham's friend and rival, conspires to capture Mitchett for her own daughter, Aggie, whose appearance of immaculate innocence immediately breaks down when it has served its purpose of qualifying her for the marriage market. Vanderbank's mixture of scrupulousness and timidity remains a permanent barrier between himself and Nanda. Mr Longdon adopts her, and they remain together in their love of truthful feeling, isolated from the sophisticated but essentially trivial society which has hitherto constituted Nanda's environment.

The novel is an example of James's interest in the survival of integrity in a materialistic society blinded by its own carefully cultivated artificiality.

### Aytoun, William Edmondstoune (1818–65)

Versatile Scottish satirist, poet and critic and contributor to ▷ *Blackwood's Magazine*. Provoked by the feverish ▷ Romanticism of much of the poetry of the early 1840s and by the enthusiasm of the critic ▷ George Gilfillan, he coined the term ▷ 'Spasmodic' to describe the work of ▷ Sydney Dobell, ▷ Philip James Bailey and Alexander Smith (1830–67). In May 1854, Aytoun instituted an elaborate hoax – publishing an anonymous critical review of a forthcoming production of *Firmilian, or the Student of Badajoz: A Spasmodic Tragedy by T. Percy Jones* and a preface to the work by its imaginary author in *Blackwood's Magazine*. *Firmilian* cleverly burlesqued the excesses of Dobell and Smith to such an extent that they disappeared from the literary scene. Aytoun also wrote the *Bon Gaultier Ballads* (1855) with Theodore Martin, a series of parodies of poets such as ▷ Tennyson and ▷ Elizabeth Barrett

Browning. His *Lays of the Scottish Cavaliers* (1849) and *The Ballads of Scotland* (1858) were very popular with their contemporary audience.

▷ Scottish literature in English.

**Bib:** Martin, T., *Memoir of William Edmonstoune Aytoun*; Weinstein, M.A., *William Edmonstoune Aytoun and the Spasmodic Controversy*.

# B

**Baedeker, Karl (1801–59)**
The author of famous guide-books, which were carried on by his son and eventually covered most of the civilized world. Their frequent mention in English 19th- and 20th-century fiction shows how indispensable they were to English middle- and upper-class tourists of the last 100 years, especially in visits to countries in which monuments and works of art are plentiful, such as Italy. He wrote in German but English editions were produced after his death, from 1861 onwards.
**Bib:** Pemble, J., *The Mediterranean Passion*.

**Bagehot, Walter (1826–77)**
A writer on political and economic affairs, best known for his book *The English Constitution* (1867) which, despite historical change, is still a classic study of the spirit of English politics and notably of the function of monarchy in providing the imaginative appeal of the state and ensuring the dignity of government without hindering desirable conflict of opinion.

Bagehot was also the author of a number of critical essays, the best known of which is *Wordsworth, Tennyson, and Browning or Pure, Ornate, and Grotesque Art in English Poetry* (1864). It is republished in *English Critical Essays* ed. by E.D. Jones (World's Classics).
**Bib:** Stephen, Leslie in *Studies of a Biographer*; Buchan, A., *The Spare Chancellor*; St John-Stevas, N.A.F., *Life*.

**Bailey, Philip James (1816–1902)**
Poet. Earliest and most significant member of a school of poets satirized by critic ▷ William Aytoun as the ▷ Spasmodics. Born in Nottingham, he was educated at Glasgow University and called to the Bar in 1840: however, he practised only as a poet. In 1839 he achieved enormous popularity with a blank verse epic drama, *Festus*, based on Goethe's (1749–1882) Faust legend. Each subsequent edition was progressively enlarged until the final *Festus* (1889) had expanded to 52 scenes and 40,000 lines. Highly emotional and religiose, *Festus* sought to portray inspiration through irregularity of form and spontaneous composition. Other, more modest, works include *The Angel World* (1850) and *The Mystic* (1855). Bailey's reputation never recovered from Aytoun's brilliant parody of his style in *Firmilian, or The Student of Badajoz: A Spasmodic Tragedy* (1854).
▷ Gilfillan, George.

**Ballad**
Traditionally, the ballad has been considered a folkloric verse narrative which has strong associations with communal dancing, and support for that link has been found in the derivation of the word 'ballad' itself (from the late Latin verb *ballare*, to dance). More recently, scholars have viewed the association between ballads and dance forms more sceptically. Generally, the term is used of a narrative poem which uses an elliptical and highly stylized mode of narration, in which the techniques of repetition with variation may play an important part. Often ballads contain repeated choral refrains, but this is not a universal feature. The great ballad collection of F.J. Child, *English and Scottish Popular Ballads*, was published at the end of the 19th century. Associated with oral tradition and song, ballads were a popular form for women poets in the 19th century, including Felicia Hemans (1793–1835), Letitia Landon (1802–38), ▷ Elizabeth Barrett Browning, ▷ Emily Brontë and ▷ Christina Rossetti, and they proved equally popular with readers. Victorian ballads often had a ▷ medieval setting, such as Barrett Browning's 'The Romaunt of the Page' (1839) and 'The Lay of the Brown Rosary' (1840).
**Bib:** Bold, A., *The Ballad*.

**Ballade**
A lyrical form favoured by French court poets of the 14th century and first used in English by Chaucer (c 1340–1400). The ballade form requires three stanzas linked by a refrain and common rhymes repeated in the same order in each stanza. It was revived in the late 19th century by poets such as ▷ Swinburne and ▷ Dante Gabriel Rossetti.

***Ballad of Reading Gaol, The (1898)***
A powerful poem by ▷ Oscar Wilde concerning the hanging of the murderer Charles Thomas Wooldridge during Wilde's own imprisonment in Reading Gaol for homosexual acts. In contrast to Wilde's earlier works it is less concerned with aesthetics than with the harshness of prison conditions and the Christian doctrine of forgiveness. It was his last work.
▷ Homosexuality.

**Ballantyne, R.M. (1825–94)**
Writer of adventure stories, aimed primarily at boys, the most famous being *The Coral Island* (1858), probably the most popular such work of the Victorian era. This story,

in which a trio of boys are shipwrecked on a Pacific island, is implicitly a ▷ colonial fable, full of blood and masculine resourcefulness. Ballantyne's life was suitably adventurous: born in Edinburgh, he received little formal education but worked as a fur trader in northern Canada from the age of sixteen. This experience produced *Hudson's Bay* (1848) and *The Young Fur Traders* (1856). After establishing himself as an author he continued to travel to research the background to his novels, which included: *Martin Rattler, Or A Boy's Adventure in the Forests of Brazil* (1858), *Pirate City* (1874), set in Algiers, and *A Tale of the London Fire Brigade* (1867).

**Balzac, Honoré de (1799–1850)**
French novelist. His *La Comédie humaine* is a panorama of French society from the Revolution to the July Monarchy (1830). It is bound together by the use of recurrent characters (Vautrin is one notable instance, Rastignac another) and recurrent motifs (notably the necessity of moral and social order contrasted with the pressures of the individual ego). Among the 100 novels which Balzac completed, drafted or projected are *Eugénie Grandet* (1833), *Illusions perdues* (1837–43), *La Cousine Bette* (1846), *Le Cousin Pons* (1847), *Le Père Goriot* (1835), *Splendeurs et misères des courtisanes* (1847).

'French society was to be the historian,' Balzac wrote, 'I had only to be the scribe.' His ways of depicting French society are geographical, historical, political and even geological insofar as all social strata find a place. These different representations, taken individually or in combination, bring into play a dynamic explained in *La Peau de chagrin* (1831) as the product of desire and power, with knowledge enlisted to restrain them. But such a restraint is rare or non-existent, and society in the *Comédie humaine* is driven by a restlessness which tends to exhaustion as it competes for the fulfilment of desire. Like society, character too is open to multiple descriptions, as a machine driven by abstracts (passion, ambition, penury, for instance) or as a representative of a human or social type. In that respect, character has a potential for expansion. It is always ready to merge into symbol (more than just the performance of symbolic actions) or be exaggerated into ▷ melodrama. Indeed, melodrama is a central Balzacian ingredient and, just as characters are actors, buildings and places too are subject to mutation into a theatre or a scene in which the novelistic events unfold.

Balzac liked myth and melodrama, and his social ▷ realism is correspondingly more than the accumulation of surface detail, since the detail acts as an indicator of underlying causes. In turn, understanding of these causes is open only to the novelist defined by his capacity for 'second sight', the capacity to perceive pattern as well as pattern destroyed. And it is considerations of this kind which distinguish Balzac from other *feuilleton* novelists such as Eugène Sue (1804–57) and help account for his pervasive influence on 19th-century fiction, particularly in England, where Balzac shaped the already strong vein of social realism.
▷ French influence on Victorian literature.
**Bib:** Prendergast, C., *Balzac: Fiction and Melodrama*; Bellos, D., *Balzac: Le Père Goriot*.

**Banks, Isabella (1821–87)**
Novelist, poet and journalist, born in Manchester, the daughter of a successful tradesman. She was sixteen years old when her poem 'A Dying Girl to Her Mother', was published in the *Manchester Guardian*. More of her work was published in *Bradshaw's Three* (1841–42), and her first collection of poems, *Ivy Leaves*, appeared in 1844. Banks then grew prolific, writing a series of novels set in the Manchester area, the best-known of which are *The Manchester Man* (1876), *Caleb Booth's Clerk* (1878) and *Wooers and Winners: A Yorkshire Story* (1880). Her novels were so rooted in her native environment that she was labelled the 'Lancashire Novelist'. They are mainly of historical interest today, seeming overloaded with detailed local description and lacking narrative pace.
▷ Regional novel.
**Bib:** Burney, E.L., *Life*.

**Barnaby Rudge (1841)**
A novel by ▷ Charles Dickens, published as part of ▷ *Master Humphrey's Clock*. The only other novel that he published in this proposed series was ▷ *The Old Curiosity Shop*; Dickens then abandoned it.

It is set in the 18th century and its central episodes are descriptions of the fierce anti-▷ Catholic disorders called 'the Gordon Riots', which terrorized London for several days in 1780. These vivid scenes, and the characters directly concerned in the riots (such as the half-wit Barnaby Rudge, the locksmith Gabriel Varden and his apprentice Simon Tappertit), constitute the part of the book which is most memorable and most representative of Dickens's style. The main story is a romantic one about the love affair of Emma Haredale, whose father has been mysteriously murdered, and Edward Chester, the son of Sir John Chester, a suave villain who helps to instigate the Riots. Sir John and Emma's uncle, Geoffrey Haredale, a Catholic, are enemies, but they unite in opposition to the marriage of Edward and Emma. During the riots, Geoffrey Haredale's house is burnt down but Edward saves the lives of both Emma and her uncle, and thus wins his approval of the match. The murderer of Emma's father turns out to be the father of Barnaby.

*Barnaby Rudge* is one of Dickens's two ▷ historical novels, the other being ▷ *A Tale of Two Cities*.

### Barnes, William (1801–86)

Poet. A clergyman from the West of England (▷ Wessex), Barnes's most important work is *Poems of Rural Life, in the Dorset Dialect* (1844), but he also wrote verse in 'Standard English'. A champion of Anglo-Saxon over the Latinate element in the English language, he greatly influenced fellow Dorsetman ▷ Thomas Hardy, who wrote the poem 'The Last Signal' (1886) on his death, and prefaced and edited an edition of his poetry in 1908.
**Bib:** Jones, B. (ed.), *The Poems of William Barnes*; Baxter, L., *The Life of Barnes by his Daughter*.

### Barrie, James Matthew (1860–1937)

Scottish playwright and novelist and the ninth of ten children. He had a very close relationship with his mother, Margaret Ogilvy, who was the eponymous heroine of his novel published in 1896 and who also appears as 'the little mother' in his autobiographical novel *Sentimental Tommy* (1896). Barrie attended Edinburgh University before working for the Nottingham *Journal* for two years, and then moved to London in 1885 to become a freelance writer. In his early writing he idealized childhood and expressed disenchantment with adult life. The sketches of Scottish life he published in various papers were collected into his first successful book *Auld Licht Idylls* (1888). His novel in the same vein, *The Little Minister* (1891), was a best-seller and was adapted for the stage in 1897. From this point on Barrie devoted himself to the theatre, producing two of his best plays, *Quality Street* and *The Admirable Crichton*, in London in 1902. His marriage to the actress Mary Ansell in 1894 was apparently unconsummated and in 1897 he became attached to Sylvia Llewellyn Davies, telling his first Peter Pan stories to her sons and publishing some of them in *The Little*

*White Bird* (1902). The play *Peter Pan*, about a boy who refused to grow up, followed in 1904 and the story was published in *Peter Pan and Wendy* (1911). Other plays include *What Every Woman Knows* (1908), *Dear Brutus* (1917) and *Mary Rose* (1920), and some excellent one-act pieces. He was knighted in 1913.
▷ Scottish literature in English.
**Bib:** Darton, F.J. Harvey, *Barrie*; Hammerton, J.A., *Barrie, the Story of a Genius*; Mackail, D., *The Story of J.M.B.*

### Barry Lyndon (1852)

A novel by ▷ William Thackeray serialized in ▷ *Fraser's Magazine* in 1844 under the title *The Luck of Barry Lyndon*. Written in the style of Fielding, it is set in the 18th century and concerns a boastful Irish adventurer who unwittingly reveals the extent of his own villany. Interesting as an example of rogue literature, and for its sustained use of an unreliable narrator.
▷ Historical novel; Newgate novel.

### Barsetshire

An imaginary English county invented by ▷ Anthony Trollope for a series of novels, some of which centre on an imaginary town in it, the cathedral city of Barchester. It is a characteristic southern English setting. The novels are the best known of his works.
Titles: ▷ *The Warden, Barchester Towers*, ▷ *Doctor Thorne, Framley Parsonage, The Small House at Allington*, ▷ *The Last Chronicle of Barset*.
▷ Wessex.

### Baudelaire, Charles (1821–67)

French poet. His best known work, *Les Fleurs du mal* (1857), points the way out of ▷ Romanticism towards modernism. Formally, it draws on the tradition of ▷ sonnet and song which Baudelaire inherited from the Renaissance. Conceptually, it springs from the perception of 'two simultaneous feelings: the horror of life and the ecstasy of life', periods of heightened sensitivity and sensibility alternating with the monotony of existence without meaning. Baudelaire's work is rich in suggestion, allowing sensation to transfuse the object as though the object were the source of the sensation rather than the occasion for it; and equally powerful value is bestowed upon the metaphorical expression of sense-experience. When the poet uncovers, invested with desire, an exotic and erotic universe in a woman's hair ('La Chevelure'), this moment is also an uncovering of the possible resonances which

the hair triggers in the poet. The contrasting
condition of 'Ennui' is a state of torpor which
saps intellectual and emotional vigour and
induces creative sterility. Everyday objects
are here commonly used to embody feelings
of failure, dejection, horror and despair.
The book's five sections explore these twin
conditions, in art and love (*Spleen et Idéal*),
in city life (*Tableaux Parisiens*), in stimulants
(*Le Vin*), in perversity (*Fleurs du mal*) and in
metaphysical rebellion (*La Révolte*), ending (in
the poem 'Le Voyage') with man's yearning
unsatisfied but finding in death a new journey
of discovery.

Baudelaire also wrote fine music and
art criticism (he championed Wagner and
Delacroix); his translations of Edgar Allan Poe
(1809–49) helped confirm, in France, interest
in tales of the fantastic; and he was the first
to investigate extensively the new genre of
prose poetry. In England, his influence has
been constant, though at the outset it raised
moral controversy. Reviewing *Les Fleurs du
mal* in the ▷ *Spectator* of 1862, ▷ Swinburne
responded to the sensualism of Baudelaire,
and this version of Baudelaire was handed
on to the late 19th-century 'decadent' poets.
T.S. Eliot (1888–1965) 'rescued' Baudelaire
and identified the French poet's sense of sin
with 'Sin in the permanent Christian sense',
even though Baudelaire himself in a letter
to Swinburne warned against easy moral
readings of his work.

▷ French influence on Victorian literature.

**Beaconsfield, Lord**
▷ Disraeli, Benjamin.

**Beardsley, Aubrey (Vincent) (1872–98)**
The leading illustrator of the 1890s and,
after ▷ Oscar Wilde, the dominant figure
in the ▷ Aesthetic movement of the period.
He became famous for his stunning black
and white illustrations to works by Wilde
and ▷ Ernest Dowson (▷ Nineties' Poets).
His styles were widely imitated and he was
responsible for a new simplicity and directness
in the art of illustrating. The flowing lines
and sumptuous compositions of his drawings
expressed what was considered most bold
and daring in the Aesthetic movement. He
was largely self-taught except for a brief spell
attending evening classes at the Westminster
School of Art which the artist Sir Edward
Burne Jones encouraged him to attend in
1891. Two years later he was commissioned
to illustrate a new edition of Sir Thomas
Malory's medieval romance, *Morte D'Arthur*,
(1469/70), and in 1894 he became art editor

of the ▷ *Yellow Book*, designing the first
four covers himself. These together with his
illustrations for Wilde's ▷ *Salome* gained him
widespread notoriety.

His art was influenced by the elegant,
curvilinear style of the Art Nouveau movement
and the bold designs of Japanese woodcuts.
Added to this was the sensuality of his
drawings of women coupled with an erotic
morbidity which shocked his critics. His
illustrations to Aristophanes' *Lysistrata* (1896)
were even more graphic. Despite his distance
from Wilde, Beardsley was dismissed from
*The Yellow Book* when the scandal surrounding
Wilde's homosexuality broke in 1895. He
joined the staff of *The Savoy* magazine as
its principal illustrator and during the last
two years of his life he illustrated Alexander
Pope's *Rape of the Lock* (1896) and Johnson's
*Volpone* (1898), wrote a number of poems
and part of a romantic novel, *Under the Hill*.
It was privately printed in an unexpurgated
version under the title *The Story of Venus and
Tannhauser* in 1907. In 1896 the tuberculosis
that had dogged his childhood flared up
again and he became an invalid. A year later
he converted to ▷ Catholicism and moved
to France, where he died at the age of
twenty-five.

**Beerbohm, Max (1872–1956)**
Essayist, cartoonist, writer of fiction. When
he began his career Beerbohm belonged to
the so-called 'decadent' generation of the
aesthetic school in the 1890s (▷ Nineties'
Poets); this included, W.B. Yeats (1865–1939)
in his Celtic Twilight phase, ▷ Oscar Wilde,
▷ Aubrey Beardsley, and the poets Lionel
Johnson (1867–1902) and ▷ Ernest Dowson.
He showed his affiliation to this school
by the playful fastidiousness of his wit,
especially in his cartoons and parodies. *A
Christmas Garland* (1912) contains parodies
of contemporary writers including ▷ H.G.
Wells, Arnold Bennett (1867–1931), and
Joseph Conrad (1857–1924). But it is in his
cartoons that his satirical wit is displayed with
most pungency and originality, eg *Caricature
of Twenty-five Gentlemen* (1896), *The Poet's
Corner* (1904), *Rossetti and his Circle* (1922).
As a writer he was above all an essayist; he
entitled his first slim volume with humorous
impertinence *The Works of Max Beerbohm*
(1896), to which he added *More* (1899), *Yet
Again* (1909), *And Even Now* (1920). He also
wrote stories (*Seven Men*; 1919), and he is
probably now most read for his burlesque
romance *Zuleika Dobson* (1911), about the
visit of a dazzling beauty to the University of

Oxford where she is responsible for a mass suicide among the students.

Beerbohm was educated at Charterhouse and Merton College, Oxford. He contributed to the ▷ *Yellow Book*, and in 1898 succeeded ▷ George Bernard Shaw as dramatic critic on the ▷ *Saturday Review*. From 1910 he lived in Italy, except during the two world wars. He was knighted in 1939. His personal and literary fastidiousness caused him to be known as 'the Incomparable Max', and as such poet Ezra Pound (1885–1972) commemorates him as 'Brennbaum the Impeccable' in section 8 of *Hugh Selwyn Mauberley* (1920).

▷ Aestheticism.

**Beeton, Mrs (1836–65)**
The author of a book on cooking and household management, published serially in *The Englishwoman's Domestic Magazine* (1859–61). The book met the needs of the rapidly broadening Victorian middle class, which was strongly attached to the domestic virtues and satisfactions. It was soon regarded as an indispensable handbook.

**Bell, Currer, Ellis, Acton**
▷ Brontë, Charlotte, Emily, Anne.

**Belloc, Hilaire (1870–1953)**
A versatile writer (novelist, poet, essayist, biographer, historian) now especially remembered for his association with G.K. Chesterton (1874–1936) in Roman ▷ Catholic propaganda. The most important phase of his career was before 1914, when he was one of a generation of popular, vivid, witty propagandists; ▷ George Bernard Shaw, ▷ H.G. Wells, and Chesterton were his equals, and the first two (as ▷ agnostic socialists) his opponents. With Chesterton, he maintained the doctrine of Distributism – an alternative scheme to socialism for equalizing property ownership. Among his best works is his earliest: *The Path to Rome* (1902), a discursive account of a journey through France, Switzerland and Northern Italy. He is now chiefly read for his light verse, eg *Cautionary Tales* (1907), *A Bad Child's Book of Beasts* (1896).

▷ Children's literature.

**Bib:** Hamilton, R., *Belloc: An Introduction to his Spirit and Work*; Speaight, R., *The Life of Hilaire Belloc*.

**Bentham, Jeremy (1748–1832)**
An extremely influential thinker, founder of the school of thought called ▷ Utilitarianism. The basis of his thought was: 1 that human motives are governed by the pursuit of pleasure and avoidance of pain; 2 that the guiding rule for society should be the greatest happiness of the greatest number; 3 that the test of value for human laws and institutions should be no other than that of usefulness. These views he expounded in *Fragment on Government* (1776) and *Introduction to Principles of Morals and Legislation* (1780). His principal associates were James Mill (1773–1836) and ▷ John Stuart Mill (1806–73); collectively they were known as the Philosophical Radicals, and together they established a practical philosophy of reform of great consequence in 19th-century Britain. But their excessive rationalism frustrated sympathy and imagination in education and the relief of poverty – see ▷ Dickens's novel ▷ *Hard Times* (1854). Bentham's thought derived from the sceptical 18th-century French 'philosophes' such as Helvetius and 18th-century English rationalists such as David Hartley (1705–57) and Joseph Priestley (1733–1804). It was, in fact, the outstanding line of continuity between 18th-century and 19th-century thinking.

**Bib:** Stephen, L., *The English Utilitarians*; Pringle-Patterson, A.S., *The Philosophical Radicals and other essays*; Atkinson, C.M., *Life*.

**Bentley, E.C. (Edmund Clerihew) (1875–1956)**
▷ Detective fiction.

**Besant, Walter (1836–1901)**
Novelist, philanthropist and journalist, born in Portsea and educated at King's College, London and Christ's College, Cambridge. Many of his novels were set in east London; for example *All Sorts and Conditions of Men* (1882) is an idealistic story about an heiress and a cabinet maker who combined to bring about the dream of 'People's Palace of Delight' in the East End (a project which Besant contributed to in real life). His novel *The Revolt of Man* (1882) is an anti-feminist dystopia, part of the debate over the ▷ New Woman.

▷ Utopian Literature.

**Best-sellers**
Novels in the Victorian period were generally published in three volumes retailing at about 10s 6d per volume. The demand for new fiction at a reasonable price was met by the ▷ circulating libraries, the chief of which after 1852 was ▷ Charles Edward Mudie's, which frequently determined a novelist's reputation by accepting or rejecting his or

her novel. In 1836, ▷ Charles Dickens rediscovered the benefits of publication in monthly numbers and ▷ *The Pickwick Papers* was published in this manner. Monthly publication meant that a novel could be bought bit by bit for considerably less than the cost of a triple-decker. The commercial success of this method improved the fortunes of Dickens's publishers, Chapman and Hall, who invested the profit they made in new technology in printing and binding, and in advertising each new novel widely. Distribution was facilitated by the developing railway system. The popularity of a novel could be gauged by the rise or fall in the monthly sales and most serial fiction was published in one volume shortly before the serial ended in order to stimulate sales. Many novelists, including ▷ Thackeray and ▷ Trollope, adopted this method of publication. By 1850 novels were mainly published in single volumes, increasing their popularity with railway travellers, who also helped to stimulate the sale of cheap reprints.

**Betham-Edwards, Matilda (1836–1919)**
Novelist, essayist and ▷ travel writer, born on a farm in Suffolk. Her mother died when she was twelve, after which Betham-Edwards educated herself, developing early an interest in France and the French. She began her first novel, *The White House by the Sea*, while still a teenager. Eventually published in 1857, it became an immediate success, reprinting continuously for the next forty years. The author went on to write more than thirty novels, of which *Forestalled* (1880) and *Love and Marriage* (1884) were her favourites. Her travel writing includes *A Winter with the Swallows* (1866) and *Through Spain to the Sahara* (1867), which record her trips with the ▷ feminist ▷ Barbara Bodichon. Betham-Edwards was a believer in women's equality and signed the 1866 petition for female suffrage. Her sympathy to socialist perspectives is evident in *The Sylvesters* (1871). In 1884, she published *Six Life Studies of Famous Women*, which included a biographical sketch of her aunt and godmother, Matilda Betham, who wrote poetry and diaries.
▷ Travel writing; Women's suffrage.

**Big Ben**
The biggest bell in the clock tower of the Houses of Parliament; often used as the name of the tower itself. The name commemorates the official under whose authority the bell was cast – Sir Benjamin Hall, Commissioner of Works, 1855–8. The loudness and

melodiousness of the chime are well known, and, from the position of the clock high above the Houses of Parliament so as to be a landmark, both the chime and the tower itself have been turned into symbols of corporate national life. They are particularly used to suggest probity, dependability and consensus: for instance, the chimes of Big Ben prefacing the BBC Radio news seem to guarantee its objectivity.

**Biography**
A selection and ordering of the known facts of a person's life written down in an attempt to create the illusion of a life actually being lived. The chief source of inspiration for English biographers was the Greek Plutarch (1st century AD), whose *Parallel Lives* of Greek and Roman men was translated by Sir Thomas North in 1579 and was widely read. Before this, biography had been practised in England with the lives of the saints in the Middle Ages and Cavendish's life of the statesman Cardinal Wolsey in the 16th century.

The regular practice of biography began in the 17th century as part of the outward-turning, increasingly scientific interest in people from all walks of life (not only saints and rulers), which in the 18th century was to give rise to the novel. Biography is a branch of history; both are concerned with tracing and evaluating the past, and the art of historical writing (▷ historical novel) advanced with the art of biography. In the 18th century the writing of biographies became habitual; at the same time biography, or ▷ autobiography, became a way of disguising pure fiction as in the novels of Daniel Defoe (1660–1731). Samuel Johnson (1709–84) was a master of biography and the life of Johnson himself, written by James Boswell (1740–95), is an outstanding example of its kind.

In the Victorian period, the historian and social critic ▷ Thomas Carlyle regarded biography as a means of recounting 'the earthly pilgrimage of a man' (*Critical and Miscellaneous Essays*, 1838). He also regarded the history of the world as 'but the Biography of great men' (▷ *On Heroes, Hero-Worship and the Heroic in History*). His edition of *Oliver Cromwell's Letters and Speeches, with Elucidations* (1845) is an attempt to portray history through the life of one of the men who helped to make it. Carlyle's sympathetic biography helped to establish Cromwell's stature. In 1851 Carlyle wrote a *Life of John Sterling* as a tribute to his 'brilliant, beautiful and cheerful friend' and followed it with a six-volumed *History of Frederick*

*the Great* (1858–65) which took him twelve
years to complete. Both of these books
are good examples of Carlyle's tendency to
'whitewash' his subjects in the service of
didacticism, in that they were designed to
support his claim that Britain was in need of
'strong men' with heroic leadership qualities.
Carlyle's own biography was written by
his great friend the historian J.A. Froude
who also edited Carlyle's *Reminiscences*
(1881): a series of biographical sketches of
famous contemporaries (such as the poets
Wordsworth and Southey), and members
of his own immediate family including his
father, James Carlyle, and his wife, ▷ Jane
Welsh Carlyle. Other biographies of the
Victorian period in which the author claims
a vital relationship between him/herself and
his/her subject include Thomas Moore's
*Letters and Journals of Lord Byron* (1830),
John Gibson Lockhart's *Memoirs* (1837–38),
a biography of his father-in-law Sir Walter
Scott, and ▷ Elizabeth Gaskell's study *The
Life of Charlotte Brontë* (1857). In each of
these cases the author had access to personal
papers and information about the subject and
frequently seasons the narrative with personal
reminiscences.

Mrs Gaskell's life of ▷ Charlotte Brontë
is characteristic of a trend among Victorian
female novelists to write sympathetic and
admiring lives of other women writers. A
favourite subject was the French novelist
▷ George Sand. Jane Williams (1806–85),
Julia Kavanagh (1824–77) and Gertrude
Mayer (1839–1932) compiled surveys of
women of letters, such as Williams's *Literary
Women of England* (1861), or collections
of articles on their lives. Anna Stoddart
(1840–1911) wrote biographies of such varied
individuals as the traveller ▷ Isabella Bird
and *Francis of Assisi* (1903).

In contrast to the personal biography is the
informative biography. This is less subjective
and may be composed of a selection of events
involving the subject, reported with as little
interpretive comment as possible. David
Masson's *Life of Milton: Narrated in Connection
with the Political, Ecclesiastical, and Literary
History of his Time* (seven vols, 1859–94), or
John G. Nicolay and John Hay's *Abraham
Lincoln: A History* (ten vols, 1890) are good
examples.

The 20th-century biographer Lytton
Strachey regarded most biographies of the
19th century as dull monuments to the
subject, whereas he considered biography to
be an art form – presenting the subject as a
human being and showing him or her from

unexpected angles. His best-known works
include *Eminent Victorians* (1918) – short
biographical studies of Cardinal Manning,
Florence Nightingale and General Gordon –
and *Queen Victoria* (1912). ▷ Edmund Gosse
wrote *The Life of Algernon Charles Swinburne*
(1917) but his most famous work is the
autobiographical *Father and Son* published
anonymously in 1907 which sheds a personal
and revealing light on the Victorian period. As
such it is a classic example of the largely new
form of autobiography for which the period is
more outstanding.
**Bib:** Gittings, R., *The Nature of Biography*.

**Bishop, Isabella Bird (1831–1904)**
▷ Travel writer. She was born in
Boroughbridge, one of two daughters of
Edward Bird, curate, and Dora Lawson,
Sunday-school teacher. She began travelling
abroad in 1854 with a visit to the United
States. *The Englishwoman in America* (1856)
was an immediate success, launching her
career as a writer. *Aspects of Religion in America*
(1859) was written during her second trip
to North America; this was followed by *The
Hawaiian Archipelago: Six Months Among the
Palm Groves, Coral Reefs and Volcanoes of
the Sandwich Islands* (1874). In 1878 she left
for Japan, returning in 1879 after travelling
through Hong Kong, Saigon, Singapore and
Malaysia. *Unbeaten Tracks in Japan* (1880)
and *The Golden Cheronese* (1883) record
these journeys. In 1889 she set out for the
Middle East, continuing through India, Tibet,
Central Asia and Persia. During this trip
she organized the building of two hospitals
in India, in memory of her father and sister.
*Journeys in Persia and Kurdistan* was published
in 1894, the year in which Bishop left Britain
on a missionary trip to China. She sailed
up the Yangtze River, rode 300 miles alone
on a mule, and built three hospitals and an
orphanage. Returning to London in 1897, she
prepared *Korea and Her Neighbours* (1898), *The
Yangtze Valley and Beyond* (1899) and *Chinese
Pictures* (1900). Her final missionary trip was
to Morocco in 1900–01. She was now severely
weakened by the ill-health that had plagued
her for many years, and she died of a tumour
in 1904. She appears as a character in Caryl
Churchill's (b 1938) play, *Top Girls* (1982).
**Bib:** Stoddart, A., *The Life of Isabella Bird
(Mrs Bishop)*.

**Blackmore, R.D. (Richard Dodderidge)
(1825–1900)**
Novelist and poet. Born in Berkshire, the
son of a clergyman, Blackmore was educated

at school in Tiverton, where he was head boy, and at Exeter College, Oxford. His mother had died when he was a baby and he spent much of his youth with an uncle in Glamorgan. A career as a barrister was cut short by epileptic fits and after an unsuccessful period as a schoolteacher, Blackmore built a house in Teddington where he lived a retired life, dividing his time between writing, and growing and selling fruit and flowers. He married Lucy Maguire in 1852; there were no children and after her death in 1888 he continued to mourn her and keep the house unchanged. He was a shy man, kind but self-centred and determined. He was fond of animals, especially dogs, and deeply absorbed in his gardening enterprise.

He published volumes of poetry, including translations of the 3rd-century Greek poet Theocritus and the Roman poet Virgil (70–19 BC). His fourteen novels include *Lorna Doone* (1869), which is rejected by eighteen publishers and is now his most famous novel, *Cradock Nowell* (1866), *The Maid of Sker* (1872), his first attempt at fiction only later finished, *Alice Lorraine* (1875) and *Springhaven* (1887). *Lorna Doone* is said to have done for Devonshire what Sir Walter Scott (1771–1832) did for the Highlands and in general Blackmore's novels abound with carefully observed and detailed descriptions of locations, wildlife and the weather along with exciting incidents, all somewhat loosely structured.

▷ Regional novel.

**Bib:** Burris, Q.G., *R.D. Blackmore: His Life and Novels*; Dunn, W.H., *R.D. Blackmore, The Author of Lorna Doone: A Biography*; Budd, K.G., *The Last Victorian: R.D. Blackmore and his Novels*.

### Blackwood's Magazine

Founded in 1817 by the publisher William Blackwood as the *Edinburgh Monthly Magazine*, it was particularly influential in the first fifteen years of its existence. Like the *Quarterly Review*, founded in 1809, it was intended as a Tory rival to the liberal ▷ *Edinburgh Review*, but called itself a 'magazine' to indicate a lighter tone than that of the 'Reviews'. It attacked poets Lord Byron (1788–1824) and Percy Bysshe Shelley (1792–1822) on political grounds, and was, like the *Quarterly*, particularly hostile to John Keats (1795–1821) because of his association with the radical journalist Leigh Hunt (1784–1859). Hunt, Keats, Charles Lamb (1775–1834) and William Hazlitt (1778–1830) were stigmatized as the 'Cockney School' of literature. *Blackwood's Magazine* began with a brilliant group of contributors, especially Sir Walter Scott (1771–1832), John G. Lockhart (known because of his fierce criticism as 'the Scorpion'), James Hogg (1770–1835), and John Wilson (1785–1854), who wrote under the pen-name of Christopher North. Between 1822 and 1835 the magazine ran a series of brilliant dialogues, *Noctes Ambrosianae*, 'Nights at Ambrose's' (a well-known inn). In 1857 it published ▷ George Eliot's ▷ *Scenes of Clerical Life*.

▷ Reviews and periodicals.

### Bleak House (1852–3)

A novel by ▷ Charles Dickens, published, like most of his novels, in monthly parts. It opens with an attack on the part of the legal system called the High Court of Chancery. The rest of the novel expands this opening into a dramatization, through a wide range of characters, of the various forms of parasitism that society lends itself to, and of the ways in which institutions (especially legal ones) falsify relationships and degrade human beings. Most of the story takes place in London. The telling of the story is shared by two contrasted narrators: the savagely sardonic but impersonal author who uses the present tense and the ingenuous, saccharine, unresentful girl, Esther Summerson, who is ignorant of her parentage, though she knows that she is illegitimate. She is adopted by a philanthropist, John Jarndyce, who also adopts two young orphan relatives, Richard Carstone and Ada Clare, who are 'wards in Chancery' (ie legally under the care of the Lord Chancellor) while the distribution of an estate to which they have claims is endlessly disputed in the Court of Chancery (the case of 'Jarndyce and Jarndyce'). Through Richard, Ada and Mr Jarndyce, Esther becomes acquainted with a large number of characters, some of whom are also despairing participants in Chancery Suits, and others (such as Skimpole, the parasitic man of letters, Mrs Jellyby, a well-meaning but incompetent philanthropist, and Turveydrop, the self-styled model of fashionable deportment) who live off society without giving anything substantial in return. Another focus in the novel is Sir Leicester Dedlock, a simple-minded but self-important land-owner, whose one redeeming feature is his devotion to his wife, the beautiful and silent Lady Dedlock. Lady Dedlock is in fact the mother of Esther Summerson, a fact known to the family lawyer, Tulkinghorn, who blackmails her. Her former lover, Captain Hawdon, is still

alive, but lives in destitution and misery. His only friend is the crossing-sweeper, Jo, who resembles Sir Leicester in that they are equally simple-minded and equally capable of one great love for another person. In social respects they are so differentiated, by the lack of any advantages in the one case and by excess of privilege in the other, that it is hard to think of them as belonging to the same species. A large number of other characters contribute to Dickens's panorama of society as mainly constituted by parasites and the victims of paraites. The theme is conveyed partly through the atmosphere of contrasted houses: Bleak House, which is in fact the cordial and life-giving home of Mr Jarndyce; Chesney Wold, the vast but empty mansion of Sir Leicester; Tom-all-alone's, the slum dwelling where Jo finds his sole refuge; the clean and orderly household of the retired soldier, Bagnet; the squalid one of the money-lender, Smallweed, and so forth. For the main characters, the story ends with the corruption of Richard Carstone, the death in despair of Lady Dedlock, the murder of Tulkinghorn and Esther's marriage to the young doctor, Woodcourt. The case of 'Jarndyce and Jarndyce' was based on an actual case centring on a Birmingham millionaire, William Jennings. The character of Skimpole is partly based on journalist and poet, Leigh Hunt, (1784–1859) and another character, Boythorn, on ▷ Walter Landor.
**Bib:** Hawthorne, J. (ed.), *An Introduction to the Varieties of Criticism: Bleak House.*

### Blind, Mathilde (1841–96)

Poet, biographer, translator and editor, who also wrote under the ▷ pseudonym Claude Lake. Born in Mannheim, Germany, she adopted the name of her stepfather, Karl Blind (a revolutionary who led the Baden revolt 1848–9). Educated by her mother and at schools in Belgium and England, she was politically committed from an early age. Her writings are eclectic: her first volume of *Poems* appeared in 1867, followed by *Shelley: A Lecture* in 1870. She edited a well-respected *Selection from the Poems of P.B. Shelley* (1872), translated Strauss's *The Old Faith and the New* (1873) and wrote a long poem based on a Scottish legend, *The Prophecy of St Oran* (1881). A biography of ▷ George Eliot followed in 1883, then came a ▷ romance, *Tarantella* (1884). *Heather on Fire* (1886) was a political protest against the clearances of the Scottish Highlands. Other works include the epic poem *The Ascent of Man* (1889), a translation of the *Journal* (1890) of Russian

*emigré* Marie Bashkirtseff (1858–84) and four further volumes of poetry. Always committed to raising the status of women and improving their educational opportunities, Blind left her estate to Newnham, the Cambridge women's college.
▷ Women's education; Women's Movement; Scottish literature in English.
**Bib:** Robertson, E.S., *English Poetesses*; Symons, A. (ed.), *The Poetical Works of Mathilde Blind.*

### Bodichon, Barbara Leigh Smith (1827–1891)

▷ Feminist and polemicist, born in London, the illegitimate daughter of a ▷ Unitarian minister and a milliner's apprentice. She enrolled in the Ladies' College in Bedford Square in 1849 and chose to study art. Later in life her drawings and paintings were widely exhibited and sold for substantial amounts. Bodichon is best-known today as an active campaigner in the fight for ▷ women's suffrage and legal reform. *A Brief Summary in Plain Language of the Most Important Laws Concerning Women* (1854) was a highly influential pamphlet that brought attention to women's powerlessness and lack of legal rights. In *Women and Work* (1857), she argued that all professions should be available to women, and in her two pamphlets on suffrage, *Reasons for the Enfranchisement of Women* (1866) and *Objections to the Enfranchisement of Women Considered* (1866), she argued lucidly for female voting rights, substantiating her points with empirical evidence she had collected. Bodichon was also concerned with ▷ education, setting up a radical school and assisting Emily Davies in establishing Girton College, Cambridge. She left £10,000 to Girton at her death. She was involved in the editing and production of *The Englishwoman's Journal* and published her *American Diary* in 1872. In this work she protested against the injustice she had seen in the American South during a trip there in 1857–8, and drew parallels between the position of slaves and the position of women.
▷ Travel writing; Marriage.
**Bib:** Herstein, S.R., *A Mid-Victorian Feminist: Barbara Leigh Smith Bodichon*; Burton, H., *Life.*

### Bohemian

Applied to artists and those who live a life supposedly dedicated to the spirit of the imaginative arts, it means living freely, refusing to observe social conventions, especially when they depend on mere habit, snobbery or fear of 'seeming different'.

In the late 20th century, it often carries a slightly mocking tone and is rarely used now without irony. Literally, Bohemian means native to Bohemia, now the western part of Czechoslovakia. In the 15th century gipsies were supposed to have come from there; in the 19th century, French students were supposed to live like the gipsies and hence to be 'Bohemian'. The word was then introduced into English with this meaning by the novelist ▷ William Makepeace Thackeray. His novel ▷ *The Newcomes* is one of the first studies in English of Bohemianism.

**Borrow, George Henry (1803–81)**
Born in Norfolk, Borrow was educated in Edinburgh and Norwich as his father, a recruiting officer in the militia, moved around. Borrow was articled to solicitors in Norfolk 1818–23, then when his father died he moved to London and worked for a publisher. He travelled in France, Germany, Russia, the East and Spain 1833–9, sending letters to the *Morning Herald* 1837–9, blazing a trail as effectively the first newspaper correspondent. In 1835 he published in St Petersburg *Targum*, translations from 30 different languages and dialects. In Russia and Spain he was an agent for the British and Foreign Bible Society. In 1840 he married Mary Clarke, the widow of a naval officer he met in Spain, and bought an estate on Oulton Broad in Norfolk, in which he had already inherited a share. There he allowed gipsies to pitch tents and live, and became friends with them. His books are in part based on his life. *The Bible in Spain* (1834) and *The Zincali or an account of the Gypsies in Spain* (1841) owed as much of their success to public interest in Borrow the man as Borrow the writer. *Lavengro* followed in 1851, losing Borrow much of his popularity due to its strong 'anti-gentility' tone. *The Romany Rye* (1857) and *Wild Wales* (1862) continued the mixture of fact with fiction, vivid portraits and revelations of the personality of the writer. He died largely unknown and little read.
▷ Travel writing; Anglo-Welsh literature.
**Bib:** Knapp, W.I., *Life, Writings, and Correspondence of George Borrow*; Collie, M., *George Borrow, Eccentric*; Williams, D., *A World of His Own: The Double Life of George Borrow*.

**Bostonians, The (1886)**
A novel by Henry James serialized in *The Century Magazine* from 1885–6. It is a satirical study of the movement for female emancipation in New England. Basil Ransom, a young lawyer from the South up on business

in Boston makes the acquaintance of his two cousins, Olive Chancellor, an ardent feminist, and her widowed sister, Mrs Lune, who is attracted to him. Olive introduces Basil to Miss Birdseye, an altruistic philanthopist, at a suffragette meeting where a beautiful young woman, Verena Tarrant, gives an inspired and arresting speech. Both Basil and Olive are immediately drawn to Verena. She is persuaded to share Olive's luxurious home and is groomed by Olive to become a leader of the ▷ feminist cause and to give up all marital aspirations. However, Basil falls in love with Verena and attempts to remove her from Olive's influence, thereby causing a split between himself and his cousin. The death of Miss Birdseye robs Verena of confidence in her purpose and Basil's appearance at the first of her series of lectures causes her to lose her nerve. Forced to choose she rejects the bitterly disappointed Olive and accepts Basil's proposal of marriage. A brilliantly sustained and complex novel, many critics place it second only to ▷ *The Portrait of a Lady* in James *oeuvre*.
▷ Women's movement; Lesbianism; Women's suffrage.

**Bowdler, Thomas (1754–1825)**
Famous for *The Family Shakespeare*, 1818; an edition in which 'those words and expressions are ommited which cannot with propriety be read aloud in a family'. He later published an edition of Edward Gibbon's *Decline and Fall of the Roman Empire* (1776–88) similarly expurgated. From these we get the word bowdlerize, meaning 'to expurgate'.

*Boys' Own Paper*
A weekly magazine for boys, founded in 1879 and published by the Religious Tract Society. It ran until 1967, reached a circulation around 250,000 and published adventure stories, often with imperialist themes, as well as essays, letters, puzzles, and competitions.
▷ Imperialism.
**Bib:** Bristow, J., *Empire Boys: Adventures in a Man's World*.

**Braddon, Mary Elizabeth (1835–1915)**
The daughter of a solicitor and privately educated, Braddon was the author of over 80 novels, twenty of which were written between 1861 and 1871, and was dubbed by her publisher the 'Queen of the Circulating Libraries'. She was born in London and brought up by her mother, who left her husband when Mary was three. In 1856 Braddon began writing in order to support the

family, the impulse also behind her taking to the stage under the name Mary Seyton. She met the publisher John Maxwell, whose wife was in a asylum, in 1860 and lived with him until they were able to marry in 1874. Her writing helped to support the five children of Maxwell's first marriage and the six from their own liaison (one of whom died in infancy). Her fourth novel, ▷ *Lady Audley's Secret* (1862), was first serialized in *Robin Goodfellow* and *The Sixpenny Magazine*, and was a sensational best-seller: a melodramatic, lurid tale of criminality and sexual passion which shocked readers by representing its deviant heroine as an angelic-looking blonde. ▷ Margaret Oliphant described Braddon as 'the inventor of the fair-haired demon of modern fiction'. Other novels include *Aurora Floyd* (1863), *The Doctor's Wife* (1864), *Henry Dunbar* (1864), *Ishmael* (1884) and *The Infidel* (1900). In addition to prolific novel writing, Braddon also wrote nine plays and edited several London magazines including *Belgravia* (1866) and *The Mistletoe Bough* (1878–92).

▷ Sensation, Novel of.

**Bib:** Wolff, R.L., *The Sensational Victorian: the Life and Fiction of Braddon*; Hughes, W., *The Maniac in the Cellar: Sensation Novels of the 1860s*.

### Bradley, F.H. (Francis Herbert) (1846–1924)

Brother of A.C. Bradley (1851–1935), the literary critic. He was himself an eminent philosopher, author of *Ethical Studies* (1876); *Principles of Logic* (1883); *Appearances and Reality* (1893), and *Essay on Truth and Reality* (1914). His position philosophically was an idealist one, and in this he has been opposed by most British philosophers ever since, beginning with G.E. Moore (1873–1958). Bradley, however, had a strong influence on T.S. Eliot (1888–1965), the poet and former philosophy student, whose early thesis on him was published in 1963.

▷ Realism.

### Bradley, Katherine (1846–1914)

Poet and dramatist who published separately, and collaboratively with ▷ Edith Cooper under the ▷ pseudonym ▷ Michael Field.

### Bray, Anna Eliza (1790–1883)

Novelist. Born in Newington, Surrey, she married the artist Charles Alfred Stothard in 1818. Her first published work, *Letters Written During a Tour Through Normandy, Brittany and Other Parts of France* appeared in 1820. This volume recorded travels with her husband, who died in an accident in 1821.

Anna married the Rev. Edward Bray in 1822, and from 1826 to 1874 published fourteen novels, as well as historical biographies and descriptive sketches. In fiction, she favoured historical ▷ romances set in the English countryside. These were extremely popular in their day, though some literary critics considered them out of date. She is best-known for her series of letters to Robert Southey, *A Description of that Part of Devonshire Bordering on the Tamar and the Tary* (1836). Subjects of her biographies include Handel (1857) and Joan of Arc (1874). She also wrote a non-fictional work for children, *A Peep at the Pixies, or, Legends of the West* (1854).

▷ Children's literature; Travel writing.

### Bridges, Robert Seymour (1844–1930)

Poet and dramatist. He was Poet Laureate from 1913–30. After medical training and work as a consultant at Great Ormond Street Children's Hospital, Bridges turned his energies fully to poetry in 1882. His first volume of verse was published in 1873, after which he wrote prolifically: his collected *Poetical Works* (1936), excluding eight dramas, are in six volumes. He was a fine ▷ classical scholar and in his experiments with classical rhythms, was something of an innovator. His most ambitious work was the long, philosophical *The Testament of Beauty*, which appeared in five parts from 1927 to 1929. Other works include: *Shorter Poems* (1890); *The Spirit of Man* (1916) and *New Verse* (1925). He was the chief correspondent and literary executor of the poet ▷ Gerard Manley Hopkins; the latter developed his poetic theories through their letters. A selection of Bridge's work, *Poetry and Prose*, has been edited by John Sparrow.

**Bib:** Smith, N.C., *Notes on The Testament of Beauty*; Guerard, A.J., *Bridges: A Study of Traditionalism*; Thompson, E., *Robert Bridges*.

### Brontë, Anne (1820–49)

Novelist and poet, sister of ▷ Charlotte, ▷ Emily and Branwell Brontë. The youngest of the family, Anne was educated largely at home, though she briefly attended school at Roe Head in 1836–7. Very close to Emily as a child, together they invented the imaginary world of ▷ Gondal, the setting for several poems and a prominent feature in their lives. Anne had more experience as a ▷ governess than either Charlotte or Emily, working for the Ingham family at Blake Hall in 1839 and 1841–5 for the Robinsons of Thorpe Green Hall. Branwell followed her there but was dismissed as a result of his obsession with Mrs Robinson, and Anne followed him home. ▷ *Agnes Grey* (1847) is a semi-autobiographical novel based on her experiences as a governess. It was published under the ▷ pseudonym Acton Bell, as were her poems in the 1846 collection, ▷ *Poems by Currer, Ellis and Acton Bell*. Her second novel, ▷ *The Tenant of Wildfell Hall*, was published in 1848. Her work is considered inferior to that of Emily and Charlotte, yet it often contains vivid and powerful descriptions. She died on a visit to Scarborough in May 1849 and was buried there.

**Bib:** Gerin, W., *Anne Brontë: A Biography*; Langland, E., *Anne Brontë: The Other One*; Knapp, B.L., *The Brontës: Branwell, Anne, Emily, Charlotte*.

## Brontë, Charlotte (1816–55)

Novelist and poet; the third of five daughters of Patrick Brontë, a Yorkshire clergyman of Irish origin, and sister to ▷ Anne and ▷ Emily Brontë. After the death of their mother in 1821, the children (including Branwell, the only son) were looked after by Elizabeth Branwell, their aunt. Charlotte attended school at Cowan Bridge, where her elder sisters Maria and Elizabeth contracted the tuberculosis from which they died in 1825, and later at Roe Head (1831–2), returning to the latter as a teacher (1835–8). She was ▷ governess to the Sidgwick family in 1839 and to the White family in 1841. In 1842 she went with Emily to Brussels to study languages, but had to return at the end of the year due to the death of her aunt. Charlotte returned to Brussels alone in 1843 and remained there a year, forming a deep attachment to her tutor M. Heger, who was fictionalized in both *The Professor* (1857) and ▷ *Villette* (1853). She wrote a great deal as a child, inventing with Branwell the imaginary world of ▷ Angria. In 1845, according to her own account, she 'discovered' Emily's poetry and included it in ▷ *Poems by Currer, Ellis and Acton Bell* (▷ pseudonyms of Charlotte, Emily and Anne Brontë), published in 1846. The book sold only two copies but Charlotte was undeterred. She wrote her first novel, ▷ *The Professor*, in the same year (it was published posthumously in 1857), and her second novel, ▷ *Jane Eyre* (1847), was an immediate success. In 1848 both Branwell and Emily died from tuberculosis, followed by Anne in 1849. Charlotte continued to write during this traumatic period, ▷ *Shirley* appearing in 1849, followed by *Villette*, regarded by many as her most mature and accomplished novel. In 1850 she met ▷ Elizabeth Gaskell who

became a great friend and who wrote her biography (1857). She married A.B. Nicholls, her father's curate, in 1854 but died from tuberculosis a few months later, in the early stages of pregnancy. She was recognized as an extraordinarily powerful and talented writer in her day, though some critics accused her of being a 'strong-minded' woman and of writing 'coarse' novels. Brontë's bold depiction of the social and psychological situation of 19th-century women has generated much late-20th-century feminist commentary which focuses on the struggle of her heroines to preserve their independence of spirit in the face of overwhelmingly adverse circumstances. In addition the confined and restless imagery of her novels is often seen as representative of the anger of suppressed and misrepresented women.

**Bib:** Gaskell, E., *Life*; Fraser, R., *Charlotte Brontë*; Gerin, W., *Charlotte Brontë: The Evolution of Genius*; Ratchford, F., *The Brontës' Web of Childhood*; Gilbert, S., and Gubar, S., *The Madwoman in the Attic*; Boumelha, P., *Charlotte Brontë*.

## Brontë, Emily (1818–48)

Novelist and poet, sister of ▷ Charlotte, ▷ Anne and Branwell Brontë, Emily lived most of her life in Haworth, Yorkshire. She briefly attended Cowan Bridge school (1824–5) and went to Roe Head in 1835, returning after a few months suffering from homesickness. A short period spent working as a ▷ governess at Law Hill and a brief excursion to Brussels with Charlotte in 1842 were the only other occasions on which she left home. With Anne, Emily created the imaginary world of ▷ Gondal, and in many of her poems she adopts the personae of Gondal characters. Charlotte 'discovered' Emily's poetry in 1845, and ▷ *Poems by Currer, Ellis and Acton Bell* appeared in 1846. Her poetry has been overshadowed by her only novel ▷ *Wuthering Heights* (1847), but she wrote many complex and interesting lyrics exploring personal identity and the poet's relationship to language and to the natural landscape. 'Loud without the wind was roaring', 'Ah! why, because the dazzling sun' and 'I am the only being whose doom' are some of her finest poetic achievments. Other lyrics such as 'O Thy Bright Eyes Must Answer Now' and 'I'll come when thou art saddest' represent a masculine muse figure with whom the poet establishes a dynamic relation.

Emily Brontë's originality and power were recognized when *Wuthering Heights* appeared, and she has been extensively discussed

ever since. The novel is so devised that
the story is told by several independent and
varyingly unreliable narrators. It sets human
passions (through the characters Heathcliff
and Catherine Earnshaw) against society
(represented by the households of Wuthering
Heights and Thrushcross Grange) with
extraordinary violence, while at the same
time retaining a cool artistic control. This
enables the reader to experience a highly
intelligent criticism of society's implicit claim
to absorb all the energies of the individual,
who potentially is larger in spirit than society
ever can be. Initially received as morbid and
too violent, it has grown in critical stature,
particularly with regard to its structure.
Bib: Sanger, C.P., *The Structure of Wuthering
Heights*; Gerin, W., *Emily Brontë: A Bibliography*;
Davies, S., *Emily Brontë: The Artist as Free
Woman*; Pykett, L., *Emily Brontë*; Stoneman,
P., *A New Casebook on Wuthering Heights*.

**Broughton, Rhoda (1840–1920)**
Novelist, the daughter of Jane Bennet
and clergyman Delves Broughton, Rhoda
Broughton grew up in Staffordshire where she
set many of her ▷ best-sellers. She began to
write at the age of twenty-two, inspired by her
admiration for ▷ Anne Thackeray Ritchie,
and was prolific and financially successful,
producing novels of sexual intrigue and
pathos, such as her first work *Not Wisely But
Too Well* (1867), which was published serially
with the help of her uncle ▷ Sheridan Le
Fanu, and *Goodbye Sweetheart* (1872). After
moving to Headington, Oxford in 1892, she
became well-known in literary and academic
circles. Altogether she wrote twenty-four
novels, mostly sensational ▷ romances
centring on 'strong-minded women', unhappy
marriages and scandalous affairs, but featuring
a new kind of tomboyish, plain-spoken
heroine which helped to make her one of
the best selling novelists of the Victorian
period in spite of ▷ Margaret Oliphant's
indignant derision. Many of her novels are
witty and malicious chronicles of 'county'
life, and speak out against ▷ marriage and
women's economic oppression. She was paid
large amounts for copyright by her publisher,
Bentley. Her works include ▷ *Cometh Up
as a Flower* (1867), *Alas* (1890) and *Scylla or
Charybdis?: A Novel* (1895). Her last novel was
*A Fool in Her Folly* (1920).
    ▷ Sensation, Novels of.

**Browning, Elizabeth Barrett (1806–61)**
Poet, the eldest child of Edward and Mary
Moulton Barrett, her reputation as a major

Victorian poet was established long before
she met ▷ Robert Browning whom she
married in 1846. An experimental writer, she
wrote ▷ ballads, political odes, allegories,
▷ sonnets, poetic dramas and an epic, as
well as publishing essays in literary criticism
and translations of Greek poetry. She spent
her childhood at Hope End in Herefordshire,
reading widely and schooling herself in the
▷ classics. Her juvenilia includes *The Battle
of Marathon* (published anonymously when she
was only fourteen), *An Essay on Mind: With
Other Poems* (1826) and *Prometheus Bound:
and Miscellaneous Poems* (1833) containing her
translation of Aeschylus' (525–456 BC) tragedy.
Her reputation was made with her first
mature collection, 'The Cry of the Children',
a famous plea to the social consciences of
the Victorian middle classes. For six years,
between 1838 and 1844, Barrett was confined
as an invalid, though during this period she
wrote extensively, culminating in ▷ *Poems*
(1844). In 1845 Robert Browning began a
correspondence with her, and a year later she
ran away from her tyrannical father in order
to marry Browning in secret. The couple left
immediately for Italy and based themselves in
Florence for the rest of Barrett's life. *Poems*
(1850) incorporates the celebrated sequence
of love-lyrics ▷ *Sonnets from the Portuguese*
written during her courtship, including the
famous and much-anthologized 'How do I
love thee? Let me count the ways', and 'The
Runaway Slave at Pilgrim's Point'. Elizabeth
gave birth to a son, known as Pen, at the age
of forty-three. In 1850 ▷ *The Athenaeum*,
to which Barrett Browning was a regular
contributor, recommended her for the Poet
Laureateship on the death of Wordsworth
(1770–1850). Although the title went to
▷ Tennyson, the fact that a woman was
considered at that time is indicative of Barrett
Browning's reputation.
    ▷ *Aurora Leigh* (1857), an epic poem
concerned with the making of a woman poet,
is now considered one of Barrett Browning's
major achievements. Other works include
*Casa Guidi Windows* (1851) and *Poems Before
Congress* (1860), which testify to her passionate
championship of Italian independence, and a
posthumously published collection, *Last Poems*
(1862). The best edition of her work is *The
Complete Works of Elizabeth Barrett Browning*
(eds. C. Porter and H. Clarke).
    ▷ Ballad; Medievalism.
Bib: Taplin, G., *The Life of Elizabeth Barrett
Browning*; Hayter, A., *Mrs Browning: A Poet's
Work and its Setting*; Leighton, A., *Elizabeth
Barrett Browning: Woman and Artist*; Mermin,

D., *Elizabeth Barrett Browning*; Stone, M.,
*Elizabeth Barrett Browning*.

## Browning, Robert (1812–89)

Poet. The son of a clerk in the Bank of
England, he married the poet Elizabeth
Barrett in 1846 under dramatic circumstances,
and lived with her until her death in 1861 in
Italy. He spent the rest of his life in London.

From the first his poetry was exuberant,
and he began as an ardent follower of Shelley
(1792–1822); *Pauline* (1833); *Paracelsus* (1835);
*Strafford* (a verse tragedy, 1837); *Sordello*
(1840). Between 1841 and 1846 he published
seven more plays, the dramatic poem *Pippa
Passes*, the collection *Dramatic Lyrics* (including
▷ 'The Pied Piper'), and *Dramatic Romances*
– all published together under the title *Bells
and Pomegranates*. During his married life
he produced *Christmas-Eve and Easter-Day*
(1850) and, his best-known work, ▷ *Men and
Women* (1855).

Nonetheless, public recognition only came
with ▷ *Dramatis Personae* (1864) and *The
Ring and the Book* (1868–9). The latter was his
most ambitious work and consists of 10 verse
narratives, all dealing with the same crime,
each from a distinct viewpoint. It was based
on an actual trial, the record of which he
discovered in Florence. The period 1850–70
was his best; the later work has endured less
well: *Prince Hohenstiel-Schwangau* (1871);
*Fifine at the Fair* (1872); *The Inn Album* (1875);
*Pacchiarotto* (1876); *La Saisia* (1878); *Dramatic
Idylls* (1879–80); *Ferishtah's Fancies* (1884);
*Asolando* (1889).

Browning was keenly aware that he
was writing poetry in an age of science, of
technology and of prose, particularly of
prose fiction. He made poetry compete with
prose in these conditions, and the curiosity
and delight in detail that were part of his
temperament fitted him to do so. Where
other poets, notably ▷ Tennyson, wrote
in a style that moved away from and above
the preoccupations of daily living, Browning
delighted in the idiom of ordinary speech
and in the peculiarities of minds and objects.
He was not the only practitioner of the
▷ dramatic monologue, but he is especially
associated with it; he chose characters
out of history or invented them in special
predicaments, and made them think aloud
so as to display their distinctive mentalities.
He was not afraid of obscurity, and both
his earlier and his later poems suffer from
it (*Sordello* and *Fifine*), although *Sordello* is
now increasingly recognized as one of his
most extraordinary and important works,

influencing, for example, Ezra Pound
(1885–1972) in his conception of the *Cantos*.
The influence of his monologues on Pound's
and T.S. Eliot's (1888–1965) early poetry
should also be noted.
▷ Medievalism.

Bib: Griffin, H.W. and Minchin, H.C., *Life*;
Miller, B., *Life*; Cohen, J.M., *Robert Browning*;
Devane, W.C., *A Browning Handbook*;
Duckworth, F.G.R., *Browning: Background
and Conflict*; Duffin, H.C., *Amphibian: a
Reconsideration of Browning*; Herford, C.H.,
*Robert Browning*; James, H., in *Notes on
Novelists*; Johnson, E.D.H., *The Alien Vision in
Victorian Poetry*; Raymond, W.O., *The Infinite
Moment*; Litzinger, B. and Smalley, D., (eds.),
*Browning: the Critical Heritage*; Langbaum, R.,
*The Poetry of Experience*; Pathak, P., *The Infinite
Passion of Finite Hearts: Robert Browning and
Failure in Love*.

## Buchan, John, 1st Baron Tweedsmuir (1875–1940)

Novelist. Buchan was born in Scotland
and educated at Glasgow and Oxford; he
contributed to the ▷ *Yellow Book* while still a
student. He is best known for his adventure
stories involving the character of Richard
Hannay, notably *The Thirty-nine Steps* (1915),
filmed by Alfred Hitchcock in 1935. Other
novels include: *Scholar Gypsies* (1896); *A
Lost Lady* (1899); *The Half-Hearted* (1900);
*Greenmantle* (1916); *Mr Steadfast* (1918); *Sick
Heart River* (1941). He had a distinguished
political career and was Governor-General of
Canada 1935–40.

## Buchanan, Robert (Williams) (1841–1901)

Poet, novelist and playwright. Buchanan
was born in Staffordshire and educated at
Edinburgh University. He moved to London
and published his first volume of poems
*Undertones* in 1863, following it with *Idylls
and Legends of Inverburn* (1865), *London Poems*
(1866), *Ballad Stories of the Affections* (1866)
and *North Coast and Other Poems* (1867). His
work is centred on the Scottish peasantry, the
rigours of northern life and, in *London Poems*,
the mean and squalid nature of city life which
is portrayed with some sympathy. In *The Book
of Orm* (1870), *Balder the Beautiful* (1877)
and *The City of Dreams* (1888) Buchanan
displays his interest in the mystical and his
affinity with the epic style favoured by the
▷ Spasmodic school. *Saint Abe and His
Seven Wives* (1872) and *White Rose and the
Red* describe life in the New World. In 1872
he published pseudonymously a pamphlet
stigmatizing ▷ Swinburne and ▷ Dante

Gabriel Rossetti as members of 'The Fleshly School of Poetry' because of their sensualism and lack of ethical awareness. Buchanan's plays were moderately successful and include *Lady Clare* (1883), *Sophia* (1886) an adaptation of Henry Fielding's (1707–54) *Tom Jones*, and *The Charlatan* (1894). Among his novels *The Martyrdom of Madeleine* is an attack on the French aestheticism of Théophile Gautier who had inspired the English Aesthetes.

▷ Scottish literature in English; Aestheticism.

## Buckingham Palace

The principal residence of the British royal family in London. The original house belonged to the Dukes of Buckingham, from whom it was bought by George III in 1762. It was rebuilt by the architect John Nash in 1825, who designed Marble Arch as a gateway to it, but the Arch was removed to its present position near the entrance to Hyde Park in 1851. It was Queen ▷ Victoria (1837–1901) who first made the palace her principal residence.

## Buckstone, J.B. (John Baldwin) (1802–79)

Actor, dramatist and theatre manager, he was born in London's East End and made his debut at the Surrey Theatre in 1823–4, establishing himself as a 'low comedian'. Between 1825 and 1850 he wrote over 100 dramatic pieces including farces, operettas and domestic melodrama – his first, *Luke the Labourer* (1826), helped to establish the genre. Comedies such as *The Wreck Ashore* (1830), *The Irish Lion* (1838), *Single Life* (1839) and the sentimental *The Green Bushes* (1845) are enlivened by low-life comic characters and champion the virtues of manly fortitude and decency. Under his management the Haymarket Theatre became the home of comedy (1853–76), and played host to dramatists such as ▷ Tom Taylor, Westland Marston and ▷ W.S. Gilbert.

## Bulwer-Lytton, Edward George Earle Lytton (1st Baron Lytton) (1803–73)

Novelist. He was the son of General Bulwer and added his mother's surname of Lytton on inheriting her estate in 1843. He was educated at Trinity and Trinity Hall, Cambridge, and was made a Baron in 1866. His novels were very famous in his lifetime, and their range is an indication of literary variety and changes in the Victorian period. His political outlook was radical when he was young; he was then a friend of the philosopher William Godwin (1756–1836), whose influence is

evident in his early novels, *Paul Clifford* (1830) and *Eugene Aram* (1832). On the other hand, he was a member of fashionable society and his first success (*Pelham*, 1828) is closer to ▷ Benjamin Disraeli's political novels of high society, for example ▷ *Coningsby*. Then in mid-career, under the influence of the strict Victorian moral code, he wrote domestic novels such as *The Caxtons – A Family Picture* (1848). He showed the influence of novelist Sir Walter Scott (1771–1832) on the Victorians in his ▷ historical novels such as *The Last Days of Pompeii* (1834), *Rienzi* (1835) and *The Last of the Barons* (1843), and the current ▷ German influence in the didacticism of his early novels and in fantasies such as *The Pilgrims of the Rhine* (1834). Bulwer-Lytton was a friend of ▷ Charles Dickens (see the biography of Dickens by Jack Lindsay) and satirized ▷ Lord Tennyson in his poem *The New Timon* (1846). He wrote some successful plays – *The Lady of Lyons* (1838), *Richelieu* (1838) and *Money* (1840). Like Disraeli, he combined his literary with a political career, for which he was rewarded with a peerage as Baron Knebworth (his mother's estate) but in his case literature had priority. His work is now little respected (he is considered as neither sincere nor original) but he is interestingly representative of his period.
**Bib:** Sadleir, M., *Bulwer: A Panorama*; Christensen, A.C., *Edward Bulwer-Lytton: The Fiction of New Regions*.

## Burnett, Frances Eliza (née Hodgson) (1849–1924)

Novelist. Burnett is known for her best-selling children's stories: *Little Lord Fauntleroy* (1886) about a boy living in New York who turns out to be the heir of an English aristocratic family, and *The Secret Garden* (1911). Burnett also wrote accomplished novels for adults: some, like *Haworth's* (1879), are set in an industrial environment in the north of England while others, like *Through One Administration* (1883), deal with American society.
**Bib:** Burnett, F.E., *The One I knew Best of All*; Burnett, V., *The Romantick Lady*; Thwaite, A., *The Life of Frances Hodgson Burnett*.

▷ Children's literature.

## Burton, Sir Richard Francis (1821–90)

Explorer and ▷ travel writer. *Scinde, or the Unhappy Valley* (1851); *First Footsteps in East Africa* (1856); *The Lake Region of Central Africa* (1860); *The Pilgrimage to Al-Medinah and Meccah* (1855). He also translated the ▷ *Arabian Nights* (*The Thousand Nights and a Night* – 1885–8) and *The Lusiads of Camoens*

(1880). For the last fourteen years of his life he worked on a translation of *The Perfumed Garden*, which his widow burned after his death.

**Bib:** Lady Burton, *Life*; Schonfield, A.L., *Richard Burton Explorer*; Wilson, A.T., *Richard Burton*.

## Butler, Samuel (1835–1902)

Satirist, scientific writer, author of an autobiographical novel, ▷ *The Way of All Flesh* (1903) in a form which became a model for a number of 20th-century writers. His satires ▷ *Erewhon* (an anagram of *Nowhere*) and *Erewhon Revisited* (1872 and 1901) are anti-utopias, ie instead of exhibiting an imaginary country with ideal customs and institutions in the manner of Sir Thomas More's *Utopia* (1516), Butler describes a country where the faults of his own country are caricatured, in the tradition of Jonathan Swift's Lilliput (*Gulliver's Travels*, 1726). He attacks ecclesiastical and family institutions; in Erewhon, machines have to be abolished because their evolution threatens the human race – a blow at Darwinism.

His scientific work concerned ▷ Charles Darwin's theory of evolution, to which he was opposed because he considered that it left no room for mind in the universe; he favoured the theory of ▷ Lamarck (1744–1829) with its doctrine of the inheritability of acquired characteristics. His disagreements and his own theories are expounded in *Life and Habit* (1877), *Evolution Old and New* (1879), *Unconscious Memory* (1880) and *Luck or Cunning?* (1886).

*The Way of All Flesh* attacks the parental tyranny which Butler saw as the constant feature of Victorian family life (despite much evidence to the contrary); so close did he keep to his own experience that he could not bring himself to publish his book in his own lifetime.

▷ George Bernard Shaw admitted a great debt to Butler's evolutionary theories and to Butler's stand against mental muddle, self-deception and false compromise in society. Writers as different from Butler and from each other as D.H. Lawrence (1885–1930) and James Joyce (1882–1941) wrote autobiographical novels after him in which the facts were often as close to their own experience.

▷ Utopian literature.

**Bib:** Cole, G.D.H., *Butler and The Way of All Flesh*; Henderson, P., *The Incarnate Bachelor*; Furbank, P.N., *Samuel Butler*; Jeffers, T.L., *Samuel Butler Revalued*; Joad, C.E.M., *Samuel Butler*; Muggeridge, M., *Earnest Atheist*; Pritchett, V.S., 'A Victorian Son' in *The Living Novel*.

# C

**Caird, Mona (1858–1932)**
Novelist, born on the Isle of Wight. She
married J.A. Henryson in 1877 and lived
in Hampstead from then until the end of
her life. From 1883 to 1915 she wrote seven
novels, as well as a non-fictional work, *The
Morality of Marriage and Other Essays* (1897).
She argued, both in this work and in her
fiction, for marriage reform. Her novels focus
on the oppression that women can suffer, yet
Caird also creates bold heroines who defy
society's expectations. Much of the fiction
is polemical in tone, with long speeches
calling for changes in attitude. Caird herself
saw ▷ marriage as a patriarchal system of
exchange, and advocated equal rights to child
custody, divorce, and proper ▷ education
for women. Her novels include *The Wings of
Azreal* (1889), *A Romance of the Moors* (1891)
and *The Daughters of Danaus* (1894). Her
last work was *Stones of Sacrifice* (1915). In
the 1890s, her work was considered ▷ 'New
Woman' fiction.
▷ Feminism; Women's movement.
**Bib:** Cunningham, G., *The 'New Woman' and
the Fiction of the 1890s*; Stetz, M.D., 'Turning
Points: Mona Caird', *Turn of the Century
Women* 2, Winter 1985.

**Candida (1898)**
One of the ▷ *Plays Pleasant and Unpleasant*
by ▷ George Bernard Shaw. Its theme is the
conflict between two views of life: the lofty,
vague one of the poet Marchbanks, and the
narrow but practical one of the Christian
Socialist clergyman Morell. Both men are
rivals for the love of Morell's wife, Candida.

**Capitalism**
The system by which the means of production
is owned privately. Production is for private
profit and productive enterprise is made
possible by large-scale loans of money
rewarded by the payment of interest. The
full triumph of capitalism came only with the
Industrial Revolution in the 19th century,
which saw, for the first time on a large
scale, mass employment in ▷ factories. The
employers, backed by a number of gifted
theorists such as Adam Smith (1723–90),
▷ Jeremy Bentham, ▷ Malthus and
David Ricardo (1772–1823), developed a
ruthless philosophy, according to which their
relationship with their workers should be
governed entirely by the economic laws of
supply and demand, with which the state
interfered, in their opinion, only at the cost
of wrecking national prosperity, even if the
interferences were dictated by the need to
save the workers from intolerable misery.
This stream of opinion among the industrialist
employers was, however, progressively
opposed by Evangelical Christians among
the politicians (eg ▷ Lord Shaftesbury), by
socialists of the school of ▷ Robert Owen
and by popular novelists between 1830
and 1860, such as ▷ Elizabeth Gaskell,
▷ Benjamin Disraeli and ▷ Charles Dickens.
The most cogent and revolutionary opposition,
however, was formulated in the work of
Friedrich Engels, *The Condition of the Working
Class* (1845) and of ▷ Karl Marx, *Das Kapital*
(1867). The two men collaborated in London
on the *Communist Manifesto* (1848). Gradually
industrial capitalism became less inhumane,
and in the last twenty years of the 19th
century, socialist opinion grew, aided by the
leadership of intellectuals such as ▷ George
Bernard Shaw and ▷ Beatrice Webb.
▷ Spencer Herbert; Anti-industrialism;
Social Problem novel.

**Carey, Rosa Nouchette (1840–1909)**
English novelist. The eighth child of a
ship-owner, she was born in Stratford-le-Bow,
London, and educated at home and at the
Ladies' Institute, St John's Wood. Her first
published novel was *Nellie's Memories* (1868),
a story she had originally told to her sister
before transcribing it several years later.
Carey was deeply religious and conservative,
believing strongly that woman's role was
domestic and maternal. This attitude is
reflected in the numerous short stories she
wrote for the *Girls' Own Paper* and in the
thirty-nine novels she published between
1868 and 1909. Her works include *Wee Wifie*
(1869); *Not Like Other Girls* (1884); *The Sunny
Side of the Hill* (1908) and *Barbara Heathcote's
Trial* (1909). She also produced a volume of
▷ biographies: *Twelve Notable Good Women of
the 19th Century* (1899).

**Carlyle, Jane Welsh (1801–66)**
Woman of letters and literary personality.
Jane Baillie Welsh was born in Haddington,
East Lothian, the daughter of a doctor who
gave her a rigorous classical education from
the age of five. At school she impressed her
tutor Edward Irving with her character and
intelligence, and he introduced her to the
historian and critic ▷ Thomas Carlyle in
1821. They married in 1826, and became
the centre of an intellectual and literary
circle. Her greatest friend was ▷ Geraldine
Jewsbury, and she knew such figures as
▷ John Stuart Mill and ▷ Harriet Taylor,
▷ Charles Dickens and ▷ Tennyson. She is

celebrated as one of the greatest letter-writers in the English language, observant and caustic but generous and kind and a witty observer of social behaviour. Her subjects include travel, books, personalities and servants and her correspondence has been published in editions by J.A. Froude (1883); L. Huxley (1924) and T. Scudder (1931). Between 1834 and 1866, the Carlyles lived at Cheyne Row, Chelsea, though they were often apart. Their relationship was fraught and difficult; some biographers have suggested that sexual impotence contributed to the marital stress. Nevertheless she was her husband's chief protector and critic. In the early 1860s Jane's health collapsed and she lived in fear of a mental breakdown, dying suddenly in 1866.
▷ Lesbianism.
**Bib:** Surtees, V., *Jane Welsh Carlyle*; Hanson, J. and E., *The Carlyles*.

**Carlyle, Thomas (1795–1881)**
Scottish essayist, historian, philosopher. The term 'philosopher' is inapppropriate to him if it implies the use of the reason for the logical investigation of truth; his friend ▷ John Stuart Mill, who was a philosopher in this sense, called Carlyle a poet, meaning that he reached his conclusions by imaginative intuition. In his old age he became known as 'the sage of Chelsea'; this is the kind of admiration that he received in England between 1840 and his death. He hated spiritual mediocrity, mere contentment with material prosperity, moral lassitude and the surrender to scientific scepticism and analytic reasoning. All these he regarded as characteristic of British civilization in the mid-19th century. Part of their cause was the overwhelming technical advances resulting from the ▷ Industrial Revolution (▷ capitalism); he also considered the immense popularity of the poet Byron (1788–1824) had helped to disintegrate spiritual wholeness because of the cynicism and pessimism of his poetry, and he distrusted equally the influence on the English mind of the coldly logical French philosophers. To counter Byron, he pointed to the spiritual health which he found in Goethe (1749–1832), and to counter the French he advocated the more emotional and intuitive 18th- and 19th-century German thinkers like Richter and Goethe.
Carlyle's influence derives even more, however, from his own character and the environment from which he sprang. His father had been a Scottish stonemason, with the moral energy and intellectual interests

which comes partly from the influence of Scottish Calvinism (▷ Presbyterianism). This religious tradition in Scotland had much in common with 17th-century Puritanism which had left such a strong mark on the English character; the resemblance between the two traditions helps to account for the hold which Carlyle established on the English imagination. His own personality was strong and individualistic; this, combined with his intention of counteracting the abstract intellectual thought of writers like ▷ Bentham, caused him to write in an eccentric prose style, distorting natural word order and using archaic language. His ▷ *Sartor Resartus* ('Tailor Repatched', 1833–4) is a disguised spiritual ▷ autobiography in which he faces the tendencies to intellectual scepticism and spiritual denial in himself, and dedicates himself to a life of spiritual affirmation. He is unable to base this affirmative spirit on the traditional religious beliefs that had supported his father, so that he has to base it on his own will, his imaginative response to nature and the inspiration provided by the lives of great men.
History was for Carlyle the storehouse of example of these great men, his 'Heroes' – and it is in this spirit that we have to approach his historical works: ▷ *French Revolution* (1837), ▷ *On Heroes, Hero-Worship and the Heroic in History* (1841), *Oliver Cromwell's Letters and Speeches* (1845) and *Frederick II of Prussia* (1858–65). In ▷ 'Signs of the Times' (1829), *Chartism* (1839) and ▷ *Past and Present* (1843) he criticized the mechanistic philosophy which he saw underlying contemporary industrial society, and in *Latter-Day Pamphlets* (1850) he attacked the quasi-scientific treatment of social questions by the rationalist political economists. *Shooting Niagara – and After?*, written at the time of the Second Parliamentary Reform Bill in 1867, reflects his total disbelief in the efficacy of mere political reform.
As a historian, Carlyle wanted history to be related to the life of the ordinary human being; as a social thinker, his advocacy of the imaginative approach to man in society relates him to the thought of Coleridge, whom he knew through his friend John Sterling (*Life of John Sterling*, 1851), and also to his own disciple, ▷ John Ruskin.
▷ Utilitarianism; Scottish literature in English.
**Bib:** Seigel, J., P., *Thomas Carlyle: The Critical Heritage*; Kaplan, F., *Thomas Carlyle: a Biography*; Tennyson, G.B., *Sartor called*

*Resartus*; Hardman, M., *Six Victorian Thinkers*; Trevelyan, G.M., *Carlyle Anthology*; Froude, J.A., *Life*; Neff, E., *Carlyle and Mill*; Harold, C.F., *Carlyle and German Thought, 1819–34*; Symons, J., *Carlyle: the Life and Idea of a Prophet*; Sanders, C.R. and Fielding, K.J. (eds.), *The Collected Letters of Thomas and Jane Carlyle*.

### Carpenter, Edward (1844–1929)

Late-19th-century writer and socialist reformer associated with the ▷ Arts and Crafts Movement and other forms of ▷ anti-industrialism. An undergraduate at Cambridge University from 1864 he was ordained in 1869 but from 1874 onwards he reacted against the social and religious conventions of his time, abandoning the church to follow his idiosyncratic form of primitive Communism. He became a travelling lecturer and part of the newly founded university extension movement which was designed to serve those unable to attend universities. He was greatly influenced by the sensual and passionately democratic writings of US poet Walt Whitman (1819–92) and by the essayist Henry David Thoreau, an advocate of civil disobedience in the face of unjust laws. Whitman, in particular, changed the course of Carpenter's life and his long unrhymed poem *Towards Democracy* (1883; expanded 1905) owes much to Whitman's verse forms. The two met in 1877 during Carpenter's visit to the United States.

Carpenter's form of Communism was based more on social reform and a return to rural crafts than on political revolution, and he shared many of the concerns and enthusiasms of ▷ John Ruskin and ▷ William Morris. He expounded his ideas in a number of prose works including *England's Ideal* (1887), and *Civilisation: its Cause and Cure* (1889; expanded 1912). He supported a number of other causes, many of them controversial, including: women's rights, sexual reform and vegetarianism. His unconventional ideas on sexuality – in particular ▷ homosexuality, which he openly advocated – brought him a number of admirers including the novelists E.M. Forster (1879–1970) and D.H. Lawrence (1885–1930). The psychologist and essayist ▷ Havelock Ellis was deeply impressed with Carpenter's writings on relationships between the sexes – in particular *Love's Coming of Age* (1896) – and homosexuality – *The Intermediate Sex* (1908). These and his other writings on the relationship between art and life, such as *Angel's Wings* (1898) and *The*

*Art of Creation* (1904), were widely read and translated bringing him many visitors to his small farm at Millthorpe, near Chesterfield, where he settled in 1883. He lived there with a succession of working-class acquaintants until 1922. His autobiography, *My Days and Dreams*, was published in 1916.

### Carroll, Lewis (Charles Lutwidge Dodgson) (1832–98)

Writer for children; author of *Alice's Adventures in Wonderland* (1865) and *Through the Looking-Glass* (1872). By profession, a mathematics lecturer at Oxford University. The 'Alice' books describe the adventures of a child in dreams, and owe their distinctiveness to the combination of childlike naivety and an authentic dream atmosphere, so that events succeed, and language is used, with dream logic instead of daylight logic. Thus these two books mark an epoch in the history of dream literature; the dream state is not merely a pretext for fantasy, but is shown to follow its own laws. Consequently Carroll's two masterpieces have had as much appeal for adults as for children. Dodgson was also a master of ▷ 'nonsense' verse which shows the same characteristics; his most famous poem is *The Hunting of the Snark* (1876). His other book for children, *Sylvie and Bruno* (1889), is less memorable.

▷ Children's literature.
**Bib:** Gardner, M., *The Annotated Alice*; Collingwood, S.D., *The Life and Letters of Lewis Carroll*; Empson, W., 'Alice in Wonderland' in his *Some Versions of Pastoral*.

### 'Castaway, A' (1870)

A 600-line prose poem by ▷ Augusta Webster. The poem is concerned with the issue of prostitution and the ▷ 'fallen woman', and ranges widely in its exploration of the sexual ideology of 19th-century Britain. Unlike ▷ D.G. Rossetti's 'Jenny', published in the same year, Webster's poem speaks from the perspective of the fallen woman rather than that of the voyeuristic observer. '[T]he silly rules this silly world/makes about women' are decried by a speaker who is branded by society as a 'thing of shame and rottenness, the animal/that feeds men's lusts'.

### Catholicism (Roman) in Victorian literature

By the 18th century religion of all kinds was becoming a mere department of life, no longer dictating ideas and emotions in all fields, even when sincerely believed. By the 19th century, writers of strong religious conviction were increasingly feeling themselves in a minority in an indifferent and even sceptical world. They therefore tended to impress their work once more with their faith, and this was especially true of the few Catholic writers, eg the poet ▷ Gerard Manley Hopkins, since Catholic faith was dogmatically so strongly defined. The century also saw the revival of Anglo-Catholicism. From the time of the Reformation (during the 16th century, when the Protestant church broke from the Roman Catholic) there had been a school of opinion which sought to remain as close to Roman Catholicism as Anglican independence allowed. The Anglo-Catholic wing of the Church was important under Charles I (1625–49), but lost prestige until it was revived by the ▷ Oxford Movement.

▷ Newman, John Henry.

## Censorship

Systematic censorship has never been an important restriction on English writing except in times of war; but English writers have not always been entirely free. In the early 19th century the government attempted a form of indirect censorship by imposing a tax on periodicals, which restricted their sale among the poor. This was especially true of those periodicals with a tendency to criticize the way the country was run. The late 18th century saw the introduction of the charge of sedition, which amounted to a form of political censorship and was a constant threat to authors, printers and booksellers. It arose in England largely as a result of the events of the French Revolution (1789–94), and it was this law that Tom Paine's *The Rights of Man* and William Blake's 'The French Revolution', both published in 1791, fell foul of. Its effects were felt until the ▷ Reform Bill of 1832 removed many of the causes of complaint.

Where sedition left off vice took over. In 1802 ▷ Thomas Bowdler formed the Society for the Suppression of Vice and issued his famous 'bowdlerized' Shakespeare in 1818, removing from the plays 'whatever is unfit to be read aloud by a gentleman to a company of ladies'. Gibbon's *Decline and Fall* (1776–88) was also subjected to the same treatment. By the 1850s the acceptability of a novel for publication, and for adoption by the ▷ circulating libraries, depended not only on its chances of becoming popular but also on its suitablity for 'family reading'. ▷ George Meredith's *The Ordeal of Richard Feverel* failed this test and it was

ten years before its author's reputation recovered.

Ten years before Meredith's novel was examined, ▷ Thackeray lamented in the Preface to *The History of Pendennis* that 'since the writer of *Tom Jones* was buried, no writer of fiction among us has been permitted to depict to his utmost power a MAN'. The powerful circulating libraries deemed it prudent not to stock 'obscene' books except on demand so it was in an author's and a publisher's best interests to think very carefully about the implications of a novel's content. Both ▷ Herbert Spencer (*Social Statics*, 1851) and ▷ John Stuart Mill (*On Liberty*, 1859) argued for freedom of speech and expression and against government intervention. However, in 1857 the Obscene Publications Act was passed. Very few cases were brought to court largely because publishers imposed a sort of self-censorship – almost by instinct – based on earlier conceptions of 'obscenity'. At the same time it was easy to misjudge what the British middle classes would tolerate. ▷ Thomas Hardy was convinced that, for a novel 'addressed by a man to men and women of full age; which attempts to deal unaffectedly with the fret and fever, derision and disaster, that may press in the wake of the strongest passion known to humanity', ▷ *Jude the Obscure* contained nothing 'to which exception can be taken'. However the *Pall Mall Gazette* reviewed it under the title 'Jude the Obscene' and Bishop How of Wakefield not only publicly burnt the novel but instigated its withdrawal from W.H. Smith's extensive circulating library.

Censorship in the theatre has been a special case since the 18th century when Henry Fielding's (1707–54) comedies attacking the Prime Minister Robert Walpole led in 1737 to the restriction of London theatres to two 'patented' ones – Covent Garden and Drury Lane. The Court Official, the Lord Chamberlain, had to license plays before they could be performed. The 1843 Theatres Act removed the restriction on theatres and confined the Lord Chamberlain's powers to the restraint of indecency.

Censorship on political grounds was much more common in the British colonies. A notable example was Din Mitra's play *Nilderpan (Mirror of the Indigo)* which sought to portray the tyranny of the British indigo planters over the rural Bengali farm labourers. Its scenes of brutality and its instigatory speeches resulted in a ban on its production. To overcome this form of censorship Indian dramatists used historical and mythological themes whose veiled symbolism would be understood by their Indian audiences.

▷ *Yellow Book*; Imperialism.

## 'Charge of the Light Brigade, The'

A famous poem by Alfred, ▷ Lord Tennyson about the episode in the battle of Balaclava (1854) in the Crimean War, between the British and the French on one side and the Russians on the other. The charge was of great heroism, but was an act of folly based on a misunderstood order. Tennyson celebrates the heroism in vivid terms. Curiously enough his poem 'The Charge of the Heavy Brigade', about an incident in the same battle that was successful, is much less well known, although it has equal merit.

## Chartist movement

A working-class political movement which flourished between 1837 and 1848. It arose because the ▷ Reform Bill of 1832 had reformed Parliament in favour of middle-class political rights but had left the working class without them. The Chartists wanted Parliament to be closely responsible to the nation as a whole and to reform an electoral system according to which the poor were excluded from membership of Parliament and denied the right to vote others into membership by their lack of the necessary property qualification. Some regions were more heavily represented in Parliament than others and all voting was subject to bribery or intimidation because votes had to be declared publicly. Consequently they put forward their Charter containing Six Points: 1 votes for all males; 2 annually elected Parliaments (instead of general elections every seven years); 3 payment of Members of Parliament (so that poor men could have political careers); 4 secret voting (voting 'by ballot'); 5 abolition of the property qualification for candidates seeking election; 6 electoral districts equal in population. The movement seemed to be a complete failure, but all these points became law between 1860 and 1914 except the demand for annually elected parliaments. The Chartists attracted an ardent following but they were badly led. Allusions are made to them in those novels between 1840 and 1860 which were concerned with 'the Condition-of-the-People Question', eg ▷ *Sybil* by ▷ Benjamin Disraeli and ▷ *Mary Barton* by ▷ Elizabeth Gaskell. This serious discussion of the social crisis of the second quarter of the 19th century was greatly stimulated by ▷ Thomas Carlyle's essay *Chartism* (1839),

one of his fiercest and most influential writings.

▷ Social Problem novel; Corn Laws, Repeal of the; Hungry Forties, The.

## 'Childe Roland to the Dark Tower Came'

One of the most famous poems by ▷ Robert Browning. He called it a 'Dramatic Romance' and it was published in ▷ *Men and Women*, 1855. It describes a journey or 'quest' (in the tradition of medieval knightly romances) which has lasted so long that Roland is almost in despair. In the poem, he reaches his destination, the tower, which stands in the middle of a great wasteland full of the signs of death. The poem ends with his sounding his horn to signal his arrival. In spite of its sombreness, the poem has a vigour of style, characteristic of Browning, which communicates itself as the most important part of its otherwise cloudy meaning. Browning, too often associated with facile optimism, is the poet here of courage and energy in the face of desperate circumstances.

The title is a quotation from Shakespeare's *King Lear* (1605), where it may be an echo of a still older ballad.

▷ Medievalism.

## Child labour

The use of children in agricultural labour was widespread, and not necessarily pernicious, up till the 19th century, but their use in factories and mines after 1800 and during the Industrial Revolution (▷ capitalism) aroused widespread indignation and led to reform. The Factory Act of 1833 limited their working hours in ▷ factories and in 1847 their hours were restricted to ten. In 1842 the Mines Act forbade the employment of women and of children under ten underground; this evil was very old, but had become much severer with the expansion of the coal industry in the 18th century after the invention of steam-powered machinery. An old abuse, too, was the employment of little boys to clean chimneys; the boys were made to climb inside the chimneys. Public indignation against the practice was aroused by ▷ Charles Kingsley's ▷ *Water Babies* (1863), but it was only effectively prohibited in 1875. The Victorian age saw the abolition of the worst abuses of children, as well as the establishment of the first universal system of ▷ education in England. Since 1939 it has been illegal to employ children under fifteen years old.

## Children's literature

Until the 19th century, children were not regarded as beings with their own kind of experience and values, and therefore did not have books written specifically for their entertainment. The literature available to them included popular versions of old romances. During the ▷ Romantic period it was recognized that childhood experience was a world of its own and, influenced by Jean-Jacques Rousseau's (1712–78) ideas on ▷ education, books began to be written especially to appeal to children. Such works as Thomas Day's *Merton and Sandford* (1783–9), Maria Edgeworth's *Moral Tales* (1801) and Mrs Sherwood's *The Fairchild Family* (1818) usually had a serious moral tone, but showed an understanding of a child's mind that was lacking in ▷ Anne and Jane Taylor's cautionary tales in verse later to be parodied by ▷ Hilaire Belloc in *The Bad Child's Book of Beasts* (1896).

It was not until the Victorian period that writers began extensively to try to please children, without attempting to improve them at the same time. ▷ Edward Lear's *Book of Nonsense* (1846) and ▷ Lewis Carroll's *Alice* books combine fantasy with humour. Romance and magic had a strong appeal for the Victorians, and fairy stories from all over the world were presented in versions for children. The collection of the brothers Grimm had appeared in 1824 as *German Popular Stories* and ▷ Hans Christian Andersen's original compositions were translated into English in 1846. Andrew Lang's *Fairy Books* were published later in the century but the most famous writer of fairy tales for children was George MacDonald, a Scot. Adventure stories for boys, such as ▷ Captain Frederick Marryat's *Masterman Ready* (1841) and ▷ Robert Louis Stevenson's ▷ *Treasure Island* (1883) became a flourishing genre. ▷ R.M. Ballantyne, who wrote best-selling children's adventure stories such as *The Young Fur-Traders* (1856) and *Coral Island* (1858), was one of the most popular writers of this kind of all time. The tradition of moral improvement still persisted, however, in such books as ▷ Charles Kingsley's ▷ *Water Babies* (1863).

Women writers produced some of the most popular and enduring books. The stress on women's maternal role in the Victorian period meant that writing children's books was less controversial for women than entering the 'serious' literary marketplace. It was viewed as an extension of their 'natural' sphere rather than a transgression. Apart from moral tales,

intended as instructional guides for young minds, a large number of adventure stories, tales of magic and fantasy, and animal stories were published. Martha Sherwood's *History of the Fairchild Family* was influential in creating a market for children's literature, but most of the famous children's books by women belong to the latter half of the century. ▷ Anna Sewell's classic horse story, *Black Beauty*, appeared in 1877 and was very much tied up with the flourishing campaigns against cruelty to animals. Animals have loomed large in children's books ever since. In Beatrix Potter's *Peter Rabbit* (1902) text and illustrations were of equal importance. ▷ Frances Hodgson Burnett's *Little Lord Fauntleroy* appeared in 1886 and ▷ Edith Nesbit began her long line of successful children's books with *The Treasure Seekers* in 1899.

Other notable children's authors include ▷ Anna Eliza Bray, ▷ Sara Coleridge, ▷ Rosa Nouchette Carey, ▷ Dinah Mulock Craik, ▷ Juliana Ewing, ▷ Jean Ingelow, ▷ Margaret Gatty, ▷ Christina Rossetti, ▷ Catherine Sinclair, ▷ Hesba Stretton, ▷ Harriet Martineau and ▷ Maria Louisa Molesworth. Following Robert Louis Stevenson's *A Child's Garden of Verses* (1885), children's verse was written by Belloc and Walter De La Mare (1873–1956).

## Cholmondeley, Mary (1859–1925)

English novelist, born in Hodnet, Shropshire, the daughter of Emily Beaumont and the Rev. Hugh Cholmondeley. She never married and lived all her life with her family. Her first novel *The Danvers Jewels* was published in 1887. *Charles Danvers* (1889); *Diana Tempest* (1893) and *The Devotee* (1897) followed. These were popular, but it was ▷ *Red Pottage* (1899) that brought Cholmondeley public recognition. Its satirical treatment of the clergy caused a minor scandal, with churchmen denouncing the book, while critics and journalists defended its humour and accuracy. None of Cholmondeley's six later novels was as successful. She faded from view, and published her last book, *The Romance of His Life* in 1921.
**Bib:** Lubbock, P., *Mary Cholmondeley: A Sketch from Memory*.

## Christmas Carol, A (1843)

A story by ▷ Charles Dickens, about a miser, Scrooge, who is converted by a series of visions from a condition of mercantile avarice and misanthropy into an embodiment of the Christmas spirit, with its generosity and good will to humankind in general. By no means one of the best of Dickens's works, it nonetheless represents entertainingly his celebration of the virtues associated with Christmas (especially characteristic of his early work). He represented these virtues as the cure of the puritan narrowness of feeling and inhumanity of outlook which were the dark side of Victorian commerce. Compare the Christmas scenes in his ▷ *Pickwick Papers* (1837) and the comments of Sleary in ▷ *Hard Times*.

### Chronicles of Carlingford, The
The collective title of a group of novels by ▷ Margaret Oliphant, including *Salem Chapel* (1863); *The Rector and the Doctor's Family* (1863); *The Perpetual Curate* (1864); *Miss Marjoribanks* (1866) and *Phoebe Junior* (1876). *The Chronicles* were Oliphant's most popular works, focusing mainly on religious life in a country town. They show the influence of Walter Scott (1771–1832), ▷ Anthony Trollope and ▷ George Eliot, although like much of Oliphant's work, they appear somewhat hurriedly written.

### Circulating libraries
Libraries in Britain from which books were borrowed by the (mostly female) reading public. The first circulating library started in 1740 and, as the institution spread, it helped to foster the growth of literacy by bringing expensive books within the reach of ordinary people. The most famous circulating libraries in 19th-century Britain were Mudie's (▷ Charles Mudie), W.H. Smith's and Boots. The three-volume or ▷ 'triple-decker' novel of the 19th century was largely supported by these libraries, although rigorous ▷ censorship was enforced.

▷ Publishing and publishers; Jewsbury, Geraldine.
**Bib:** Leavis, Q.D., *Fiction and the Reading Public*.

### City of Dreaming Spires
Oxford, from a description in ▷ Matthew Arnold's poem, *Thyrsis* (1867), an elegy for ▷ Arthur Hugh Clough.

### Clarke, Mary Cowden (1809–98)
Critic, novelist and poet, born in London. She was the daughter of composer Vincent Novello and Mary Sabilla Hehl, and was educated at home and in France. Her father's literary acquaintances included Keats (1795–1821), Leigh Hunt (1784–1859), and Charles Cowden Clarke, whom she married in 1828. In 1829 she began a project that was to occupy her for sixteen years. *The Complete Concordance to Shakespeare* was eventually published in 1845, and remained the standard concordance until the end of the 19th century. Other work on Shakespeare includes *Shakespeare Proverbs* (1848) and a collection of stories based on *The Girlhood of Shakespeare's Heroines* (1852). She also wrote several volumes of verse biographies of her father and her husband; an autobiography, *My Long Life* (1896); a series of novels and a collection of *Short Stories in Metrical Prose* (1873). She was the editor of the *Musical Times* from 1853–6.
**Bib:** Altick, R.D., *The Cowden Clarkes*.

### Classic, classics, classical
These words are apt to cause confusion. The term 'classic' has been used to denote a work about whose value it is assumed there can be no argument, *eg* ▷ *David Copperfield* is a classic. The word particularly implies a changeless and immutable quality; it has sometimes been used to deny the need for reassessment, reinterpretation and change. Because only a few works can be classics, it may be argued that the term is synonymous with the best. This is not necessarily the case, especially with regard to changes in literary taste and a constantly moving canon of texts.

'Classics' is the study of ancient Greek and Latin literature. 'Classic' is used as an adjective as well as a noun, *eg* ▷ Dickens wrote many classic novels. 'Classical' is mainly used as the adjective for 'classics', *eg* classical scholarship.

### Clive, Caroline (1801–73)
Novelist and poet. Born Caroline Meysey-Wigley, her father was an MP. She published her poems in 1840 (as 'V'), though more interest was aroused by her first (and anonymous) novel, *Paul Ferroll* (1855), whose hero murders his first wife and is able to keep his secret for eighteen years through a happy and prosperous second marriage. The novel entered into the wider debate about ▷ divorce (leading up to the 1857 Divorce Act), while the moral ambiguities arising from the author's apparent unwillingness to condemn her hero, combined with the novel's interest in secrecy, make *Paul Ferroll* an important forerunner of the ▷ sensation novel of the 1860s. In the sequel, *Why Paul Ferroll Killed His Wife* (1860), Clive adopts a more conventionally moralistic tone.

▷ Marriage.

### Clough, Arthur Hugh (1819–61)
Poet. He was the son of a Liverpool cotton

merchant, and was educated at ▷ Rugby School under ▷ Thomas Arnold, and at Balliol College, Oxford. At Oxford he came for a time under the influence of ▷ Newman, afterwards a Roman ▷ Catholic but at the time one or the leaders of the Anglican religious revival known as the ▷ Oxford Movement; later, when Clough was a senior member (Fellow) of Oriel College, he became a sceptic in religious belief. It was necessary (until 1871) to accept the doctrines of the Church of England in order to be a senior member of an Oxford College; thus Clough's religious doubts caused him to resign. He travelled in Europe, was for a short time principal of a students' hostel in London University (where no religious restrictions operated) and lectured in the USA. Finally (1853) he accepted a post under the government in the Education Office. He was the close friend and correspondent of the poet and critic ▷ Matthew Arnold, who commemorated his death with the elegy *Thyrsis* (pub. 1867). Almost all of Clough's letters to Arnold have disappeared, but Arnold's letters to him (see *Letters to Clough*, ed. H.F. Lowry) are interesting for what they reveal of the minds of the two men. Both were religious doubters, and both were dismayed by the course of 19th-century civilization. Arnold was desolated by the loss of his friend, and attributes his death to premature despair ('Too quick despairer, wherefore wilt thou go?').

Clough's long poems have a light, though scarcely serene, spirit. The best-known ones are the two verse novels, *The Bothie of Tober-na-Vuolich* (1848) and *Amours de Voyage* (1849; pub. 1858), and the uncompleted dramatic dialogue *Dipsychus* (1850; pub. 1869). The first two are written in a metre unusual in English, the Latin hexameter. *Dipsychus* employs a wide variety of metres. The subject of the first poem is a young man of advanced intellectual opinions but emotional immaturity, and his love affair with a Scottish Highland peasant girl who has the emotional maturity that he lacks; published in the revolutionary year of 1848, it also explored ▷ Chartism and class differences. *Amours* is about a self-doubting man who loses the girl he loves through his inability to arrive at conclusions as to the truth of his own feelings. *Dipsychus*, 'the man in two minds', is a colloquy between a self-doubter and the spirit who haunts him, who admits to the name 'Mephistophilis' and yet is not certainly evil. The other poets of the age were as much afflicted by the torments of doubt as Clough was, but Clough differed

from them in relating doubt to the conduct of ordinary daily life, and in his use of a kind of irony which is much more characteristic of 20th-century poets than it is of 19th-century ones. He has consequently attracted much more critical interest in the 20th century than he received in the past; see for example the claims made on his behalf in the Introduction to Tom Paulin's *Faber Book of Political Verse* (1986).
**Bib:** Chorley, K., *Clough: The Uncommitted Mind*; Houghton, W.E., *The Poetry of Clough*; Goode, J., Hardy, B., essays in *The Major Victorian Poets* (ed. Isobel Armstrong).

### Cobbe, Frances Power (1822–1904)

Essayist and ▷ travel writer. Born in Newbridge, Dublin, she was educated by ▷ governesses until 1836 when she went to school in Brighton. Her first published work, *Essays on the Theory of Intuitive Morals*, appeared anonymously in 1855. One reviewer described it as 'the work of a lofty and masculine mind'. Cobbe wrote prolifically on religious and moral issues and was deeply involved in social reform, advocating ▷ women's suffrage and arguing that women were not contributing all that they might to society. Her works include *Essays on the Pursuits of Women* (1863); *The Cities of the Past* (1864); *Italics* (1864); *Darwinism in Morals and Other Essays* (1872); *The Moral Aspects of Vivisection* (1875); *The Duties of Women* (1881); *The Scientific Spirit of the Age* (1888) and an autobiography, *Life of Frances Power Cobbe* (1904).

▷ Women's Movement.

### Coleridge, Mary (1861–1907)

Poet, novelist and great-great niece of poet and critic Samuel Taylor Coleridge (1772–1834). Born in London, she lived with her parents who played host to a number of distinguished literary figures including ▷ Tennyson, ▷ Browning, ▷ Ruskin and ▷ Fanny Kemble. In 1895 she taught at the Working Women's College. She wrote a number of novels including *The Seven Sleepers of Ephesus* (1893) and a historical ▷ romance *The King with Two Faces* (1897). Her poetry, which she wrote continuously throughout her life, was admired by ▷ Robert Bridges but Coleridge herself was reluctant to publish it. She produced two volumes, *Fancy's Following* (1896) and *Fancy's Guerdon* (1897), both of which appeared under her ▷ pseudonym 'Anodos'. After her death from appendicitis a collection of 200 poems was gleaned from her letters and notebooks

by fellow poet Henry Newbolt (1862–1938)
and published in 1907 (expanded 1954).
Her themes are those of female friendship
and spinsterly solidarity, love's elusiveness
and the fragility of identity. Others briefly
record psychic and dream states. Her most
famous poem is 'The Other Side of the
Mirror' which 20th-century feminist critics
Sandra Gilbert and Susan Gubar regard as
an examination of the monstrous alter-ego of
the female (▷ *Jane Eyre*). Her other works
include: a collection of short prose sketches,
*Non Sequiter* (1900); three novels, *The Fiery
Dream* (1901), *The Shadow on the Wall* (1904),
*The Lady on the Drawing Room Floor* (1906),
and a ▷ biography of Holman Hunt (1908).
*Gathered Leaves* (1910) contains extracts from
her letters and diaries.
**Bib:** Gilbert, S. and Gubar, S., *The Madwoman
in the Attic*; Leighton, A., *An Anthology of
Victorian Women Poets*, Bernikow, L. (ed), *The
World Split Open*.

### Coleridge, Sara (1802–52)

Writer, the daughter of poet and critic Samuel
Taylor Coleridge (1772–1834). She educated
herself, with the help of poet Robert Southey
(1774–1843), acquiring six languages and a
good knowledge of Classics and philosophy.
Wordsworth described her as 'remarkably
clever'. In 1822 she translated Dobrizhoffer's
Latin *Account of the Abipones* and in 1825 the
*Memoirs* of the Chevalier Bayard. She married
her cousin, Henry Coleridge, in 1829, and
lived in Hampstead, London, where she wrote
*Pretty Lessons in Verse for Good Children* (1834)
and the fantastical poem *Phantasmion* (1837).
In 1843 Henry died, after which Coleridge
devoted herself to organizing, editing and
annotating her father's works, a task which
she performed with great skill. She was greatly
admired in London literary society, and her
*Memoir and Letters* was published in 1873.
**Bib:** Wilson, M., *These Were Muses*; Woolf,
V., 'Sara Coleridge' in *Death of the Moth and
Other Essays*.

### Collins, Wilkie (1824–89)

Novelist; one of the first ▷ detective novelists
in English. His two famous novels are *The
Woman in White* (1860), first published in
▷ *Household Words*, a magazine edited by
▷ Charles Dickens, and ▷ *The Moonstone*
(1868). These novels of ▷ sensation
established a pattern for English detective
fiction. His mastery was especially over plot-
construction in which he influenced Dickens.
His characterization is less distinguished
but in *The Woman in White* he excels in

this, too, and in the creation of disturbing
atmosphere. He collaborated with Dickens
in a few stories in *Household Words* and in
▷ *All the Year Round*: *The Wreck of the Golden
Mary*, *A Message from the Sea*, *No Thoroughfare*.
Collins's other novels include *No Name* (1862)
and *Armadale* (1866), which has been praised
for its ▷ melodrama.
**Bib:** Robinson, K., *Life*; Phillips, W.C.,
*Dickens, Reade and Collins: Sensation Novelists*;
Ashley, R., *Wilkie Collins*; Eliot, T. S., Preface
to *The Moonstone*, World's Classics edition;
Lonoff, S., *Wilkie Collins and His Victorian
Readers*; Peters, C., *The King of Inventors: A
Life of Wilkie Collins*; Rance, N., *Wilkie Collins
and Other Sensation Novelists*; Hetler, T., *Dead
Secrets: Wilkie Collins and the Female Gothic*.

### Colonialism

'Colonization' is normally understood to
mean the process of annexation of a country
or countries by an imperial power and the
establishment of colonies or settlements fully
or partly subject to that power. 'Colonialism'
can therefore be glossed as the process by
which those settlements are maintained in
a subordinate relationship to that imperial
power. The most aggressively colonial
European countries were France, Portugal,
Spain and Britain, and the areas most subject
to colonization included the Indian sub-
continent, Africa, Australasia, the Americas
and the Caribbean.

Colonialism does not have to imply
formal annexation, however. Colonial status
involves the imposition of decisions by one
people upon another, where the economy or
political structure has been brought under the
overwhelming influence of another country.
Western colonialism was most active from
1450 to 1900. It began in the Renaissance
with the voyages of discovery; the new
territories were annexed for their material
resources and for the scope they offered to
missionary efforts to extend the power of the
Church. The last independent non-Western
territories were parcelled out in 1900.

There was a strong tradition, founded
on the imperialist myth of the Victorian
era (▷ Imperialism), of which ▷ Thomas
Carlyle, ▷ Rudyard Kipling and ▷ Rider
Haggard were the most famous exponents,
that white intervention was made in the
interests of the native inhabitants. Carlyle's
essay 'An Occasional Discourse on the
Nigger Question' (1849) claimed that the
abolition of slavery in the British Empire
in 1833 had led to the negroes becoming
'sluggards' and 'scoundrels'. In reality, freed

slaves were refusing to work the plantations unless they were paid a decent wage. For Carlyle however, the negro was 'an idle Black gentleman, with his rum-bottle in his hand . . . breeches on his body, pumpkin at discretion, and the fruitfulest region of the earth going back to jungle around him'. His answer was to advocate the use of the whip to compel them back to work.

Carlyle's views alienated those more liberal Victorians such as ▷ John Stuart Mill, and his isolation was made even more acute when he demonstrated his support for the controversial British colonial officer Governor John Edward Eyre (1815–1901). Eyre emigrated to Australia for reasons of health, where he became a sheep farmer and explored much of the continent. He served as a magistrate and protector of the Australian Aborigines and was later appointed Governor of New Zealand (1846–53). In 1853 he became Acting Governor of various of the Caribbean islands (1853–64) and permanent governor of Jamaica. Shortly after his appointment to Jamaica there was a black rebellion at Morant Bay (October 11, 1865). Eyre used extreme measures to crush the rebellion and also took excessive reprisals. In all there were over 400 executions. In the end Jamaica became a crown colony and Eyre was recalled by the British government in 1866. Although he was commended for overcoming the revolt his methods were censured. Prominent British intellectuals of the time such as Mill, ▷ Herbert Spencer and ▷ Thomas Henry Huxley called for his trial for murder. In addition to Carlyle, Eyre's supporters also included ▷ John Ruskin and ▷ Alfred, Lord Tennyson. Eyre was not indicted for murder and was also found innocent in a civil case brought against him by a Jamaican (▷ Jane Eyre).

Carlyle's friend and future biographer the novelist James Anthony Froude (1818–94) visited the Caribbean in 1886 and subsequently wrote The English in the West Indies, or, The Bow of Ulysses (1888) which strongly advocates government intervention to protect white settlers from being 'crowded out by the blacks'. Froude also supported Eyre, claiming he had been 'unworthily sacrificed to public clamour'. Another visitor to the West Indies was the novelist ▷ Charles Kingsley and his At Last: A Christmas in the West Indies (1871) is an enthusiastic account of the natural history of the West Indian colonies.

The colonization of Africa began in earnest in response to the demand for raw materials and markets caused by the ▷ Industrial Revolution. The 'scramble for Africa' between the various European powers in 1884 led to the Berlin West Africa Conference (1884–5) which agreed on an orderly partitioning of the continent and in particular the territory of the Congo. Despite this, tensions were rife between the British, Dutch and French and, towards the end of the 19th century, the Germans. The British colonial effort was aided by the explorations of David Livingstone (1813–73) from 1841 until his death, and the Welsh explorer Henry Morton Stanley in the late 1870s. The British financier and empire builder Cecil Rhodes helped to maintain a colonial presence for Britain in Africa in the mid 1880s. Kingsley's neice, ▷ Mary Kingsley, travelled extensively in West Africa between 1893 and 1895 recording her experiences in a number of books on the subject.

By 1818, after the successful resolution of the Napoleonic wars had removed the French threat, Britain was the dominant European power in India. Under the Governor Generalship of the ▷ Utilitarian Lord William Bentinck, who was instrumental in the suppression of sati (the sacrifice of Hindu widows on their husband's funeral pyres) and thagi (ritual murder and robbery by gangs), India was encouraged to absorb and adopt Western learning and culture through the medium of English and by 1857 Britain had established complete political control of the Indian sub-continent. However, in 1857 the Bengal army mutinied and what began as a military incident soon escalated into a full-scale popular revolt. Britain did not regain supremacy until 1859, threatening the fragile peace with vicious and often indiscriminate reprisals. The 60 years between the suppression of the mutiny and the end of the First World War saw both the rise of British imperial power in India, and nationalist agitation against it. It was characterized by British racial arrogance and often violent abuse of 'native' Indians. ▷ Rudyard Kipling coined the phrase 'the white man's burden' to describe the duties incumbent upon British officials sent to serve in India. The British government of India became 'the world's largest imperial bureaucracy' (Encyclopaedia Britannica) and transfer of power was effected only after partition in 1947.

British colonization of Australia began in earnest in 1788 with the landing of 730 convicts and 250 free persons at Botany Bay in January of that year. By 1830 the number of convict settlers in the country had reached 58,000, a third of which were Irish rebelling against British colonial policy in Ireland. The Australian Marcus Clarke's novel *For the Term of His Natural Life* (1874) remains a vivid description of convict experience. Between 1829 and 1859 four of Australia's six states were established: Western Australia, South Australia, and the Northern and Southern portions of New South Wales. However, led by New South Wales all the colonies achieved self-government by 1856.

▷ Karl Marx wrote articles specifically about the colonization of Ireland by England and about the British Empire in India, stressing the link between capitalism and colonialism.

▷ Kemble, Fanny.
**Bib:** Johnston, H.H., *History of the Colonization of Africa by Alien Races*; Gopal, S., *British Policy in India, 1858–1905*; Shaw, A.G.L., *Convicts and the Colonized (1830–60)*; Memmi, A., *The Colonizer and the Colonized*; Said, E., *Orientalism*; Spivak, G.C., *In Other Worlds*; Bolt, C., *Victorian Attitudes to Race*; Fieldhouse, D.K., *The Colonial Empire*; Parry, J.H., *Trade and Dominion*; Wiliams, P. and Chrisman, L. (eds), *Colonial Discourse and Post-Colonial Theory*; Brewer, A., *Marxist Theories of Imperialism: A Critical Survey*.

### Cometh Up as a Flower (1867)

A novel of ▷ sensation by ▷ Rhoda Broughton. The heroine, Nell le Strange, is left as the head of a motherless household and delights in her father's affection. She is later attracted to a handsome guardsman, but he is already married and Nell has to accept a marriage of convenience to a rich old man, Sir Hugh. The novel is noteworthy for its description of Nell's revulsion, both at her aged husband and her situation as a 'bought' woman. She decides not to leave Sir Hugh after reading ▷ Mrs Henry Wood's ▷ *East Lynne*, and eventually dies of consumption.

### Comic verse

In direct contrast to the tendency towards earnestness and social responsibility championed by ▷ Thomas Carlyle, the Victorians also produced a large body of light literature including excellent comic verse, parodies and ▷ nonsense. The Victorian's love of humour is perhaps best exemplified in ▷ *Punch* magazine, founded in 1841, which claimed, despite its Radical politics, to be primarily a 'Guffawgraph'.

One of the most successful and gifted parodists was ▷ William Aytoun whose *The Book of Ballads: Edited by Bon Gaultier* (1845), published jointly with Theodore

Martin (1816–1909), satirizes the inflated sentiment of ▷ Tennyson among others. However, Aytoun's most influential parody was his *Firmilian, or the Student of Badajoz: A Spasmodic Tragedy by T. Percy Jones* (1854) which helped to destroy the reputation of the ▷ Spasmodic school of poets. The novelist ▷ Thackeray parodied the weaknesses of ▷ Disraeli, ▷ Bulwer-Lytton, ▷ Mrs Gore and many others in his *Mr Punch's Prize Novelists* (1847). Other parodies include C.S. Calverley's *Verses and Translations* (1862), W.S. Gilbert's *Bab Ballads* (1869), which contains a skit on Coleridge's *The Ancient Mariner*, and Lewis Carroll's *Alice in Wonderland* (1865) and *Through the Looking Glass* (1872) which contain imitations of Tennyson and ▷ Southey. W.S. Gilbert's collaboration with Arthur Sullivan, which began in 1871, resulted in the Savoy Operas which raised farce to a totally new level.

Nonsense verse was pioneered by ▷ Edward Lear, who borrowed the limerick form from an anonymous collection entitled *Anecdotes of Fifteen Gentlemen* (c 1821), and went on to popularize it. The tradition was continued by Carroll in such poems as 'The Hunting of the Snark' (1876) and *Dreamland* (1882). The Victorian age's talent for self-ridicule can be summed up in ▷ Swinburne's own *Seven Against Sense* (1880).
**Bib:** Henkle, R.B., *Comedy and Culture; England 1820–1900*; Huggett, E. (ed), *Victorian England as Seen by 'Punch'*; Sewell, E., *The Field of Nonsense*.

### Comte, Auguste (1798–1857)

French philosopher. He sought to expound a scientifically based philosophy for human progress called positivism, which deduced laws of development from the facts of history and excluded metaphysics and religion. His chief works were translated into English. In them he sought to establish a system that would be the scientific equivalent of the Catholic system of philosophy. In this he failed, but his work led to the modern science of sociology. In England, his chief disciple was Frederick Harrison (1831–1923), but he also deeply interested the philosopher ▷ John Stuart Mill and the novelist ▷ George Eliot. The character of his beliefs suited radically reformist and religiously sceptical English intellectuals such as these; on the other hand, his systematization of ideas was alien to English habits of mind, and was criticized by the philosopher ▷ Herbert Spencer.

*Coningsby, or The New Generation* (1844)
A political novel by ▷ Benjamin Disraeli. By
means of it, the rising politician, Disraeli,
expresses his contempt for the lack of
principle behind the contemporary Tory
(right-wing) party, whose side he nonetheless
took against the expediency and materialism
of the ▷ Whigs and ▷ Utilitarians. Against
them he advocates a revived, platonically
idealized aristocracy with the interests of the
people at heart and respected by them as their
natural leaders. Such a new aristocrat is the
hero of the novel, Coningsby, and he and
his friends form a group comparable to the
Young England group which Disraeli himself
led in Parliament. Coningsby is the grandson
of Lord Monmouth, a type from the old,
unprincipled, predatory aristocracy, whose
inveterate enemy is the industrialist Millbank,
representing the new and vital middle class.
Coningsby falls in love with Millbank's
daughter, is disinherited by his grandfather
and eventually is elected to Parliament with
Millbank's support. The novel is essentially
one of propaganda of ideas, but written with
great feeling, liveliness and intelligence.
Lord Monmouth was based on the actual
Lord Hertford, also used as the basis of
Lord Steyne in ▷ Thackeray's ▷ *Vanity
Fair*. Another excellently drawn character is
the detestable Rigby, based on John Wilson
Croker, politician and journalist, and author
of the notoriously abusive review of Keats's
*Endymion* (1818).

**Contagious Diseases Acts**
   ▷ Women's Movement, The.

*Contemporary Review, The*
It was founded in 1866 and has Sir Percy
Bunting as its most famous editor. It covered
a variety of subjects and in 1955 incorporated
▷ *The Fortnightly Review*.

**Cook, Eliza (1818–89)**
Poet, essayist and ▷ feminist. The youngest
of eleven children, she was born in London
and grew up in Horsham, Sussex. She
educated herself and published her first
verses, *Lays of a Wild Harp*, in 1835. The
collection was well-received, and encouraged
her to contribute poems to the *Metropolitan
Magazine*, the *New Monthly Magazine* and the
*Weekly Dispatch*, the last of which printed her
most famous poem, 'The Old Arm Chair', in
1837. Her work varies between sentimental,
domestic verse, fiery political ▷ ballads and
satirical poetry. Her second collection, *Melaia
and Other Poems* (1838), sold well both in

Britain and North America, and three further
volumes followed: *Poems: Second Series* (1845);
*I'm Afloat: Songs* (1850) and *New Echoes, and
Other Poems* (1864). From 1849–54 she wrote
and edited ▷ *Eliza Cook's Journal*, a feminist
miscellany addressing topics such as work,
marriage and the law. The 1860 publication
*Jottings From My Journal* includes much of
this material. Cook also wrote a collection of
aphorisms, *Diamond Dust* (1865). She never
married, but was passionately attracted to
Charlotte Cushman, an actress.
   ▷ Women's movement; Lesbianism.
**Bib:** Hickok, K., *Representations of Women:
19th Century British Women's Poetry*.

**Cooper, Edith (1862–1913)**
Poet and dramatist who published separately,
and collaboratively with ▷ Katherine Bradley
under the ▷ pseudonym ▷ Michael Field.

**Copyright, The law of**
The right of writers, artists and musicians
to refuse reproduction of their works. The
right is now established law in every civilized
country. The first copyright law in England
was passed under Queen Anne in 1709.
Before this, it was possible for publishers to
publish books without the author's permission,
and without allowing him or her any profits
from sales, a practice very common during
the lifetime of Shakespeare (1564–1616).
Until 1909, the laws of the United States
did not adequately safeguard British authors
against having their works 'pirated' there,
ie published without their permission and
without giving them suitable financial return.
▷ Dickens suffered from this state of affairs,
and it greatly angered him.

**Corelli, Marie (1855–1924)**
▷ Pseudonym of novelist Mary Mackay, born
in London the illegitimate daughter (though
she claimed to be adopted and born in 1864)
of Scottish songwriter Charles Mackay.
Educated by ▷ governesses and for a while
at a convent, she was a gifted pianist and
had intended to take up a musical career, for
which she adopted the name Corelli. In 1885
a psychic experience led her to start writing
and her novels are sensational, full of trances,
swoons, religious conversions and visions.
Her first novel, *A Romance of Two Worlds*
(1886), was so successful that she abandoned
music to become a professional writer. Her
great popularity occured with *Barabbas: A
Dream of The World's Tragedy* (1886), despite
unfavourable reviews, and of her twenty-eight
best-selling novels, *The Sorrows of Satan* (1895)

had a greater initial sale than any previous English novel. After 1901 she lived with her friend, Bertha Vyver, in Stratford-upon-Avon, and never married. Her popularity declined into ridicule before her death. Other novels include *The Mighty Atom* (1896) and *Boy* (1900)

▷ Sensation, Novel of.

Bib: Coates, E.G., *Life*; Bigland, E., *Marie Corelli: The Woman and the Legend*; Masters, B., *Now Barabbas Was a Rotter: The Extraordinary Life of Marie Corelli*.

### Cornhill Magazine, The

A monthly periodical, at the height of its fame soon after its foundation by ▷ William Thackeray, the novelist, in 1860. Contributors included ▷ John Ruskin, ▷ Matthew Arnold, ▷ Mrs Gaskell, ▷ Anthony Trollope and ▷ Leslie Stephen, besides Thackeray himself. It continued in the 20th century to publish the work of many writers.

### Corn Laws, Repeal of the, 1846

The Corn Laws existed to protect English home-grown corn from competition from imported foreign corn. Their existence made for higher food prices and assumed the superior importance of agricultural interest over urban industrial interests. In the first half of the 19th century the Tory party derived its main support from landowners, whereas the ▷ Whigs owed much of their support to the new industrialists of the rapidly growing industrial towns. The Whig Anti-Corn Law League consequently represented not merely opposition to a particular measure but rivalry between main segments of society; moreover, the workers, anxious above all for cheap food, supported the urban middle class and the Whigs. It was nonetheless a Tory Prime Minister, ▷ Robert Peel, who repealed the Corn Laws under pressure of a severe famine in Ireland. The abolition of the Corn Laws was of historic importance in several ways: 1 it divided the Tory party, sending its younger leader, ▷ Benjamin Disraeli, into opposition, with his supporters, against Peel; 2 it began the era of ▷ free trade (ie trade unrestricted by import or export taxes); 3 it acknowledged implicitly that industrial interests were henceforth to be regarded as more important than agricultural interests; 4 it relieved the almost revolutionary restlessness of the working class, so that England was one of the few countries in Europe not to undergo upheaval or serious threat of upheaval in the Year of Revolutions, 1848.

▷ Hungry Forties, The.

### Court of Chancery

A Court of law under the Lord Chancellor, head of the English judicial system. The Court grew up in the 15th century to deal with cases which for any reason could not be dealt with efficiently by the established law courts administering Common Law. The practice developed a system of law supplementary to Common Law, known as Equity. Few things so neatly demonstrate the disadvantage of women in English law as the fact that they are treated as the legal equivalents of orphans and lunatics, through one of the special fields of jurisdiction Equity was created to cover. There have been recent attempts, by means of 'equal opportunities' legislation, for instance, to remedy this long-standing disability. By the 19th century Chancery procedure became excessively complex, its relationship with other courts of law was ill-defined, and judgements were often delayed for years – hence the satire to which ▷ Charles Dickens subjected the Court in his novel, ▷ *Bleak House*. The system was reformed by the Judicature Act, 1873. (The idiom 'in chancery' means 'remaining undecided indefinitely'; a 'ward in Chancery' is an orphan whose interests are in the care of Chancery.)

### Craik, Dinah Mulock (1826–87)

Novelist and essayist, who also wrote poetry and short stories. She was born in Stoke-on-Trent, the daughter of a nonconformist clergyman who was feckless and eccentric and was committed as a pauper lunatic in the 1830s. She wrote prolifically – novels, plays, poetry, biography, ▷ travel books, didactic essays and children's stories – to help support her family. After an unsettled childhood she lived with her brother in London, becoming well-known in literary society and marrying George Craik, a partner in Macmillan's publishing house, in 1865. Her first novel was *The Ogilvies* (1849), and her most famous ▷ *John Halifax, Gentleman* (1856). Craik's fiction is predominantly sentimental and romantic, but it also questions traditional sex roles and often depicts female characters attempting to discover autonomous identities. Her novels include *The Head of the Family* (1852), *Agatha's Husband* (1853), *Christian's Mistake* (1865) and *The Woman's Kingdom* (1869). Her non-fiction includes *A Woman's Thoughts About Women* (1858), *Plain Speaking* (1882), and *Concerning Men and Other Papers* (1888). These essays address the need for female self-reliance, offering advice to women on ways to gain independence. She was not a radical writer, but nevertheless contributed to the exploration of woman's role in the Victorian period. She was also a shrewd negotiator and businesswomen, but a generous one, using a pension granted to her in 1864 to help needy authors.

▷ Women's Movement; Children's literature.

**Bib:** Foster, S., *Victorian Women's Fiction: Marriage, Freedom and the Individual.*

### Cranford (1853)

A novel by ▷ Elizabeth Gaskell first published in ▷ *Household Words* (ed. ▷ Charles Dickens) 1851–3. It is the best known of her novels. The town of Cranford is actually based on Knutsford, some seventeen miles from Manchester. The book describes the life of the predominantly feminine genteel society of the place. Though apparently very slight, it contains graphic description, subtle, ironic humour resembling Jane Austen's (1775–1817), and acute discernment in discriminating between the vulgar arrogance of the merely rich and the sensitive, humane pride of the gentility. Its most famous characters are the blatant and ostentatious Honourable Mrs Jamieson and, in contrast, the timid, retiring, yet distinguished Miss Matty.

### Cricket on the Hearth, The (1846)

A Christmas book by ▷ Charles Dickens, one of a series started by ▷ *A Christmas Carol*, 1843. It is a tale in which the evil schemes of old Tackleton to injure the married love of Peerybingle and his young wife, Dot, and to marry May Fielding are frustrated by the magic of the Cricket and by a mysterious stranger.

### Crimean War

A war between the Russians and the British, French and Ottoman Turkish which took place between October 1853 and February 1856, and was fought mainly on the Crimean Peninsular. It was caused primarily by an act of aggression by Russia against the Ottoman sultan and by a dispute between Russia and France concerning the holy lands in Palestine. Britain fought in defence of the Turks and major engagements took place at the Alma River on September 20, at Balaklava on October 25, and at Inkerman on November 5, 1854. In addition to high war casualties, disease accounted for the deaths of over a quarter of a million of the men lost on both sides. The British conscience was stirred by reports of the appalling conditions endured by sick and wounded servicemen, and women were urged to join the troops as nurses.

Among those who volunteered was the pioneer of the nursing profession Florence Nightingale (1820–1910). She arrived at the barrack hospital at Scutari, Turkey on November 5, 1854 where she was put in charge of nursing. Due to the initial hostility of doctors to female presence on the wards, Nightingale and her nurses were forced to stand by and watch as casualties died in overcrowded and insanitary conditions plagued by fleas and rats. When finally allowed to help she began by scrubbing down the wards and washing the patients' clothes. Her individual care of the wounded soldiers earned her the soubriquet 'The Lady with the Lamp'. Nightingale became a national hero and her efforts helped establish the Royal Commission on the Health of the Army in May 1857. This in turn led to the founding of the Army Medical School in the same year. Using her considerable private funds, and money raised by public subscription to commemorate her work in the Crimea, she set up the Nightingale School for Nurses at St Thomas' Hospital in 1860, which was the first nursing school of its kind.

The Crimean War stirred a certain amount of jingoism in England. ▷ Gladstone, then Chancellor of the Exchequer, defended it as necessary to the maintenance of public law in Europe and doubled income tax in 1854 in order to pay for Britain's involvement. Just prior to the outbreak of hostilities in the Crimea, Tennyson wrote of 'the blood-red blossom of war' in his long poem *Maud* but added six lines in 1856 to suggest that the speaker of these lines was deranged. *Maud* nevertheless retains its bellicosity and is suffused with references to the Crimean War. Tennyson also marked the disastrous events at Balaklava in his patriotic poem ▷ 'The Charge of the Light Brigade' (1854). An opposing point of view is expressed by ▷ Sydney Dobell, a member of the so-called ▷ Spasmodic school of poetry. In his *England in Time of War* (1856), jingoism gives way to compassion for the tragic personal consequences of war. In similar vein ▷ Newman, moved and enraged by reports concerning the state of the British army in the Crimea, wrote a series of letters to the *Catholic Herald* in 1855 entitled 'Who's to Blame?'. Minor novelist Thomas William Robertson (1829–71) wrote *Ours* (1866) which deals with the private lives of British officers serving in the Crimea. It also exploits the pathos and ironies of war in general, and the

Crimean War in particular. The Crimean War features in the play *Birth* (1870) by Thomas William Robertson, ▷ Thackeray's *The Rose and the Ring* (1855) and ▷ Charles Kingsley's *The Heroes* (1856).

### Crowe, Catherine (?1800–72)

Novelist and short story writer, born in Kent. She married Lt Col John Crowe in 1822 and moved to Edinburgh until the death of her husband in 1860, after which she went to live in Folkestone. A prolific writer, she is best-known for her collection of supernatural stories, *Night Side of Nature or Ghosts and Ghost Stories* (1848), which ran to several editions. She also wrote plays, her first work being the tragedy *Aristomedus*, published anonymously in 1838. Her novel *Susan Hopley* (1841) was successfully adapted for the stage, and *The Cruel Kindness* (1853), a drama, was performed at the Haymarket Theatre. Other novels include *Manorial Rights* (1839), *Linny Dawson* (1847) and, for children, *Adventures of a Monkey* (1861).
**Bib:** Sergeant, A., *Women Novelists of Queen Victoria's Reign.*

### Cruikshank, George (1792–1878)

Illustrator, with a strong satirical and moralistic bent; famous especially for his illustrations to ▷ Charles Dickens's novel ▷ *Oliver Twist.*

### Crystal Palace

▷ Exhibition, The Great.

### Culture and Anarchy (1869)

A volume of essays by ▷ Matthew Arnold, originally published as articles in ▷ *The Cornhill Magazine.* It is subtitled *An Essay in Political and Social Criticism* and was designed to demonstrate that culture was the best remedy for the political, social and religious unrest that, in his view, characterized England at that time. Arnold defined the main purpose of culture as the stimulation of intelligence and reason. Its advance was blocked by certain inequalities, confusions and imbalances within English life which, unchecked by an adequate centre of authority, threatened to slide towards anarchy. Arnold distinguishes between two categories of mind in contemporary society: the Hebraic, with its emphasis on the virtues of private conduct and practical achievement; and the Hellenic, which valued contemplation, reason and critical discrimination. England, he considered, was becoming barbarous owing to the preponderance of the former over the latter, with which he identified. The answer to the conflict lay in culture with its emphasis on the development of the individual within the broader framework of society, its commitment to the growth of the moral life and its aspirations towards perfection.

### Curzon, Sarah Anne (1833–98)

Born Sarah Vincent in Birmingham, England, she married Robert Curzon, and emigrated with him to Canada in 1862. She was a strong advocate of suffrage and education, contributed to many journals, and wrote a column on women's issues. *Laura Secord, the Heroine of 1812: A Drama, And Other Poems* (1887) and *The Story of Laura Secord, 1813* (1891) are both historical representations of Laura Secord's heroic actions in crossing enemy lines to warn the British of impending American attack in the war of 1812. The earlier volume includes *The Sweet Girl Graduate*, a comic play about a woman who disguises herself as a man in order to graduate from the University of Toronto.

▷ Women's Movement.

D

### Daisy Miller (1879)

A story by ▷ Henry James. It concerns the visit of girl from the USA to Europe, and is one of the stories in which James contrasts US freshness of impulse, moral integrity, and naivety with the complexity and deviousness of the European mentality. The girl's innocence and candour is misinterpreted as moral turpitude by the North Americans who are long settled in Europe, including the young man who acts as a focal character for the narrative.

▷ Novel of manners.

### Dame schools

Schools for poor children in the 18th and 19th centuries, especially in country towns and villages. Unlike the charity schools, they were run by private initiative, especially by single women supplementing their income by teaching reading and writing.

▷ Education.

### Daniel Deronda (1876)

A novel by ▷ George Eliot (Mary Ann Evans). It contains a double story: that of the hero, Daniel Deronda, and that of the heroine Gwendolen Harleth. Daniel is the adopted son of an aristocratic Englishman, and a young man of gracious personality and positive values; he discovers that he is of Jewish parentage, and ends by marrying a Jewish girl, Mirah and devoting himself to the cause of establishing a Jewish homeland. Gwendolen belongs to an impoverished upper-class family and marries (under pressure from her clergyman uncle) a rich and entirely self-centred aristocrat, Henleigh Grandcourt, to redeem their fortunes. Her story is the discovery of the truth of her own nature, just as Deronda's story is the discovery of his origin and vocation. Their stories are linked by the almost casual but entirely beneficent influence of Deronda over Gwendolen, whom he saves from despair after the death of her husband in circumstances that compromise her conscience.) The theme of artistic dedication is central.) Critics have observed that the story of Gwendolen is one of the masterpieces of English fiction, but that that of Daniel is comparatively flat and unconvincing.

▷ Jews in Victorian literature.

### Darwin, Charles Robert (1809–82)

Biologist. His book *On the Origin of Species by means of Natural Selection* (1859) not only expounded the theory of the evolution of natural organisms (which in itself was not new, for it had been held by, among others, Darwin's grandfather, the poet Erasmus Darwin) but presented persuasive evidence for the theory. In brief, this was that species naturally tend to produce variations and that some of these variations have better capacity for survival than others, which in consequence tend to become extinct. Darwin's conviction partly began with his study of ▷ Malthus on population, and it thus belongs to the rationalistic tradition which the 19th century inherited from the 18th. The book greatly disturbed many religious people, since it apparently contradicted the account of the creation of the world of *Genesis* in the Bible; it also raised serious doubts about the existence of the soul and its survival after the death of the body. However, it is possible to exaggerate the importance of the Darwinian theory as a cause of religious disbelief: on the one hand, ▷ Charles Lyell's *Principles of Geology* (1830–3) had already done much to upset traditional beliefs (those, for instance, of the poet ▷ Tennyson) and so had scientific scholarship on biblical texts by men like Charles Hennell (as in the case of the novelist ▷ George Eliot); on the other hand, intelligent believers such as the poet Samuel Taylor Coleridge (1772–1834) had long ceased to accept the Bible as a sacred record of fact in all its books. The effect of Darwin's ideas was probably rather to extend religious doubt from the intelligentsia (who were already deeply permeated by it) to wider circles. Another kind of effect was to produce in the popular mind a naive optimism that man was subject to a general law of progress; it thus encouraged an uncritical view of history and society.

Darwin wrote a number of other scientific works, including *The Descent of Man* (1871). His *Journal of Researches into the Geology and Natural History of the various countries visited by H.M.S. 'Beagle'*, a report of his first important scientific expedition (1831–6), is a fascinating travel book. He also wrote a brief but interesting *Autobiography* (edited with additions by Nora Barlow, 1958).

▷ Agnosticism.

**Bib:** Huxley, L., *Charles Darwin*; Stevenson, L., *Darwin among the Poets*; West, G., *Darwin: the Fragmentary Man*; Darwin, F., *Life and Letters*; Beer, G., *Darwin's Plots*.

### David Copperfield (1849–50)

A novel in ▷ autobiographical form by ▷ Charles Dickens. 'Of all my books I like this the best; like many fond parents I have a favourite child and his name is David Copperfield.' Some commentators have thought that the hero is representative of Dickens himself, and point to the resemblance of initials: C.D. and D.C. It is true that in outline Copperfield's experiences – his sense of early rejection, ▷ child labour in a warehouse, experience as a journalist and final success as a novelist – are similar to Dickens's own. But Dickens's purpose was to present an imaginative picture of growth from childhood to manhood in his own period of history, using his own experience as some of its material but without intending a biographical record. The social landscape of this novel is broader than an autobiography would be likely to achieve. It includes the moralistic and sadistic oppressiveness of Copperfield's mercantile step-father, Murdstone, and the intimate study of selfish hedonism in Copperfield's aristocratic friend, Steerforth; the spontaneous cordiality of the humble Yarmouth boatman, Peggotty, and his sister, and the cunning deviousness of Uriah Heep, whose servile humility is disguise for his total ruthlessness in making his way from bleak beginnings to a position of power. The novel is strong in dramatic contrast, and particularly interesting in the counterbalancing of the women characters in a series of feminine archetypes. Copperfield is fatherless, and his gentle, guileless mother (who becomes victim in matrimony to Murdstone) is like an elder sister to the child; both are children to the motherly, protective servant, Clara Peggotty. She is replaced by the harsh and loveless Miss Murdstone who plays the role of cruel stepmother. Copperfield runs away and takes refuge with his idiosyncratic aunt, Betsey Trotwood, who has shaped for herself an eccentric independence of men, retaining for a harmless lunatic (Mr ▷ Dick) a compassionate tenderness which she now extends to her nephew, in spite of having rejected him at birth because he was a boy. Copperfield's first wife, Dora Spenlow, is a simulacrum of his mother – a child wife, on whom ▷ Ibsen seems to have based Nora in A Doll's House. Two other representatives of Victorian womanhood are Agnes Wickfield (whom he eventually marries), the stereotype of defenceless womanly sanctity and nearly a victim of Heep's rapacity, and Little Em'ly who is first under the protection of Peggotty and then becomes 'the ▷ fallen woman' when she is seduced by Steerforth. Another very striking portrait is Rosa Dartle, companion to Steerforth's mother and poisoned by vindictive hatred of him because of his cool assumption of social and masculine privilege. Though not the richest and deepest of Dickens's novels, it is perhaps psychologically the most revealing, both of Dickens himself and of the society of his time.

**Bib:** Storey, G., *David Copperfield: Interweaving Text and Fiction.*

### Davidson, John (1857–1909)

Poet. Best remembered for his ▷ ballads and songs, in particular *Thirty Bob a Week*, he also wrote plays, novels and philosophical works. A friend of poet W.B. Yeats (1865–1939) and fellow member of the ▷ Rhymer's Club, a group of ▷ Nineties poets which met to read their poetry from 1890–94 at the Cheshire Cheese, a pub in Fleet Street. Davidson was also influenced by ▷ Nietzsche in his passionate ▷ atheism, exemplified by *God and Mammon* (1907), a trilogy of which only two parts were complete when Davidson committed suicide. He contributed to the ▷ *Yellow Book*, and was an important figure in the development of the 20th-century Scottish Renaissance (▷ Scottish literature in English).

**Bib:** Turnbull, A. (ed.), *Poems*; Lindsay, M. (ed.), *John Davidson: A Selection of his Poems* (Preface by T.S. Eliot).

### Decadents

A term attributed to the French poet Paul Verlaine in 1885, who contributed to a review, *Le Decadent*, founded by Anatole Baju, from 1886–9. The French Decadents were inspired by ▷ Charles Baudelaire and counted Arthur Rimbaud (1854–91), Stephane Mallarmé (1842–98) and Tristran Corbière among their number. J.K. Huysmans' novel *A rebours (Against the Grain*, 1894) was called 'the breviary of the Decadence' by poet Arthur Symons (1865–1945). In England the term 'Decadents' was applied to a group of poets at the end of the 19th century, which included ▷ Arthur Symons, ▷ Oscar Wilde, ▷ Ernest Dowson and Lionel Johnson (1867–1902), who constituted the later generation of the ▷ Aesthetic Movement and included the English followers of the French ▷ Symbolist poets. Their aim was to set art free from the claims of life and their art is characterized by a 'world weariness' brought on by the death of the century, a sense of social decline and spiritual dispossession. G.L. van Roosebroeck gives an account of the term in *The Legend of the Decadents.*

▷ Rhymer's Club; *Yellow Book*; French influence on Victorian literature.

*Deerbrook* (1839)

The only novel by journalist and feminist ▷ Harriet Martineau, *Deerbrook* is set in a tranquil English village in the early 19th century. Two orphaned sisters, Hester and Margaret Ibbotson, come to stay with their cousins, the Grey family. The personal lives of the sisters become entwined with the life of the village – portrayed as a hotbed of personal rivalries, gossip and intrigue. The sisters are contrasted in personality: Hester is beautiful but prone to jealousy, Margaret less physically attractive but more intelligent. Romances develop between the sisters and the two most eligible men in the village. The novel also contains ▷ feminist sentiments, expressed mainly by Maria, the crippled ▷ governess, who protests against the restricted opportunities available to middle-class women. *Deerbrook* was well-received, being favourably compared to Jane Austen's (1775–1817) novels. ▷ Charlotte Brontë later claimed that Martineau's honest portrayal of passion had influenced her own writing.

Deism

A form of religious belief which developed in the 17th century as an outcome of the Reformation. The poet and philosopher Edward Herbert (1583–1648) evolved the idea that, while the religion revealed in the Gospels was true, it was preceded by 'natural' religion, according to which by his own inner light a man could perceive all the essentials of religious truth. Herbert's deism was further expounded in the 18th century by others (often in such a way as to suggest that the Christian revelation as presented in the Gospels was redundant), and it suited the 18th-century cool and rational habit of mind which tended to see God as abstract and remote. Bishop Butler among the theologians and David Hume (1711–76) and Immanuel Kant (1724–1804) among the philosophers exposed the unsoundness of deistic arguments in the 18th century, and in the 19th century the growth of the genetic sciences demolished the basic assumptions of deism, ie that human nature and human reason have always been constant, in a constant environment.

*Demos: A Story of English Socialism* (1886)

A novel by ▷ George Gissing in which he questions the validity of socialism and the qualities of its leaders. The story centres on the founding of an Owenite ironworks in an unspoilt valley.
▷ Owen, Robert.

*De Profundis* (1905;1949)

A prose piece by ▷ Oscar Wilde written during the author's imprisonment in Reading Gaol (1895–97) for ▷ homosexual practices. It takes the form of an extended letter written to Wilde's erstwhile companion Lord Alfred Douglas ('Bosie'), whose father, the Marqess of Queensberry, was instrumental in securing Wilde's incarceration. In it, Wilde upbraids Douglas for distracting him from his work and encouraging him in dissipation. He also criticizes Douglas for his shallowness and neglect and accuses him of being a petty parasite, greedy, extravagant and over-indulged. At the same time the letter praises the devotion of Robert Ross, who finally became Wilde's executor. It was sent to Douglas, who destroyed it after reading the opening pages. Afterwards he denied having received it. A drastically edited version of the letter was published by Ross in 1905 under the title *De Profundis* (taken from the opening line of Psalm 130). It was revised and reprinted in a more complete form in 1949.

*Desperate Remedies* (1871)

▷ Thomas Hardy's first published novel in which he adopted the formulae of the popular ▷ sensation novel of the time.

Detective fiction

This branch of literature is usually easy to distinguish from the much wider literature of crime and retribution in drama and in the novel. Unlike the latter, detective fiction seldom relies on the presentation of deep emotions or on subtle and profound character creation. Character, emotion, psychological analysis of states of mind and social reflections will all be present as flavouring, and may even be conspicuous, but the indispensable elements are always a mysterious – but not necessarily horrible – crime, and a detective, who is commonly not a professional policeman, but who has highly developed powers of scientific deduction. It is essential that the surface details should be convincing, and that the author should keep no clues from the reader who thus may enjoy the satisfaction of competing with the detective at his own game. In the detective story proper, as opposed to the crime novel, the criminal's identity is not revealed until the end, and provides the focus of attention.

Precursors of the form are ▷ Wilkie Collins's novel ▷ *The Moonstone* (1868) and the stories of the US writer Edgar Allan Poe (1809–49), featuring the French detective Dupin. But the widespread popularity of detective fiction began with ▷ Arthur Conan Doyle's Sherlock Holmes stories (1887). The staggering perspicuity of the amateur detective from Baker Street, and his superiority to the police and to his companion and foil, Dr Watson, won him a world-wide audience. Another early exponent of the detective short story was G.K. Chesterton (1874–1936), whose detective, Father Brown, is a modest and intuitive Catholic priest who first appeared in *The Innocence of Father Brown* (1911).

The first women detectives in fiction appeared in the 1860s; the stereotype of women's 'nosiness' and obsessive interest in gossip and trivia was often used to explain the female detective's skill in ferreting out crimes and criminals. By the end of the 19th century a number of women writers were producing detective and mystery fiction for an increasingly profitable market.
**Bib:** Sleung, M., *Crime on her Mind*; Craig, P., *The Lady Investigates*; Wing, G., Ed. 'Edwin Drood and Desperate Remedies: prototypes of Detective Fiction in 1870', *Studies in English Literature* 13 677–87 Autumn 1973.

### Diana of the Crossways (1885)
A novel by ▷ George Meredith in which the central character Diana Warwick is accused of adultery by her husband. His action for divorce fails but the couple agree to separate. Diana forms a relationship with Percy Dacier, a rising young politician, but their affair ends after Diana's betrayal of a political secret to the press. Diana eventually marries an old admirer after the death of her husband. The character of Diana Warwick has much in common with ▷ Hardy's Sue Bridehead, the heroine of ▷ *Jude the Obscure*, and is an example of the ▷ 'New Woman' fiction of the period.

### Diaries
As a form of literature diaries began to be significant in the 17th century. The spirit of criticism from the Renaissance and the stress on the individual conscience from the Reformation combined with the political and social turbulence of the 17th century to awaken people to a new awareness of personal experience and its possible interest for general readers. The private nature of the diary form also led to many women taking up this form of writing. Thus the art of the diary arose with the art of biography and ▷ autobiography.

Diaries may first be divided into two classes: those clearly meant to be strictly private and those written more or less with

an eye to eventual publication – although ▷ Oscar Wilde was quick to see the disingenuousness of such a division. In his play *The Importance of Being Earnest* (1895) Cecily Cardew hides her diary from Algernon claiming that it is 'simply a young girl's record of her own thoughts and impressions, and consequently meant for publication'. A further division may be made between those diaries which are interesting chiefly as a record of the time in which the writer lived and those which are mainly a record of the writer's personality. In the 19th century the diaries of Thomas Creevey (1768–1838) and Charles Greville (1794–1865) are famous as records of public affairs, and that of Henry Crabb Robinson (1775–1867) for impressions of the leading writers who were his friends. Hannah Culwick, a Victorian maidservant, wrote seventeen diaries running from 1854–73, providing a fascinating account of a life in service in the Victorian period. The socialist and reformer Beatrice Webb wrote diaries which are a major source for English social and political history and a record of the difficulties encountered by women wishing to work on an equal level with men. ▷ George and Weedon Grossmith's *Diary of a Nobody* (1892) is a comic novel of late Victorian manners which parodies the form, claiming to be the diary of city clerk Charles Pooter.
▷ Allingham, William.

### Dick, Mr
A character in ▷ Charles Dickens's novel ▷ *David Copperfield*. A harmless lunatic, he has an obsession with King Charles's head (ie ▷ Charles I, decapitated in 1649) – hence his name is commonly used as a synonym for obsession, like the idiom 'a bee in one's bonnet'.

### Dickens, Charles (1812–70)
The most popular and internationally known of English novelists. His father was a government clerk who liked to live prosperously, and his sudden impoverishment and imprisonment for debt in the ▷ Marshalsea was a drastic shock to the boy Dickens; prisons recur literally and symbolically in many of his novels, which are also filled with attacks on the injustice of social institutions and the inequalities between the rich and the poor. He began his writing career as a journalist, and all his novels were published serially in periodicals, especially in two edited by himself – ▷ *Household Words* started in 1850, and ▷ *All the Year Round*, started in 1859, both of them weeklies.

His first book, ▷ *Sketches by Boz* (1836), was a collection of stories and descriptive pieces written for various papers in the tradition of the essayists – Charles Lamb (1775–1834), William Hazlitt (1778–1830), Leigh Hunt (1784–1859) – of the previous generation, with the especial difference that Dickens wrote about the hitherto neglected lower middle class. ▷ *The Pickwick Papers* (1836–7), at first loosely connected but gathering unity as it proceeded, was immensely successful. There followed: ▷ *Oliver Twist* (1837–8), ▷ *Nicholas Nickleby* (1838–9), ▷ *The Old Curiosity Shop* and ▷ *Barnaby Rudge* (1840–1). This concludes the first, comparatively light-hearted phase of Dickens's writing, in which he developed his characteristic comedy and melodrama. ▷ *Martin Chuzzlewit* (1843–4) begins a more impressive style of writing in which the comedy and melodrama deepen into new intensity, though critics observe that the beginning of the novel is still in the earlier manner. In 1843 begins his series of Christmas Books, including ▷ *A Christmas Carol* and ▷ *The Cricket on the Hearth*. Thereafter come his mature masterpieces: ▷ *Dombey and Son* (1846–8); ▷ *David Copperfield* (1849–50); ▷ *Bleak House* (1852–3); ▷ *Hard Times* (1854); ▷ *Little Dorrit* (1855–7); ▷ *A Tale of Two Cities* (1859); ▷ *Great Expectations* (1860–1); ▷ *Our Mutual Friend* (1864–5). Dickens was writing ▷ *Edwin Drood* when he died.

**Bib:** Forster, J., *Life*; Johnson, E., *Life*; Wilson, E., in *The Wound and the Bow*; Chesterton, G.K., *Charles Dickens*; Gissing, G., *Charles Dickens: A Crucial Study*; House, H., *The Dickens World*; Leavis, F.R., in *The Great Tradition*; Collins, P., *Dickens and Crime*; *Dickens and Education*; Gross J., *Dickens and the Twentieth Century*; Leavis, F.R. and Q.D., *Dickens the Novelist*; Wilson A., *The World of Charles Dickens*; Carey, J., *The Violent Effigy: A Study of Dickens' Imagination*; Kaplan, F., *Dickens: a Biography*; Jaffe, A., *Vanishing Points: Dickens, Narrative and the Subject of Omniscience*.

## Dismal science, The

Political economy; so called by ▷ Thomas Carlyle because the social thought of such writers as Adam Smith (1723–90) ▷ Jeremy Bentham, ▷ Thomas Malthus and David Ricardo tended to be pessimistic about the alleviation of poverty and inhumanly indifferent to the consequences of economic laws as they saw them.

## Disraeli, Benjamin (Lord Beaconsfield) (1804–81)

Statesman and novelist. He was of Spanish-Jewish descent; his grandfather settled in England in 1748. His political career was brilliant; he entered Parliament in 1837; in the 1840s he was the leader in the House of Commons of a small number of Tory (▷ Whig and Tory) politicians who, as the 'Young England' group, wanted a revival of the party and of the national spirit in an alliance between a spiritually reborn aristocracy and the common people; by 1848 he was leading the Conservatives in the House of Commons; in 1868 and in 1874–80 he had his two periods as one of the most brilliant of English Prime Ministers. Both politically (he secured the vote for the urban working class) and socially (eg his trade union legislation) he at least partly succeeded in securing support for his party from the working class. He was made Earl of Beaconsfield in 1876.

The novels which now chiefly hold attention are his 'Young England Trilogy': ▷ *Coningsby* (1844); ▷ *Sybil* (1845) and *Tancred* (1847). All were written to promulgate his doctrine of Tory Democracy and they all have imperfections, partly because for Disraeli literature was second to politics. On the other hand they have great liveliness of characterization and show keen insight into the structure of society with its cleavage between rich and poor, which Disraeli called 'the two nations'. His other novels are: *Vivian Grey* (1826); *The Young Duke* (1831); *Alroy* and *Ixion in Heaven* (1833); *The Infernal Marriage* and *The Rise of Iskander* (1834); *Henrietta Temple* and *Venetia* (1837); *Lothair* (1870) and *Endymion* (1880).

▷ Social problem novel.

**Bib:** Blake, R., *Life*; Moneypenny, W.F. and Buckle, G.E., *Life*; Jerman, B.R., *The Young Disraeli*; Holloway, J., in *Victorian Sage*; Dahl, C., in *Victorian Fiction* (ed. L. Stevenson); Pritchett, V.S., in *The Living Novel*; Schwartz, D.R., *Disraeli's Fiction*; Brava, T., *Disraeli the Novelist*; Harvie, C., *The Centre of Things: Political Fiction in Britain from Disraeli to the Present*.

## Dissenters' Schools and Academies

In the 18th century, Protestants who did not belong to the Church of England (ie Dissenters or Nonconformists) were not allowed to attend its schools. They could enter Scottish but not English universities. They therefore set up their own educational institutions which provided efficient education, often more up-to-date than that in the schools attended by Anglicans. Dissenting schools and academies became steadily less important in the 19th century, especially after London University was opened in 1828. The last restrictions on non-Anglicans at Oxford and Cambridge were removed in 1871.

▷ Religious groups; Education.

## Divorce

Until 1857 divorce was possible only through Church courts which had kept their authority over matrimonial relations since before the Reformation, while losing it in nearly all other private affairs of laymen. Even after a marriage had been dissolved by a Church court, a special ('private') act of Parliament was necessary before the divorce was legalized. In consequence, divorces were rare and only occurred among the rich and influential. Adultery and cruelty were the accepted grounds, and the wife was commonly in an unfavourable position, so that no divorce was granted on account of a husband's adultery until 1801. The law of 1857 added desertion as a ground for divorce, and proceedings were taken out of the hands of the Church courts and put under the courts of the realm. Since 1938, unsoundness of mind may also be pleaded as a cause of divorce, and it has been further facilitated in other ways, perhaps the most important of which is the concept of 'marital breakdown'. This abolishes the idea of one of the partners being 'guilty' and the other 'injured'.

▷ Marriage.

## Dixon, Ella Hepworth (1855–1932)

Journalist, short story writer and feminist. Dixon's one novel, *The Story of a Modern Woman* (1894), is an autobiographical account of the loneliness suffered by a woman who leads an independent life as a journalist. It is one of the most moving of the ▷ 'New Woman' novels.

## Dobell, Sydney (Thompson) (1824–74)

Poet, born in Kent, the son of a wine merchant. Precocious as a child, he never attended school or university but was privately educated in Cheltenham. He married at the age of twenty after a five-year engagement and was said to have never been separated from his wife for more than thirty hours during their thirty years of marriage. His dramatic poem *The Roman* (1850) supported the cause of Italian nationalism but the publication of the first part of *Balder* (1854) qualified him for inclusion in the ▷ Spasmodic school of poetry identified and ridiculed

by ▷ William Aytoun, who parodied the ludicrous plot in his *Firmilian* (1854). Dobell never completed his epic poem. Other, less sensationalist, works include *England in Time of War* (1856), notable for its compassionate and non-jingoistic treatment of the ▷ Crimean War, and a collection of essays, *Thoughts on Art, Philosophy, and Religion*, which appeared posthumously in 1876.

▷ Gilfillan, George.

## Doctor Thorne (1858)

The third novel in ▷ Anthony Trollope's ▷ Barsetshire sequence. It was his most popular novel during his lifetime and extends the sequence to take account of county society.

## Doll's House, A (1879)

A bold and controversial play by Norwegian dramatist ▷ Henrik Ibsen written in 1879 and first performed in London in 1889. In it Ibsen describes the financial and intellectual enslavement of Nora by her husband and the play discusses notions of individual freedom and social conformity, and in particular the relationship of this debate to the position of women. The play provoked a storm of controversy. It was criticized for its 'immorality' – a point of view satirized by ▷ George Bernard Shaw as 'Ibsenism' – and praised by supporters of the ▷ Women's Movement for its daring and emancipated conclusion.

## Dombey and Son (1847–8)

One of the earliest of the mature novels by ▷ Charles Dickens. Dombey is a proud and heartless London merchant whose sole interest in life is the perpetuation of his name in connection with his firm. For this reason he neglects his deeply affectionate daughter Florence for the sake of his little son, Paul, whom, however, he values not for himself but as the future embodiment of his firm. The boy is motherless, deprived of affection and physically delicate – he dies in childhood. To prevent Florence from marrying a mere clerk in his firm, Dombey sends her lover – Walter Gay – on business to an unhealthy colony in the West Indies. Dombey's pride makes him susceptible to flattery; he is preyed upon by Carker, his manager, one of Dickens's most notable villains, and by Major Joe Bagstock. He is led into marriage with a cold, disillusioned girl, Edith Granger, who runs away from him with Carker. Both his pride and his wealth are eventually taken from him and he finds himself in the end dependent on the forgiving Florence and Walter Gay. A particular interest of the book is that railways play an important part in it just at the time when they were transforming English life. The sombreness of Dombey's mansion is opposed to the warm-hearted if unbusinesslike environment of the shop of Solomon Gills, Gay's uncle.

### 'Dover Beach'
A poem of religious doubt and despair by ▷ Matthew Arnold, published in *New Poems* (1867), and probably the best known of all his works. It contains the line 'Ah, love, let us be true to one another', and is a classic statement of the transitory nature of religious faith to which the speaker opposes love and faithfulness.

### Dowden, Edward (1894–1913)
Critic and scholar born in Cork and educated at Queen's College and Trinity College, Dublin where he was appointed Professor of English Studies in 1867. He is distinguished for his work on Shakespeare, editing twelve plays for the original Arden edition and writing *Shakspeare: A Critical Study of His Mind and Art* (1875), which was the first book in English to attempt a study of Shakespeare's development as a dramatist, although he sentimentalized his poetry. He also wrote *A Shakspeare Primer* (1877), a study of the poet Southey (1879) and biographies of Shelley (1886) and ▷ Browning (1905). He was also one of the earliest admirers of Walt Whitman, and his own *Poems* appeared in 1876.
   ▷ Irish Literature in English.

### Dowson, Ernest (Christopher) (1867–1900)
Poet, born in Kent and one of the most talented of the circle of late 1890's English poets known as the ▷ Decadents. He was an active member of the ▷ Rhymers' Club (1891–4), which included W.B. Yeats (1865–1939), ▷ Arthur Symons (1865–1943), Richard Le Gallienne (1866–1947), Lionel Johnson (1867–1902), ▷ Aubrey Beardsley and occasionally ▷ Oscar Wilde. He contributed poems to the ▷ *Yellow Book* and the *Savoy*. He left Queen's College, Cambridge without a degree, due to a decline in his family's fortunes and worked at his father's dock. His literary idols were Edgar Allen Poe, ▷ Baudelaire, Verlaine (1844–96) and ▷ Swinburne and in 1891 he met the twelve-year-old Adelaide Foltinowicz, who became the inspiration for much of his poetry and a symbol of love and innocence which counteracted his world-weariness, despite her

refusal of his offer of marriage. In the same year he converted to Roman ▷ Catholicism and published his best-known poem 'Non Sum Qualis Eram Bonae sub Regno Cynarae', remembered for its refrain 'I have been true to you Cynara, in my fashion'. After the deaths of his parents in 1894 he discovered symptoms of his own tuberculosis. Adelaide married a waiter in her father's restaurant and Dowson moved to France where he was discovered wretched, penniless and addicted to absinthe by his friend R.H. Sherard, in whose house he died. The poet of ennui and idealized love, his verse first achieved attention in *Poems* (1896). *Decorations*, which included experimental prose poems, followed in 1899. Dowson's output, as were his themes, was limited, but his poems are remarkable for their lyricism and cadence and he had a significant influence on Yeats and Rupert Brooke (1887–1915). Dowson also published two novels in collaboration with Arthur Moore – *A Comedy of Masks* (1893) and *Adrian Rome* (1899) – and a one-act verse play, *The Pierrot of the Minute* (1897). His *Letters* were published in 1967.
**Bib:** Davidson, D., *British Poetry of the 1890s.*

### Doyle, Sir Arthur Conan (1859–1930)
Novelist; chiefly noted for his series of stories and novels about the amateur detective, Sherlock Holmes, a genius in minute deduction and acute observations. His friend, Dr Watson, is represented as the ordinary, ingenuous man, who needs to have everything pointed out to him and explained; and this offsets the ingenuity of the detective. The combination of acute detective and obtuse colleague has been imitated in many detective stories ever since. The stories include: *A Study in Scarlet* (1887); *The Adventures of Sherlock Holmes* (1891); *The Memoirs of Sherlock Holmes* (1893); *The Hound of the Baskervilles* (1902); *The Return of Sherlock Holmes* (1905). Conan Doyle also wrote historical novels of merit; eg *Micah Clarke* (1888), *The White Company* (1891), and *Rodney Stone* (1896).
   ▷ Detective fiction; Historical novel.
**Bib:** Lamond, J., *Conan Doyle: a Memoir;* Conan Doyle, A., *The True Conan Doyle;* Carr, J.D., *The Life of Conan Doyle;* Roberts, S.C., *Holmes and Watson;* Pearsall, R; *Conan Doyle: A Biographical Solution.*

### *Dracula* (1897)
A novel by ▷ Bram Stoker which has become, like Mary Shelley's *Frankenstein* (1818), a modern myth. The story opens with the diary of Jonathon Harker, who falls victim

to Count Dracula whilst acting as his solicitor. Dracula then travels to Whitby where the story is resumed in letter form by Harker's fiancée, Mina Murray, who witnesses her friend Lucy Westenra fall under Dracula's spell. A stake through the heart restores Lucy to peace and Dracula is thwarted in his pursuit of Mina and finally destroyed. Elaine Showalter reads the novel as a 'decadent fantasy of reproduction through transfusion', with strong hints of homoeroticism, and as an attack on the sexual daring of the ▷ 'New Woman'.

▷ Horror fiction.

**Bib:** Showalter, E., *Sexual Anarchy: Gender and Culture at the Fin de Siècle.*

## Dramatic monologue

A poetic form in which the poet invents a character, or, more commonly, uses one from history or legend, and reflects on life from the character's standpoint. The dramatic monologue is a development from the conversation poem of Coleridge (1772–1834) and Wordsworth (1770–1880), in which the poet reflects on life in his own person.

▷ Tennyson was the first to use the form, eg ▷ *The Lotos-Eaters* (1833), *Ulysses* (1842) and *Tithonus* (pub. 1860). In these poems, he takes the standpoint of characters in Greek myth and causes them to express emotions relevant to their predicaments. The emotions, however, are really more relevant to those of Tennyson's own age, but the disguise enables him to express himself without inhibition, and particularly without involving himself in the responsibility of having to defend the attitudes that he is expressing. His most ambitious poem in this form is the monodrama ▷ *Maud* (1855).

However it was ▷ Robert Browning who used the form most profusely, and with whom it is most associated, eg 'My Last Duchess' (1845), 'Fra Lippo Lippi', ▷ 'Andrea del Sarto', 'The Bishop Orders His Tomb', 'Bishop Blougram's Apology', all in ▷ *Men and Women* (1855); 'Mr Sludge the Medium' in ▷ *Dramatis Personae* (1864); and *The Ring and the Book* (1869). Browning used it differently from Tennyson: his characters are more detached from his own personality; the poems are attempts to explore a wide variety of attitudes to art and life. His monologues have little to do with drama, though superficially they resemble soliloquies in plays of the age of Shakespeare. They have an even closer resemblance, though still a rather superficial one, to the medieval convention of public confession by characters

such as the Wife of Bath and the Pardoner in Chaucer's (c 1340–1400) *Canterbury Tales*. Most of all, however, they emulate the exploration of character and society in the novel of Browning's own day, and his *The Ring and the Book* is really an experiment in the novel; the tale unfolds through monologues by the various participators in and spectators of the events. Still another use for the dramatic monologue is that to which ▷ Arthur Clough puts it in his poem *Dipsychus* (*Divided Mind*, 1850). This poem is in the form of a dialogue, but it is a dialogue between the two parts of a man's mind: that which tries to sustain moral principle, and that which is sceptical of principle, seeking only pleasure and material well-being.

A more searching irony was brought to the dramatic monologue by ▷ T.S. Eliot in *The Love Song of F. Alfred Prufrock* (1915) and *Gerontion* (1920).

### Dramatic Studies (1866)

The first collection of poetry by ▷ Augusta Webster, including the much-admired poem 'Snow-waste'. The ▷ dramatic monologues of the collection show the influence of ▷ Robert Browning, but Webster's subjects tend to be related specifically to women's experience, as in 'By The Looking Glass', a poem about spinsterhood. The ▷ realism and directness of the verse disturbed some Victorian critics.

### Dramatis Personae (1864)

A collection of poems by ▷ Robert Browning, including a number of his more famous ones: 'Abt Vogler', 'Rabbi Ben Ezra', 'A Death in the Desert', 'Caliban upon Setebos', 'Mr Sludge the Medium'.

### Dream of John Ball, A (1888)

A story by ▷ William Morris serialized in *The Commonweal*, 1886–7, in which the protagonist describes a dream in which he is transported back to Kent during the peasant's revolt of 1381. John Ball, a dissenting priest, inspires the peasants to victory and later discusses their hopes and plans for change with Morris. Morris describes the 19th century and the Industrial Revolution, whereupon John Ball realizes he is, in fact, dreaming of the future. *A Dream of John Ball* anticipates Morris's *News From Nowhere* (1890) in its use of the dream motif to link past, present and future.

### Du Maurier, George (1834–96)

Graphic artist and novelist; born in Paris. His grandparents had been refugees in England from the French Revolution (1789–94); his

father was a naturalized British subject; his mother was English. In 1865 he joined the staff of ▷ *Punch* and became one of the best known British humorous artists, satirizing the upper classes rather in the style of ▷ William Thackeray. He wrote three novels: *Peter Ibbetson* (1891), ▷ *Trilby* (1894) and *The Martian* (posthumous, 1896). The first two were extremely popular, but their sentimentality has put them out of fashion.
**Bib:** Ormond, L., *George Du Maurier.*

# E

### Earthly Paradise, The (1868–70)

A poem by ▷ William Morris published in three volumes, consisting of twenty-four tales written in verse with a prologue and a linking narrative, and describing a medieval ▷ Utopia which offers an alternative to the industrial society of the mid-19th century. One of the verse tales, *Atalanta's Race*, tells the story of the legendary Atalanta, a beautiful girl famed for her speed. To win her, suitors had to beat her in a race or else be killed by her dart. She was eventually beaten by Milanion, who distracted her by throwing down three golden apples. Atalanta is also celebrated by ▷ Swinburne in ▷ *Atalanta in Calydon*. The poem proved popular with the Victorian public and helped establish Morris as one of the leading poets of the day.

▷ Pre-Raphaelite Brotherhood; medievalism.

### East Lynne (1861)

A novel of ▷ sensation by ▷ Mrs Henry Wood. Lady Isabel Vane mistakenly believes her husband to be having an affair, and runs away with rakish Frank Levison. Her fate as a ▷ 'fallen woman' is one of the most appalling in Victorian literature. She has a child, is deserted, crippled in a train crash and reported dead, then returns home in disguise to become ▷ governess to her own children. In the meantime, her husband has married the woman Isabel believed he was involved with. Her final punishment is having to watch her son die without revealing her identity to him. The book was favourably reviewed in *The Times*, sold over 2.5 million copies by 1900, was translated into several languages and adapted into a stage melodrama. Conventional Victorian values towards ▷ marriage and the family are forcibly driven home, and Wood displays an almost sadistic relish in her punitive treatment of Isabel.

▷ *Cometh Up as a Flower*.

### Eden, Emily (1797–1869)

The daughter of William Eden, the first Baron Auckland, Emily Eden was born in Westminster. She was a close friend of Prime Minister Melbourne, who appointed her brother George Governor General of India in 1835. She went with him and her sister Frances, and acted as his hostess until their return in 1842, and in London till 1849. She was a member of the highest social circles and many celebrities visited her house where she held morning gatherings. She was unable to go out due to ill health. In 1844 she published *Portraits of the People and Princes of India*, and

then in 1866 and 1872 *Up the Country; Letters Written from the Upper Provinces of India*. In 1919 her great-niece edited a further selection of her letters. Her novels, *The Semi-detached House* (1859), published anonymously, and *The Semi-attached Couple* (1860), by 'E. E.', were written some thirty years previously. They portray fashionable society with good-humoured wit and owe something to Jane Austen (1775–1817), whom Eden much admired.

▷ Colonialism.

### Edinburgh Review (1807–1929)

A quarterly periodical founded by critics Francis Jeffrey (1773–1850), Sydney Smith (1771–1845) and Henry Brougham (1778–1868) in 1802. It introduced a new seriousness into literary criticism and generally took a moderate ▷ Whig position in politics. Jeffrey's literary taste was rigidly classicist and he had little sympathy with the 'Lake Poets', William Wordsworth (1770–1850), Samuel Taylor Coleridge (1772–1834) and Robert Southey (1774–1843). The term originates in the *Edinburgh Review*, Oct. 1807. Later contributors were ▷ Thomas Babington Macaulay, William Hazlitt (1778–1830), ▷ Thomas Carlyle and ▷ Matthew Arnold.

▷ *Blackwood's Magazine*; Romanticism; *The Spectator*.

### Education

In 19th-century England *laissez faire* policies meant that the state was reluctant to undertake national systems of education of any sort. England was well behind the most advanced European countries, especially Prussia, in this respect. Wealthy and middle-class children were usually educated at home by ▷ governesses or private tutors and the boys were then sent to boarding schools. Private boarding schools for girls were rare but increased in number after the middle of the century. Grace Melbury in ▷ Thomas Hardy's ▷ *The Woodlanders* attends a boarding school in 'a fashionable suburb of a fast city' and her education places her in a different class from that occupied by her lover Giles Winterbourne. Rosamund Vincy, from ▷ George Eliot's ▷ *Middlemarch*, is similarly elevated by her boarding school education at Miss Lemon's school. Lowood School, where ▷ Charlotte Brontë's Jane Eyre suffers disgusting food, cold and cruelty, is based on the Clergy Daughters School at Cowan Bridge established for the daughters of poor Evangelical clergy and is an altogether different establishment. It has its counterpart in Dotheboys Hall in ▷ Charles Dickens's ▷ Nicholas Nickleby, where the master Wackford Squeers also starves and ill-treats his pupils.

The education of the poorer sections of society was placed entirely in the realm of private or philanthropic enterprise and, at the beginning of the period, it was unsystematic and inconsistent. The principal reason for this slow development was the religious divisions of public opinion. The medieval assumption that education must fundamentally be the concern of the Church faded very slowly in England. The schools for the majority of children in the first part of the 19th century were controlled by rival Anglican and Dissenting movements (▷ Religious groups): the National Society for the Education of the Poor in the Principles of the Established Church (which provided National Schools), and the British and Foreign School Society respectively. Until 1870, the National Society was responsible for most of the schools for the poor. It gave a fairly intensive education in the Bible as well as elementary education of a general description. Richard Phillotson in ▷ Thomas Hardy's ▷ Jude the Obscure is a National schoolmaster and Jude is one of the most powerful indictments of the education of the poor in the Victorian period. Since the Church of England was the established Church of the state, it claimed that it should have a monopoly of religious instruction in any state system, a claim that was strongly resisted by the Dissenters. In ▷ Charlotte Brontë's ▷ Shirley (1849) there is an account of rival school feasts organized by the Church and by the Dissenters in which the Church gets decidedly the better of the fray (▷ Dissenter's Schools and Academies). In 1829 the ▷ Catholics also joined in the provision of voluntary schools. Sunday Schools had been in existence since 1780 for the education of the children of the poor on the one day in the week on which they were likely to be free from employment. In 1833, the government for the first time acknowledged some responsibility independent of the Churches by granting a subsidy of £20,000 for school buildings, to whichever society chose to build them. Since Britain was, by then, the richest country in the world, the sum was contemptibly small. In 1839 these grants became annual and were administered by a committee of the Privy Council, voluntary schools in receipt of grants were inspected, and this was the beginning of the ministry of education. Mr McChoakumchild's performance in Thomas Gradgrind's model school is assessed by a school inspector in ▷ Charles Dickens's ▷ Hard Times.

Until 1870, the important advances towards nationwide state education remained in private hands. The most important of these advances, though it affected only a minority, was in the ▷ public school system. By the early 19th century many of the public schools had been allowed to decline. Others, including Winchester, Eton, Harrow, Westminster and ▷ Rugby, drew their pupils predominantly from the upper classes and suffered from serious discipline problems. The character of these schools changed largely due to the influence of ▷ Thomas Arnold, headmaster of Rugby from 1828 to 1842, and father of ▷ Matthew Arnold. Thomas Arnold believed that education should train the whole character of a boy and not merely his mind. The guiding principle of the public schools became that of the Roman poet Juvenal (AD ?60–?130), writing at a time when the Roman Empire had a corresponding greatness to that of Britain after Arnold: 'mens sana in corpore sano' – 'a healthy mind in a healthy body' (▷ Imperialism). A consequence of this maxim, though Arnold himself never emphasized it, was that athletics became an essential element in public school education. Hitherto, sport had been discouraged rather than otherwise by educational institutions, as tending to disorderly conduct, but public schools gave it such importance that in many of them it came to exceed the prestige of scholarship (▷ Tom Brown's Schooldays). Arnold's Rugby not only introduced new standards into the public schools, but it had two further important results. One was that it gave real significance to boarding school education; the boys lived at the school for three-quarters of the year, not, as before, merely because conditions of travel were difficult, but because the school could thereby educate the boy during his leisure as well as in the classroom, an important consideration when it was a question of educating his whole character, and when sport was an essential part of this character training. The second result was that many new schools were founded, so that until 1950 a public school education became the norm, not only for upper-class boys, but for the sons of professional men and the more prosperous businessmen as well.

There were special social and political reasons for this adoption of public school education by the middle classes. One was the continuing prestige of the English aristocracy. The middle-class businessman, especially if he had raised himself from a lower rank in society, wanted his son to be a ▷ 'gentleman', and was prepared to take on the burden of high public school fees. In many cases the secondary education of girls was sacrificed in order to pay for that of their brothers. In some families girls were sent to finishing schools where the emphasis was on behaviour and artistic accomplishments. Many of these were situated in France, Germany or Switzerland to facilitate the learning of a foreign language. The Pensionnat de Demoiselles in Charlotte Brontë's ▷ *Villette* is an example of a modest finishing school. There was a more important reason for the popularity of the public schools. Britain, by 1850, was the centre of the largest overseas empire that the world had ever seen. This great empire required an unprecedented number of administrators, who had to be men of high moral quality and courage, as well as of good ability. The aristocracy could not provide them all itself, and would have aroused social resentment had it tried; they came, therefore, from preponderantly middle-class backgrounds, and it was the public schools which gave them the education considered necessary to qualify them for the function.

In some respects, however, the expansion of the public schools had an unfortunate effect on the development of English society and education. By giving the governing classes the recruits they needed, the public schools tended to prolong the complacent indifference of the state to its educational responsibilities. Secondly, since the public school tradition was almost entirely an Anglican one, the public schools also prolonged the opposition between the Dissenters and the Anglicans over education. Thirdly, but most importantly, the public schools made more conspicuous the social gulf between the richer and poorer classes.

Universal elementary education was introduced by Forster's Elementary Education Act of 1870, which provided state education for all at the primary level (to the age of eleven) by means of Board Schools, wherever the Church schools were inadequate. Primary education became compulsory for all children throughout England and Wales in 1880 and fees were abolished in the majority of schools by 1891. Secondary education was still administered by voluntary and private organizations, and by the public schools until 1902 when Balfour's Act provided compulsory education up to the age of fourteen, and placed secondary schools under the authority of the local government County Councils.

The 19th century witnessed the founding of several new universities as well as a number of girl's high schools and boarding schools where the education on offer approached that in boy's grammar and public schools (▷ Education of Women). The period also saw the establishment of teacher training colleges such as the Training School at Melchester attended by Sue Bridehead in *Jude the Obscure*. Towards the end of the century departments of education were provided in universities and university colleges to train postgraduates to become teachers. Technical schools offered industrial and craft skills from the second half of the 19th century. They had their origins in the voluntarily established Mechanics' Institutes designed to provide further education for the new class of skilled worker: the 'mechanics' of the iron, steel and engineering industries who were a product of the Industrial Revolution, and who had been enfranchised by the ▷ Reform Bill of 1867. They began in Scotland, where education in general since the Reformation was more widely extended and popularly sought than in England. It was the Scottish lawyer, statesman, and man of letters Henry Brougham (1778–1869) who brought the movement to England. By 1824, the London Institute had 1500 artisans subscribing one guinea a year for their instruction, which was conducted in the evenings.

## Education of Women

During the pre-Victorian period, middle-class girls' education took place either under the tutelage of ▷ governesses or family members, or at schools where 'feminine accomplishments' were taught. The education of working-class girls was even more limited and haphazard. It was possible to attend a Church school and receive elementary instruction, but the majority did not. The first investigation of girls' schools – *The Report of the Taunton Commission* in 1867 – revealed the parlous state of female education.

The 1830s saw the first significant protest against the inadequacy of educational opportunity, but as with the ▷ women's suffrage campaign, these protests tended to issue from the middle classes, who were generally unconcerned about their poorer sisters. ▷ Tennyson's ▷ *The Princess* (1850) advocates educational opportunities for women and the eponymous heroine actually founds a university for this purpose. Campaigners were primarily concerned with improving the education of governesses; this group formed the majority of students at Queen's College in London when it opened in 1848. Queen's was more like a secondary school than a college, but it nevertheless offered a range of courses previously unavailable to women. It was also open to all 'ladies' over the age of twelve, and among its first students were writers ▷ Jean Ingelow and ▷ Adelaide Procter.

In 1869 Emily Davies launched the campaign for higher education; in the same year ▷ Frances Power Cobbe read a conference paper calling for 'University Degrees for Women'. Despite fierce resistance from large sections of society who felt that women were constitutionally incapable of intellectual achievement, the campaigners slowly gained ground. In 1878 London University awarded its first degrees to women. 1892 saw the universities of Edinburgh, Glasgow, St Andrew's and Aberdeen following suit, but Oxford and Cambridge did not give such degrees before 1920 and 1921 respectively, although both had affiliated women's colleges (Girton, 1869 and Newnham, 1875 were founded in Cambridge and others followed at Oxford). All this was despite warnings from medical men that cerebral development in the female must be at the cost of physiological, ie child-bearing, aptitude. Women writers actively involved in the campaign for education included ▷ Mathilde Blind, ▷ Barbara Bodichon, ▷ Mona Caird, ▷ Harriet Martineau, ▷ Emily Pfeiffer, ▷ Catherine Sinclair and ▷ Elizabeth Wolstenholme-Elmy. Since the commencement of state education in 1870, the status of women teachers has been brought equal to that of men teachers, and since 1902 equal secondary education has been provided for both sexes.

▷ 'Woman Question, The'; Education; Woman's Movement, The.
**Bib:** Kamm, J., *Hope Deferred: Girl's Education in English History*.

### Edwards, Amelia (1831–92)

Novelist, short story and ▷ travel writer. She was born in Weston-super-Mare and educated at home by her mother. After working as a journalist, she published her first novel, *My Brother's Wife*, in 1855. She subsequently wrote several more romantic novels and two historical works, *The History of France* (1856) and *A Summary of English History* (1858), before editing a collection of poetry, *Home Thoughts and Home Themes* (1865). She contributed a number of notable ghost stories to leading periodicals of the day

before turning her attention to travel writing in the 1870s. *A Thousand Miles up the Nile* (1877) was a highly successful account of her journey through Egypt to the Nubian desert. Edwards then became an enthusiastic and learned Egyptologist, publishing a further work, *Pharaohs, Fellahs and Explorers* (1892), as well as translating a manual on Egyptian archaeology and lecturing on the subject in Britain and North America, earning herself an honorary doctorate from Columbia University.

### Edwin Drood, The Mystery of (1870)

A novel by ▷ Charles Dickens, unfinished at his death. The novel begins in a cathedral town (based on Rochester); the plot turns on the engagement of Edwin and Rosa Bud, who do not really love each other, and the rivalry for Rosa's love of Edwin's sinister uncle, John Jasper, and an exotic newcomer to the town, Neville Landless. Edwin disappears and Neville is arrested for his murder; Rosa flees to London to escape Jasper; on her behalf the forces for good are rallying in the shape of Rosa's guardian, Mr Grewgious, a clergyman called Crisparkle and a mysterious stranger, Mr Datchery, when the story breaks off. The fragment is quite sufficient to show that Dickens was not losing his powers. The sombreness and the grotesque comedy are equal to the best in his previous works. There have been numerous attempts to end the novel but none of any particular note.

### Egdon Heath

A gloomy tract of country which is the Dorsetshire setting for ▷ Thomas Hardy's novel ▷ *The Return of the Native*. As often in Hardy's novels, the place is not merely a background to the events but exercises an active influence upon them.

### Egerton, George (1859–1945)

The ▷ pseudonym of novelist and short story writer Mary Chavelita Dunne. She was born in Melbourne, Australia, and travelled widely as a young woman. In 1887 she eloped with Henry Higginson to Norway. She later married George Egerton Clairmonte and moved to Ireland where she began to write seriously. Her most successful works were two volumes of short stories, ▷ *Keynotes* (1893) and *Discords* (1894). The stories challenged patriarchal attitudes, and Egerton became associated with the ▷ 'New Woman' movement. Her later writing did not live up to her early potential and she faded from view. Later works include *Fantasias* (1898); *Rosa Amorosa* (1901) and *Flies in Amber* (1905).

Bib: Cunningham, G., *The New Woman and the Fictions of the 1890s*.

## Egoist, The (1879)

One of the most admired novels by ▷ George Meredith. The 'egoist' is the rich and fashionable Sir Willoughby Patterne, who is intolerably self-centred and conceited. The story concerns his courting of Clara Middleton and her fight for independence from his assertiveness. Willoughby is opposed by Vernon Whitford, who is austere, honest and discerning, the tutor of Willoughby's poor relation, Crossjay, a boy whose vigorous animal spirits are accompanied by deep and spontaneous feeling. Partly owing to Crossjay, Clara is eventually enabled to evade Willoughby's advances, which have been backed by her father whose luxurious tastes Willoughby has indulged. She marries Whitford, a conclusion which is a victory for integrity over deceitful subtlety. The story is told with the brilliance of Meredith's rather mannered wit and is interspersed with exuberant passages of natural description symbolically related to the theme. Though Meredith's mannerism has lost the book some of its former prestige, his analysis of self-deceit and his understanding of the physical components of strong feeling make *The Egoist* an anticipation of kinds of fiction more characteristic of the 20th century.
▷ Gentleman.

## Eliot, George (1819–80)

Pen-name of the novelist Mary Ann Evans (at different times of her life she also spelt the name Mary Anne, Marian and Marianne). She was the daughter of a land-agent in the rural midlands (Warwickshire); her father's work (the management of estates) gave her wide experience of country society and this was greatly to enrich her insight and the scope of her novels. Brought up in a narrow religious tradition, in her early twenties she adopted ▷ agnostic opinions about Christian doctrine but she remained steadfast in the ethical teachings associated with it. She began her literary career with translations from the German of two works of religious speculation (▷ German influence on Victorian literature); in 1851 she became assistant editor of the ▷ *Westminster Review*, a journal of great intellectual prestige in London. Her friendship with ▷ George Lewes led to a union between them which they both regarded as amounting to ▷ marriage; this was a bold decision in view of the rigid opposition in the English society of the time to open unions not legalized by the marriage ceremony.

Her first fiction consisted of tales later collected together as ▷ *Scenes of Clerical Life*. Then came her series of full-length novels: ▷ *Adam Bede* (1859), ▷ *The Mill on the Floss* (1860), ▷ *Silas Marner* (1861), ▷ *Romola* (1862–3), ▷ *Felix Holt* (1866), ▷ *Middlemarch* (1871–2) and ▷ *Daniel Deronda* (1876). Up till *Romola* the novels and tales deal with life in the countryside in which she was brought up; the society is depicted as a strong and stable one, and the novelist combines in an unusual degree sharp, humorous observation and intelligent imaginative sympathy. *Romola* marks a dividing point; it is a ▷ historical novel about the society of the Italian city of Florence in the 15th century. As a work of imaginative literature it is usually regarded as scholarly but dead; however, it seems to have opened the way to the more comprehensive treatment of English society in her last three novels, in which the relationship of the individual to society is interpreted with an intelligence outstanding in the history of the English novel and often compared with the genius of the Russian novelist, ▷ Leo Tolstoy (1828–1910). Her critical reputation has varied; it declined somewhat after her death, her powerful intellect being considered to damage her creativity. She was defended by ▷ Virginia Woolf (1882–1941) in an essay in 1919, but was really re-established by inclusion in F.R. Leavis's *The Great Tradition* (1948). With the rapid strides in feminist criticism in the 1980s, however, Eliot has been reclaimed as a major influence on women's writing and her works have been the focus of numerous feminist critiques, eg S. Gilbert and S. Gubar, *The Madwoman in the Attic* (1979).

George Eliot's poetry (*The Spanish Gipsy*, 1868, and *The Legend of Jubal*, 1870) is now little regarded but her essays for the *Westminster Review* include work of distinction and she published a collection, *The Impressions of Theophrastus Such*, in 1879.

In 1880, George Lewes having died, she married John Walter Cross, but she died in the same year.

Bib: Haight, G.S., *Life*; Leavis, F.R., in *The Great Tradition*; Bennett, J., *George Eliot: Her Mind and her Art*; Harvey, W.J., *The Art of George Eliot*; Pond, E.J., *Les Idées Morales et Réligieuses de George Eliot*; Hardy, B., *The Art of George Eliot*; Roberts, N., *George Eliot: Her Beliefs and Her Art*; Newton, K.M., *George Eliot*; Norbelie, B.A., *Oppressive Narrowness: A Study of the Female Community in George Eliot's Early Writings*.

### *Eliza Cook's Journal* (1849–54)

A journal written and edited (almost single-handedly), by ▷ Eliza Cook, English poet and essayist. It was aimed at middle-class women and attempted to inform and entertain as well intervene in debates around the ▷ 'Woman Question'. It included reviews, essays, poetry and sketches, and treated such subjects as the position of working women, the need for legal reform, the construction of the 'old maid' and the inadequacy of girls' ▷ education. It ceased publishing after five years due to Cook's ill-health, but much material was later included in *Jottings from My Journal* (1860).

### Ellis, Henry Havelock (1859–1939)

Psychologist and essayist. Part of his work was scientific: *Man and Woman* (1894); *Studies in the Psychology of Sex* (1897–1910). Part of it was literary and expressed in reflective essays: *Little Essays in Love and Virtue* (1922); *Impressions and Comments* (1914–23); *The Dance of Life* (1923). In the latter work he exemplified the revival of the essay as a reflective form early in this century. He was a friend of the novelist ▷ Olive Schreiner. **Bib:** Calder Marshall, A., *Life*; Collis, J.S., *An Artist of Life*.

### 'Empedocles on Etna' (1852)

A poem by Matthew Arnold, and the most famous account of the legendary death of Empedocles, philosopher and statesman of the Greek colony of Agrigentum in Sicily, who is said to have led the people against the tyrannical government of a powerful class and then to have refused to become their king. According to legend he met his death in the volcano of Etna, though in reality he seems to have died in Greece. In the poem the philosopher is counselled by a physician, Pausanias, and a poet, Callicles, but neither is able to dispel his despair and he throws himself into the crater of Mount Etna – a disillusioned and banished political leader. Arnold's own scepticism is expressed within the poem.

### Endymion (1880)

▷ Benjamin Disraeli's last novel. Set in the period between the end of Lord Liverpool's government in 1827 and the start of Disraeli's own political career, it traces the fortunes of the twin children of a promising politician who dies penniless. Myra Pitt Ferrars succeeds due to her beauty and wit and her husband, the Foreign Secretary Lord Roehampton, intervenes on behalf of her brother Endymion. Lord Palmerston is thinly disguised as Lord Roehampton and the character St Barbe bears a resemblance to ▷ Thackeray.

### 'Enoch Arden'

A poem by ▷ Tennyson written in 1861 and 1862 and published in *Enoch Arden and Other Poems* in 1864, which brought its author £6000 in one year. It was one of the most popular of Tennyson's poems in its day. Based on a story furnished by his sculptor friend, Thomas Woolner, it tells of a man who returns from a voyage of many years, having undertaken to save his wife and children from penury, to find her happily remarried. Rather than destroy her happiness he conceals the fact of his return and lives alone for the rest of his life. His literal and symbolic isolation is powerfully realized in the description of his shipwreck on a lonely island, and in the moment when he renounces his wife and children after seeing the new family through the window. Enoch Arden is associated with Christ, and with Ulysses, who figures again in Tennyson's powerful lyric 'Crossing the Bar'. The theme is common to ▷ Elizabeth Gaskell's *Sylvia's Lovers* and ▷ Adelaide Anne Procter's poem 'Homeward Bound'.

### Erewhon (1872) and Erewhon Revisited (1901)

Satirical anti-utopias by ▷ Samuel Butler. Sir Thomas More's *Utopia* is a description of an ideal country as different as possible from England. Erewhon (an anagram of 'Nowhere') represents a country many of whose characteristics are analogous to English ones, caricatured and satirized. Thus Butler satirizes ecclesiastical institutions through the Musical Banks and parental tyranny through the Birth Formulae; machinery has to be abolished before it takes over from human beings. In *Erewhon Revisited*, Higgs, the English discoverer of Erewhon, finds that his previous departure by balloon has been used by Professors Hanky and Panky ('hanky-panky' is deceitful practice) to impose a new religion, according to which Higgs is worshipped as a child of the sun. Butler's method in these satires resembles Jonathan Swift's satirical technique in the Lilliput of *Gulliver's Travels* (1726).
  ▷ Utopian literature.

### Essays in Criticism (1865, 1888)

The two volumes (First Series 1865; Second Series 1888) that contain much of the most important of ▷ Matthew Arnold's literary critical work. The first volume opens with 'The Function of Criticism at the Present Time', a discussion of the relevance of criticism both to creative literature and to society and civilization; it is an example of what the poet T. Eliot (1888–1965) was later to call Arnold's 'propaganda for criticism', and it has been influential among 20th-century critics. The second essay, 'The Literary Influence of Academies', makes a case for authoritative standards in culture, and constitutes an implicit criticism of the habits of English culture, again in a way that is still relevant. The remainder of the first volume comprises essays on foreign writers and literature. The Second Series opens with a striking essay on 'The Study of Poetry', in which Arnold puts his view that poetry will supply to the modern world the kind of inspiration that was afforded by great religions in the past – a view which has also been put forward in the 20th century, notably by I.A. Richards in *The Principles of Literary Criticism* (1924), though he expresses the view in other terms. The remainder of the Second Series consists principally of studies of English poets of the 18th and 19th centuries. On the whole, Arnold's fame rests more on the broad themes of the relationships of literature and society than on his particular studies, though some of these, eg on the German poet Heinrich Heine in the First Series, are of great interest.

### Esther Waters (1894)

A novel by ▷ George Moore, this sympathetic treatment of a servant girl seduced brought him instant success. Esther is a member of the Plymouth Brethren who goes into service at Woodview for the Barfield family to escape her drunken father. Aged only seventeen, she is seduced and deserted by the footman William Latch. Dismissed from her position, Esther endures a bitter and humiliating struggle to rear her son. She rejects an offer of marriage from a respectable Salvationist and marries William Latch for the sake of their son. In addition to being a good husband and father Latch is also a publican and bookmaker and is ruined both physically and financially by his involvement in horse racing. He dies leaving the family destitute, but Esther's son soon becomes independent. Esther returns to Woodview at the close of the novel and to the widowed and impoverished Mrs Barfield who was previously kind to her. Here she finds peace and fulfilment. *Esther Waters* shares many similarities with ▷ Hardy's ▷ *Tess of the d'Urbervilles* (1891) but the former is less naturalistic and its

heroine is resourceful and enduring rather than tragic.

▷ 'Fallen Woman, The'.

### Ethnography

The term used in the 19th century for what later came to be known as anthropology: it refers to the descriptive studies of customs of particular tribes or peoples of particular regions. Pioneered in Britain by J.C. Prichard (1786–1848), it did not simply study cultural phenomena but implicitly ranked them in a hierarchy of degrees of civilization. Philology, one of the disciplines included in the science, was also subject to this politicization.

### Europeans, The (1878)

A novel by ▷ Henry James, first published serially in *The Atlantic Monthly* from July to October 1878. Alongside ▷ *Daisy Miller*, which appeared in same year, it opened up the international theme in James's writing, using the ▷ 'novel of manners' style to contrast two cultures – Europe and the USA.

### Eustace Diamonds, The (1873)

A novel by ▷ Anthony Trollope initially serialized in ▷ *The Fortnightly Review* from 1871–73, and forming the third in the ▷ Palliser sequence. The novel shares many of the concerns of ▷ Wilkie Collins's *The Moonstone* (1868).

### Evangelical Movement

A movement for Protestant revival in the Church of England in the late 18th and early 19th century. It was stimulated partly by John Wesley's (1703–91) Methodist revival and the activities of other sects (especially among the working classes) outside the Church of England; it was also a reaction against the rationalism and scepticism of the 18th-century aristocracy and against the ▷ atheism of the French Revolution (1789–94). Politically, the movement tended to be conservative and was therefore strong among the Tories, whereas the ▷ Whigs (especially their aristocratic leaders such as Charles James Fox, 1749–1806) retained more of the 18th-century worldliness and scepticism. In doctrine the Evangelicals were inclined to be austere, to attach importance to strength of faith and biblical guidance and to oppose ceremony and ritual. Socially they developed a strong sense of responsibility to their fellow human beings, so that one of their leaders, William Wilberforce (1759–1833), devoted his life to the cause of abolishing slavery and the slave trade in British dominions, and

later Lord Shaftesbury (1801–81) made
it his life-work to alleviate the social and
working condition of the working classes.
The leaders of the movements were
laymen rather than clergy, and upper
class rather than lower class, amongst
whom the Nonconformist sects were more
actively influential. As the Noncomformists
were to contribute to English socialism
later in the century a religious rather
than a ▷ Marxist inspiration, so the
Evangelicals later led to generations of
highly responsible, independent-minded
intellectuals such as historians Thomas
Babington Macaulay and G.M Trevelyan
(1876–1962).
  ▷ Religious Groups.

**Ewing, Juliana Horatia (1841–85)**
Writer of ▷ children's literature. Born in
Ecclesfield, Yorkshire, the daughter of
▷ Margaret Gatty. Her first published story
was in ▷ Charlotte Yonge's *Monthly Packet*
in 1861. She also contributed to her mother's
periodical for children, *Aunt Judy's Magazine*,
taking over its editorship in 1873. She was an
extremely prolific writer and very popular in her
time, though her sentimental and moralizing
tone makes her less liked by children today. Her
stories include: *Mrs Overtheway's Remembrances*
(1866–8); *The Brownies* (1865); *Jan of the
Windmill* (1872) and *Jackanapes* (1879).
**Bib:** Eden, Mrs H.F.K., *Juliana Horatia
Ewing and her Books.*

# F

**Fabian Society**

A large society of socialistic intellectuals, closely bound up with the British Labour Party. It was founded in 1884 and named after the Roman general Fabius Cunctator – 'Fabius the Delayer' – who in the 3rd century BC saved Rome from the Carthaginian army under Hannibal, by using a policy of attrition instead of open battle, ie he destroyed the army by small attacks on isolated sections of it, instead of risking total defeat by confronting Hannibal with the entire Roman army. The Fabian Society similarly advocates socialism by piecemeal action through parliamentary reform instead of risking disaster by total revolution; this policy has been summarized in the phrase 'the inevitability of gradualness'. The Fabians were among the principal influences leading to the foundation of the Labour Party in 1900. The years between 1884 and 1900 were those of its greatest distinction; they were led by ▷ George Bernard Shaw, and Sidney and ▷ Beatrice Webb, and made their impact through the Fabian Essays on social and economic problems. They always advocated substantial thinking on solid evidence, in contrast to the more idealistic and 'utopian' socialism of such writers as ▷ William Morris.

**Factories**

In the sense of industrial buildings in which large numbers of people were at work under one roof, as opposed to domestic industry with the workers in their own homes, factories existed to some extent in the 16th century. It was in the 18th century, however, with the invention of labour-saving machines and then of steam power to drive them, that the factory system became general. Pockets of domestic industry continued well into the 19th century, but it became increasingly the exception. Large industrial towns grew up haphazardly to accommodate the new factories; there is a vivid description of an extreme example in ▷ Benjamin Disraeli's novel ▷ Sybil. The employment of masses of labour tended to dehumanize relations between employer and employees, and instigated a new kind of class war; ▷ Elizabeth Gaskell's novels ▷ North and South and ▷ Mary Barton, and ▷ Charles Dickens's ▷ Hard Times illustrate this. The first Factory Act to have an important effect on the improvement of conditions was that of 1833; by then the public conscience was truly aroused and the Ten Hours Act of 1847 restricted hours of labour. The main intention of the early Factory Acts was to prevent the employment of young children and to limit the hours of employment of women; they were made effective by the use of Factory Inspectors. Later Factory Acts have sought to prevent the use of dangerous machinery and to ensure that factories were healthy places to work in. Some employers came to see that it was in their own interests to make factory conditions as healthy and pleasant as possible: Andrew Undershaft in ▷ George Bernard Shaw's play *Major Barbara* is an example of an enlightened factory owner of the 20th-century sort.

Another use of the word 'factory' is to denote a centre for 'factors', ie men of commerce who transact trade on behalf of their employers. In the 18th century the East India Company established such factories in India, eg at Madras.

▷ Anti-industrialism; Capitalism.

**'Fallen Woman, The'**

A number of British women writers addressed the subject of the 'fallen woman' in the latter half of the 19th century. Sympathetic representations include ▷ Elizabeth Gaskell's ▷ *Ruth*, and Marion Erle in ▷ Elizabeth Barrett Browning's ▷ *Aurora Leigh*. Both these works brought attention to the sexual double standard, and both figure maternal love as the path of redemption for the woman. In other novels such as ▷ Mrs Henry Wood's ▷ *East Lynne* the errant woman was cruelly punished in the course of the narrative, serving as a warning to women readers.

▷ 'Castaway, A'; Orphans; Webster, Augusta; *Tess of the d'Urbervilles; Adam Bede; Esther Waters*.

**Far from the Madding Crowd (1874)**

A novel by ▷ Thomas Hardy. The title is a quotation from *Elegy Written in a Country Churchyard* (1751) by Thomas Gray (1716–71). It is one of Hardy's ▷ Wessex novels, and the first of real substance, following the comparatively slight ▷ *Under the Greenwood Tree*. The central character is Bathsheba Everdene, who is loved by three men: Farmer Boldwood, a solid but passionate squire; Gabriel Oak, a shepherd, who loves her with quiet constancy and wins her in the end, and the glamorous soldier, Sergeant Troy, whom she marries first. Troy combines fascinating gallantry with ruthless egoism; he allows his wife-to-be, Fanny Robin, to die in a workhouse, and is capricious and cruel to Bathsheba; he is eventually murdered by Boldwood. A crude outline such as this brings out the ballad-like quality of the story, characteristic of all Hardy's novels but more subtly rendered in later ones. Its distinction of substance is in Hardy's intimate understanding and presentation of the rural surroundings of the characters, and in the contrast between the urbane attractions of Troy and the rough but environmentally vigorous qualities of Boldwood and Oak. Bathsheba herself is a capricious and colourful heroine, not presented with psychological depth but with confident assertiveness which makes her convincing.

## Fashionable Novel, The (The 'Silver-fork' School)

A genre popular in Britain between 1825 and 1850. Typically, such novels concentrate on describing the lives of the wealthy and feature glamorous heroines in search of love, marriage and luxury. Even at the time there was debate as to whether these novels unquestioningly praised the seemingly empty lives of their heroes and heroines (the term comes from 'silver-fork polisher', which means to compliment those wealthy enough to possess such cutlery), or whether they were in fact subtle satires. A significant aspect of the genre is its focus on contemporary fashion; the novels often served as handbooks on the latest styles, referring explicitly to particular London shops and dressmakers. Practitioners of the genre include Susan Ferrier (1782–1854), ▷ Catherine Gore and ▷ Frances Trollope. In *The Silver-Fork School: Novels of Fashion Preceding Vanity Fair*, M.W. Rosa discusses the work of male and female 'fashionable' authors and argues that the genre reached its apotheosis in ▷ Thackeray's ▷ *Vanity Fair* (1847–8).
**Bib:** Adburgham, A., *Silver Fork Society: Fashionable Life and Literature 1814–1840*.

## Felix Holt the Radical (1866)

A novel by ▷ George Eliot. The hero is a talented young working man who makes it his vocation to educate the political intelligence of his fellow-workers. His rival for the love of Esther Lyon, the daughter of a Nonconformist (▷ religious groups) minister, is the local landowner, Harold Transome, also a radical politician, though pursuing a more conventional career. George Eliot makes Holt utter high-minded speeches which weaken the reality he is supposed to possess. On the other hand, a subsidiary theme which concerns Harold Transome's mother, the secret of Harold's illegitimacy, and his hostility to the lawyer, Jermyn, who is really his father,

is treated so well that it is among the best examples of George Eliot's art.

## Feminism

The term 'feminist' was not in general use until the last decade of the 19th century. The word *'feministe'* was used in 1894 in an article in the *Daily News* to describe a supporter of 'feminism': the 'advocacy of the rights of women based on the theory of the equality of the sexes'.
▷ Women's Movement, The.

## Feminist publishing

The history of feminist publishing in Britain can be traced back to the mid-19th century, when Emily Faithfull founded the Victoria Press in 1860, and went on to co-found, with Emma Anne Paterson, the Women's Printing Society in 1876. The latter had a distinct agenda with clearly defined feminist goals. The ▷ women's suffrage movement had the greatest generating effect for feminist publishing. The Woman's Press was responsible for publishing the work of the Women's Freedom League, and the Women's Writers' Suffrage League, founded in 1908 by Cicely Hamilton (1872–1952) and Bessie Hatton, published many pamphlets for the suffrage cause – most notably May Sinclair's 'Feminism' (1912).

## Fenians

An Irish patriotic and revolutionary society founded by Irish immigrants to the USA in 1858; its aim was to unite Irishmen all over the world to secure the independence of Ireland from British rule. The original Fenians were a semi-legendary band of warriors under the leadership of Finn Mac Coul, said to have lived in the 3rd century AD.
▷ Irish literature in English.

## Field, Michael (Katherine Bradley, 1846–1914 and Edith Cooper, 1862–1913)

Collaborative poets and dramatists. Katherine Bradley moved to the home of her niece, Edith Cooper, in 1865, and thereafter the two women were devoted and constant companions, viewing themselves as a spiritual partnership – 'closer married' than their friends the Brownings – until Edith's death in 1913. Although they sometimes published separately under the ▷ pseudonyms Arran (Katherine) and Isla (Edith) Leigh, they first collaborated, using these pseudonyms, in a volume of poems, *Bellerophon*, and in the first 'Michael Field' play, *Callirrhoe* (1884), which

was widely acclaimed. Enjoying a private income they produced twenty-seven tragic dramas and eight volumes of verse, all written in partnership and often published in limited editions. Centring mostly on classical and historical subjects, only one of their plays was ever performed, but their poetry is notable for its sensuousness, passion and mysticism, and includes love poems to each other. Their verse collections include *Long Ago* (1889) based on poems by Sappho the Greek poet; (7th–6th century BC) *Underneath the Bough* (1893); *Wild Honey from Various Thyme* (1908); *Poems of Adoration* (1912) written by Edith, and *Mystic Trees* (1913), written mainly by Katherine. The two women also co-wrote a journal, *Works and Day*, extracts from which were published in 1933 (ed. T. and D.C. Moore). In 1907 they converted to Catholicism. They lived together almost all their lives, dying of cancer within months of each other.
  ▷ Lesbianism
**Bib:** Sturgeon, M., *Michael Field*; Hickok, K., *Representations of Women: 19th Century British Women's Poetry*; Faderman, L., *Surpassing the Love of Men*; Leighton, A., *Victorian Women Poets: Writing Against the Heart*.

### Fitz-Boodle, George Savage

The pen-name assumed by the novelist ▷ William Makepeace Thackeray for the 'Fitz-Boodle Papers' he contributed to ▷ *Fraser's Magazine*, 1842–3.

### FitzGerald, Edward (1809–93)

Translator and poet; chiefly known for his extremely popular translation of the Persian poem ▷ *The Rubaiyat of Omar Khayyam* (1859). He also published *Euphranor* (1851), a ▷ Platonic dialogue; translations of *Six Dramas of Calderon* (1853), and in 1865, a translation of ▷ Aeschylus' *Agamemnon*. His delicate praise of a life of pleasure and his enjoyment of beauty, evident in his *Rubaiyat*, countered the moral earnestness of the age and influenced the 'anti-Victorian' ▷ Pre-Raphaelite and ▷ Aesthetic movements later in the century.
**Bib:** Benson, A. C., *FitzGerald*; Terhune, A. M., *Life*; Campbell, A. Y., in *Great Victorians*, eds. Massingham, A. J. and H.

### Flaubert, Gustave (1821–80)

French novelist. His first novel, *Madame Bovary*, involved him in a court action for immorality on its publication in 1857. The story of the adultery of a doctor's wife in Normandy, it ironizes not only the

▷ Romanticism of the principal character, but also the unappealing bourgeois values of the characters around her and the parochial milieu from which she attempts to escape. The book is equally notable for its contribution to psychological realism in the form of *style indirect libre*, a version of the 'stream of consciousness' technique regularly employed by Virginia Woolf (1882–1941) and James Joyce (1882–1941). Flaubert's 1869 novel, *L'Education sentimentale*, intended as the moral history of his generation, portrays the fruitless love of Frédéric Moreau for Mme. Arnoux, against the background of 1840s Paris and the 1848 Revolution; love and politics prove comparable in misdirected and misrecognized opportunities, which defuse both the dynamism of character and the fulfilment of plot. History, together with religion, comes under renewed investigation in *Salammbô* (1862), *La Tentation de Saint Antoine* (1874) and *Trois Contes* (1877). These end in further equivocation, with the reader left uncertain about what values are to be derived from works so pervaded by irony and authorial impersonality. In the unfinished *Bouvard et Pécuchet* (1881), the work's eponymous protagonists are composed of the novels, guide books and folk-lore they avidly read, and conversely they take for reality what are only representations of it. In addition to foregrounding fictive processes, this novel also dwells on the stupidity of bourgeois society and the received ideas on which this society feeds, a Flaubertian theme since *Madame Bovary*.
  In the 19th century, Flaubert was prized for his ▷ realism (he was also claimed by naturalism and rejected both labels), understood as psychological representation or the accumulation of circumstantial detail (called the 'reality effect' by 20th-century literary critic Roland Barthes). Yet such detail in Flaubert tends to overwhelm rather than sharply define the character. Accordingly, the 20th century has valued him for his challenges to mimesis, including the traditional privileged ties between author and reader, writer and character, individual and society.
  ▷ French influence on Victorian literature.

### Fleet Prison, The

A royal prison in London from the 12th century (Falstaff is sent there at the end of Shakespeare's *Henry IV, Part II*, 1600), used for debtors after 1641 and demolished in 1848. It is described in ▷ Charles Dickens's ▷ *The Pickwick Papers*. Clergymen imprisoned in the Fleet sometimes conducted secret marriages, ie without the formalities of licence or 'banns'. Such marriages were legal though the clergyman was liable to a fine – a penalty which was no deterrent to one already bankrupt.

### 'Fleshly School of Poetry, The'

A term taken from an article by ▷ Robert Buchanan (who signed himself 'Thomas Maitland'), published in ▷ *The Contemporary Review* in October 1871. In it Buchanan links ▷ Dante Gabriel Rossetti, ▷ Algernon Swinburne and ▷ William Morris together as poets perversely loyal to each other and united against the common decencies. His main criticism was that their work was too obsessed with the body and with aesthetics in general. Buchanan also claimed that their work was morally irresponsible. Rossetti, against whom the main thrust of Buchanan's criticism was directed, replied in a dignified article entitled 'The Stealthy School of Criticism' published in ▷ *The Athenaeum* in December of the same year. However, he was deeply affected by the 'fleshly school' controversy. For Swinburne it provided yet more ammunition in his private war with Buchanan, who finally defeated Swinburne's publisher in a libel suit. However, Buchanan's literary career was irreparably damaged by the controversy. In their comic opera *Patience*, ▷ Gilbert and Sullivan based the character of Bunthorne, a 'fleshly poet', partly on ▷ Oscar Wilde, who was delighted by the association.
**Bib:** Buckley, J.H., *The Victorian Temper*; Doughty, O., 'The Fleshly School of Poetry: 1871–72' in *Dante Gabriel Rossetti*.

### Forsyte Saga, The

A sequence of novels constituting a study of Victorian and Edwardian society by John Galsworthy (1867–1933). They comprise: *The Man of Property* (1906): *The Indian Summer of a Forsyte* (1918); *In Chancery* (1920); *Awakening* (1920); *To Let* (1921). A television serialization of the work in 1967 was extremely popular.

### Fortnightly Review, The

*The Fortnightly Review* was founded in 1865 by, among others, the novelist ▷ Anthony Trollope. It was a vehicle of advanced liberal opinion, and included amongst its contributors the scientist ▷ T.H. Huxley, the political scientist ▷ Walter Bagehot, the positivist philosopher Frederick Harrison, the critics ▷ Matthew Arnold and ▷ Leslie Stephen, the novelists ▷ George Eliot and ▷ George Meredith, the poets ▷ D.G. Rossetti and ▷ Algernon Swinburne, and ▷ Walter Pater

and ▷ William Morris, the last two both leaders of social and critical thought.

### Fothergill, Jessie (1851–91)

Novelist, born in Chetham Hill, Manchester. She was sent to boarding school in Harrogate after her father's death, and began her literary career with *Healey* (1975). Eleven novels followed, including *The First Violin* (1877), *The Lasses of Leverhouses* (1888) and her last work, *Oriole's Daughter* (1893). Much of her fiction concerns romantic involvements between people of different social classes.

### Fourth Estate, The

Traditionally, and for political purposes, English society was thought until the 20th century to have three estates: the lords spiritual, the lords temporal and the commons. ▷ Thomas Carlyle alludes to a Fourth Estate, ie the press, implying that the newspapers have an essential role in the political functions of society. He attributed the phrase to the 18th-century statesman. Edmund Burke (1729–97).

### Franchise

Normally understood as the right to vote for a representative in Parliament. From the reign of Edward I (1272–1307), when representatives of the Commons were first summoned to Parliament, until 1832, this right was possessed by landowners whose land was worth at least forty shillings a year and by the citizens of certain towns (parliamentary boroughs) in which the qualifications varied. The first Parliamentary Reform Bill of 1832 arranged a property qualification which enfranchised the middle classes uniformly throughout Britain. The Reform Bill of 1867 enfranchised the working classes of the towns and the third, in 1884, extended the franchise to include men of all classes everywhere. In 1918 women were enfranchised on reaching the age of thirty and in 1928 they were accorded the vote, like men, at twenty-one. Enfranchisement was one of the main demands made by the suffragette movement. The franchise today is said to be 'universal', ie it excludes only minors (people under eighteen), certified lunatics, criminals serving a sentence or Peers of the Realm (holders of titles of nobility and bishops, who are entitled to sit in the House of Lords).
▷ Reform Bills; women's suffrage.

### Fraser's Magazine

It started in 1830 as an imitator of *Blackwood's*, but after the mid-19th century it became

Liberal. It published ▷ Thomas Carlyle's ▷ *Sartor Resartus* in 1833–4; at this time it was under the influence of S.T. Coleridge's (1772–1834) Conservative philosophy. In 1848 it published ▷ Charles Kingsley's novel of idealistic reform, *Yeast*. The historian J.A. Froude was its editor 1861–74, and tried to publish ▷ Ruskin's radical treatise on the nature of wealth, *Munera Pulveris* (1862–3), but this proved unpopular with the public, and the treatise was left unfinished. ▷ William Allingham was its editor between 1874 and 1879. The magazine folded in 1882.

### Frazer, Sir James G. (1854–1915)

Anthropologist. His *Golden Bough* (1890–1915; abridged edition 1922) is a vast study of ancient mythology; it influenced 20th-century poetry such as T.S. Eliot's *The Waste Land* (1922). Other publications include: *Totemism (1887); Adonis, Attis, Osiris, Studies in the History of Oriental Religion* (1906); *Totemism and Exogamy* (1910); *Folklore in the Old Testament* (1918). Frazer was a major influence on the development of 20th-century anthropology and psychology, and in addition edited works by William Cowper (1731–1800) and Joseph Addison (1672–1719).

### Free Trade

Nowadays the term is understood to mean trade between nations without restrictions either in the form of the prohibition of certain commodities or in duties (taxes) on their importation. The view that trade should be so conducted was expressed most influentially in Adam Smith's *Wealth of Nations* (1776). In the 19th century free trade particularly suited English industrialists and it became a leading issue between the ▷ Whigs, who represented industrial interest, and the Tories who wished to protect agricultural ones. The repeal of the ▷ Corn Laws, which had imposed taxes on imported corn, was a decisive victory for the free traders, though the policy of governments has always fluctuated, and trade has never been entirely free.

In the early 17th century the term was used for trade unrestricted by the monopolies granted (for a price) by the Crown to certain individuals. In the 18th century the term was a euphemism for smuggling.

### French influence on Victorian literature

One of the most important influences on the development of literature in the Victorian period came from a group of artists and writers in mid-19th-century France who formulated between them a new theory concerning the purpose of art which was to have far-reaching effects on the development of the novel – destined to become the dominant literary genre of the second half on the 19th century. ▷ Honoré de Balzac (1799–1850) and the brothers Edmond and Jules de Goncourt (1822–96, 1830–70) believed that literature served society better by revealing the truth of contemporary life rather than providing an escape from it. Balzac's *La Comédie Humaine* was the medium for recording and classifying the social life of France in all its aspects: 'French society was to be the historian,' he declared, 'I had only to be the scribe.' Balzac saw himself as accurately and exhaustively representing the 'truth' through detailed reportage of even the most minute aspects of everyday life – clothes, furniture, food – coupled with the social classification of characters into types and a fundamental analysis of the economic basis of society. However, as the Goncourt brothers declared, different novelists may subscribe to different criteria of 'truth'. At the same time confusions arose over the role of the artist and that of the historian or sociologist. These debates formed the basis of the theory of ▷ realism which was imported from France into England in the 1880s, along with ▷ naturalism, which took the argument a stage further by positing the post- ▷ Darwinian idea that human beings were wholly determined by heredity and environment. This methodology was employed with varying degrees of success in the novels of ▷ Emile Zola (1840–1902) who was to have a strong influence on ▷ George Gissing, ▷ George Moore and, towards the end of his novel-writing career, ▷ Thomas Hardy.

Although there were similar debates concerning the function of art in England before 1880, critics and novelists such as ▷ Charles Dickens, ▷ George Eliot and ▷ Henry James were more concerned with investigating the moral behaviour of men and women in society rather than representing material reality. The theory of realism in England was much less coherent and scientific than in France. The work of the novelist ▷ Gustave Flaubert (1821–80), with its emphasis on objectivity, exactness of rendition and taking inspiration from the ordinary, was claimed by both realism and naturalism although Flaubert himself rejected both labels. After the publication of novels such as *Madame Bovary* (1857) and *L'Education sentimentale* (1869) he became the prose writer to whom all serious young writers in France and Britain put themselves to school. At the same time, writers like Flaubert were concerned in their fiction with the sexual as well as the social pressures surrounding women trapped by the repressive social mores of 19th-century Europe, and British writers, including Hardy, Gissing, ▷ Meredith and the ▷ 'New Woman' novelists of the 1890s, were encouraged by his example. Likewise, the novelist ▷ George Sand was admired, and vilified, for her revolt against contemporary social norms and for her championship of passion. Both of these themes are amply illustrated in her novels. Flaubert's pupil Guy de Maupassant (1850–1903), who was by the end of his life the most famous ▷ short story writer in the world, also helped to initiate the revolt against Victorian values – especially the conspiracy of silence on sexual matters. De Maupassant developed the short story form almost single-handedly, striving within the constraints of this new and concentrated genre to penetrate below the surface of the 'banal, photographic view of life' to reveal a deeper, underlying and more appalling truth which, he believed, was the only truth an artist should be concerned with. French novels, conventionally considered daring, were commonly printed on yellow paper. Therefore subscribers to the ▷ *Yellow Book*, the voice of the British ▷ Aesthetic Movement, could have no doubt as to the nature of its contents.

The main influence as far as poetry was concerned came in the mid-19th century with ▷ Baudelaire, whose *Les Fleurs du Mal* (1857) inspired ▷ Swinburne and through him the ▷ Nineties poets such as ▷ Ernest Dowson and, later, Arthur Symons (1865–1945), who alternately regarded Baudelaire as deliciously decadent and frankly satanic. Symons was deeply influenced by the ▷ Symbolist movement of late 19th-century France, which was a reaction against the documentary precision of realism and the scientific determinism of naturalism. The Symbolists included Baudelaire, Paul Verlaine (1844–96), Mallarmé (1842–98), Rimbaud (1854–91) and Jules Laforgue (1860–87). Symons introduced their work to English readers through his influential study *The Symbolist Movement in Literature* (1899).

The doctrine of ▷ Aestheticism which arose in England in the 1880s as a conscious revolt against high Victorian optimism and belief in the morality of art, was also shaped and influenced by contemporary developments in France. Apart from ▷ Walter Pater and his predecessors, the Aesthetes owed much to the French doctrine of '*L'Art pour L'Art*' (art for art's sake) which stressed the morality of the senses against more conventional virtues and deified the intensity of the moment.
**Bib:** Starkie, E., *From Gautier to Eliot: the Influence of France on English Literature, 1851–1939.*

## French Revolution, The: A History (1837)

Published almost fifty years after the French Revolution (1789–94), this historical account by ▷ Thomas Carlyle was generally regarded in its time as his masterpiece. It was intended as a warning to the British aristocracy and renders Carlyle open to the charge of bending history to fit his moral purpose. Published in the year that saw the rise of the ▷ Chartist movement, the message of Carlyle's book was that unless the upper classes behaved more responsibly toward the working classes an English Revolution would soon erupt. He emphasized the limited understanding of people involved in a particular historical process by presenting events as if he were an onlooker.
**Bib:** Cumming, M., *A Disemprisoned Epic: Form and Vision in Carlyle's 'French Revolution'.*

# G

**Gamp, Sarah**
A drunken nurse in ▷ Charles Dickens's novel ▷ *Martin Chuzzlewit*. She always carried an unbrella and her name 'gamp' has therefore come to mean umbrella in colloquial usage.

**Gaskell, Elizabeth Cleghorn (1810–65)**
Novelist, short story writer and biographer. Elizabeth Cleghorn Stevenson was the daughter of a ▷ Unitarian minister and spent her childhood with her aunt in Knutsford, Cheshire after her mother's death in 1811. In 1832 she married William Gaskell, also a Unitarian minister, based in Manchester, with whom she had four daughters, and a son who died in infancy. She and her husband first intended to write the annals of the Manchester poor in the manner of George Crabbe (1754–1832, who wrote about rural life in Suffolk with uncompromising realism); and her first novel, ▷ *Mary Barton* (1848), presented the outlook of the industrial workers with justice and sympathy sufficient to anger some of the employers. It won the attention of ▷ Charles Dickens and most of her later work was published in his periodical magazines ▷ *Household Words* and ▷ *All the Year Round*. ▷ *Cranford* began to appear in 1851, and ▷ *Ruth* in 1853, the latter novel causing a scandal because of its sympathetic treatment of a ▷ 'fallen woman'. *Cranford*, a study of a small circle in a small town based on Knutsford, has been compared with the work of Jane Austen in its ability to endow smallness of circumstance with large implications. Social issues are also at the heart of ▷ *North and South* (1854–5) and many of Gaskell's short stories. In 1863 the ▷ historical novel ▷ *Sylvia's Lovers* appeared and *A Dark Night's Work: Cousin Phyllis and Other Tales*. Her masterpiece ▷ *Wives and Daughters*, though unfinished, was published posthumously between 1864 and 1866. Other works include the celebrated biography of her friend ▷ Charlotte Brontë (1857), and ghost stories, a selection of which has recently been reprinted as *Lois the Witch and Other Stories* (1989).

Mrs Gaskell's work reveals a commitment to humanitarian principles and to Unitarianism. The ▷ 'social problem' novels call for reconciliation between employers and workers, for Gaskell was always reforming rather than radical. She advocated motherhood as woman's mission in life, but her fiction often exposes the contradictions in Victorian attitudes and calls for more 'nurturing' men. Recent feminist critics have re-assessed Gaskell's portrayal of 'marginalized women' – the spinsters, widows, ▷ orphan girls and madwomen who figure largely within her work. Her novels are an interesting connecting link between those of Jane Austen and ▷ George Eliot.

**Bib:** Hopkins, A.B., *Life*; Cecil, D., *Early Victorian Novelists*; Haldane, E., *Mrs Gaskell and her Friends*; Tillotson, K. (on Mary Barton) in *Novels of the Eighteen-Forties*; Gerin, W., *Elizabeth Gaskell: A Biography*; Easson, A., *Elizabeth Gaskell*; Stoneman, P., *Elizabeth Gaskell*.

**Gatty, Margaret (1809–73)**
Writer of ▷ children's literature and a keen botanist. She was born Margaret Scott in Burnham vicarage, Essex, and moved to Yorkshire after marrying the Rev. Alfred Gatty in 1839. Of her ten children, ▷ Juliana Horatia Ewing worked most closely with her on *Aunt Judy's Magazine*, a periodical for children. Gatty's works include *The Fairy Godmothers* (1851); *Parables from Nature* (a series of five books published between 1855 and 1871); *Aunt Judy's Tales* (1859); *Christmas Crackers* (1870), and a two-volume *History of British Seaweeds* (1863), which became the standard source of information about seaweeds for the next 80 years. Gatty's writing for children reveals a good sense of humour, but contains too much moralizing to appeal to 20th-century readers. She was, however, highly popular in her day.

**Gentleman**
Before the 14th century the French *gentil homme* meant 'nobleman', man of aristocratic descent. By the 19th century the title was allowed to all men of the educated classes, though being occupied in trade was still regarded as a barrier. ▷ Anthony Trollope's novels show it as a site of contest: everyone wanted to claim they were a gentleman and its moral connotations were quite unstable. Though in theory it was behaviour that counted, appearances for most people counted still more, as is shown in Magwitch's notions of a gentleman in ▷ Charles Dickens's novel ▷ *Great Expectations*. The ▷ public schools, at least since the 17th century, had associated the idea of gentleman with ▷ education, especially a ▷ classical education in Greek and Latin literature; in the 19th century the public schools were greatly increased in numbers and the association of the rank of gentleman with a public school education persists to this day. In ▷ George Meredith's novel ▷ *The Egoist* the name of the character

reference to his conception of himself as the 'pattern' of a gentleman.

### Germ, The (1850)

The literary magazine of the ▷ Pre-Raphaelite Brotherhood lasting for only four issues from January to April 1850. ▷ Dante Gabriel Rossetti, ▷ Christina Rossetti, ▷ Coventry Patmore and Thomas Woolner (▷ 'Enoch Arden') published poetry in it. Dante Gabriel Rossetti's short story *Hand and Soul* was also printed in it. It was edited by the Rossettis' brother, William Michael Rossetti.

### German influence on Victorian literature

Unlike other European literatures, such as French or Italian, the literature of the German-speaking world did not begin to make itself felt in Britain to any great extent until the late 18th and 19th centuries. There are two reasons for this. The first is that the great flowering of literature written in the modern form of the German language did not take place until the second half of the 18th century; the second is that Germany did not begin to assume the status of a major foreign language for the English until the second decade of the following century, and even then it remained far behind French in importance. In the cultural interchange between the two literatures Britain has on balance been the dominant partner. German men of letters during the 18th century were far more likely to have a lively awareness of current developments in English literature than were their English counterparts of developments in Germany. In this way English literature was able to play a crucial role in the process by which German writers of the late 18th century succeeded in exerting their independence from the prevailing standards of neo-classical decorum which French models seemed to dictate. The writers of the *Sturm und Drang* (Storm and Stress) – a German literary movement, identified in the late 1770s – looked to Britain rather than France for support and justification of their revolutionary project, and early attempts to provide a repertoire for the German national theatre owed a great deal to the influence of Shakespeare. So when German theatre first made an impression in Britain, the new stimulus contained many, though unrecognized, indigenous elements.

In the theatre the leading German naturalist dramatist Gerhart Hauptmann (1862–1946) may not have had the impact of the Scandinavian dramatists ▷ Ibsen and August Strindberg (1849–1912), but in intellectual left-wing circles, at least, he was read and admired. The presentation of industrial class conflict in *Die Weber* (*The Weavers*, 1892) where Hauptmann succeeds in creating a 'social' drama without individualized heroes, renewed interest in German theatre and in some ways foreshadowed the political commitment associated with Bertolt Brecht (1898–1956). In England as in Germany Georg Buchner (1813–37) came to be valued only long after his premature death, and Frank Wedekind (1864–1918) provided in his *Frühlings Erwachen* (*Spring's Awakening*, 1891) a masterpiece which has survived translation.

However, it was in the novel that the first impact of the new German literature was felt. The discovery of such works as ▷ Goethe's epistolary *Die Leiden des jungen Werthers* (*The Sorrows of Young Werther*, 1774) by an English audience in 1799 unfortunately soon met an insurmountable obstacle in the form of war. In the wake of the French Revolution (1789–94) a climate of opinion was created in England which was deeply and indiscriminately suspicious of all mainland European influence. When English interest was reawakened, it was once again Goethe who was at the centre of controversy. The first part of *Faust* (1808) was felt then to be quite shocking in terms of the way sexuality and religious matters were treated and Goethe's reputation as an immoral author was revived. The poet Coleridge's (1772–1834) thought was deeply indebted to German philosophy, and his younger contemporaries Shelley (1792–1822) and Byron (1788–1824) were great admirers of *Faust*. Sadly Byron, whose works were widely read and admired in Germany, did not live to see the tribute Goethe paid him in the second part of *Faust* (1832).

For ▷ Thomas Carlyle, Goethe and Byron signified opposite moral and artistic poles, and it was Carlyle who was the single most important conduit of German literature and thought in the 19th century. He had already published his translation of Goethe's *Wilhelm Meister* when, in 1839, his *Critical and Miscellaneous Essays* appeared, containing the many articles on German literature which he had written for the journals of the day. The work was seminal and inaugurated what was the great age of German influence in Britain. Probably inspired by Carlyle, ▷ Matthew Arnold immersed himself in the works of Goethe and was deeply influenced by him. His discovery and admiration of Heinrich Heine (1797–1856)

Heine (1797–1856) on the other hand was quite independent and an appreciative essay on the later poet is included in *Essays in Criticism* (1865). For Arnold, Goethe and Heine were great modern spirits in comparison with whom the English ▷ Romantics were insular and intellectually deficient. Arnold's German culture extends far beyond these two authors however and, in scope at least, he is like ▷ George Eliot in this regard.

It is now appreciated that the profound influence of the so-called 'Higher Criticism' in Britain does not commence with the publication in 1846 of Eliot's translation of Strauß's *Das Leben Jesu* (1835) but has roots which reach back into the last quarter of the 18th century, and that Coleridge was ahead of his time in his appreciation of the significance to religion and philosophy of the German school of biblical criticism. George Eliot is less a beginning than a culmination. Arnold had recognized in Goethe a figure who was working to 'dissolve' the dogmatic Christianity which had once been the bedrock of European civilization. It is now clear, however, that it was the Higher Criticism which, by mythologizing Christianity, undermined its claims more surely even than ▷ Charles Darwin, the geologists and positivist science. From this it is clear that when considering the massive response of English writers to German literature at this time, no sharp line can be drawn between works of imagination on the one hand and works of historical scholarship, cultural history and philosophy on the other. If a novel of ideas such as ▷ *Daniel Deronda* could hardly have been written without Strauß (1808–74) and Feuerbach (1804–72), then Goethe's *Wilhelm Meister* is scarcely less crucial. The relevance here of ▷ G.H. Lewes, whose *Life of Goethe* appeared in 1855, is obvious. In the last decade of the century another admirer of Goethe, ▷ Oscar Wilde, with inspired flippancy, could show young Cecily earnestly studying her German grammar under the eyes of Miss Prism and the Reverend Chasuble, but for many the loss of religious faith which followed the encounter with German thought brought great anguish before it brought serenity.

It is one of the paradoxes of the Victorian era that, while a series such as Bohn's Standard Library made available to a reading public a large number of German classic texts in translation, there were still many gaps and absences. The imaginative literature of the middle and second half of the century, represented by writers such as the Austrian Franz Grillparzer (1791–1872), E. Mörike

(1804–75), A. Stifter (1805–68), Friedrich Hebbel (1813–63), T. Storm (1817–88), Theodor Fontane (1819–98), and the Swiss writers G. Keller (1819–90) and C.F. Meyer (1825–98) did not reach the wider audience it deserved. Because this literature is in a sense provincial, its failure to make much impression in Britain is less surprising than the British blindness to the considerable achievements of important earlier figures such as Heinrich von Kleist (1777–1811) or E.T. A. Hoffmann (1776–1822), though the latter was not unknown and certainly influenced Edgar Allen Poe (1809–49). Of this generation it was perhaps the figure of Richard Wagner (1813–83), more associated with music than literature, whose work has had most influence on English literature. In some ways he was an important precursor of the Celtic revival, and his aesthetic theories as much as his use of the *leitmotif* influenced subsequent writers throughout Europe.

During the 19th century the figures of ▷ Walter Scott, ▷ William Thackeray and ▷ Charles Dickens exercised a profound influence on the development of ▷ realist fiction in Germany. Thomas Mann (1875–1955) was closest to this tradition in his novel of the decline of a bourgeois family, *Buddenbrooks* (1901), and for many years was held in high esteem.

### Ghosts (1890)

A play by ▷ Henrik Ibsen originally produced in Norwegian as *Gengangere* in 1881. One of the major plays of his ▷ realist period its early performances in London caused outrage and controversy. Its main character, the widowed Mrs Alving, has vigorously suppressed the truth concerning her profligate husband. However the truth comes back to haunt her in the form of her son Oswald who returns from Paris suffering from hereditary syphilis. The play tackles such taboo subjects as incest and euthanasia, and examines the dead conventions that smother the living society.

### Gilbert, Sir William Schwenck (1836–1911)

English dramatist most famous for his partnership with Sir Arthur Sullivan. Together they produced the famous Savoy operas, so called because they were produced at the Savoy Theatre; Gilbert wrote the libretti and Sullivan composed the music. The partnership began with *Thespis; or, The God Grown Old* in 1871 and concluded with *The Grand Duke* (1896). The best known of these light operas are *HMS Pinafore* (1878),

*The Pirates of Penzance* (1880), *Iolanthe* (1882), *The Mikado* (1885) and *The Gondoliers* (1889). Gilbert's plays are rarely performed now, although *Engaged* (1887) has received attention for its influence on ▷ Oscar Wilde's *The Importance of Being Earnest*.
**Bib:** Cox-Ife, W., *Gilbert: Stage Director*; Sutton, M., *Gilbert*.

### Gilfillan, George (18?–18?)

An enthusiastic and exuberant reviewer and critic who frequently wrote under the name 'Apollodorus'. He championed the work of ▷ Philip James Bailey, Alexander Smith and ▷ Sydney Dobell, later satirized by ▷ William Aytoun as the ▷ 'Spasmodic' school of poetry. A Scots burgher minister in Dundee, he shared ▷ Carlyle's dogmatism and tendency to pontificate and his influence on early Victorian poetic taste was as powerful as Carlyle's, although their views on art differed significantly. He rapidly established a wide reputation with his *Galleries of Literary Portraits* (1845–54) and his articles in the *Quarterly*, the *Eclectic*, *Tait's Magazine* and *Hogg's Instructor*. His reputation waned, however, as a result of Aytoun's satiric portrait of him in *Firmilian, a Spasmodic Tragedy*. His *Letters and Journals* were published in 1892.
**Bib:** Nicoll, W. Robertson, *Gilfillan's Literary Portraits*; Buckley, J.H., *The Victorian Temper*.

### Gilfil's Love-Story, Mr

One of ▷ George Eliot's ▷ *Scenes of Clerical Life*.

### 'Girl of the Period, The' (1868)

An essay by ▷ Eliza Lynn Linton, published in *The Saturday Review*. It caused much controversy, was sold worldwide and was described as 'an epoch-making essay'. The 'Girl of the Period' is depicted as a frivolous, extravagant creature 'who dyes her hair and paints her face . . . whose sole idea of life is fun' and who shows no respect for men, ▷ marriage or motherhood. Linton laments this 'pitiable mistake and . . . grand national disaster' and calls for a return to a past ideal of womanhood. The essay does not touch upon issues central to women's lives in the 1860s such as higher ▷ education, work, or ▷ women's suffrage, but it caused a furore and sparked numerous imitations.
▷ 'Woman Question, The'.

### Gissing, George Robert (1857–1903)

Novelist; author of: *Workers in the Dawn* (1880); *The Unclassed* (1884); ▷ *Demos* (1886);

*A Life's Morning* (1888); *The Nether World* (1889); *The Emancipated* (1890); ▷ *New Grub Street* (1891); *Born in Exile* (1892); ▷ *The Odd Women* (1893); *The Town Traveller* (1898); *The Crown of Life* (1899); *Our Friend the Charlatan* (1901); *By the Ionian Sea* (1901); *The Private Papers of Henry Ryecroft* (1903). Posthumous: the historical novel *Veranilda* (1904) and *Will Warburton* (1905). Of these, much the best known is *New Grub Street*, a study of literary life in late 19th-century London. Gissing saw with deep foreboding the spread of a commercialized culture which would so oppress the disinterested artist and so encourage the charlatan that, in his view, national culture was bound to deteriorate, with concomitant effects on the quality of civilization as a whole. The partial fulfilment of his predictions has given this novel in particular a greatly revived prestige. His vision was serious and sombre, and he depicted the enclosed, deprived world of the poor of his time in *Demos* and *The Nether World*. *Thyrza* and *Henry Ryecroft* are other novels which are singled out from his work. He was deeply interested in ▷ Charles Dickens and his study of that novelist (1898) is among the best on the subject; but he had also been affected by the austere, scrupulous artistry of the French 19th-century novelists ▷ Flaubert and ▷ Zola. His best work often has a strong autobiographical content, characteristic of some of his contemporaries, such as ▷ William Hale White and ▷ Samuel Butler
▷ Newspapers and periodicals.
**Bib:** Donnelly, M., *Gissing, Grave Comedian*; Org, J., *Gissing*; Roberts, M., *The Private Life of Henry Maitland* (novel based on Gissing's life); Poole, A., *Gissing in Context*; Pollie, M., *The Alien Art: A Critical Study George Gissing's Novels*.

### Gladstone, William Ewart (1809–98)

One of the principal British statesmen of the 19th century and a leader, first of the Tories (Conservatives) and later, Prime Minister four times, of the Liberals (formerly ▷ Whigs). His strength lay in finance – he was an advocate of ▷ free trade – and domestic reform; late in life he advocated and came near to bringing about self-government for Ireland (Irish Home Rule). His personality was impressive and his ardour and energy very great, but he lacked the intimate charm and subtle wit of his opponent ▷ Benjamin Disraeli, whom he fought with almost religious dedication. Their rivalry is often recalled as a golden age of English parliamentarianism by those who see public competition and conflict between individuals as the most productive form of political activity.

Gladstone was a man of deep culture, a classical scholar who published studies of ancient Greek literature. His reforms were important in removing abuses and improving justice and equality in the universities, the army, the ▷ franchise, the right to form and maintain ▷ trade unions, and recruitment to the military and civil services.

### Goblin Market and Other Poems (1862)

The first published collection of poems by ▷ Christina Rossetti. The title poem is a narrative concerning two sisters; Laura, who succumbs to the temptation to eat the luscious fruit of the rapacious goblin men which she pays for with a lock of her hair, and Lizzie, who saves her from the physical and psychological decline of unassuaged addiction by seeking out the goblins' fruit but refusing to consume it herself. Enraged by her resistance, the goblins press the fruit on to her body. When Laura eats and drinks the fruit from Lizzie it acts as an antidote, the goblins' power is defeated and she is cured. The poem is a rich blend of fantasy, allegory, fairytale and Victorian Christian morality, erotically suggestive and linguistically complex. It has generated much psychoanalytic and feminist criticism, being interpreted as a ▷ lesbian fantasy, a female myth and a poem concerned with women's relationship to language. It is Rossetti's most famous work and a strong and sinister Victorian evocation of desire, fear and compulsion.

Other notable poems in the collection include the enigmatic and elusive 'Echo', 'Winter: My Secret', and 'A Triad', in which Rossetti criticizes the amatory possibilities available to women. The collection established Rossetti as a significant voice in Victorian poetry.
**Bib:** Moers, E., *Literary Women*; Mermin, D., 'Heroic Sisterhood in *Goblin Market*', *Victorian Poetry*, 21 (1983), 107–18; Galligani Casey, J., 'The Potential of Sisterhood: Christina Rossetti's *Goblin Market*', *Victorian Poetry*, 29 (1991), 63–78; Leighton, A., *Victorian Women Poets: Writing Against the Heart*.

### Goethe, Johann Wolfgang von (1749–1832)

German poet; the greatest European man of letters of his time. His fame was due not only to the wide scope of his imaginative creation, but to the many-sidedness and massive independence of his personality. From 1770 to 1788 he was an inaugurator and leader of the passionate outbreak known in ▷ German as the *Sturm und Drang* – 'storm and stress' – movement, but from 1788 (after his visit to Italy) he represented to the world a balanced harmony inspired by the ▷ classicism he had found there. But he did not lose his sense that the spirit is free to find its own fulfilment according to its own principle of growth. At the same time, from 1775 he was prominent in the affairs of the German principality of Weimar (whose prince was his friend), concerning himself with practical sciences useful to the state, and thence with a serious study of botany and other natural and physical sciences, to the point of making significant contributions to scientific thought. His commanding mind was admired in France, England, and Italy, with whose literatures Goethe was in touch; he corresponded with the poet Byron (1788–1824); poet and novelist Walter Scott (1771–1832) translated his *Goetz von Berlichingen*, which dated from the ▷ Romantic phase of Goethe's career; he encouraged the young ▷ Thomas Carlyle. For Carlyle (▷ *Sartor Resartus*) Goethe was the spirit of affirmation that the age needed, to be set against the spirit of denial and withdrawal which he saw manifested in Byron. For ▷ Matthew Arnold, one of the most influential critics of the mid-19th century, Goethe's serene and responsible detachment represented the needed outlook for the practice of criticism.

Goethe is most famous for his double drama, *Faust* (1808 and 1832), but other works that became famous in England include the Romantic drama *Goetz von Berlichingen*; the epic *Hermann and Dorothea*; a study in Romantic sensibility, *The Sorrows of Young Werther* (1774); the novel *Wilhelm Meister* and a large body of lyrical verse.

### Gondal

An imaginary world created by ▷ Emily and ▷ Anne Brontë around 1834 when they broke away from ▷ Charlotte and Branwell, who were engaged in the creation of ▷ Angria. None of the prose writings of Gondal survive, although many of Emily's poems take on the persona of a Gondal character such as Augusta Geraldine Almeda or Julius Brenzaida. Gondal continued to be a source of imaginative engagement for Emily and Anne as late as 1845, when Emily was twenty-seven and Anne twenty-five.
**Bib:** Ratchord, F., *Gondal's Queen*.

**Gore, Catherine Grace Frances (1799–1861)**
Born Moody, the daughter of a wine
merchant in East Retford, Nottinghamshire,
Catherine Gore showed literary ability at an
early age and was nicknamed 'the Poetess'
by her peers. She wrote some 70 novels
between 1824 and 1862, of the 'silver-fork
school' (▷ Fashionable Novel); novels of
fashionable and wealthy life. They include
*Theresa Marchmont or the Maid of Honour*
(1824), *Manners of the Day, or Woman as the
game* (1830), which was praised by George IV,
*Mothers and Daughters* (1830), *Mrs Armytage:
or Female Domination* (1836), possibly her
best, *Cecil, or the Adventures of a Coxcomb*
(1841) and *The Banker's Wife, or Court and
City* (1843), which was dedicated to Sir John
Dean Paul, portrayed as a swindler, as he in
fact turned out to be in 1855 when Gore lost
£20,000. She also wrote poems, plays – *The
School for Coquettes* (1831), *Quid pro Quo or the
Day of Dupes* (1844) – and short stories, and
composed music. Her writing is characterized
by shrewd observation and perceptive insight,
together with satire and invention, and gives
an interesting portrait of life in a certain class
and time.

**Gosse, Sir Edmund (William) (1849–1928)**
Critic, biographer and poet. He is especially
known for his ▷ autobiography *Father and
Son* (1907), one of the classic works for
interpreting the Victorian age. He was born
in London, the son of Philip H. Gosse, a
distinguished zoologist and devout member of
the Plymouth Brethren. Privately educated, he
worked as a librarian, at the British Museum
and later at the House of Lords, a translator
and a lecturer at Cambridge University.
A central figure in London literary life, he
was friends with ▷ Swinburne, ▷ Robert
Louis Stevenson, ▷ Thomas Hardy and
▷ Henry James. As a critic he was one of
the first to introduce ▷ Ibsen to the English
stage and translated two of his plays, *Hedda
Gabler* (1891) and *The Master Builder* (with
▷ William Archer, 1893). He wrote a number
of critical studies of 17th-century literature, a
biography of Swinburne and a study of Ibsen.

**Gothic novel**
The Gothic novel was a type of fiction
popular in the late 18th and early 19th
centuries which generally dealt with tales of
the macabre and the supernatural. The term
'Gothic' originally implied 'medieval', or
rather fantasized versions of what was seen
to be medieval. Later 'Gothic' came to cover
all areas of the fantastic and the supernatural.

Gothic novels are usually set in a foreign
country and/or the remote past. Locations
include monasteries, castles, dungeons,
graveyards and mountainous landscapes. The
Gothic was originally cultivated in reaction
to the sedate neoclassicism and elevation of
reason which characterized the 18th century.
    The first Gothic novel was Horace
Walpole's *The Castle of Otranto* (1794) and the
influence of the Gothic carries on through
Mary Shelley's *Frankenstein* (1818) and on
into the Victorian period to surface in the
novels of ▷ Emily and ▷ Charlotte Brontë
and ▷ Charles Dickens; the poetry of
▷ Tennyson and the ▷ 'Spasmodic' poets
and the short stories of ▷ Sheridan Le Fanu
and ▷ Thomas Hardy.
    ▷ Sensation, Novel of; Gothic revival;
Medievalism.
**Bib:** Baldick, C., *In Frankenstein's Shadow*;
Ellis, K.F., *The Contested Castle: Gothic
Novels and the Subversion of Domestic Ideology*;
Milbank, A., *Daughters of the House*; Varma,
D.P., *The Gothic Flame: Being a History of the
Gothic Novel in England*.

**Gothic revival**
An architectural style now chiefly associated
with the reign of ▷ Queen Victoria
(1837–1901). A taste for Gothic had in fact
started in the 18th century; its starting point
is associated with Horace Walpole's (1717–97)
design of his home, Strawberry Hill (1747).
The taste for Gothic spread between 1750
and 1830; as an artistic style it remained a
minority cult, but as a sentiment it grew with
the popularity of the sensationalism of the
▷ Gothic novels and with the rise of the
▷ Romantic cultivation of the sensibility. In
the 18th century, the taste for Gothic tended
to be fanciful and sensational rather than
deeply serious, although it gained seriousness
from such a publication as Thomas Percy's
*Relique of Ancient English Poetry* (1765); the
19th-century Romantic revival, especially
the novels of Walter Scott, (1771–1832),
produced a deeper and much more genuine
feeling for the Middle Ages (▷ Medievalism).
From about 1830, the Gothic revival became
a genuine cultural re-direction; in literature
it was advanced by ▷ Thomas Carlyle (*Past
and Present*) and by ▷ John Ruskin (*The
Stones of Venice*); in religion by the ▷ Oxford
Movement; in architecture and painting by
the Catholic architect Pugin (through his
writings rather than his buildings) and the
▷ Pre-Raphaelites. Ruskin, especially in his
famous essay 'The Nature of Gothic', was
the most eloquent of these exponents; he

used the spirit of Gothic to challenge the materialistic spirit of the time consequent to the mass production methods of the Industrial Revolution. Nonetheless, in architecture and design the Victorian Gothic revival was vitiated by the technology of the new industrial methods, which could elaborate Gothic ornament mechanically. In poetry and fiction, ▷ Tennyson's revival of Arthurian legend in ▷ *Idylls of the King*, ▷ Browning's delight in elaborate descriptive detail, and ▷ Dicken's vivid idiosyncrasies in the presentation of character and environment, can all be ascribed to a prevailing neo-Gothic appeal to the imagination. But in the 1870s, a reaction set in: neo-Gothic architectural styles were succeeded by a return to ▷ classicism, generally known as the new 'Queen Anne' style, though it was often much more eclectic and exuberant. Eclecticism can be seen to dominate artistic taste in both the plastic arts and literature until the emergence of modernism in the 20th century.
Bib: Milbank, A., *Daughters of the House: Modes of the Gothic in Victorian Fiction*.

## Governesses

The governess was a familiar figure to Victorians, as she is to readers of ▷ *Jane Eyre* and ▷ *Agnes Grey* today. Governesses were drawn from the ranks of the middle classes; from families whose economic circumstances demanded that their daughters seek employment, yet remain respectable. The range of professions deemed suitable for middle-class women narrowed during the early 19th century so that by the Victorian period governessing was virtually the only path open to them. Pay and conditions, however, were often poor, as the ▷ Brontë novels testify. In 1841 a Governesses' Benevolent Institution was founded to assist the unemployed and needy. It was increasingly recognized that the 'plight' of the governess was a social problem, and many periodical essayists addressed the issue during the 1840s. It was the governess's status as a middle-class woman that fired such concern; no similar attention was directed to working-class women's conditions of employment. The preoccupation with the figure of the governess was crucially linked to the ideal of womanhood that she was supposed to embody and reproduce in her charges. The anomaly of her position was that at the same time as she ideally conformed to all the standards of middle-class femininity, she was competing for jobs in the marketplace and therefore threatened to undermine the ethos of separate spheres of activity for women and men upon which Victorian society depended. Practically as well as ideologically she was often in a difficult position – barely educated herself yet required to teach others. The need for governesses to be better informed led to a series of evening lectures held at King's College, London, in 1847. These fed directly into the campaign for higher education for women, and in 1848 Queen's College for women was founded in London.

▷ Hall, Anna Maria; Jameson, Anna; Education of Women; *Deerbrook*; *Lady Audley's Secret*; *Shirley*; *Villette*.

## Grahame, Kenneth (1859–1932)

Children's writer and essayist. Grahame is remembered for his animal fable *The Wind in the Willows* (1908), which was based on stories made up for his son and which, after receiving little attention when first published, subsequently became a classic of children's fiction. Previously Grahame had contributed to the ▷ *Yellow Book* and had published several works primarily concerned with childhood experience: *Pagan Papers* (1893), *The Golden Age* (1895) and *Dream Days* (1898). He was born in Edinburgh, went to school in Oxford and worked in the Bank of England until 1908 when he retired because of ill-health.

▷ Children's literature.

## Grand, Sarah (1854–1943)

▷ Pseudonym of novelist Frances McFall, née Clark. She was born in Donaghadee, County Down, and moved to Yorkshire after her father's death in 1861. At sixteen she married Major David McFall, a surgeon. She later left her husband and moved to London where she became involved in ▷ feminist activity. Her first novel was *Ideala* (1888), her second ▷ *The Heavenly Twins* (1893), which was a sensational success. It attacked the sexual double standard in marriage, called for emancipation and protested against the immorality of the Contagious Diseases Act. She is said to have coined the term ▷ 'New Woman' in 1894. In 1897 her semi-autobiographical novel *The Beth Book* appeared. In 1898 she became President of the Tunbridge Wells branch of the National Union of ▷ Women's Suffrage Societies, and between 1922 and 1929 was mayoress of Bath. She died in Bath at the age of 88.

▷ Women's Movement.
Bib: Kersley, G., *Darling Madame: a Portrait of Sarah Grand*; Cunningham, G., *The 'New Woman' and the Fiction of*

*the 1890s*; Showalter, E., *A Literature of Their Own*.

## Great Exhibition, The

Held in 1851, in Hyde Park in London, it was the first international exhibition of the products of industry and celebrated the peak of the British Industrial Revolution. It was regarded as a triumph for British prosperity and enlightenment, though by some critics, eg the philanthropist ▷ Lord Shaftesbury, as concealing the scandal of immense urban slums. Its principal building, the Crystal Palace, was a pioneer construction in the materials of glass and cast-iron. The architect was Joseph Paxton.

▷ Albert of Saxe-Coburg-Gotha.

## Great Expectations (1860–1)

A novel ▷ Charles Dickens. Its title refers to expectations resulting from wealth anonymously donated to Philip Pirrip (shortened to Pip) who has been brought up in humble obscurity by his half-sister and her husband, the village blacksmith, Joe Gargery. His 'expectations' are to be made a ▷ 'gentleman' – understood in social terms as holding privilege without responsibility. He supposes his money to be the gift of the rich and lonely Miss Havisham, who has in fact merely used him as an experimental victim on whom her ward, Estella, is to exert her charm with the aim of breaking his heart. Pip's great crisis comes when he discovers his real benefactor to be the convict Magwitch, whom he had helped in an attempted escape when he was a child. Magwitch, who had been made into a criminal by the callousness of society in his own childhood, has built up a fortune in Australia (to which he was deported) and has tried the experiment of 'making a gentleman' out of another child. His assumption is essentially that of society as a whole – that appearances, and the money that makes them, are what matters. Magwitch returns to England illegally to see the fruit of his ambition, and Pip has to decide whether he will be responsible for his unwanted benefactor or escape from him. His decision to protect Magwitch and help him to escape again produces a revolution in Pip's nature: instead of assuming privilege without responsibility he now undertakes responsibility without reward, since he will also divest himself of his money. 'Expectations' are important in other senses for other characters: Estella expects to become a rich lady dominating humiliated admirers, but she becomes enslaved to a brutal husband; Pip's friend, Herbert Pocket, dreams of becoming a powerful industrialist, but he has no capital until Pip (anonymously) provides it; Wopsle, the parish clerk in Pip's village, imagines himself a great actor and becomes a stage hack; Miss Havisham is surrounded by relatives whom she depises and who nonetheless live in expectation of legacies after her death; Miss Havisham herself, and Magwitch also, live for expectations (in Estella and Pip) which are frustrated – in these instances fortunately. In its largest implications, *Great Expectations* is concerned with the futility of a society in which individuals live by desires powered by illusion. This view of the novel gives emphasis to those characters who are free of illusion: the lawyer Jaggers who exerts power by his cynical expectation of human folly; his clerk, Wemmick, who divides his life sharply between the harshness demanded by his profession and the tenderness of his domestic affections; Joe Gargery and his second wife Biddy, survivors from an older social tradition, who remain content with their own naive wisdom of the heart. Dickens was persuaded by his friend ▷ Bulwer-Lytton to change the end of the novel: in the first version Pip and Estella, older and wiser, meet again only to separate permanently; in the revised one, Dickens leaves it open to the reader to believe whether they will be permanently united, or not.

## Greenaway, Kate (1846–1901)

Born in Hoxton, the daughter of a wood-engraver, Greenaway began nature drawing as a child. She went to the Royal College and the Slade, and became a writer and illustrator of children's picture books in which she portrays an idealized world of sweetly pretty children in floral surroundings. She was encouraged by ▷ John Ruskin, whom she met in 1882 and who lectured on her art at Oxford in 1883, praising its innocent view of childhood and in effect its lack of ▷ realism. ▷ George Eliot also admired her art. Greenaway liked the ▷ Pre-Raphaelites and disliked contemporaries such as James Whistler. A strong, though unorthodox, religious instinct is evident in her search for beauty and goodness. She rejected the ▷ woman's movement, and enjoyed considerable commercial success, influencing design and children's dress. Her first success was *Under the Window* (1878), a collection of rhymes she wrote and illustrated. Her later work includes *Marigold Garden* (1885) and an illustrated edition of ▷ Robert Browning's

▷ *The Pied Piper of Hamelin*. She also wrote poetry, much of it still unpublished.
**Bib:** Engen, R.K., *Kate Greenaway*; Holme, B., *The Kate Greenaway Book*.

**Gregory, Lady Augusta (1852–1932)**
Promoter of Irish drama, she founded the Irish Literary Theatre, with W.B. Yeats (1865–1939) and Edward Martyn in 1898. This became the Irish National Theatre Society in 1902 and led to the establishment of the Abbey Theatre in Dublin. She wrote several plays for it and collaborated with Yeats in *The Pot of Broth* and *Cathleen ni Houlihan* (both 1902). Of her own plays the best known are *Spreading the News* (1904), *The Gaol Gate* (1906), *Hyacinth Halvey* (1906), *The Rising of the Moon* (1907) and *The Workhouse Ward* (1908). She also translated Molière (1622–73) into Irish idiom in *The Kiltartan Molière*.
▷ Irish literature in English.
**Bib:** Kohfeldt, M., *Lady Gregory: The Woman behind the Irish Renaissance*.

**Grein, Jack Thomas (1862–1935)**
Dramatist, critic and manager who helped introduce the work of European dramatists to English audiences at the end of the 19th century. He founded the Independent Theatre Club in 1891, 'to give special performances of plays which have a literary and artistic rather than a commercial value'. The first production was ▷ Ibsen's ▷ *Ghosts* which met with a storm of abuse, and thereafter little of Ibsen's work was shown; although ▷ George Bernard Shaw's contribution to the controversy, *Widowers' Houses*, his first London production, was put on in 1892. Grein's dramatic criticism has been published in five volumes.
**Bib:** Orme, M., *J.T. Grein; the Story of a Pioneer*.

**Grimm's Fairy Tales**
German folk-tales collected by the brothers Jacob (1785–1863) and Wilhelm (1786–1859)

Grimm, and published 1812–15. They first appeared in English in a volume illustrated by ▷ George Cruickshank and containing such stories as 'Snow White', 'Hansel and Gretel' and 'Rumpelstiltskin'. They were the first collectors to write down the stories just as they heard them, without attempting to improve them.
▷ Children's literature.

**Grossmith, George (1847–1912) and Weedon (1853–1919)**
The brothers were both involved with the theatre, coming from a theatrical family, friends of the Terrys and ▷ Henry Irving. They are remembered, however, for *The Diary of a Nobody* (1852), initially serialized in ▷ *Punch*, written by both brothers and illustrated by Weedon. The nobody in question, Mr Pooter, sensitive to the slightest humiliation, conveys the events and contemporary background detail in a life striving for gentility. The book was immediately successful, with a wide readership, and has remained popular.
▷ Diaries.

*Group of Noble Dames, A* **(1891)**
A collection of ten short stories by ▷ Thomas Hardy, published initially in various periodicals from 1889–90 and collected together in 1891. A series of historical narratives set in mansions and castles in ▷ Wessex, many of the stories were inspired by John Huchins' *History and Antiquities of the County of Dorset* (1861–73) which Hardy read. The dominant themes are taken from Hardy's earlier work, especially love between a poor man and a lady, and sexual temptation. The stories were rewritten and ▷ bowdlerized in order to make them acceptable for volume publication.
▷ Historical novels.

**Haggard, Sir H. (Henry) Rider (1856–1925)**
Son of a Norfolk squire, he spent several
years in South Africa as a young man, writing
books on its history and farming, but he is
famous for his numerous adventure novels set
in such exotic locations as Iceland, Mexico
and ancient Egypt. They are characterized
by gripping narrative and strange events, as
well as evocative descriptions of landscape,
wildlife and tribal society, particularly in
Africa. He has had a world-wide readership
and some of his stories have been filmed. *King
Solomon's Mines* (1886) and *She* (1887) are the
most famous novels. *The Days of My Life: an
Autobiography* appeared in 1926.
**Bib:** Haggard, L.R., *The Cloak that I Left*;
Ellis, P.B., *H. Rider Haggard: A Voice from the
Infinite*; Higgins, D.S., *Rider Haggard: The
Great Storyteller*.

**Hall, Anna Maria (1800–81)**
Irish novelist and journalist. Born Anna Maria
Fielding in Dublin she moved to England
in 1815 and married Samuel Carter Hall
in 1824, who managed her literary salon
from their home. She befriended many
young writers including ▷ Dinah Craik and
▷ Margaret Oliphant whilst publishing her
own stories of Irish character and society,
such as *Sketches of Irish Character* (1829) and
*Lights and Shadows of Irish Life* (1838). She
also produced three dramas, some children's
stories, and fiction which dealt sympathetically
with the peculiar problems of women's lives.
These include *Tales of Women's Trials* (1835)
and *The Old Governess* (1858), which describes
the miseries of the ▷ governess profession.
She helped to found the Governesses'
Institute and the Home for Decayed
Gentlewomen, which she supported with
much of the profit from her writings, although
she was unsympathetic to women's rights. She
was awarded a Queen's Pension in 1868.
  ▷ Irish literature in English; Women's
Movement.

**Hard Times (1854)**
A novel by ▷ Charles Dickens. It is the
only one by him not at least partly set in
London. The scene is an imaginary industrial
town called Coketown. One of the main
characters, Thomas Gradgrind, is based
on the ▷ Utilitarian leader James Mill
(1773–1836); as such he is an educationist
who believes that education should be merely
practical and hence factual, allowing no place
for imagination or emotion. He marries his
daughter Louisa to a ruthless manufacturer,
Josiah Bounderby, who puts Gradgrind's

philosophy into practice in that he has no
place for humane feeling in the conduct of
his business. Louisa accepts him in order
to be in a position to help her brother Tom
who becomes, under the influence of his
upbringing, callous, unscrupulous and meanly
calculating. Louisa is nearly seduced by a
visiting politician. James Harthouse, who is
cynically concerned only to find amusement in
a place with no other charms. The opposition
to this world of calculating selfishness is
a travelling circus called 'the horse-riding'
owned by Sleary. Sissy Jupe, a product
of the circus and the human fellowship
that it engenders, is found ineducable by
Gradgrind, whose dependant she becomes,
but she has the inner assurance required to
face Harthouse and compel him to leave the
town. Gradgrind's world falls apart when he
discovers that he has ruined his daughter's
happiness and turned his son into a criminal.
A subplot concerns a working-man, Stephen
Blackpool, a victim of the Gradgrind-
Bounderby system, and of young Gradgrind's
heartless criminality.
  ▷ Social Problem novel; Anti-industrialism.
**Bib:** Samuels, A., *An Introduction to the
Varieties of Criticism: Hard Times*.

**Hardy, Thomas (1840–1928)**
Novelist and poet. Hardy was born in Higher
Bockhampton, the son of a master mason and
builder, Thomas Hardy senior, and his wife
Jemima, who encouraged his early interest
in literature. As a child he was immersed in
country life, legend and folklore and became
acquainted with the harshness of rural
living, which contributed to his sympathy for
country workers and animals. From 1856–62
he was apprenticed to a local architect and
met the Dorsetshire dialect poet ▷ William
Barnes, and the intellectual Horace Moule,
who encouraged his intellectual aspirations
and later introduced him to the theories
of ▷ Charles Darwin: Hardy claimed that
after reading Darwin he gave up his plan to
become a country parson and he spent the
rest of his life trying to reconcile the orthodox
notion of a benevolent God with Darwin's
theory of evolution through natural selection.
At the same time he witnessed the growing,
impoverishment of the south-west of England,
an area which was to feature so strongly in his
novels as ▷ Wessex. From 1862–7 he joined
the architectural offices of Arthur Blomfield
in London and published his first article 'How
I built myself a House'. He also made an
unsuccesful foray into poetry.
  His first novel, *The Poor Man and the Lady*

(1867), was rejected by ▷ George Meredith, a reader for Chapman and Hall, on the grounds that it was too socialistic. His first published novel was *Desperate Remedies* (1871), a ▷ sensation novel in the style of ▷ Wilkie Collins, and while writing it he met Emma Lavinia Gifford in St Juliot, Cornwall, where he had been sent by his employer to survey the mouldering parish church of which her father was the rector. They married in 1874 and though their relationship was extremely troubled Hardy wrote a flood of poems 'in expiation' on her death in 1912. These are collected in *Satires of Circumstance, Lyrics and Reveries* (1914), and remain amongst Hardy's finest literary works.

Between 1871 and 1898 Hardy wrote fourteen novels; three volumes of short stories: *Wessex Tales* (1888), *A Group of Noble Dames* (1891), and *Life's Little Ironies* (1894); and a volume of poetry, *Wessex Poems* (1898). His best known novels are the group he named his 'Novels of Character and Environment'. They include ▷ *Under the Greenwood Tree* (1872); ▷ *Far from the Madding Crowd* (1874); ▷ *The Return of the Native* (1878); ▷ *The Mayor of Casterbridge* (1886); ▷ *The Woodlanders* (1887); ▷ *Tess of the d'Urbervilles* (1891); ▷ *Jude the Obscure* (1895). The remaining seven he classed as 'Romances and Fantasies' (▷ *A Pair of Blue Eyes*, 1873; *The Trumpet Major*, 1880; *Two on a Tower*, 1882; *The Well-Beloved*, 1897), and 'Novels of Ingenuity' (▷ *Desperate Remedies*, 1871; *The Hand of Ethelberta*, 1876; *A Laodicean* 1881). Many of these are the subject of serious critical re-evaluation, in particular the much underrated *A Pair of Blue Eyes*. His remaining works include: *Poems of the Past and Present* (1902); *Time's Laughingstocks and Other Verses* (1909); *Late Lyrics and Earlier* (1922); *Human Shows, Far Phantasies, Songs and Trifles* (1925) and the posthumous *Winter Words in Various Moods and Metres* (1928).

Hardy's poetry is as distinguished as his novels; indeed he regarded himself primarily as a poet. His diction is distinctive and he experimented constantly with form and stresses, and the singing rhythms subtly respond to the movement of his intense feelings; the consequent poignance and sincerity has brought him the admiration of poets ever since. His lyrics nearly always centre on incident, in a way that gives them dramatic sharpness. Hardy also wrote a three-part epic verse drama, *The Dynasts* (1903–8), and a verse drama about Tristram and Iseult, *The Famous Tragedy of the Queen of Cornwall* (1923). His work is continually under scrutiny

by feminist scholars, some of the more discerning of whom have interrogated the crude simplification of his works as fatalist or pessimistic and exposed the criticism of social institutions that underpins his remarkable portrayals of women.
**Bib:** Gittings, R., *Young Thomas Hardy*, *The Older Hardy*; Millgate, M., *Thomas Hardy*: *A Biography*, *Thomas Hardy: His Career as a Novelist*; Seymour-Smith, M., *Hardy*; Morgan, R., *Women and Sexuality in the Novels of Thomas Hardy*; Boumelha, P., *Thomas Hardy and Women*; Widdowson, P., *Hardy and History*; Johnson, T., *A Critical Introduction to the Poems of Thomas Hardy*.

### Hazlewood, Colin Henry (1823–75)
A comedian on the Lincoln, York and western circuits, Hazlewood began his career as a dramatist in 1850 with a successful farce. He is chiefly remembered for his successful dramatization of ▷ M.E. Braddon's ▷ sensation novel ▷ *Lady Audley's Secret* in 1863.
**Bib:** Wolff, R.L., *Sensational Victorian: The Life and Fiction of M.E. Braddon*.

### *Heavenly Twins, The* (1893)
A novel by ▷ Sarah Grand. The first half of this immensely successful book describes the lives of two twins, Angelica and Diavolo. As children they are both irrepressible, energetic and daring, but as they grow older they are forced to take different paths. Diavolo is given a good ▷ education and finally leaves home for an army career, while Angelica follows a conventionally female path and becomes trapped in domestic routine. The second half of the book concentrates on two women, Edith and Evadne. Religious and naive, Edith unknowingly marries a syphilitic naval officer, and both she and her child contract the disease. After a period of mental degeneration, Edith dies. Evadne, who has studied anatomy, physiology and pathology, refuses to consummate her marriage after discovering that her husband has had a previous affair, and lives a sexless life. She is frustrated as a result and has a mental breakdown, but she recovers from this after the death of her husband and marries again. Like Grand's *The Beth Book*, the novel explicitly addresses sexual/political issues. The lives of the twins reflect the inequality of educational opportunity, while Edith and Evadne represent the 'old' and ▷ 'New Woman' respectively. Despite Evadne's learning, however, she becomes trapped in a life of repression after promising her

husband that she will not become active in the ▷ women's movement.

### Hedda Gabler (1890)

A play by Norwegian dramatist ▷ Henrik Ibsen which marks his development away from an expressly social and moralist mode of drama and towards a more psychological and symbolic style. The play questions the conventional ideology of womanhood through the portrayal of its central character – Hedda – who finds her potential for effective activity limited and instead is forced to exercise an emotional power over those who enter her orbit.

### Heir of Redclyffe, The (1853)

A novel by ▷ Charlotte Yonge, informed by the religious principles of the ▷ Oxford Movement and much admired by prominent literary figures of the day such as ▷ Tennyson, ▷ D.G. Rossetti and ▷ William Morris. The novel contrasts genuine and superficial goodness of character through the story of two cousins, Guy and Philip Morville. Guy appears brash, but is deeply generous and ultimately self-sacrificing, whereas Philip is greatly admired but undeserving of accolades. Philip's machinations almost succeed in thwarting Guy's marriage. Guy later nurses Philip through a fever, catches it himself and dies. Philip repents of his sins and inherits the ancient house of Redclyffe.

### Hellas

In Greek, the name of Greece. Hellenes were the Greeks. Hellenism: the influence of ancient Hellenic or Greek culture, especially in what was understood as its ideals of intellectual enlightenment and the cultivation of beauty. ▷ Matthew Arnold for example, in *Culture and Anarchy* (1869), contrasted Hellenism, in which he thought Victorian England was deficient, with Hebraism, or primary concern with right and wrong conduct, of which he thought it had quite enough.

*Hellas* is also the title of a poetic drama by Shelley (1792–1822) and inspired by the proclamation of Greek independence in 1821.

### Henry Esmond, The History of (1852)

A ▷ historical novel by ▷ William Makepeace Thackeray. It is a very careful reconstruction of early 18th-century English aristocratic and literary society. The hero's father has been killed fighting for James II, ie he was a Jacobite. The politics of the book are involved with Jacobite plotting by the Roman Catholic branch of the House of Stuart to recover the throne of Britain from the Protestant branch. There are portraits of some of the distinguished personalities of the time – the Duke and Duchess of Marlborough, and the writers Sir Richard Steele (1672–1729), Joseph Addison (1672–1719) and Jonathan Swift (1667–1745). The style emulates that of Addison himself. The theme is the devotion of the young Henry Esmond to his relatives, Lady Castlewood, eight years older than himself, and her proud and ambitious daughter, Beatrix. These relationships are complicated by political intrigues and by family mysteries – Esmond is in reality himself the heir to the title and properties inherited by Lady Castlewood's husband. In the end, Esmond marries the widowed Lady Castlewood and emigrates to Virginia; his story continues in *The Virginians* (1857–9).

### Hereward the Wake (1865)

A ▷ historical novel by ▷ Charles Kingsley written after he became Regius Professor of History at Cambridge and based on the story of a half-legendary Anglo-Saxon hero who held out against William the Conqueror until 1070 in the town of Ely. The fame of Hereward depends a good deal on Kingsley's novel which is a colourful but inadequate story of battle, disguise and witchcraft.

### Historical Novel

A novel set in a well-defined historical context, generally before the author's own life (and therefore, in that sense at least, not based on the author's own experiences, but on other sources, whether literary or historical). Historical novels often include versions of real people and events and descriptions of social customs, clothing, buildings etc, to give an effect of verisimilitude. However, there are also more fantastical versions of the form, such as the Gothic novel. In Britain it was Sir Walter Scott (1771–1832) who established the popularity of the form and who influenced its development long after his death. Examples include ▷ Eliza Lynn Linton's *Azeth the Egyptian* (1847), ▷ George Eliot's ▷ *Romola* (1862–3) and ▷ *Middlemarch* (1871–2), ▷ Wilkie Collins's *Antonina* (1850), J.H. Shorthouse's *John Inglesant* (1881), the novels of ▷ William Ainsworth and ▷ Charlotte Yonge, ▷ Charles Kingsley's ▷ *Hypatia* (1852–53), *Westward Ho!* (1855) and ▷ *Hereward the Wake* (1865) and the novels of ▷ R.D. Blackmore. As old traditions crumbled and values changed, the Victorians

looked back to the past as a golden age of
stability, or to furnish them with lessons for
the present and future. Some, like Blackmore
and Kingsley, sought sensationalist or merely
new and lucid plots in the activities of the
past. In ▷ *Henry Esmond* (1852) ▷ Thackeray
sought to make 'history familiar rather than
heroic', whereas ▷ Dickens meant his ▷ *A
Tale of Two Cities* (1859) – a novel set at the
time of the French Revolution (1789–94) – to
be read with contemporary politics in mind.
George Eliot's *Middlemarch* demonstrates how
the past moulds the present and ▷ Thomas
Hardy's *The Trumpet Major* (1880) is written
out of the slowly growing awareness,
characteristic of the Victorian period, of the
individual as an historical person belonging to
a particular time.
**Bib:** Lukacs, G., *The Historical Novel*; White,
H., *Metahistory: The Historical Imagination in
Nineteenth Century Europe*; Sanders, A., *The
Victorian Historical Novel, 1840–1880*; Easson,
A. (ed.) *History and the Novel*.

### Histories and chronicles

Histories and chronicles are important in the
study of literature in two ways: as sources
for imaginative material and as literature in
their own right. However, with the exception
of the Venerable Bede (673–735), it was not
until the 17th century that English historians
began to achieve the status of major writers.
An early and prominent 19th-century
historian was ▷ Thomas Carlyle, who was
influenced by the re-creation of the daily
life of the past in the ▷ historical novels
of Sir Walter Scott (1771–1832). Carlyle's
historical works (the most notable of which
is his ▷ *French Revolution*, 1837, are more
imaginative than factual. ▷ T.B. Macaulay
was a better historian and not inferior as
an imaginative writer. ▷ *Macaulay's History
of England* is the only historical work which
comes near Gibbon's *Decline and Fall of the
Roman Empire* (1776–88) in reputation, and
Macaulay was responsible for the so-called
'Whig view of history' as steady progress in
material welfare and political advance. Other
eminent 19th-century English historians
were J.A. Froude, who is, however, notorious
for his prejudices in *A History of England
from the Fall of Wolsey to the Spanish Armada*
(1856–70), and J.R. Green, whose *Short
History of the English People* (1874) was for
some time a popular classsic owing to the
breadth of Green's social sympathies. It
was, however, in the 19th century that the
controversy about history as an art or as a
science developed, and other distinguished

historians of the period tended to become
comparatively specialized scholars without
the breadth of appeal of such men as Gibbon
and Macaulay. The latter's great-nephew,
G.M. Trevelyan (1876–1962) continued
the broader humane tradition of historical
writing. Recent theoretical developments have
led to renewed questionings of the terms of
historical knowledge: see, for example, H.
White, *Metahistory: The Historical Imagination
in Nineteenth Century Europe*.

### Hobbes, John Oliver (1867–1906)

▷ Pseudonym of Mrs Pearl (Mary Teresa)
Craigie who was born near Boston,
Massachusetts and moved with her family
to London as a baby. She was educated
in Berkshire and Paris, read widely, and
published her first stories at the age of
nine. She began writing regular drama
and art columns soon after her marriage
to Reginald Walpole Craigie in 1887. Her
first novel *Some Emotions and A Moral*
(1892) established her reputation as a
clever and caustic writer, and set a pattern
for her subsequent fiction in its treatment
of ill-matched marriages and disillusioned
idealism. Her output spans ten novels,
including: *The Sinner's Comedy* (1892), *The
Gods, Some Mortals and Lord Wickenham*
(1895), *The Scheme For Saints* (1897), *Robert
Orange* (1899), an idealized fictional portrait
of ▷ Disraeli, and *The Serious Wooing*
(1901); several successful plays such as *The
Ambassador* (1898); sketches and ▷ travel
essays as well as essays on George Eliot
(*Encyclopaedia Britannica*, 1901) and George
Sand (1902). She was a figure in London's
literary life and was admired by writers such
as ▷ Thomas Hardy. She became President
of the Society of Women Journalists in 1895
– the same year as her highly publicized
divorce following the birth of her son, of
whom she gained custody after a public
trial. Paradoxically she was also a member
of the Anti-Suffrage League (▷ Women's
suffrage). She converted to ▷ Catholicism
in 1892 and her last novel *The Dream and
the Business* (1906) deals obliquely with the
'clever' woman's predicament.
▷ 'Woman Question, The'.
**Bib:** Maison, M., *Life*; Richards, J.M., *Life*.

### Holdsworth, Annie (d?1910)

Novelist, feminist and editor. Born in Jamaica,
Holdsworth's book *Joanna Traill, Spinster*
(1894) addresses the ▷ New Woman theme
of female independence. She was co-editor of
*The Woman's Signal*. Her later novels include:

*The Years That the Locust Hath Eaten* (1896) and *The Gods Arrive* (1897).
▷ Women's Movement.

## Holiday House (1839)

A novel for children by Scottish writer ▷ Catherine Sinclair, which helped to develop a taste for books representing mischievous rather than moral children. Sinclair described her intentions thus: 'In these pages the author has endeavoured to paint that species of noisy, frolicsome, mischievous children, now almost extinct, wishing to preserve a sort of fabulous remembrance of days long past, when young people were like wild horses on the prairies, rather than well-broken hacks on the road.'
▷ Children's literature.

## Holmes, Sherlock

▷ Detective fiction; Doyle, Sir Arthur Conan.

## Homosexuality

Accorded a marginal place in literary representation and, when it has been shown, usually hedged about with implications of the exotic, the abnormal or at least the exceptional. According to Ronald Pearsall (*The Worm in the Bud: The World of Victorian Sexuality*) the term 'homosexual' was first used by a Hungarian physician named Benkert in 1869, and there was enormous interest in the phenomenon in the later years of the 19th century. Between 1898 and 1908 more than 1000 works on homosexuality were published. Homosexuality as a concept began to take shape in the 1880s in the work of John Addington Symonds (1840–93) and Richard von Krafft-Ebing, and in the research of Victorian sexologists such as ▷ Havelock Ellis. Legal prohibition at the time led to almost universal repression, except in the ▷ public school system where it appears to have thrived, if undercover. The editor William Stead declared in his *Review of Reviews*: 'Should everyone found guilty of Oscar Wilde's crime be imprisoned, there would be a very surprising emigration from Eton, Harrow, ▷ Rugby and Winchester to the jails of Pentonville and Holloway.' There were several attempts to make homosexuality respectable, including a number of books written by homosexuals advocating a change of terminology. Euphemisms such as 'homogenic love', 'contrasexuality', 'homoeroticism', 'similisexualism', 'sexual inversion', 'intersexuality' and 'the third sex'

were all used as substitutes. Carl Heinrich Ulrich invented the term 'uranism' in the 1860s and exponents were known as 'urnings' and 'dionings'. The philosophical form 'uranismus' indicated the female soul in the male body and the term 'urning', used to describe homosexual activity, was noted by J.A. Symonds as appearing in a number of novels of the time. Until 1828 sodomy was punishable by death if the activity had been witnessed by another, and such was the repression and fear that blackmail, especially of public figures, and self-mutilation were common.

In the 1850s Fleet Street, Holborn and the Strand were favourite places for homosexual prostitutes, who were known in early and mid-Victorian times as 'margeries' and 'pooffs'; the act itself was referred to as 'backgammon'. Politicians suspected of homosexuality but tolerated neverthless, as people in high office tended to be, included George Canning and ▷ Disraeli. One celebrated homosexual was the painter and poet Simeon Solomon, a friend of ▷ Algernon Swinburne. He eventually died in squalor in a ▷ workhouse in 1905. J.A. Symonds and ▷ Edmund Gosse were more discreet about their sexual preferences, and the affection of ▷ Tennyson for Arthur Hallam, celebrated in ▷ *In Memoriam* (1850) has been seen by some critics as evidence of adolescent homosexual anguish. After the 1885 Criminal Law Amendment Act the penalty for procuration was two years imprisonment with or without hard labour. It was this law that ▷ Oscar Wilde fell foul of in 1895. His is perhaps the most famous example of the persection of homosexuals at this time. Many historians follow the pioneering work of philosopher Michel Foucault (1926–84) in claiming that male homosexuality and the role of the male homosexual were 'invented', ie named and pathologized, in the 19th century in an attempt to distinguish between acceptable and abhorrent behaviour. For an account of sexual ambiguity in the literature of the late 19th century see Elaine Showalter's *Sexual Anarchy*.
▷ Lesbianism.

**Bib:** Montgomery Hyde, H., *The Love That Dared Not Speak its Name: A Candid History of Homosexuality in Britain*; Weeks, J., *Coming Out: Homosexual Politics in Britain from the Nineteenth Century to the Present*; Reade, B., *Sexual Heretics: Male Homosexuality in English Literature from 1815 to 1900*; Croft-Cooke, R., *Feasting With Panthers: A New Consideration of Some Late Victorian Writers*; d'Arch Smith, T., *Love In Earnest: Some Notes on the Lives and*

*Writings of English 'Uranian' Poets from 1889 to 1930.*

## Hopkins, Gerard Manley (1844–89)

Poet. He was converted to Roman ▷ Catholicism in 1866, and entered the Jesuit Order in 1868. He then gave up poetry, but resumed writing in 1875 with ▷ *The Wreck of the Deutschland*, his first important poem. So unusual were Hopkins's poems that they were not published in his own lifetime; after his death they passed to his friend, ▷ Robert Bridges, who delayed their publication until 1918, and even then Hopkins's fame did not become widespread until the second edition of 1930. The date of his publication, the interest he shared with modern poets in the relationship between poetry and experience and his technical innovation and intense style, has caused him to be thought of as belonging more to the 20th century than to the 19th. His ▷ 'sprung rhythm' is a technical term meaning the combination of the usual regularity of stress patterns with freely varying numbers of syllables in each line. This was not new, but was contrary to the practice that had predominated in English poetry since Edmund Spenser (?1552–99), which required a uniform pattern of syllabic counts, as of stresses. In Hopkins's poetry, the rhythm of the verse could more easily combine with the flow and varying emphasis of spoken language, so that the two kinds of expressiveness unite. A kindred sort of concentration is obtained by his practice – natural to the spoken language but uncommon in writing – of inventing compound words, especially adjectives, eg 'dappled-with-damson west' for a sunset, 'lovely-asunder starlight' for stars scattered over the sky.

Keats (1795–1821) was a strong influence upon him (as upon so many of the later Victorians) and Hopkins shared Keats's gift for evoking in words the physical response suitable to the thing they express. This was the more conspicuous in Hopkins because of his intense interest (for which he found support in the 13th-century philosopher Duns Scotus) in the qualities which give any object its individual reality, distinguishing it from other objects of the same class. For these qualities he invented the term 'inscape'. He also invented 'instress' for the force of these qualities on the mind. This intensity of response to the reality and beauty of objects was akin to the intensity of his feeling about the relationship between God and man.

All Hopkins's poetry is religious, and in quality recalls the early 17th-century devotional poets, John Donne (1572–1631) and George Herbert (1593–1633); in his 'terrible sonnets', for instance, Hopkins engages in direct dialogue with God as does Donne in his *Holy Sonnets*, or Herbert in a lyric such as *The Collar*. Thus Hopkins unites the rhythmical freedom of the Middle Ages, the religious intensity of the early 17th century, the response to nature of the early 19th, and he anticipated the 20th century in challenging conventional encumbrances in poetic form.

**Bib:** Gardner, W.A., *Life*; Hartman, G.H. (ed.), *Hopkins*; Bottrall, M. (ed.), *Gerard Manley Hopkins: Poems*; Bergonzi, B., *Gerard Manley Hopkins*: Roberts, G. (ed.), *Gerard Manley Hopkins: The Critical Heritage*; Oug, W.J., *Hopkins, the Self and God*; Weyland, N. (ed.), *Immortal Diamond: Studies in Gerard Manley Hopkins*.

## Horror fiction

Although horror fiction has undergone astonishing changes since the earliest ▷ 'Gothic' novels in the 1760s, the themes of transgression with which the genre deals have remained largely unchanged. Returning obsessively to taboo subjects (death, sex, incest, decay, bodily corruption, psychosis) horror novels have been described both by critics and champions as an 'undergrowth of literature' whose function is to speak the unspeakable. In his critical book *Supernatural Horror in Literature* H.P. Lovecraft declares: 'The oldest and strongest emotion of mankind is fear, and the oldest and strongest kind of fear is of the unknown. These facts few psychologists will dispute, and their admittedness must establish for all time the genuiness and dignity of weirdly horrible tales.' Sixty years later leading contemporary horror novelist Stephen King writes: 'Horror appeals to us because it says, in a symbolic way, things we would be afraid to say . . . It offers us a chance to exercise (not exorcise) . . . emotions which society demands we keep closely in hand' (*Danse Macabre*, 1981). Similarly, British horror novelist Ramsey Campbell has described the genre as 'the branch of literature most often concerned with going too far. It is the least escapist form of fantasy. It shows us sights we would ordinarily look away from or reminds us of insights we might prefer not to admit we have.'

Whilst much early horror fiction is rooted in US literature (Edgar Allan Poe, 1809–49, is frequently cited as the godfather of modern Gothic), Britain produced a number of key texts in the 19th century. ▷ Sheridan Le

Fanu published as early as *1838* in the *Dublin Magazine* and his *Ghost Stories and Tales of Mystery* (*1851*) combined the sensational and the Gothic to new and terrifying effect. Mary Shelley's *Frankenstein* (*1817*) has become the genre's single most re-worked (and indeed abused) text and ▷ Bram Stoker's ▷ *Dracula* (*1897*), itself influenced by Sheridan Le Fanu's vampire novel *Carmilla* (*1872*), set the tone for future tales of vampirism. Of the longevity of these horror icons David Punter writes: *'Frankenstein and Dracula are still granted fresh embodiments [because of] both their own imagistic flexibility and . . . the essential continuity under capitalism of the anxieties about class and gender warfare from which they sprang.'* *Dracula* has been read as dramatizing masculine fears of the insatiable sexual demands of the new generation of 'emancipated' women, and as a covert study in homoeroticism. The question of whether classic horror fiction alludes to contemporary rather than timeless fears has been of central import in recent years.
**Bib:** Sullivan, J., (ed.), *The Penguin Encyclopaedia of Horror and the Supernatural.*

### Household Words

A weekly periodical edited by ▷ Charles Dickens from 1850 to 1859. It emulated the magazine tradition of ▷ *Blackwood's* (started 1817) but aimed at a wider public. Among works published in it were Dickens's novel ▷ *Hard Times* and ▷ Mrs Gaskell's ▷ *North and South*. It was followed by ▷ *All the Year Round*.
   ▷ Reviews and periodicals.

### Hughes, Thomas (1822–96)

In his time a prominent public figure as a lawyer, leading Christian Socialist and Radical MP, Hughes is now remembered for his *Tom Brown's Schooldays* (1857), which launched a whole genre of boys' school tales. The novel records how Tom Brown triumphs over various schoolboy trials (including the

archetypal bully, Flashman) finally to captain the school cricket team and become a solid citizen. As well as spinning a good yarn, the book is also interesting for its first-hand (if fictionalized) account of ▷ Thomas Arnold's reform of the ▷ public school system at ▷ Rugby. The sequel, *Tom Brown at Oxford* (1861), is of interest for its evocation of the ▷ Oxford Movement.
   ▷ Lawrence, G.A.; Education.

### Hungry Forties, The

The decade 1840–50, so called because bad harvests caused serious food shortages, leading to mass agitation for abolition of the tax on imported corn (Anti-Corn Law League) and for a more democratic political system (the ▷ Chartist movement). It was in the years 1845–51 that the Irish famine took place: about 10 per cent of the population died from hunger and disease, and mass emigration ensued from those remaining.
   ▷ Corn Law, Repeal of the; Free Trade; Social Problem novel.

### Huxley, Thomas Henry (1825–95)

Biologist. He was a supporter of ▷ Darwin's theory of evolution and combined philosophical speculation with technical exposition. His many works, essays, lectures and articles included the influential publications: *Man's Place in Nature* (1863), *The Physical Basis of Life* (1868), *Science and Culture* (1881) and *Science and Morals* (1886). He held that scientific discoveries had neither given support to nor discredited religious faith, and he invented the term ▷ agnosticism for this attitude to religion.

### Hypatia, or, New Foes with an Old Face (1853)

An ▷ historical novel by ▷ Charles Kingsley, originally published in ▷ *Fraser's Magazine* 1852–53 and set in Alexandria in the 5th century AD.

# I

**Ibsen, Henrik (1828–1906)**
Norwegian dramatist; his working life
(1850–1900) began in a period when the
art of the theatre had fallen low everywhere
in Europe, and perhaps lowest of all
in Britain. By the end of the century
Ibsen's example had revived interest in
drama everywhere and had profoundly
influenced a number of other important
dramatists, such as August Strindberg
(1849–1912) in Sweden, Anton Chekhov
(1860–1904) in Russia, and ▷ Shaw in
Britain. Ibsen began by writing romantic
and historical dramas. Then, in self-
imposed exile, he wrote his two great
poetic dramas, *Brand* (1866) and *Peer
Gynt* (1867). About ten years later he
started on the prose dramas, the sequence
of which continued to 1900. The first
group of these treated social problems
with startling boldness: *Pillars of Society*
(1877), ▷ *A Doll's House* (1879); ▷ *Ghosts*
(1881); *An Enemy of the People* (1882).
After this, his work became increasingly
psychological, anticipating the 20th century
in the handling of inner conflicts, self-
deceptions, and frustrations: *The Wild Duck*
(1884); *Rosmersholm* (1886); *The Lady from
the Sea* (1888); ▷ *Hedda Gabler* (1890). So
far these plays had been extremely realistic,
but the psychological phase showed a new
and interesting dramatic use of symbols.
In the last group of plays the symbolism
takes precedence over the ▷ realism:
*The Master Builder* (1892); *Little Eyolf*
(1894); *John Gabriel Borkman* (1896), and
*When We Dead Awaken* (1900). It was the
social realist phase which most influenced
Shaw, and it was Shaw who was the most
eloquent introducer of Ibsen's art to the
British public, particularly in his book
*Quintessence of Ibsenism* (1891). The English
dramatic revival of 1890–1914 (as distinct
from the Anglo-Irish one by W.B. Yeats,
1865–1939, and J.M. Synge, 1871–1909,
happening at the same time) thus consisted
predominantly of realist plays dealing with
social problems, by such writers as Shaw,
Galsworthy (1867–1933) and Granville
Barker (1877–1946). The psychological
and symbolical phases of Ibsen's work
have had, together with the writing of
Chekhov and Strindberg, greater influence
since 1920.

▷ Archer, William.

Bib: Beyer, E., *Ibsen: The Man and his Work*
(trans. Wells. M.); Meyer, M., *Henrik Ibsen:
A Biography*, 3 vols.: Williams, R., *Drama from
Ibsen to Brecht*.

**Idylls of the King, The**
A series of poems by ▷ Alfred Tennyson on
episodes from the legends of King Arthur.
The earliest and most famous fragment is
the *Morte D'Arthur* (1842), but the series
really begins in 1859 with *Enid, Vivien,
Elaine, Guinevere*, followed by (1869) *The
Coming of Arthur, The Holy Grail, Pelleas and
Ettare, The Passing of Arthur*; (1871) *The Lost
Tournament*; (1872) *Gareth and Lynette*; (1885)
*Balin and Balan. Enid* was later divided into
*The Marriage of Geraint* and *Geraint and Enid*.
*Morte D'Arthur* was included in *The Passing of
Arthur*. The whole series was intended to have
a loose epic structure; single-minded virtue
ideally conceived is gradually overcome by evil
through the sinful passion of Lancelot and
Arthur's wife, Guinevere. Extremely popular
at the time, the *Idylls* have chiefly harmed
Tennyson's reputation since. They were
written under the influence of the ▷ Pre-
Raphaelite movement with its romanticization
of the Middle Ages. Later the poems struck
readers as bodiless, with the life neither of the
Middle Ages nor of 19th century. However,
parts of the *Idylls*, notably *Vivien* with its
powerful evocation of unleashed sexuality
and *Morte d'Arthur* with its impotent image
of kingship, have recently demanded a less
complacent response.

▷ Medievalism.

**Imperialism**
A desire to build up an empire; that is, to
dominate politically and assimilate other
countries and to extend the influence of the
colonizing nation through trade, diplomacy
and cultural dominance. It has a long history
from Rome to the present day, although
the main period of imperialism began with
the 17th-century conquests of the Americas
and reached its height in the 1880s and
90s, by which time Britain's dominance and
influence extended to Africa, Hong Kong,
India, Canada, Australia and New Zealand,
the Caribbean, Egypt and the Sudan.
Critics of the 'post-colonial' period and its
literatures have identified the development
of cultural imperialism with the growth of
English as a privileged academic subject in
the 19th century. The valorization of English
literary study as it developed in India, for
example, was useful in terms of propaganda,
and in naturalizing constructed values
such as 'civilization' and 'humanity', which
established 'savagery', 'native', 'primitive'
'as their antithesis and as the object of a
reforming zeal' (Ashcroft, Griffiths, Tiffin;
see bibliography). Hand in hand with this

goes one of the main features of imperial oppression which is control over language. British imperialism led to the spread of English as the official language of commerce and culture across the globe. Literature which reflects British imperialism includes *Plain Tales From the Hills* (1888), ▷ *The Jungle Book* and *Second Jungle Book* (1894, 1895) by ▷ Rudyard Kipling; *King Solomon's Mines* (1885), *Allan Quatermain* (1887), *She: A History of Adventure* (1887) by ▷ H. Rider Haggard.

▷ Colonialism.

**Bib:** McCrum, R., *The Story of English*; Bodelsen, C. A., *Studies in Mid-Victorian Imperialism*; Ashcroft, B., Griffiths, G., Tiffin, H., *The Empire Writes Back: Theory And Practice in Post-Colonial Literatures*; Eldridge, C.C., *The Imperial Experience From Kipling to Forster*.

## Importance of Being Earnest, The (1895)

A comedy by ▷ Oscar Wilde subtitled *A Trivial Comedy for Serious People*, and first performed in 1895. The title is a subtle play on the word 'earnest' which functions as a man's name – one which 'inspires absolute confidence' – and an indication of one of the most pervading characteristics of the era. It was ▷ Thomas Carlyle who urged the Victorians to 'earnestness' in thought and deed and Wilde satirizes the condition mercilessly. The play contains sharp social observation delivered in apparently throwaway lines and covers such topics as the morals and marriages of the upper and lower classes, lady novelists and the early ▷ feminist movement. It was Wilde's last and most enduring play.

## Industrial Revolution, The

Normally understood as the succession of changes which transformed England from a predominantly rural and agricultural country into a predominantly urban and manufacturing one in the 18th and 19th centuries, and especially between 1750 and 1850. It was the first such revolution in the modern world.

England was already a great trading nation by the beginning of the 18th century, with much private capital ready for investment. Its oceanic position, which ensured easy access to overseas markets, coupled with the fact that its irregular indented coastline meant that most places were within reach of water transport, contributed to its rapid development. In addition Britain was relatively rich in natural resources such as water, salt, iron, clay and, above all, coal.

Not only was trade free to move throughout the British Isles but there was considerable freedom of movement between the social classes. English middle-class religious belief emphasized the individual conscience as the guide to conduct as well as the moral excellence of sober, industrious employment. These values encouraged self-reliance and enterprising initiative. Although those who belonged to the Nonconformist or Dissenting sects which rejected the Church of England were barred from political rights, and Parliament (controlled by the aristocracy) was far from truly representative, the political leaders of the country were extremely interested in commerce, which they were ready to participate in and profit from. The bent of the whole nation from the early 17th century had been increasingly practical and the steadily growing population provided a market which invited exploitation by various methods of improved production. Once the process started, it gathered its own momentum, which was increased by the existence of large supplies of convenient fuel in the country's coalfields. Agriculture also contributed to industrial growth: the landowners were zealous farmers and their improved methods of cultivation not only freed much labour which then became available for employment in the town factories, but increased the food supplies available for the towns. Finally, the 18th century (in contrast to the 17th) was a time of relative peace and stability in Britain, undisturbed by the wars in which her armies and money were engaged across the sea.

In the textile industry, already established since the 15th century as the principal industry, a number of machines were invented which increased production and reduced labour but were too large for the cottages where the processes had hitherto been carried out. They therefore had to be housed in ▷ factories and mills where large numbers of employees worked together. These machines were at first operated by water power. In the iron industry, the principal fuel used had been charcoal, the supply of which was becoming exhausted. However, improved methods of smelting by coal were discovered and ironmasters set up their blast furnaces in the neighbourhood of the coalfields of the north Midlands and north of England.

Most important of all, in 1769 James Watt patented an adaptation of his steam engine to the machines used in the textile industry;

this consequently ceased to depend on water power and concentrated itself in the north of England to be near the coalfields. An important result was the immense expansion in the manufacture of cotton cloth. An extensive system of canals was constructed in the 18th century for the transport of goods and fuel, and the modern methods of road and bridge building were introduced, but the decisive advance in communications was the invention of the steam rail locomotive by George Stephenson (1814); by 1850 a railway system covered the country. The Industrial Revolution was a period of epic excitement, especially in the development of rail transport. It produced inventors and engineers, such as Isambard Kingdom Brunel (1806–59), who had to force their projects against established prejudice and ignorance. The other side of the epic story was the meteoric emergence of great financial speculators such as George Hudson (1800–71), the 'Railway King', who rose from being a York draper to controller of a third of the railway system, but whose career ended in disgrace. The social changes were unprecedently dramatic, in the rapid growth of the Midland and northern industrial towns and the opening of new opportunities for wealth for ambitious men from humble backgrounds. This heroic and extraordinary aspect of industrialism was a great motivating power in Victorian culture.

By 1850, Britain was the 'workshop of the world'; no other country was ready to compete with it in industrial production. The towns were the source of the country's wealth, though the landowners retained their social prestige and often became much richer by ownership of coalfields. The north of England became the most advanced region in Britain; its towns grew rapidly, unplanned and frequently characterized by ugliness and dirt. Economic motives often outran a sense of social conscience and the new urban proletariat worked and lived in evil conditions under employers who had often risen from poverty and had the ruthlessness which was the consequence of their own struggle. England was divided as never before; the industrial north from the agricultural south, the industrial working classes from their employers, and both from the long-established gentry, particularly of the south.

Many Victorian novels are eloquent testimony to the social conditions; the title of ▷ Elizabeth Gaskell's ▷ North and South, and the subtitle of ▷ Benjamin Disraeli's ▷ Sybil, or the Two Nations are evidence in themselves. Josiah Bounderby in ▷ Charles

Dickens's ▷ Hard Times is a portrait of the unprincipled kind of industrial employer; Sir Leicester Dedlock and Rouncewell the ironmaster in ▷ Bleak House exemplify the old order's failure to understand the new. ▷ Charles Kingsley's ▷ Alton Locke: Tailor and Poet (1850), and Mrs Gaskell's ▷ Mary Barton drew attention to the wretched living and working conditions of the urban poor.

▷ Anti-industrialism; Hungry Forties, The; Chartist movement; Carlyle, Thomas, Capitalism; Child Labour; Smiles, Samuel; Social Problem novel; Trade Unions.

## Ingelow, Jean (1820–97)

Poet, novelist and writer of ▷ children's literature. Born near Boston, Lincolnshire she was educated at home and wrote poetry from a very young age. The family moved to London where, driven by financial need, Ingelow published A Rhyming Chronicle of Thoughts and Feelings (1850) following it a year later with Allerton and Dreux, the first of her five novels. She also wrote Off the Skelligs (1879), Fated to be Free (1875) and Sarah de Berenger (1879).

She joined a small literary group, 'The Portfolio', whose members included ▷ Adelaide Procter and ▷ Christina Rossetti, and contributed, under the ▷ pseudonym 'Oris', to the evangelical Youth's Magazine which she also edited for a year. These contributions were published later in book form in Studies For Stories (1864), Stories Told to a Child (1865) and A Sister's Bye-Hours (1868). She achieved enormous success with her twenty-five books which included verse, children's stories and novels. Her second volume of Poems (1863) ran to thirty editions and included the much anthologized 'Divided', and 'The High Tide on the Coast of Lincolnshire, 1571', which established her reputation as a poet. Other popular poems include 'A Story of Doom' (1867) from the collection of the same name. Her most successful children's book was Mopsa the Fairy (1869).

Her literary acquaintances included ▷ Tennyson, Christina Rossetti, ▷ Jane and Ann Taylor and the poet and feminist essayist Dora Greenwell (1821–82). An edition of her poems was edited in 1908 by ▷ Alice Meynell. She has been described as 'A lost Pre-Raphaelite' unjustly excluded from literary history.

**Bib:** Anon., Some Recollections of Jean Ingelow (1901); Peters, M., Jean Ingelow, Victorian Poetess; Hickok, K., Representations of Women: 19th Century British Women's Poetry.

*In Memoriam A. H. H.*
A sequence of poems by ▷ Alfred Tennyson
inspired by the death of Arthur Henry
Hallam, at twenty-two, in 1833. He was a
brilliant young man of great promise and
hopefulness; Tennyson a year or two older,
had found in his friendship with Hallam a
strong resource against his own disposition
to despondency and scepticism. Hallam's
death crystallized for him the difficulty of
spiritual affirmation in an age of upheaval
in established ideas. Science was already
shaking traditional certainties and contributing
to the feeling that the reality of nature itself
was perpetual flux: there are echoes in *In
Memoriam* of ▷ Lyell's *Principles of Geology*
(1830–3).

The poem was written between 1833 and
1850 and is structurally loose or fragmented
– it was to be called 'Fragments of an Elegy'.
It consists of 130 sections, each section being
lyric in stanzas of four eight-syllable lines
rhyming *abba* – a form used by Ben Jonson
(1572–1637) in his elegy 'Though Beauty
be The Mark of praise'. The sequence is
a single poem arranged in three sections
divided by Christmas Odes, and the whole
concluded by a marriage-song for the wedding
of Tennyson's sister; another sister, Emily,
had been engaged to Hallam. Various moods
of grief are expressed, and a reaching out
to restored confidence and hope; in places
Tennyson engages in debate between religion
and science. Despite much disagreement
about the work as a whole, *In Memoriam* is
usually acknowledged to be Tennyson's finest
achievement.

▷ Atheism; Agnosticism; Homosexuality.

**Irish literature in English**
Ireland – England's first and closest colony –
presents a recent history of literary movements
and concerns that is very differently paced
from that of its colonizer. From 1171, the
year of Ireland's conquest by Henry II,
until the latter years of the 19th century, the
history of Irish literature in English is, largely
speaking, part of the general history of English
literature. Since the Irish literary revival
began in the 1880s, however, the existence
and the memory of a literature in Ireland's
original tongue, Gaelic, has interacted with
the country's adopted vernacular at every
level: in the detail of syntax; in the choice –
or rejection – of subject-matter; and in each
writer's struggle with identity.

Throughout the 18th and 19th centuries –
and into the 20th – writers from Anglo-Irish
Ireland made a rich and vigorous contribution

to English literature. ▷ Bram Stoker,
▷ Oscar Wilde, ▷ George Moore and
▷ George Bernard Shaw are amongst the
better-known Irish writers of the Victorian
period. Their writings are not primarily
concerned with the matter of Ireland or
their own Irishness, although George Moore
published a trilogy of reminiscences, in the
early 20th century, of the years he spent in
Ireland. Those who did write of Ireland,
like Dion Boucicault (1820–90), who is held
by many to be the inventor of the 'stage
Irishman', and Thomas Moore (1779–1852),
the purveyor to the drawing rooms of London
of an Ireland sugared by sentiment and exile,
capitalized on what looks with hindsight
like caricature. The collaborative novelists.
▷ Somerville and Ross are representative
of the Anglo-Irish tradition of exploiting the
attitudes of the indigenous Irish towards their
landed masters to comic effect in collections
such as *Some Experiences of an Irish RM*
(1899), its sequel *Further Experiences of an
Irish RM* (1908), *A Patrick's Day Hunt* (1902)
and *All on the Irish Shore* (1903). All these
writers of Anglo-Irish Ascendancy, coming
from their background of landed privilege,
seemed to be unaware of the still surviving
Gaelic tradition of native Irish literature, with
its long ancestry and close connections with
mainland Europe – a tradition eloquently
evoked in Daniel Corkery's *Hidden Ireland*
of 1924, and recently made available anew
in Seán Ó Tuama's and Thomas Kinsella's
1981 anthology *An Duanaire: Poems of the
Dispossessed*.

Moreover, during this pre-revival period
only a handful of creative writers mirrored
the growing interest that folklorists like T.
Crofton Croker (1798–1849), travellers (again
many of them from Europe) and diarists
were taking in Irish peasant life. Maria
Edgeworth (1767–1849) and William Carleton
(1794–1869) stand almost alone in the
seriousness with which they looked at their
native land and its inhabitants. Edgeworth's
*Castle Rackrent* (1800) and Carleton's *Traits
and Stories of the Irish Peasantry* (1830–3) are
isolated landmarks; and Carleton, an adopted
member of ascendancy culture was born
a Catholic peasant, has been read in recent
years with renewed interest and recognition.
▷ Sheridan Le Fanu was well-known for
his publication of the Irish ballads 'Phaudrig
Croohoore' and 'Shamus O'Brien' (1837)
and for his novels, stories and verse such as
'Beatrice', 'The Legend of the Glaive' and
'Song of the Bottle'. He is best known for
his contributions to the development of the

▷ short story with his skilfully constructed tales of mystery and terror.

In the decades that followed the devastation of native Gaelic culture by the famine and mass emigration of the 1840s, a new sense of Ireland's nationhood began, paradoxically, to emerge. The poets and dramatists of the literary revival of the 1880s and 1890s regarded Standish O'Grady (1846–1928) as its prime mover. His two-volume history of Ireland – *The Heroic Period* (1878) and *Cuchullin and His Contemporaries* (1880) – sent them back with a new authority to the ancient matter of Ireland. It was on this material, and on a new attention to the distinctive English actually spoken in Ireland, that the renaissance of Irish letters was founded. Its chief authors – the most notable being W.B. Yeats (1865–1939) and ▷ Lady Gregory (1852–1932) – were still, to begin with, the sons and daughters of the Ascendancy, but before long they were joined in their work of forging the soul of the soon-to-be-independent nation by writers who sprang from the native and Catholic population. A common task was perceived.

In the 100-odd years since the poet and translator Douglas Hyde (1860–1949) gave a lecture to the newly-formed National Literary Society in Dublin entitled 'The Necessity of De-Anglicizing Ireland' (1892), Irish writers have had continually to ask themselves and each other quite how, and to what extent, de-Anglicization is to be carried out – and who they are when they have done it.

Ireland's writers began by looking to their country's heroic past and its idealized idea of the west, the non-anglicized land of saints,

scholars and a noble peasantry, but they also looked, from the very start, to the literatures of Europe. ▷ Ibsen was a profound influence on the dramatists of Dublin's Abbey Theatre; ▷ George Egerton (Mary Chavelita Dunne) translated Knut Hamsun's *Hunger* and wrote about the ▷ 'New Woman' in her novel *Keynotes* (1893) before the 19th century ended.

▷ Allingham, William.

**Bib:** *Macmillan Dictionary of Irish Literature*; Foster, J.W., *Fictions of the Irish Literary Revival: A Changeling Art*; Hyde, D., *A Literary History of Ireland*.

### Irving, Sir Henry (1838–1905)

Actor. His original name was Brodribb, but he adopted the name of Irving when he gave up a commercial career for acting in 1856. For ten years he performed over 500 parts in provincial companies. He made his name in London in 1871 with the part of Mathias in the melodrama *The Bells* by Leopold Lewis (adapted from *Le Juif Polonais* by Erckmann-Chatrian). This was at the Lyceum Theatre, which later became famous under his management. His reputation grew by his performance in a great variety of roles (including two in plays by the poet ▷ Tennyson, *The Cup* and *Becket*), especially Shakespearean ones: his performances of Hamlet and Shylock became legendary. Irving's style was strongly romantic and powerfully eloquent; he and Ellen Terry, with whom he was associated at the Lyceum from 1878 to 1902, gave English theatre its main distinction at the time.

**Bib:** Bingham, M., *Henry Irving and the Victorian Theatre*.

## James, Henry (1843–1916)

Novelist. Born in New York; his father was an original writer on philosophy and theology, and his brother, William James, became one of the most distinguished philosophers and psychologists of his day. His education was divided between America and Europe. Europe drew him strongly, and he finally settled in Europe in 1875 after a series of long visits. He was naturalized British in 1915. Towards both continents, however, he had mixed emotions. As to the US, he belonged to the eastern seaboard, New England, which had its own well-established traditions originating in English Puritanism, and he was out of sympathy with the American ardour for commercial enterprise and westward expansion. As to Europe, he was fascinated by the richness of its ancient societies and culture, but he brought an American, and especially a New England, eye to the corruption which such advanced development generated. The conflict was fruitful for his development as an artist, and it was not the only one; he was also aware of the contrast between the contemplativeness of his father's mind and the practical adventurousness characteristic of his brother's outlook and of Americans in general. And in his close study of the art of the novel, he felt the difference between the intense interest in form of the French tradition and the deeper moral interest to be found in the English tradition.

In the first period of his work, his theme is preponderantly the clash between the European and the American outlooks: *Roderick Hudson* (1875); *The American* (1877); *The Europeans* (1878); ▷ *Daisy Miller* (1879); ▷ *The Portrait of a Lady* (1881). To this period also belong two novels about American life: *Washington Square* (1881); ▷ *The Bostonians* (1886); and two restricted to English life, *The Tragic Muse* (1890); *The Princess Casamassima* (1886). His second period shows a much more concentrated and difficult style of treatment, and it concerns English society only: *The Spoils of Poynton* and ▷ *What Maisie Knew* (1897); ▷ *The Awkward Age* (1899). Between his first and second periods (1889–95) he experimented in drama; this was his least successful episode, but the experiment helped him to develop a dramatic technique in the writing of his novels. He wrote twelve plays in all. In his last period, the most intensive and subtle in style, James returned to the theme of the contrast of US and European values: *The Wings of the Dove* (1902); ▷ *The Ambassadors* (1903); ▷ *The Golden Bowl* (1904). On his death he left unfinished *The Ivory Tower* and *The Sense of the Past*. Some of his best fiction is to be found among his short stories, and he was particularly fond of the 'novella' form – between a story and usual novel in length; *The Europeans* and *Washington Square* come into this class, and so does his well-known ghost story, ▷ *The Turn of the Screw* (1898).

In his criticism, James is important as the first distinguished writer in English to give the novel and its form concentrated critical attention. His essays have been collected under the title *The House of Fiction* (1957), edited by Leon Edel. He also wrote books on ▷ travel, the most notable of which is *The American Scene* (1907), and ▷ autobiographical pieces – *A Small Boy and Others* (1913); *Notes of a Son and a Brother* (1914) and *Terminations* (1917). (The last is also the title of a story published in 1895.) ▷ Novel of manners.

Bib: Edel, L., *Henry James*; Matthiessen, F.O., *Henry James: The Major Phase*; Anderson, Q., *The American Henry James*; Leavis, F.R., in *The Great Tradition*; Dupee, F.W., *Henry James*; Bewley, M., in *The Complex Fate* and in *The Eccentric Design*; Wilson, E., in *The Triple Thinkers*; Krook, D., *The Ordeal of Consciousness in James*; Gard, R. (ed.), *James: The Critical Heritage*; Tanner, T., *Henry James*; Berland, A., *Culture and Conduct in the Novels of Henry James*; Freedman, J., *Professions of Taste: Henry James, British Aestheticism, and Commercial Culture*.

## Jane Eyre (1847)

This best-known and most popular of the novels of ▷ Charlotte Brontë is in the form of a fictionalized ▷ autobiography containing some authentic autobiographical information. The earlier and most generally admired part of the book details the experiences of the penniless and unattractive eponymous heroine, first in the household of her unfeeling aunt, Mrs Reed, and later at Lowood Asylum – a charitable school based on Cowan Bridge, which Charlotte and her sisters attended. Following this, Jane takes up the position of governess to the household of the Byronic Mr Rochester, to whom she becomes increasingly attracted, finally agreeing to marry him. Unbeknown to her, however, he has a mad wife, Bertha Mason, who is locked in the attic and who escapes the evening before the wedding and tears Jane's wedding veil before her eyes. In church the next day Rochester is exposed as a potential bigamist by his wife's brother. In the third section Jane flees, finding sanctuary with Mary, Diana and their brother

St John Rivers – a cold and passionless clergyman who proposes marriage to her. Jane refuses him after a telepathic communication from Rochester because, unlike the passionate but morally flawed Rochester, Rivers does not love her. The fortuitous bequest of a legacy by an unknown uncle in Madeira reveals the hitherto unsuspected kinship between Jane and the Rivers family and, armed with a family and independent means, she returns to Rochester to discover that his house has burned down and that he has been blinded and maimed trying to save his wife. His equal at last, she marries him.

The novel is a mixture of ▷ Romantic, ▷ Gothic and ▷ realist forms, a female *Bildungsroman* (a novel describing the youthful development of a central character, usually male) that challenged contemporary attitudes in its portrayal of a 'strong-minded' and desiring woman. *Jane Eyre* was the catalyst for feminist criticism of the 1980s, beginning with S. Gilbert and S. Gubar's *The Madwoman in the Attic* (1979), in which unstable female characters in texts written by women were seen as doubles of the sane heroine and products of the suppression of the feminine. Another re-reading occurred several years earlier in Jean Rhys's *The Wide Sargasso Sea* (1966) which tells the story sympathetically from the perspective of the first Mrs Rochester and places the novel in the context of 19th-century colonialism.
▷ Imperialism.
**Bib:** Chakravorty Spivak, G., 'Three Women's Texts and a Critique of Imperialism'; Nestor, P., *Charlotte Brontë's Jane Eyre*.

### Janet's Repentance
One of ▷ George Eliot's ▷ *Scenes of Clerical Life*.

### Jefferies, Richard (1848–87)
Essayist and novelist. He wrote about the English countryside and its life and presented it plainly, without affection but with force. This has caused his reputation to rise in the 20th century, with its intensified interest in preserving natural surroundings and in understanding their environmental influence in society. He is well known for his volumes of essays: *Gamekeeper at Home* (1878); *Wild Life in a Southern County* (1879); *Round About a Great Estate* (1880); *Wood Magic* (1881); *The Life of the Fields* (1884). His novels are *Greene Ferne Farm* (1880); *The Dewy Morn* (1884); *Amaryllis at the Fair* (1887); *After London, or Wild England* (1885). His best-known books are probably *Bevis* (1882), a children's

story (▷ Children's literature), and his autobiography, *The Story of my Heart* (1883).
▷ Regional Novel.
**Bib:** Taylor, B., *Richard Jefferies*.

### Jekyll and Hyde
▷ *Strange Case of Dr Jekyll and Mr Hyde, The.*

### Jewsbury, Geraldine Endsor (1812–80)
Novelist, critic and journalist born in Measham, Derbyshire, the fourth of six children. Her elder sister Maria, also a writer, cared for the family until her marriage when Geraldine took over, looking after her father until his death in 1840 and her brothers until her marriage in 1853. Fêted in social and intellectual circles her friends included ▷ Charles Kingsley and his wife, the ▷ Rossettis, ▷ Ruskin and ▷ Huxley. Her first novel, *Zoë*, was published in 1845, and is one of the first Victorian novels to examine religious scepticism. It was followed by *The Half-Sisters* (1848) and ▷ *Marian Withers* (1851) both arguing strongly for changes in the upbringing of women. Jewsbsury moved to London to be close to her great friend ▷ Jane Welsh Carlyle and, despite ill-health, she contributed articles and reviews to periodicals such as ▷ *The Westminster Review* and ▷ *The Athenaeum* and was a reader for the publisher, Bentley's, influencing the choice of books selected for Mudie's ▷ circulating library. She wrote three further novels: *Constance Herbert* (1855), *The Sorrows of Gentility* (1856) and *Right or Wrong* (1856), as well as two stories for children. She was well known for her wit and conversation, and in 1892 *A Selection from the Letters of Geraldine Jewsbury to Jane Welsh Carlyle* was published (ed. Mrs A. Ireland). Both women had wanted their letters destroyed. Virginia Woolf wrote an article, 'Geraldine and Jane', for *The Times Literary Supplement* (28 February 1929) concerning the women's friendship.
▷ Women's Movement.
**Bib:** Howe, S., *Geraldine Jewsbury*.

### Jews in Victorian literature
Archetypal images of Jewish people, including the moneylender and the social outcast, have their roots in religious prejudice. In the medieval period usury was a reason for excommunication and Jews were quick to recognize it as an economic necessity. At the same time the exclusive policy of the guilds drove the Jews from handicrafts towards the retail trades, trade in second-hand goods and peddling. Their deviation from the status quo in terms of their religious practices,

occupations and appearance led to their
identification as scapegoats. Continuous
persecution and exile contributed to the
myth of the 'Wandering Jew' which was
prominent in the 19th century and helped to
feed the notion of a Jewish world conspiracy.
By 1850 Jewish immigrants who had arrived
from Europe at the turn of the century had
become a permanent part of the community
in England. Until 1860 Jews were unable
to take up a seat in Parliament because of
the explicitly Christian oath every new MP
was obliged to swear. By this time, however,
▷ Benjamin Disraeli – a Jew who had
been received into the Church of England
– was already one of the country's leading
statesmen.

By 1880 the Jews sought acceptance
through integration, and, although massive
immigration from Eastern Europe and
Russia caused overcrowding in certain areas
of England, there was little or no violent
anti-semitism. The Victorians approved of
Jewish dedication to the family, morality,
tradition and upward social mobility through
hard work. In 19th-century fiction Jews are
commonly depicted in extremes of good
or bad. Against the evil criminal Fagin of
▷ Charles Dickens's ▷ *Oliver Twist* there
is Riah of ▷ *Our Mutual Friend*, ▷ George
Eliot's idealized ▷ *Daniel Deronda* and the
godlike Sidonia in Disraeli's ▷ *Coningsby*.
▷ W.H. Ainsworth's ▷ sensation novel *Jack
Sheppard* (1839) depicts the London Jewish
criminal fraternity. ▷ Anthony Trollope's
*Nina Balatka* (1867) examines anti-semitism
through its portrayal of the love between the
Jew Anton Trendellsohn and Nina who is a
Christian. The magazine ▷ *Punch* regularly
portrayed Jews as vulgar, pushy, dishonest
and obsessed with money, while ▷ Thackeray
depicts them as ostentatious and equally
vulgar snobs (*The Book of Snobs*, 1869).

▷ Aguilar, Grace; Levy, Amy.
**Bib:** Naman, A.A., *The Jew in the Victorian
Novel: Some Relationships Between Prejudice
and Art.*

### John Halifax, Gentleman (1856)

A highly successful novel by ▷ Dinah
Mulock Craik. The tale is narrated by
Phineas Fletcher, a crippled man of sensitive
character. He relates the story of John
Halifax, who begins his working life as a
tanner's apprentice, but rises in the world
through his hard work, heroic deeds and
good fortune. By the end of the novel he has
married an heiress, bought property and a
business, and is given the opportuniy to run

for Parliament. Phineas Fletcher, unable to
pursue the material rewards of the world as a
result of his physical disability, has been seen
as symbolizing women's position in society.
Phineas does not, however, revolt against his
lot, but shows profound admiration for the
achievements of Halifax.

### Jones, Henry Arthur (1851–1929)

Dramatist. He wrote some 60 plays, and is
notable for beginning an English dramatic
revival in the later years of the 19th century
along with ▷ T.W. Robertson, ▷ Arthur
Pinero and ▷ Shaw. For instance, *Saints
and Sinners* (1884) was not only a dramatic
success, but aroused controversy by discussing
religious issues in a study of middle-class
provincial life. Other plays of comparable
note are *The Middleman* (1889) and *Judah*
(1890). His lectures and essays on drama
were collected in *The Renascence of the English
Drama* (1895).
**Bib:** Jones, A.D., *Life*; Archer, W., *The Old
Drama and the New*; Cordell, R.A., *Henry
Arthur Jones and the Modern Drama.*

### Jude the Obscure (1895)

The last novel by ▷ Thomas Hardy. In
Hardy's words the theme is the 'deadly war
. . . between flesh and spirit' and 'the contrast
between the ideal life a man wished to lead
and the squalid real life he was fated to lead'.
Jude Fawley is a village mason (like Hardy's
father) who has intellectual aspirations. He
is seduced into marriage by Arabella Donn;
when she abandons him, he turns back to
learning, but falls in love with Sue Bridehead,
whose contradictory nature seeks freedom and
yet frustrates her own desire. She runs away
from her schoolmaster husband, Phillotson,
who disgusts her, and joins with Jude in an
illicit union. Their children die at the hands
of Jude's only child by Arabella, who takes
his own and their lives because he believes
that he and they had no right to be born. Sue
returns in remorse to Phillotson, while Jude is
beguiled back by Arabella, who deserts him on
his deathbed.

The setting and the four main characters
are so representative that the novel is almost
an allegory. Jude's native place is Marygreen,
a run-down village which is a kind of emblem
of decayed rural England. His ambition is to
enter the University of Christminster, which
is Oxford, but so named as a reminder by
Hardy that the way of learning had once also
been a goal of the spirit. Jude uproots himself
from Marygreen but is unable to enter the
university because of his social origins, though

university because of his social origins, though he lives in the town (where he meets Sue) and works there as a mason. Hardy's point is not so much the social one that the old universities of Oxford and Cambridge were all but closed to working men; he is more concerned to show that the decay of spiritual goals in the England of his day matches the decay of the countryside. Jude himself is a complete man – physically virile as well as spiritually aspiring; it is his very completeness which the modern world, both Marygreen and Christchurch, is unable to accept. Sue Bridehead represents the ▷ 'New Woman' of the day, emancipated in her own theory but not in body. Sue is all mind; Arabella all body, and Phillotson a kind of walking death – a man of the best intentions who is nonetheless helplessly destructive in consequence of his lack of both physical and spiritual vitality. The novel epitomizes Hardy's longing for spiritual values and his despair of them; its pessimism has a strong poetic quality, and after completing

it he gave himself entirely to poetry. Like many of Hardy's novels, *Jude the Obscure* is set in the recent past – about twenty years before the time of writing. Publication of the book caused an uproar; after its hostile reception Hardy wrote no further novels.

▷ Censorship.

### Jungle Book, The (1894) and Second Jungle Book, The (1895)

Two sequences of ▷ short stories and poems by ▷ Rudyard Kipling concerning the boy Mowgli, who grows up in the jungle separated from the human community. He grows from dependency into dominance over the animals and eventually returns to his kind as a forest ranger. Humanity is portrayed as crude and unrestrained in comparison with the animals who exhibit a strong sense of social responsibility in accordance with the jungle law.

▷ Imperialism.

**Kavanagh, Julia (1824–77)**
Novelist. Born in Thurles and educated at
home, Julia Kavanagh was the daughter of
a writer who later claimed to have written
her novels and that his own worst work was
hers. She lived with her parents, remaining
single to care for her invalid mother. Much
of her youth was spent in France, and the
French character and way of life are reflected
in her novels. On the death of her mother
she returned to France and lived in Nice
until her death. Her first novel, *The Montyon
Prizes* (1846) was very popular. The best
known are perhaps *Madeleine* (1848), *Nathalie*
(1850) and *Adèle* (1858). Her biographical
sketches, *French Women of Letters* (1862) and
*English Women of Letters* (1863), have been
much praised. Her other publications include
a volume of ▷ short stories, *Forget-me-
nots* (1878).

**Kemble, Frances (Fanny) (1809–93)**
Actress, poet and ▷ autobiographer, born in
London. She was the niece of actress Sarah
Siddons and the daughter of actor-manager
Charles Kemble. In 1832 she left Britain to
tour North America with her father, recording
her experience in her *Journal* (1835). She
married Pierce Mease Butler in 1834, but
the relationship became problematic when
Fanny realized that her husband was a
slave-owner. She was horrified by a visit she
made to his Georgia plantation in 1838, and
became increasingly estranged from him.
Eventually they separated in 1845 and were
divorced in 1849. In 1863 she published
*Journal of a Residence on a Georgia Plantation*,
in which she attacks slavery, describes the
living and working conditions of the people
and decries her own unwitting involvement
in the system. For the rest of her life she
travelled between Europe and North America,
writing and giving public readings. Her works
include *Poems* (1844); *Records of a Girlhood*
(1878); *Records of Later Life* (1882), and *The
Adventures of Mr John Timothy Homespun in
Switzerland* (1889).
▷ Colonialism.
**Bib:** Driver, L.S., *Life*, Marshall, D., *Life*.

**Keynotes and Discords (1893 and 1894)**
Two volumes of ▷ short stories by ▷ George
Egerton which explore female oppression as
well as celebrating women's potential. Notable
stories in *Keynotes* include 'Now Spring Has
Come', which deals with the transitory nature
of romance, 'The Spell of the White Elf'
and 'A Cross Line'. The *Discords* collection
is graver and darker, focusing on women's

anger and describing the effects of women's
emotional and economic dependence on men.
In 'Gone Under' a woman's lover arranges
to have their illegitimate child murdered by
the midwife, in 'Wedlock' a women murders
her three stepchildren because her husband
has separated her from her own child. 'Virgin
Soil' describes the lasting damage caused to
a young girl by her lack of sex education.
Egerton's writing is characterized by a use of
symbolism influenced by dramatists ▷ Ibsen
and August Strindberg (1849–1912).
▷ 'New Woman, The'; Irish literature in
English.

**Kilvert, Robert Francis (1840–79)**
Diarist. He was curate in the village of
Clyro, Radnorshire. His candour and
responsiveness to people and environment
make his ▷ diaries valuable records of
rural environment in the mid-Victorian era.
Selections were published in 1938–40, edited
by William Plomer.

**Kim (1901)**
A novel by ▷ Rudyard Kipling. Kim, whose
real name is Kimball O'Hara, is the orphan
son of an Irish soldier in India, and he spends
his childhood as a waif in the city of Lahore.
He meets a Tibetan holy man in search of a
mystical river, and accompanies him on his
journey. Kim falls in with his father's old
regiment, and is adopted by them, eventually
becoming an agent of the British secret
service under the guidance of an Indian,
Hurree Babu. In spite of the ingenuousness of
Kipling's British chauvinism, conspicuous in
the later part of the book, the earlier part is an
intimate and graphic picture of the humbler
reaches of Indian life.

**Kingsley, Charles (1819–75)**
Novelist, clergyman, reformer. He belonged
to a movement known as Christian Socialism,
led by F.D. Maurice. He is now remembered
chiefly for his children's book, ▷ *The Water
Babies* (1863). His novels *Yeast* (1848) and
▷ *Alton Locke* (1850) are concerned with the
theme of social injustice. ▷ *Hypatia* (1853),
*Westward Ho!* (1855) and *Hereward the Wake*
(1865) are ▷ historical novels. His retelling
for the young of Greek myths, *The Heroes*
(1856) is still well known.
▷ Social problem novel, Children's
literature; Lawrence, G.A.
**Bib:** Pope-Hennessy, U., *Canon Charles
Kingsley*; Martin, R.B., *The Dust of Combat: A
Life of Kingsley*; Thorp, M.F., *Life*; Barry, J.D.,
in *Victorian Fiction* (ed. L. Stevenson); Chitty,

S., *The Beast and the Monk: A Life of Charles
Kingsley*; Collom, S.B., *Charles Kingsley: The
Lion of Eversley*.

### Kingsley, Mary (1862–1900)

▷ Travel writer and ▷ ethnologist. She was
born in Islington, London, the daughter of
Mary Bailey and George Henry Kingsley, and
niece of the novelist ▷ Charles Kingsley. She
is remembered today as an explorer of West
Africa, having travelled widely in that area
between 1893 and 1895. She recorded her
experiences in *Travels in West Africa, Congo
Francaise, Corisco, and Cameroon* (1897), in
which she writes of the customs and traditions
of peoples such as the Ajumba, Adooma
and Fan, as well as describing natural
environments in great detail. Two further
works, *The Story of West Africa* (1899) and
*West African Studies* (1899), are respectively
historical and anthropological in focus.
Kingsley died of enteric fever in Cape Town
in 1900, during her third trip to Africa. She
was celebrated as a great ethnologist; a society
was founded in her name to promote the
study of African peoples and culture.

▷ Colonialism.

**Bib:** Campbell, O., *Mary Kingsley: A Victorian
in the Jungle*; Clair, C., 'Female Anger and
African Politics: The Case of Two Victorian
"Lady Travellers"', *Turn-of-the-Century Women*
2, 1, Summer 1985.

### Kipling, Rudyard (1865–1936)

Poet, short-story writer, novelist. He was born
in India, educated in England, and returned to
India at seventeen as a journalist. In 1889 he
came to England to live.

Kipling's poetry is striking for his success
in using, vividly and musically, popular forms
of speech, sometimes in the ▷ Browning
tradition of the ▷ dramatic monologue,
eg *McAndrew's Hymn*, or in the ▷ ballad
tradition, eg *Barrack-Room Ballads* (1892).
He was also able to write poetry appropriate
to public occasions and capable of stirring
the feelings of a large public, eg his famous
*Recessional* (1897). His poetry is generally
simple in its components but, when it rises
above the level of doggerel, strong in its
impact. It needs to be read in selection: *A
Choice of Kipling's Verse* (ed. T.S. Eliot) has a
very good introductory essay.

Kipling's stories brought him fame, and,

partly under French influence, he gave
close attention to perfecting the art of the
▷ short story. The volumes include: *Plain
Tales from the Hills* (1887); *Life's Handicap*
(1891); *Many Inventions* (1893); *The Day's
Work* (1898); *Traffics and Discoveries* (1904);
*Actions and Reactions* (1909); *A Diversity of
Creatures* (1917); *Debits and Credits* (1926) and
*Limits and Renewals* (1932). The early stories
in particular show Kipling's capacity to feel
with the humble (common soldiers, Indian
peasants) and the suffering. But he admired
action, power, and efficiency; this side of his
character brought out much of the best and
the worst in his writing. Some of his best
stories show his enthusiasm for the triumphs
of technology, and are about machines
rather than people, eg in *The Day's Work*.
On the other hand he was inclined to be
crudely chauvinistic, and to show unpleasant
arrogance towards peoples ruled by or hostile
to Britain, though he also emphasized British
responsibility for the welfare of the governed
peoples. Yet again, he sometimes engaged in
delicate if sentimental fantasy, as in *They* and
*The Brushwood Boy* (1925); some of his later
stories show a sensitive and sometimes morbid
insight into abnormal states of mind, eg *Mary
Postgate* (1917). The stories, like the poems,
are best read in selection: *A Choice of Kipling's
Prose* (ed. Somerset Maugham).

Kipling is not outstanding as a full-length
novelist. His best novel is ▷ *Kim* (1901),
based on his childhood in India; *Stalky and
Co* (1899) is well known as a tale about
an English public school, and is based on
Kipling's own schooldays at the United
Services College. *The Light that Failed* (1890)
shows his more sensitive and sombre aspect.
An autobiographical fragment, *Something of
Myself*, was published in 1937.

Kipling's children's stories are minor
classics of their kind: ▷ *The Jungle Books*
(1894–5); *Just So Stories* (1902); *Puck of Pook's
Hill* (1906). *Rewards and Fairies* (1910) is less
celebrated.

▷ Children's literature; Imperialism.

**Bib:** Birkenhead, Lord, *Rudyard Kipling*
(biography); Page, N., *A Kipling Companion*;
Carrington, C.E., *Life*; Dobree, B., *Kipling*;
Orwell, G., in *Critical Essays*; Wilson, E., in
*The Wound and the Bow*; Green, R.L. (ed.),
*Kipling: The Critical Heritage*.

## Labour Party

Since 1923, one of the two main political parties in Britain, the other being the Conservative Party. The Labour Party was founded in 1900, and was called the Labour Representation Committee until 1906, when it took its present name. It claims to represent the interests of the working classes, and it favours state ownership of the means of production and distribution (state socialism) but it is not committed to complete socialization of the economy. The majority of its supporters are working class, but it also has fairly extensive middle-class support among intellectuals.

It was under the Labour government of 1945–50 that the Welfare State was set up and under Harold Wilson's Labour administration (1966–70) that important legal reforms were made, including the facilitating of birth control and divorce, the permitting of homosexuality and abortion, the abolition of hanging and theatre ▷ censorship.

Origins of the Labour Party:

**1** The 19th-century working-class movements. The most important of these was the growth of ▷ trade unions, which began a process of confederation in 1866; it was in consequence of a resolution by the Trades Union Congress (TUC) in 1899 that the Party was founded. Earlier movements which contributed to the origins of the party were those of the socialist ▷ Robert Owen; the ▷ Chartist Movement which, though it failed in its objectives, educated the working class in political consciousness; the Philosophical Radicals or ▷ Utilitarians, led by ▷ John Stuart Mill, who appealed to intellectuals among the workers, and elsewhere.

**2** The Liberal Party. Throughout the 19th century the ▷ Liberals (formerly the ▷ Whigs) claimed to be the party of reform, although important social reforms were often initiated by Conservatives (Tories) such as ▷ Shaftesbury and ▷ Disraeli. It was in alliance with the Liberal Party that the Workmen Members first entered Parliament in the last twenty years of the 19th century. The Liberals, however, received much support and money from employers of labour in the towns, so that a split caused by workers leaving the Liberal Party became inevitable.

**3** The Nonconformist sects. The Protestant churches which refused conformity with the Church of England included Baptists, Congregationalists, ▷ Presbyterians, Quakers, ▷ Unitarians and Methodists. Most of their support was from the lower social classes and, though they were predominantly non-political, they inevitably encouraged thoughtful discussion of political questions, especially social justice; they also assisted by helping to educate their members in social cooperation (▷ religious groups).

**4** ▷ The Fabian Society. This was a society of socialist intellectuals, founded in 1884. It was led by some brilliant minds, including ▷ Bernard Shaw and ▷ Beatrice Webb, and became very influential.

**5** ▷ Marx and the growth of Social Democracy in Europe. The European Social Democratic Federation was founded in 1881. However, although the British Labour Party has always had affinities with Social Democracy, in its origins it was not predominantly Marxist; its socialism derived more from earlier thinkers such as Owen.

**6** The leadership of the Scottish Labour Movement – Keir Hardie. Scotland was not so bound by tradition to the existing political parties as England was, and the Scottish working class was on the whole better educated. The Scotsman Keir Hardie was one of the finest leaders of the British Labour Party at the time of the foundation of the party.

## *Lady Audley's Secret* (1862)

A novel of ▷ sensation by ▷ Mary Braddon. Abandoned by her husband, the heroine deserts her child, leaving it to the care of her father. She adopts a new identity and gains work as a ▷ governess, later accepting an offer of marriage from Sir Michael Audley and thereby becoming a bigamist. When her first husband returns, she attempts to murder him by pushing him down a well, but he survives and Lady Audley is discovered. She is sent to a lunatic asylum, having pleaded hereditary insanity.

The novel was a huge success and has been dramatized, filmed and adapted for television. Feminist critics have read the work as a subversive attack on domestic ideals and feminine stereotypes, and commented on Braddon's use of an angelic-looking blonde as a deviant woman.

▷ Hazlewood, Colin Henry.
**Bib:** Showalter, E., *A Literature of Their Own*.

## 'Lady of Shalott, The' (1832)

One of the best-known poems by ▷ Alfred Tennyson. The story is an episode from the Arthurian legend of Sir Lancelot, and is to be found in Malory's *Morte d'Arthur* (1469/70) and in the 13th-century French romance *Lancelot*. Tennyson's poem is popular as an example of his extremely musical verse; it is also an example of his recurrent theme of withdrawal from deathly reality into a world of reverie. He expanded the story in his *Lancelot and Elaine* (1859), one of the ▷ *Idylls of the King*.

## Lady Windermere's Fan (1892)

A play by ▷ Oscar Wilde which brought him his first success in the theatre.

## Lamarck, Jean-Baptiste (1744–1829)

French pioneer biologist who formulated an explanation of evolutionary change based on the supposition that physical and mental characteristics developed by an individual in response to changes in its environment were physically inherited by its offspring. His theory of evolution through the inheritance of acquired characteristics was highly influential throughout most of the 19th century, despite being usurped by ▷ Darwin's theory of evolution through natural selection. It formed the basis of much of ▷ Herbert Spencer's early thought.

## Landor, Walter Savage (1775–1864)

Poet. Of upper-class background he was expelled from Oxford University for his intemperate radicalism, and lived for many years in Florence. He wrote the blank verse epic, *Gebir* (1768), the tragedy *Count Julian* (1812), and collections of verse: *Hellenics* (1847), *Italics* (1848), *Heroic Idylls* (1863). He was a fine classical scholar, producing a Latin version of *Gebir*, and his imagination was essentially literary in its inspiration. He is now chiefly remembered for his prose *Imaginary Conversations* (1824, 1828, 1829) between such figures of the past as Dante and Beatrice, and Elizabeth and Mary Tudor. His quarrelsome but generous personality was caricatured by ▷ Charles Dickens as Boythorn in ▷ *Bleak House*.
**Bib:** Pinsky, R., *Landor's Poetry*.

## Langham Place Group, The

▷ Women's Movement.

## Last Chronicle of Barset The (1867)

The last of the ▷ Barsetshire novels, about the politics of the imaginary cathedral town of Barchester, by ▷ Anthony Trollope. It centres on one of Trollope's best characters – the Reverend Josiah Crawley, the curate of Hogglestock. A poor, proud, isolated man with rigorous standards, he is accused of theft and persecuted by the arrogant Mrs Proudie, wife of the bishop. A minor theme is the

engagement of Major Grantly to Mr Crawley's daughter, Grace, in defiance of the wishes of his father the Archdeacon. It is often considered to be the best of Trollope's novels.

## Lawrence, G.A. (George Alfred) (1827–76)

Novelist. Lawrence's first novel was the enormously successful *Guy Livingstone* (1857), whose fighting, hunting, womanizing hero was the most extreme example of the glorification of masculinity common to a group of writers in the 1840s and 1850s sometimes known as the 'muscular' school (other novelists included ▷ Charles Kingsley and ▷ Thomas Hughes). Lawrence had attended ▷ Thomas Arnold's ▷ Rugby, and his portrayal of the school in *Guy Livingstone* is even more violent than that in Hughes's *Tom Brown's Schooldays*, published the same year. His subsequent novels were largely written in a similar vein, and include *Maurice Dering* (1864) and the nationalistic *Brakespeare* (1868), set in the Hundred Years' War.
▷ Historical novel.

## Lear, Edward (1812–88)

Comic poet. He wrote *The Book of Nonsense* (1846) and *Nonsense Songs, Stories, and Botany* (1870) for the grandchildren of the Earl of Derby. Like ▷ Lewis Carroll, who wrote the *Alice* books for children, Lear's poems for children show remarkable freedom of fantasy; in consequence, the 20th century, with its new science of psychoanalysis, has seen in them unsuspected depths of interest. The poems combine grotesque comedy with haunting melancholy. He did much to popularize the limerick. He illustrated the poems himself with extremely witty line drawings. Lear was by profession a landscape painter, but his elaborate landscape paintings have much less distinction and interest than his drawings and sketches.
▷ Nonsense literature; Children's literature.
**Bib:** Davidson, A., *Life*; Noakes, V., *Life*; Sewell, E., *The Field of Nonsense*.

## Lee, Vernon (1856–1935)

▷ Pseudonym of essayist, novelist and short story writer Violet Paget. She was born near Boulogne, France, and travelled around Europe as a young girl, receiving her education from various ▷ governesses. Lee's literary career was full of eccentric oscillations between fame and infamy. Her first major work was *Studies of the 18th Century in Italy* (1880), which was a great success, but her first novel (*Miss Brown*, 1884) damaged her reputation, as did the short story 'Lady Tal' (*Vanitas*, 1892), which contained an ill-considered and barely disguised portrait of novelist ▷ Henry James. Thereafter she turned her attention to essays, and *Genius Loci: Notes on Places* (1899) was a success. During the First World War she wrote a pacifist trilogy, *Satan the Waster* (1920), which was generally condemned, although it was better received when re-issued in 1930. Lee left England to avoid the disapproval of her family and friends of her ▷ lesbianism. In Paris she was a frequent visitor at Natalie Barney's (1876–1972) famous Rue Jacob salon. Other works by the prolific Lee include *Gospels of Anarchy* (1980), *The Tower of Mirrors* (1914), and two volumes of *Supernatural Tales*, published posthumously in 1955 and 1956.

**Le Fanu, J.S. (Joseph Sheridan) (1814–73)**
Novelist and journalist. Born in Dublin of an old Huguenot family related by marriage to Richard Sheridan's (1751–1816) family, he wrote poetry as a child, including a long Irish poem at the age of fourteen. After education by his father and tutors, he went to Trinity College, Dublin, in 1833, writing for the *Dublin University Magazine* and in 1837 joining the staff. He later became its editor and proprietor. In 1837 he published some Irish ▷ ballads and in 1839 was called to the Bar, although he did not practise, soon turning to journalism. He bought *The Warden*, *Evening Packet* and part of the *Dublin Evening Mail*, later amalgamating the three into the *Evening Mail*. In 1844 he married Susan Bennett and withdrew from society after her death in 1858, when he wrote most of his novels, many in bed, on scraps of paper. His writing is ingeniously plotted, shows an attraction to the supernatural and has been increasingly well received this century. The novels include *The House by the Churchyard* (1863), *Wylder's Hand* (1864), *Uncle Silas* (1864), *Guy Deverell* (1865), *The Tenants of Malory* (1867), *A Lost Name* (1868), *The Wyvern Mystery* (1869), *Checkmate* (1871), *The Rose and the Key* (1871) and *Willing to Die* (1873) which was finished a few days before his death. The short stories, *In a Glass Darkly*, appeared in 1872 and a collection of neglected stories, *Madam Crowl's Ghost and Other Tales of Mystery*, in 1923.
▷ Horror fiction; Irish literature in English.

**Lesbianism**
The Criminal Law Amendment Act of 1885, amended to outlaw homosexual acts in private, referred only to men. Lesbianism has never

been a crime in Britain. This was not due to a permissive or enlightened attitude on the part of the state, but because legislators were apparently at a loss to explain to Queen Victoria what homosexual acts existed between women, who were conventionally credited with little sexual awareness in middle-class circles. Male ▷ homosexuality came to prominence through newspaper reports of court cases but, as Ronald Pearsall (see bibliography) has suggested, if male homosexuality was 'the love that dared not speak its name', female homosexuality could not speak its name because it was undefined. There was a conspiracy of silence or professed and outraged ignorance, concerning possible sexual activity between women. ▷ Swinburne's *Poems and Ballads* (1866) was violently condemned by John Morley in the ▷ *Saturday Review* because it contained poems such as 'Anactoria', in which Sappho reproaches a fickle female lover. Morley expressed relief that such poems 'will be unintelligible to a great many people, and so will the fevered folly of "Hermaphroditus", as well as much else that is nameless and abominable'. His greatest wish was that young women should remain in ignorance of the existence of such matters lest they became corrupted. Lesbianism was identified as a medical problem in Germany, but even there authors were unperceptive and inaccurate about the reality and potential of sexual love between women. Towards the end of the century passionate attachments between women were championed by the more radical ▷ New Women, a fact noted by Edward Carpenter in *Love's-Coming-of-Age* (1896). Carpenter discusses the use of the term 'urnings' (coined by the Austrian writer K.H. Ulrichs) to describe people born 'on the dividing line between the sexes . . . while belonging distinctly to one sex as far as their bodies were concerned they may be said to belong *mentally* and *emotionally* to the other'. Carpenter himself preferred the use of the term 'The Intermediate Sex'.

Close emotional and even physical friendships between women were sentimentalized, yet at the same time many women sought the emotional and spiritual closeness, and often the sexual satisfaction they missed in their marriages, in their friendships with other women. Novelists like ▷ George Meredith were charmed and completely unthreatened by powerful emotional relationships between women. In his ▷ *Diana of the Crossways* (1885) the passionate but possibly asexual friendship between Antonia and Lady Emma

Dunstane offers sustenance and a refuge from the dismal failure of Antonia's marriage. In ▷ Charlotte Brontë's ▷ *Villette* Lucy Snowe cures herself of her passion for Dr John by 'redirecting' it to Ginevra Fanshawe under the temporary licence offered by the part she is coerced into performing in the school play.

The writer and reformer Edith Simcox was passionately involved with a largely unresponsive ▷ George Eliot who was the unwitting inspiration for much of Simcox's reforming zeal. Other such relationships that went beyond simple friendship include the attachment between ▷ Jane Welsh Carlyle and ▷ Geraldine Jewsbury, and Lillian Faderman (see bibliography) believes their love was reinforced by a 'mutual struggle to transcend the role allotted to Victorian women'. The heroines of ▷ Christina Rossetti's poem ▷ 'Goblin Market' enjoy a close and sensuous relationship which went unremarked by the censors. The same is true of Cytherea Aldclyffe's passionate response to Cytherea Graye in ▷ Thomas Hardy's novel *Desperate Remedies* (1871). The term 'Boston Marriage' was commonly used in late 19th-century New England to describe a long-term monogamous relationship between two unmarried women. ▷ Henry James's novel ▷ *The Bostonians* (1885) is a largely unsympathetic study of such a relationship between Olive Chancellor and Verena Tarrant, although James himself had no prejudice against lesbianism, having viewed it at close range in the relationship between his sister Alice and Katharine Loring in Boston. Other women who formed close, passionate and supportive relationships with each other include the sensation novelist ▷ Marie Corelli and Bertha Vyver and the poet ▷ Eliza Cook and Charlotte Cushman. Lesbianism is explicitly condemned in ▷ Eliza Lynn Linton's *The Rebel of the Family* (1880).

▷ Field, Michael; Somerville and Ross.
**Bib:** Pearsall, R., *The Worm in the Bud: The World of Victorian Sexuality*; Faderman, L., *Surpassing the Love of Men*; Cox, D.R. (ed.), *Sexuality and Victorian Literature*.

### Lesson of the Master, The (1892)

A story by ▷ Henry James. Its theme is the barrier set up against the true artist by supposedly cultivated society, which can understand nothing about the artist's dedication and can therefore only hinder him by its unintelligent praise based on false standards.

▷ Short story.

### Lever, Charles James (1806–72)

Irish novelist. Famous in the 19th century for his vigorous comic novels about Irish country life and life in the army, eg *Harry Lorrequer* (1837), *Charles O'Malley* (1841), *Tom Burke of Ours* (1843). He was criticized for perpetuating the Englishman's comic notion of the Irish character – the 'stage Irishman' caricature – but ▷ William Makepeace Thackeray, who was a friend of Lever and parodied him in *Novels by Eminent Hands*, declared (in *A Box of Novels*) that Lever was true to Irish nature in being superficially humorous but sad at heart.

▷ Irish literature in English.
**Bib:** Stevenson, L., *Dr Quicksilver: The Life of Charles Lever*.

### Levy, Amy (1861–89)

Jewish novelist and poet, the daughter of Lewis Levy and Isabelle Levin, she was born in Clapham, London, and was the first Jewish woman to attend Newnham College, Cambridge. While still a student, she published her first volume of poetry, *Xantippe and Other Verse* (1881). *A Minor Poet and Other Verse* appeared in 1884, and in 1888 *The Romance of a Ship* and *Rueben Sachs*, a novel describing the London Jewish community in which she grew up. *Miss Meredith* and *A London Plane Tree and Other Verse*, both published in 1889, mark the end of Levy's literary career. She killed herself in the same year. She was actively involved in ▷ feminist and radical debates as well as deeply concerned about the position of Jewish people in Europe.

▷ Jews in Victorian literature; Women's Movement.

### Lewes, George Henry (1817–78)

Philosopher and critic. He wrote on a wide variety of subjects but his most remembered work is his *Life of Goethe* (1855), researched with ▷ George Eliot's help. Other works include *The Biographical History of Philosophy* (1845–6), studies in biology such as *Studies in Animal Life* (1862), two novels, *Ranthrope* (1847) and *Rose, Blanche and Violet* (1848), critical essays on the novel and the theatre, and, his most important philosophical book, *Problems of Life and Mind* (1873–8), the last volume of which was completed by George Eliot after his death. He collaborated with Thornton Leigh Hunt in founding the *Leader* and was first editor of the *Fortnightly Review* (1865–6). In 1854 he left his wife, who had had three sons by Hunt, and lived with Mary Ann Evans (George Eliot) until his death.

**Bib:** Kitchell. A.T., *George Lewes and George Eliot*; Ashton, R., *G.H. Lewes: A Life*.

## Liberal Party

The Liberals were the successors of the ▷ Whig Party. In its political sense, the word 'Liberal' was first applied to what were considered to be extreme or even revolutionary reformers. Byron and Leigh Hunt collaborated to found the short-lived *Liberal* magazine in 1822. In the meantime, the Philosophical Radicals, led by ▷ Bentham and the ▷ Mills, were collaborating with the Whigs to secure the passing of the first Parliamentary ▷ Reform Bill (1832). The Whigs, who had formerly consisted preponderantly of landed aristocracy, then found themselves supported by the newly enfranchised industrial middle class, and it became increasingly clear that a new name had to be adopted. By the end of the 1830s the Whigs were increasingly calling themselves Liberals, and it became the accepted name for the party by the 1860s. Until 1923 the Liberals and the Conservatives were the principal political parties in Britain: the Liberals tended to be more representative of town and industrial interests, and more inclined to strive for reform. The disastrous decline of Liberal strength since 1923 has been due to a realignment of social interests.

## Linton, Eliza Lynn (1822–98)

Novelist, journalist and poet, born in Keswick, the sixth daughter and twelfth child of her mother, who died when Eliza was five months old. Self-taught, she rebelled against her conservative family background and moved at the age of twenty-three to a boarding house in London where she began a career as a journalist contributing to newspapers and periodicals such as ▷ Dickens's ▷ *Household Words*. She published two ▷ historical novels, *Azeth the Egyptian* (1846) and *Anymone* (1848), a radical attack on double sexual standards, *Realities* (1850), and wrote for the ▷ *Morning Chronicle* (1848–51) before moving to Paris where she lived until 1854. In 1858 she married William Linton in order to look after his seven children. They separated in 1867. Her later fiction, in particular *Sowing the Wind* (1867) and *The One Too Many* (1894), displays an increasingly reactionary attitude towards the early feminist movement and this tendency is even more pronounced in her journalistic writings for the ▷ *Saturday Review*. Her articles from 1866 to 1868 form a series of sensationalist attacks on the ▷ 'New Woman', and those who campaigned for women's rights, which were reprinted in 1883 under

the title of her most notorious essay ▷ 'The Girl of the Period'.

Her other works include *Ourselves: Essays on Women* (1869), *Rebel of the Family* (1880), and *The True History of Joshua Davidson, Christian and Communist* (1872) which, alongside *Under Which Lord* (1879), attacks the hypocrisy of the church. Despite her intense attachments to other women she explicitly condemned ▷ lesbianism in *The Rebel of the Family*. Her ▷ *Autobiography of Christopher Kirkland* (1885) records her own life through a masculine persona. She was close friends with ▷ Walter Savage Landor, ▷ Thomas Hardy, ▷ George and Agnes Lewes, ▷ George Eliot, the novelist and suffragist Beatrice Harraden (1864–1936) and Annie Hector, and she sold the house she inherited at Gad's Hill to Charles Dickens. She was made a member of the Society of Women Authors two years before her death and became the first woman to serve on its committee. Her own memoir *My Literary Life* appeared posthumously in 1899 and contains an acid attack on George Eliot.

▷ Women's Movement.

**Bib:** Anderson, N.F., *Women Against Women in Victorian England: A Life of Eliza Linton*; Layard, G.S. (ed), *Mrs Eliza Lynn Linton. Her Life, Letters and Opinions*.

## Little Dorrit (1855–7)

A novel by ▷ Charles Dickens. It centres on the theme of imprisonment, both literal and symbolic. William Dorrit (with his children and his brother Frederick) has been so long in the ▷ Marshalsea Prison for debtors that he is known as 'the Father of the Marshalsea' – a title that gives him a spurious social prestige. Arthur Clennam, who befriends him in the belief that the Dorrit family has been victimized by the commercial interests of his own family, is eventually confined in the same prison. But outside, the characters inhabit prisons without visible walls: William Dorrit inherits a fortune, and he and his family are constricted by social ambition under the gaolership of Mrs General who instructs them in fashionable ways; Mrs Clennam, Arthur's supposed mother, inhabits a gloomy house, confined to her chair and her bad conscience, under the gaolership of her servant Flintwinch who knows her guilty secrets; Merdle, the financier of reputedly enormous wealth, is the prisoner of his false position, and his gaolers are his fashionable wife and his arrogant butler; the servant girl, Tattycoram, is at first the prisoner of the well-intentioned but misguided Mr and

Mrs Meagles, and then escapes to the worse prison of Miss Wade, herself a prisoner of her self-inflicted loneliness. The nation is under the imprisoning control of a government department, the Circumlocution Office, which exists to gratify the interests of the enormous Barnacle family. Three characters stand out in independence of this conspiracy to confine and frustrate: Frederick Dorrit, who lives out an existence of passive misery by refusing to share (in or out of the Marshalsea) the self-deceptions of his brother William; Amy ('Little Dorrit') who consistently follows the compassion of her affections and the duties this imposes on her; and Daniel Doyce, the engineer whose enterprise is baffled by the Circumlocution Office but who perseveres in his vocation with humble and disinterested reverence for the demands that it makes on him. The self-interested Circumlocution Office at the top of society is balanced by the inhabitants of Bleeding Heart Yard, people who are themselves prisoners of the exorbitant property owner, Casby, but who live in the freedom of their own equal and open-hearted society. The blackmailer Rigaud is a figure of menacing evil and a dramatic counterpart to Mrs Clennam's hypocrisy and pretence, which is at the heart of the imaginative scheme of the novel. *Little Dorrit* is often regarded as Dickens's finest work, both in dramatic impressiveness and in richness of psychological insight.

**'Locksley Hall'**
A poem by ▷ Alfred Tennyson, first published in *Poems* (1848). It contains the famous line 'Let the great world spin forever down the ringing grooves of change' which epitomizes the Victorian equation of change with progress. It was begun after an unhappy love affair between Tennyson and Rosa Baring and bears traces of misogyny. The poem is a ▷ dramatic monologue and its structure is unusual in that it is composed of trochaic couplets with eight stresses.

**'Lotos-Easters, The'**
A poem by ▷ Alfred Tennyson, first published in *Poems* (1832) which contains much of his most distinguished work. Its subject is the ancient Greek myth of the *lotophagi* ('lotus-eaters' – Tennyson used the Greek spelling, 'lotos') who appear in Homer's *Odyssey*. Those who visit the land where the lotus fruit grows and eat some of it lose all desire to return home. The theme of

Tennyson's poem is the temptation to reject the world of activity, change and stress, in favour of a trancelike existence measured only by the more languorous rhythms of nature and a leisured absorption in sense perceptions. Along with ▷ 'The Palace of Art' it dramatizes the conflict in Tennyson between his ▷ 'Romantic' inclination towards sensation and philosophical aloofness and the demands that art should address itself to the issues of the day. It is in the tradition of Spenser (?1552–99) and the more luxuriant Keats (1795–1821): the rhythms have a hypnotic music, and the imagery is strongly and unsettlingly sensuous.

**Lyall, Edna (1857–1903)**
▷ Pseudonym of novelist Ada Allen Bayly. She was born in Brighton, Sussex, and after the deaths of both her parents moved to her uncle's home in Caterham. Lyall supported women's suffrage, was a committed Liberal and involved herself in charitable and social work. Her novels reflect her Christian religious views, but are more than simple moral tracts. With her second work, *Donavan* (1882), she became an extremely popular writer and her subsequent works ran to numerous editions. *We Two* (1884) and *Hope the Hermit* (1898) were especially successful. Other works include *Doreen* (1894), in which she supported the movement for Irish Home Rule, and her last novel *The Hinderers* (1902), which protested against the Boer War.
**Bib:** Escreet, J.M., *Life;* Payne, G.A., *Life.*

**Lyell, Sir Charles (1797–1875)**
Geologist. His principal work, *The Principles of Geology* (1830–33), revolutionized ideas about the age of the earth, and was as much of a challenge to current theological thinking as ▷ Darwin's *Origin of Species* (1859) was to be. He also contributed the idea of change as continous and ceaseless instead of sudden, intermittent and catastrophic, which had been the prevailing view. This added to the sense of flux and instability which haunted such contemporary imaginative writers as ▷ Matthew Arnold, ▷ Clough and ▷ Tennyson, whose ▷ *In Memoriam* shows traces of Lyell's influence.

**Lytton, Edward George Earle Lytton, Bulwer- (1st Baron Lytton)**
▷ Bulwer-Lytton, Edward George Earle Lytton (1st Baron Lytton).

**Macaulay, Thomas Babington (1800–59)**
Historian, essayist, politician and poet. He was
actively on the ▷ Whig side politically; that
is to say, without being a radical reformer,
he had strong faith in the virtue of British
parliamentary institutions. He was, from
the publication of his essay on the poet
John Milton (1608–74) in 1825, a constant
contributor to the main Whig periodical,
the ▷ Edinburgh Review, and his History of
England (1848 and 1855) is strongly marked
by his political convictions. He was trained
as a lawyer and became an eloquent orator;
his writing has corresponding qualities of
persuasiveness and vividness. As a historian he
was best at impressionistic reconstruction of
the past, and the same gift served him in his
biographical essays on writers John Bunyan
(1628–88), Oliver Goldsmith (1730–74),
Samuel Johnson (1709–84), Fanny Burney
(1752–1840) and the younger William Pitt.
He represented the most optimistic strain of
feeling in mid-19th-century England – its faith
in the march of progress.

Macaulay's Lays of Ancient Rome (1842)
were an attempt to reconstruct legendary
Roman history in a way that might resemble
the lost ▷ ballad poetry of ancient Rome.
Though not major poetry, they are very
vigorous verse with the kind of appeal that is
to be found in effective ballad poetry.

Macaulay was raised to the peerage in 1857.
▷ Macaulay's History of England.
**Bib:** Trevelyan, G.M., Life and Letters; Bryant,
A., Macaulay; Firth, C., A Commentary on
Macaulay's History of England; Trevelyan,
G.M. in Clio: a Muse; Stephen, L., in Hours
in a Library; Clive, J., Thomas Babington
Macaulay: The Shaping of the Historian.

**Macaulay's History of England from the
Accession of James II**
The history (Vols. 1 & 2, 1848; 3 & 4, 1855;
5, 1861) is a thorough, detailed account of
two reigns: James II (1685–8) and William
III (1689–1702). It is unfinished and was
originally intended to extend to the time
of George I (1714–27) and further. The
period covered is perhaps the most crucial
for English political development. James II,
a ▷ Catholic, tried to enforce his will in the
Catholic interest against Parliament, which
frustrated him and expelled him from the
throne in the Revolution of 1688. Parliament
then summoned William from Holland to
reign jointly with his wife, who was also
James's daughter, Mary II (1689–94). William
was the champion of the Protestant cause in
Europe, and Mary was also Protestant.

Macaulay's politics were strongly in the
▷ Whig parliamentary tradition and his
history is an epic of the triumph of the ideas
which to him gave meaning to English history.
Considered as history, the work is accordingly
one-sided, much more a work of historical
art than of historical science; it represents
what historians have come to call 'the Whig
interpretation of history'.
▷ Histories and Chronicles.

*Macmillan's Magazine*
It was founded in 1859 and published a
variety of material, including pieces by
▷ Tennyson, ▷ Matthew Arnold, ▷ Henry
James and ▷ Thomas Hardy. It folded
in 1907.

**Maeterlinck, Maurice (1862–1949)**
Belgian ▷ symbolist dramatist, influential in
the development of 'serious' drama at the end
of the 19th century. His most famous work is
Pelleas et Melisande, produced in London in
1898, and again in 1904 with Sarah Bernhardt
as Pelleas and Mrs Patrick Campbell as
Melisande. His plays were admired by the
poet W.B. Yeats (1865–1939) and actor
and dramatist Harvey Granville Barker
(1877–1946); Aglavaine and Selysette was given
six performances at the ▷ Court Theatre
in 1904.
**Bib:** Knapp, B., Maurice Maeterlinck.

**Malet, Lucas (1852–1931)**
▷ Pseudonym of novelist Mary Kingsley, the
daughter of novelist ▷ Charles Kingsley. The
pseudonym was adopted to avoid capitalizing
on the family's literary fame. Mrs Lorimer: A
Sketch in Black and White (1882) was Malet's
first novel, and she continued to write until
her death, producing more than twenty works,
including Colonel Enderby's Wife (1885); The
Wages of Sin (1891); The Gateless Barrier
(1900); The Far Horizon (1906); Deadham Hard
(1919); The Survivors (1923) and The Dogs
of Want (1924). Her style is prolix and often
sentimental, her characterization and detail
typically 19th- rather than 20th-century, yet her
contribution to literature was recognized when
she was awarded a civic pension in 1930.

**Mallarmé, Stéphane**
▷ Symbolism.

**Mallock, W.H. (1849–1923)**
A ▷ Catholic controversialist now best
known for his satirical novel The New Republic,
portraying leading members of the Victorian
intelligentsia, including ▷ John Ruskin,

▷ Matthew Arnold, ▷ Walter Pater and ▷ Thomas Huxley. He wrote a number of books on social questions against socialism. His *Memoirs of Life and Literature* was published in 1920.

**Bib:** Adams, A.B., *The Novels of W.H. Mallock*; Wolf, R.L., *Gains and Losses: Novels of Faith and Doubt in Victorian England.*

### Malthus, Thomas Robert (1766–1834)

Economist; particularly famous for his *Essay on Population* (1798), which he reissued in an expanded and altered form in 1803. Its original title was: *An Essay on the Principle of Population as it affects the Future Improvement of Society, with Remarks on the Speculations of Mr Godwin, M. Condorcet, and other Writers.*

The essence of his view was that social progress tends to be limited by the fact that population increases more rapidly than means of subsistence, and always reaches the limits of subsistence, so that a substantial part of society is doomed to live beyond the margin of poverty. The 'natural checks' which prevent population increase from exceeding the means of subsistence are war, famine, and pestilence, to which he added human misery and vice. In the second edition he added a further possible check by 'moral restraint', ie late marriages and sexual continence. These arguments made a strong impression on public opinion; an important practical consequence of them was the replacement of the existing haphazard methods of poor relief by the harsh but reasoned and systematic ▷ Poor Law system of 1834.

Malthus's relentless and pitiless reasoning led to political economy becoming known as the ▷ 'dismal science'. His conclusions were contested by humanitarians, and later seemed belied by factors he did not foresee, such as cheap imports of food from newly exploited colonies like Canada. Since 1918 'Malthusian' theories of the dangers of over-population have revived.

▷ Darwin, Charles Robert.

### Manchester Guardian, The

It was started in 1821 as a weekly paper, becoming daily in 1855. As the leading Liberal publication outside London, it was edited from 1872 to 1929 by C.P. Scott. Its title was changed to *The Guardian* in 1959, and since 1961 it has been published from London.

### Manchester School, The

A group of politicians in the 1840s, led by Richard Cobden and John Bright; they advocated the reduction or abolition of import duties (▷ Free Trade) and the prevention of all political interference in the development of commerce ('Laissez-faire'). The heart of the movement was in the rapidly growing industrial towns of the north, especially Manchester. The name was first applied to the group by their opponent, the Conservative politician ▷ Benjamin Disraeli.

### Marian Withers (1851)

A novel by ▷ Geraldine Jewsbury. Considered to be her best work of fiction, it is concerned with issues such as female ▷ education and societal expectations of women. Set in Manchester, the narrative focuses on the life of Marian Withers, detailing her social background and describing her passage to maturity.

### Marius the Epicurean (1885)

A philosophical novel by ▷ Walter Pater tracing the spiritual journey of a young Roman of the second century AD who moves from Epicureanism (the doctrine of the philosopher Epicurus, 342–270 BC, who is best known for his principle that pleasure is the beginning and end of life – although for him pleasure meant the acquisition of a mind at peace), through Stoicism (a philosophy founded in 4th-century-BC Greece which underlined the significance of the soul and advocated indifference to bodily suffering) and finally to the aesthetic pleasure of Christianity. However Marius remains faithful to his Epicurean philosophy to the end. The novel was enormously influential on Pater's contemporaries, as well as on later writers such as W.B. Yeats (1865–1939) as an analysis of aesthetic religiosity.

### Marriage

The first significant Marriage Act of the Victorian period was the Marriage Act of 1836 which permitted legal wedding ceremonies to be held in ▷ Catholic or ▷ Protestant Dissenting churches, provided that the registrar was notified. Prior to this only a Church of England parson had the legal right to marry people. No one under the age of twenty-one could marry without parental consent and there were heavy penalties for clergymen who defied these injunctions. Divorce with the option of remarriage was not available except by private Act of Parliament, which only the rich could afford. For the poor the only substitutes for ▷ divorce were ritualized wife-sales (as in ▷ Thomas Hardy's

▷ *The Mayor of Casterbridge*: the last recorded example was in 1887) or desertion. In 1857 the Matrimonial Causes Act introduced civil divorce for adultery: again only the rich could afford it and only men could petition for divorce. Wives were not permitted to divorce their husbands for adultery until 1923.

Before the Married Women's Property Acts of the late Victorian period a woman's property became her husband's on marriage, despite the wedding vow, in which the man promised to endow his wife with all his worldly goods. The review of the English marriage laws, which stated that a wife, her property, earnings and children were all in the power of her husband, was initiated in 1836 by ▷ Caroline Norton, who separated from her husband after his unsuccessful petition for divorce on the grounds of her adultery with Lord Melbourne. Prevented from having access to her children she published a number of pamphlets condemning the marriage laws and in particular the obliteration of a woman's legal personality on becoming a wife. These coupled with the publicity surrounding her trial gave impetus to the first organized ▷ feminist effort to challenge the marriage laws and became one of the great women's rights campaigns of the Victorian period. Norton induced Thomas Talford to introduce the Infant Custody Act allowing women to sue for custody of children under seven and access to those under sixteen. It became law in 1839. The Infant Custody Act of 1886 made separated or divorced parents jointly responsible for their children; however, the children of parents living together were still under the control of the father.

In 1854 Barbara Leigh Smith, inspired by Norton's case and that of Anna Murphy Jameson, wrote *A Brief Summary in Plain English of the Most Important Laws of England Concerning Women*, which was a plea for married women's rights. She formed a small committee to draw up and circulate a petition to Parliament asking for the amendment of the laws of property affecting wives. This group was the core of the Langham Place Group (▷ Women's Movement). From the spring of 1856–7 the issue of married women's property and divorce law reform were inextricably linked, although proposals for divorce reform were issued quite independently of women's rights activists. Women had to wait until the 1870 Married Women's Property Act before their right to earn money and keep it for their own use was recognized by the law. However, in 1870 most middle-class women were unable to obtain remunerative occupations. After 1870 improvement in the status of married women was closely allied with the ▷ women's suffrage campaign, each hampering the progress of the other. A full Married Women's Property Law was not passed until 1882. This was the single most important change in the legal status of women in the Victorian period and allowed women to act as independent legal personages. It was fought for by women's rights campaigners such as Elizabeth ▷ Wolstenholme-Elmy and Ursula Bright.

▷ 'Woman Question, The'.
**Bib:** Shanley, M.L., *Feminism, Marriage and the Law in Victorian England: 1850–1895*; Holcombe, L., *Wives and Property: Reform of the Married Women's Property Law in 19th Century England*.

**Marryat, Florence (1838–99)**
Novelist, the daughter of ▷ Captain Frederick Marryat, author of *Children of the New Forest* (1847). Florence was educated by ▷ governesses and at sixteen married T. Ross Church, with whom she had eight children. A prolific writer of ▷ sensation novels, her first work, *Love's Conflict*, was published in 1865. Between 1865 and 1899 she wrote over forty volumes, including works on spiritualism, such as *There Is No Death* (1891) and *The Spirit World* (1894). Marryat's novels are mostly melodramatic ▷ romances with stereotypical characters who become involved in crimes of passion. They include *Woman Against Woman* (1865); *Her Lord and Master* (1871); *A Crown of Shame* (1888) and *How Like a Woman* (1892).

**Marryat, Captain Frederick (1792–1848)**
Novelist. He was a Captain in the Royal Navy and his novels are chiefly about the sea. The best known of them are: *Frank Mildmay* (1829); *Peter Simple* (1834); *Jacob Faithful* (1834); *Mr Midshipman Easy* (1836). *Japhet in Search of a Father* (1836) is the story of a child of unknown parents who eventually achieves prosperity. Others of his books were intended for boys; the best known of these is *Masterman Ready* (1841). Marryat continued the 18th-century realistic tradition of narrative, the most famous examples of which are the novels of Tobias Smollett (1721–71). Marryat's other well-known novel, *Children of the New Forest* (1847), was one of the first ▷ historical novels to be written for children.

▷ Realism; Children's literature.
**Bib:** Marryat, F., *Life and Letters of Captain Marryat*; Conrad, J., 'Tales of the Sea' in

*Notes on Life and Letters*; Warner, O., *Captain Marryat: a Rediscovery*.

## Marshalsea

A prison in Southwark, London. It was opened in the 13th century as a prison for the Marshalsea Court, which dealt with cases involving a member of the royal household. After the ▷ Restoration it was kept for petty debtors. ▷ Dickens's father was imprisoned there for debt, and it is described in ▷ *Little Dorrit* (1858). The prison was abolished in 1849.

## Martin Chuzzlewit, The Life and Adventures of (1843–4)

A novel by ▷ Charles Dickens. The Chuzzlewit family includes old Martin, a rich man grown misanthropic owing to the selfishness and greed of the rest of his family; young Martin, his grandson, who begins with the family selfishness but is eventually purified by hardship and the good influence of his servant, Mark Tapley; Anthony, old Martin's avaricious brother, and Jonas, Anthony's son, who, by the end of the book, has become a figure of the blackest evil; Pecksniff, at first a trusted friend of old Martin, is one of Dickens's most effective hypocrites; ▷ Mrs Gamp, the disreputable nurse, is one of his most famous comic creations. The novel is divided rather sharply by the episode in which young Martin temporarily emigrates to America. This episode is a self-sufficient satire on American life; moreover, not only is young Martin's character radically changed by it but the story thereafter takes on a denser substance. Pecksniff, Jonas and the fraudulent financier Tigg Montague cease to be merely comic and become substantially evil. These changes mark the transition from the earlier Dickens, the comic entertainer, into the later Dickens, of sombre power. The novel is thus a transitional work but it is also, as his comic masterpiece, the climax of Dickens's first phase.

## Martineau, Harriet (1802–76)

Critic, novelist, journalist, essayist and biographer. Born in Norwich, the sixth of eight children, her youth was marked by illness, poverty and morbidity and increasing deafness; her Huguenot parents insisted on educating the children to earn their own living, which became essential after their father went bankrupt in 1826. She supported herself initially by writing reviews for the *Monthly Repository* and by needlework. A devout ▷ Unitarian, she published *Devotional Exercises for the Use of Young Persons* in 1823, followed by *Addresses with Prayers* (1826). In 1830 she won all three prizes in a competition set by the Central Unitarian Association to write essays aimed at converting the Roman Catholics, Jews and Mahommedans. Between 1832 and 1834 she published a series of social reformist tales, *Illustrations of Political Economy*, influenced by the ideas of ▷ J.S. Mill, ▷ Jeremy Bentham, and David Ricardo (1772–1823). The tales were highly successful, as were her stories for 'Brougham's Society for the Diffusion of Useful Knowledge', which sold some 10,000 copies. She became a literary celebrity, turning increasingly away from religion, and was consulted on social and economic matters by her friends including ▷ Malthus and Sydney Smith; she suggested and managed ▷ Thomas Carlyle's first course of lectures in 1837.

She travelled to North America in 1834, supporting the Abolitionists despite threats to herself, and published *Society in America* (1837) and *A Retrospect of Western Travel* (1838). A trip to Venice in 1839 was cut short by illness and from 1839–44 she was an invalid, but produced her first and best novel, *Deerbrook*, in 1839, an historical work which celebrates women's intellectual aspirations and bonds. *The Hour and the Man* (1840), on Toussaint l'Ouverture, and children's stories collected in *The Playfellow* (1841) followed. *Life in the Sickroom* appeared in 1843, followed by *Letters on Mesmerism*, an account of the treatment she claimed had cured her illness, in 1845. She settled in the Lake District in a house she designed and built herself, where she received William Wordsworth (1770–1850), ▷ Matthew Arnold, ▷ Charlotte Brontë, and ▷ George Eliot. She visited Palestine in 1845.

Other publications include numerous articles for the *London Daily News* and the ▷ *Edinburgh Review*, supporting ▷ divorce reform and attacking the Contagious Diseases Act (▷ Women's Movement); a radical *History of the Thirty Years' Peace* (1849–50), and the anti-theoretical *Laws of Man's Social Nature and Development* (1851). She was influenced by ▷ Comte, and her free translation, *The Positivist Philosophy of Comte*, appeared in 1853. Her *Autobiography*, begun in 1855, was eventually published in 1877. A staunch advocate of ▷ education for women, she also supported ▷ women's suffrage movements in England and the US.

▷ Children's literature; Travel writing; Feminism.

**Bib:** Miller, F., *Life*; Pichanick, V.K., *Harriet*

*Martineau: The Woman and Her Work*; Webb, R.K., *Harriet Martineau: A Radical Victorian*.

## Marx, Karl (1818–83)

Born in Trier of German-Jewish parentage, attended university in Berlin and Bonn where he first encountered Hegelian dialectic. He met Friedrich Engels (1820–95) in Paris in 1844, and in 1848, the Year of Revolutions, they published *The Communist Manifesto* together. In that year Marx returned to Germany and took part in the unsuccessful revolution there before fleeing to Britain where he was to remain until his death in 1883. In 1867 he published *Capital*, the voluminous work for which he is best known. Marx is justly renowned for his adaptation of the Hegelian dialectic for a ▷ materialist account of social formations, which is based upon an analysis of the opposition between different social classes. He is, arguably, the most prolific thinker and social commentator of the 19th century whose work has had far-reaching effects on subsequent generations of scholars, philosophers, politicians and analysts of human culture. In the political ferment of the 1960s, and especially in France, his work was subject to a series of extraordinarily productive re-readings, especially by philosophers such as Louis Althusser (1918–90), which continue to affect the understanding of all aspects of cultural life. In Britain Marx's work is what lies behind a very powerful literary and historical tradition of commentary and analysis, and has informed much work in the areas of sociology, and the study of the mass media. *Capital* and a range of earlier texts, have come to form the basis of the materialist analysis of culture.

## *Mary Barton* (1848)

The first novel by ▷ Elizabeth Gaskell, subtitled *A Tale of Manchester Life*, and written to counteract her deep distress at the death of her infant son. The background to the story is Manchester during the ▷ 'Hungry Forties', a decade during which working-class protest came to the attention of the middle classes. Mary Barton is the daughter of John Barton, a man employed by the Carson family as a mill hand and driven by desperation to join a militant ▷ Chartist group which requires him to assassinate Harry Carson, one of the most unpopular employers. However, Jem Wilson becomes the principal suspect. Mary has been involved with Carson, lured by the appeal of his wealth, but is in danger of following her beloved Aunt Esther's inevitable descent into prostitution. Ultimately she saves

working-class Jem from the death penalty and recognizes her real love for him. The novel provoked much hostility from Manchester mill owners and the Tory (▷ Whig and Tory) press, yet it has also been criticized by ▷ Marxist commentators for its naive treatment of class struggle and its sentimental ending. Recent feminist readings have emphasized the novel's critique of masculinist politics of confrontation, its exploration of the process of socialization and its call for an ethic of caring and nurturing in the community, which is seen to bind women and the working class. It was admired by ▷ Charles Dickens and ▷ Thomas Carlyle.

▷ Social Problem novel

**Bib:** Tillotson, K., *Novels of the Eighteen-Forties*; Williams, R., *Culture and Society 1780–1950*, Spencer, J., *Elizabeth Gaskell*; Stoneman, P., *Elizabeth Gaskell*; Homans, M., *Bearing the Word*; Nestor, P., *Female Friendships and Community*.

## *Master Humphrey's Clock*

The title of what ▷ Charles Dickens intended to be an inclusive serial linking distinct tales – ▷ *The Old Curiosity Shop* and ▷ *Barnaby Rudge*. Master Humphrey is the narrator of the early pages of the former, but Dickens abandoned the idea.

## *Master of Ballantrae: A Winter's Tale* (1889)

A novel by ▷ Robert Louis Stevenson set immediately after the Jacobite Rebellion of 1745, telling the story of the Marquis of Tullibardine. Stevenson intended it as 'a drama in a nutshell', a chronicle of domestic enmity.

▷ Historical novel.

## Materialism

The philosophical theory that only physical matter is real and that all phenomena and processes can be explained by reference to it. Related to this is the doctrine that political and social change is triggered by change in the material and economic basis of society.

▷ Marx, Karl.

## *Maud* (1855)

One of the best-known poems by ▷ Alfred Tennyson. It is called 'A Monodrama', and is in fact an example of the ▷ dramatic monologue, a form particularly characteristic of Victorian poetry, especially in the work of ▷ Browning and Tennyson.

It is in three parts. Part I tells of the mysterious death of the narrator's father, who has been ruined by the contrivances of 'that old man, now lord of the broad estate and the Hall'. But the narrator gradually falls in love with the old lord's daughter, and here occurs the famous lyric 'Come into the garden, Maud'. The young lord, her brother, treats him with contempt, however, and Part II opens with their duel and the death of the brother. The narrator flies abroad, and falls into the depths of morbid despair. In Part III he recovers, and seeks salvation through the service of his country in war: the poem was written in the year in which the Crimean War broke out.

*Maud* exemplifies the versatility of Tennyson's craftsmanship by the variety of its metrical and stanzaic form, and the brilliant distinctness of his vision in some of the imagery. It contains bitter criticism of the temper of the age. The poem has been held to betray Tennyson's confusion about his age; criticizing it, yet swimming with its tide. *Maud* is a Gothic conflation of images of disease, mental aberration and sexual repression.

### Mayor, Flora M. (1872–1931)

Novelist and ▷ short story writer who also wrote under the ▷ pseudonym of Mary Stafford. The twin daughter of intellectual parents, and born into an Anglican clerical household that respected women's ▷ education, Mayor was educated at Surbiton High School and Newnham College, Cambridge. She initially pursued an acting career without parental consent. Mayor's first publication appeared during this period, a collection of short stories entitled *Mrs Hammond's Children* (1901). Mayor's career as an actress was terminated through illness, brought on by the sudden death of her fiancé in 1903. Mayor never married, and lived largely in the company of members of her family.

Mayor's writings champion the rights of middle-class unmarried women and widows at a time when the English spinster was regarded as a problem by political commentators and the ▷ women's movement alike. Her first two novels take as their central theme different facets of spinsterhood, focusing particularly on psychological issues. In *The Third Miss Symons* (1913) Mayor explores the stereotype of the 'spurned' and unlikeable spinster in relation to a sensitive apprehension of the self-destructive effects of apparent social, sexual and emotional failure. *The Rector's Daughter* (1924) redresses the stereotype, detailing the complexity of the unconsummated but reciprocated passion between Mary Jocelyn

and the neighbouring clergyman. *The Squire's Daughter* (1929) formulates an analysis of the disintegration of late-Victorian class boundaries, a concern which draws attention to Mayor's own conservative political beliefs. Mayor's novels are significant in their close examination of the inner life of women, and interestingly straddle late 19th- and early 20th-century gender ideologies. Mayor's only other publication is *The Room Opposite and Other Tales of Mystery and Imagination* (1935).
**Bib:** Oldfield, S., *Spinsters of this Parish*; Williams, M., *Six Women Novelists*.

### Mayor of Casterbridge, The (1886)

A novel by ▷ Thomas Hardy. Its hero is the country labourer, Michael Henchard. At the beginning of the book, when times are hard, he gets drunk at a fair and sells his wife and child (▷ marriage) to a sailor called Newson. He bitterly repents and renounces strong drink for twenty years. His wife returns after eighteen years, supposing Newson to be drowned, and by this time Henchard has prospered so far as to have become Mayor of Casterbridge (Dorchester). At the same time as her return Henchard takes on as his assistant in his business of corn-dealing a wandering Scotsman, Donald Farfrae. The rest of the novel is the story of the rivalry between Farfrae and Henchard. Farfrae is never deliberately his enemy, yet merely by virtue of living in the same town he deprives Henchard of everything, and the latter leaves the place at the end of the novel as poor as when he started, and far more wretched. Hardy seems to have intended a kind of ▷ Darwinian study of the survival of the fittest among human beings. Henchard is a monolithic character, who puts all his energy and passion into every relationship and activity; Farfrae has a flexible personality and is able to devote to every predicament exactly what it demands, without excess. Henchard's crowning sadness is the loss of the girl he has supposed to be his daughter but who is in fact Newson's; he loves her nonetheless, but Newson returns and claims her.

### Medievalism in Victorian literature

The nostalgia for an idealized medieval period that animated several writers of the Victorian period had its roots in a profound dissatisfaction with and rejection of aspects of the society and culture of the time. Enthusiasm for things medieval was stimulated by the ▷ Oxford Movement's interest in the medieval background of the Church. For ▷ Thomas Carlyle the 12th century was epitomized by everything he found missing in his own society: universal religious belief, a society based on community feeling rather than cash, electoral systems which resulted in the appointment of the best candidate, and a benevolent and uncorrupted dictatorship free from what he saw as the inefficiency of parliamentary democracy. His essay ▷ *Past and Present* (1843) contains a finely realized study of the 12th-century Abbot Samson of Bury St Edmunds.

The poet ▷ Elizabeth Barrett Browning disguises her analysis of contemporary sexual politics by placing the action of her ▷ ballad 'The Romaunt of the Page' (1839) in a picturesque medieval setting. 'The Lay of the Brown Rosary' (1840) is also set in the medieval period as are many of ▷ Robert Browning's poems, such as 'The Statue and the Bust', which deals obliquely with the possessiveness, both in material and sexual terms, which he saw as characteristic of his age. ▷ Tennyson was likewise possessed by 'the Passion of the past' and reacted to the problem of producing 'contemporary poetry' by adapting ancient genres to the treatment of modern subjects. His poem 'Morte d'Arthur', based on Sir Thomas Malory's long prose romance of the same name written around 1469/70, uses a medieval form to examine contemporary issues such as the collapse of political, intellectual, and religious orthodoxy. Tennyson developed this project in his ambitious Arthurian epic ▷ *The Idylls of the King*. Malory's original text was reprinted at the end of the 19th century with illustrations by ▷ Aubrey Beardsley.

However, it was the ▷ Pre-Raphaelites – ▷ William Morris, ▷ Dante Gabriel Rossetti and ▷ John Ruskin – ▷ who raised nostalgia for the Middle Ages to a creed. They upheld the strong moral tone of Victorian art and believed in a medieval world (largely of their own invention) in which culture was serious, satisfying, and integrated into the fabric of society. 'Apart from the desire to produce beautiful things,' wrote Morris in 1894, 'the leading passion of my life has been and is hatred of modern civilization.' Much of Morris's early verse such as 'The Defence of Guinevere' has a medieval setting. At the same time he was dedicated to the revival of domestic crafts, in reaction to an increasingly mechanized age. The Pre-Raphaelites were also attracted to the ideals of courtly love (passionate yet unconsummated love which could take on a sacramental quality as the sublime experience) embodied in the medieval period.

The ▷ Aesthetes, influenced by ▷ Pater, supplanted an idealized Middle Ages as a source of inspiration with an equally idealized Renaissance.

**Bib:** Morris, K.L., *The Image of the Middle Ages in Romantic and Victorian Literature*; Cheney, L.D.G. (ed.), *Pre-Raphaelitism and Medievalism in the Arts*.

## Melodrama

The prefix 'melo' derives from the Greek *melos*, music. Orignally, melodrama was a play in which there was no singing but the dialogue had a musical accompaniment; the first example is said to be Rousseau's *Pygmalion* (1775). As the musical accompaniment gradually died out, the word came to denote romantic plays of extravagantly violent action, and it now covers any work of literature with a sensational plot and a penchant for lavish spectacle. The word has also been used to denote popular ballad operas in which spoken dialogue is used extensively. This use, however, is much less common. In the Victorian theatre, melodramas were usually concerned with the sufferings of the innocent at the hands of the wicked, who were usually vanquished by the end of the play after a series of fearsome adventures involving sensational risks. Tension is sustained by constantly exposing the innocent characters to peril and effecting their rescue in the nick of time. The rise of technical innovation in the theatre led to spectacular staging in which train crashes, snowstorms, earthquakes and battles were presented with increasing realism.

Thomas Holcroft's *Tale of Mystery* (1802), a translation of Guilbert de Pixérécourt's *Coelina, ou l'enfant de Mystère* (1800), established the genre in England. As the century progressed, music and singing gradually faded from the plays and was replaced by the demand for more ingenious and technically complex visual effects. The Irish dramatist Dion Boucicault (▷ Irish literature in English) produced two of the best-known melodramas – *The Octoroon* (1859) and *The Colleen Bawn* (1860). Other, even more sensational productions such as *London by Night* (1844) and *Under the Gaslight* (1867) anticipated the naturalist theatre of the late 19th century in their realistic staging and focus on social evils. Victorian melodramas have their roots in the English Gothic and the German *Sturm und Drang* (Storm and Stress) movements so prominent in the late 18th and early 19th centuries.

**Bib:** Rowell, G., *The Victorian Theatre 1792–1914*; Rees, T., *Theatre Lighting in* *the Age of Gas*; Booth, M.R. (ed.). *Victorian Spectacular Theatre 1850–1910*; Bingham, M., *Henry Irving and the Victorian Theatre*.

## Men and Women (1855)

A volume of poems by ▷ Robert Browning. It contained fifty pieces, nearly all ▷ dramatic monologues, a form in which a character soliloquizes about himself, his predicament or his relationship with another. The book contains much of Browning's best-known work, such as 'Any Wife to Any Husband', 'Andrea del Sarto', 'Fra Lippo Lippi'. In the *Collected Works* of 1868, the poems were dispersed, and only thirteen remained under the title *Men and Women*.

## Meredith, George (1828–1909)

Novelist and poet. Born at Portsmouth, the son of a tailor and naval outfitter; his grandfather, Melchizedeck, had had the same business and is the basis of the character Old Mel in the novel *Evan Harrington* (1861). George Meredith was educated in Germany and his writings were influenced by ▷ Germans, especially the novelist Jean Paul Richter (1763–1825), who stimulated his conception of comedy. Meredith was even closer to ▷ French culture, especially the radical thinking of the 18th-century Philosophes. On his return to England he began to study law but soon took to journalism and serious literature.

He began by publishing verse: *Poems* (1851). In 1855 he published his eastern romance *Shaving of Shagpat*, and in 1857 a romance in German style, *Farina, a Legend of Cologne*. ▷ *The Ordeal of Richard Feverel* (1859) was his first real novel, followed by *Evan Harrington*, which is now regarded as one of his best. In 1862 he produced his most famous volume of poems, ▷ *Modern Love*. Other publications included: *Sandra Belloni* (1864; originally called *Emilia in England*); *Rhoda Fleming* (1865); *Vittoria* (1867 – a sequel to *Sandra*); *The Adventures of Harry Richmond* (1871); *Beauchamp's Career* (1875 – his own favourite); *The Idea of Comedy* (1877 – a critical essay, important for understanding his work); ▷ *The Egoist* (1879 – one of his best known novels); *The Tragic Comedians* (1880); *Poems and Lyrics of the Joy of Earth* (1883); ▷ *Diana of the Crossways* (1885 – the first of his novels to reach a wide public); *Ballads and Poems of Tragic Life* (1887); *A Reading of Earth* (1888 – verse); *One of Our Conquerors* (1891); *The Empty Purse* (1892 – a poem); *Lord Ormont and his Aminta* (1894); *The Amazing Marriage* (1895). His concluding works were

all poetry: *Odes in Contribution to the Song of French History* (1898); *A Reading of Life* (1901); *Last Poems* (published in 1910 after his death). His unfinished novel, *Celt and Saxon*, was also published posthumously.

Meredith's reputation at present rests chiefly on his novels but, like ▷ Thomas Hardy, he seems to have been a novelist who preferred poetry. His prose is poetic in its use of metaphor and ▷ symbolism, and both his poetry and his prose are often expressed in concentrated and difficult language which invites comparison with ▷ Robert Browning. The impulsiveness and ruggedness of his prose also recalls ▷ Thomas Carlyle, whom Meredith resembled in his hostility to the mechanistic qualities of his age. Of all the Victorian novelists who ever had a major reputation, his has perhaps sunk the lowest in this century: both his prose and his poetry tend to be regarded as intolerably mannered and he is accused of fixing his attention on style as an end, instead of using it as a medium. Nonetheless, his intense interest in psychological exploration (again recalling Browning), his use of metaphor and symbol from the natural world to express states of mind and the freshness of some of his characters (especially women) were all original in his own time and keep him from being forgotten.

**Bib:** Stevenson, L., *Life*; Lindsay, L., *Life*; Trevelyan, G.M., *Poetry and Philosophy of George Meredith*; Sassoon, S., *Meredith*; Sitwell. O., *Novels of Meredith*; Lees, F.N., in *Pelican Guide 6: Dickens to Hardy*; Cline, C.L., *Letters*; Woolf. V., in *Common Reader*; Williams, D., *George Meredith: His Life and Lost Love*.

## Methodism

A religious movement founded by John Wesley (1703–91). The name was at first applied derisively to himself and his associates when he was a student at Oxford in 1729, referring to the strict rules that they made for themselves in order to follow a religious life; however, he early accepted the designation. From 1739, a time when the Church of England was particularly apathetic, the movement spread rapidly among the poor all over England, and it became especially strong in the industrial towns. Wesley himself had no desire to separate Methodism from the Anglican Church, but the demands on his energies forced him to ordain preachers whom the Church felt it could not accept as clergymen; consequently the Methodists developed an independent organization.

The later movement divided into a number

of distinct organizations. It spread abroad, especially to the USA where the membership numbers about 13 million, as compared with rather more than half a million in Britain.

### Mew, Charlotte (1869–1928)

Poet and ▷ short story writer, born in London to a genteel but oppressive middle-class family. Mew's life was overshadowed by the mental illness of two siblings and the death of her father, which was to leave her impoverished in her late twenties. Despite limited educational advantages she published her first poems and a short story, 'Passed', in the ▷ *Yellow Book* shortly before the public scandal of ▷ Oscar Wilde's arrest in 1895 left the magazine greatly discredited. She also published in *The English Woman* and *The Egoist*. Her work was well received by ▷ Thomas Hardy, John Masefield (1878–1967), publisher Harold Monro (1879–1932) and Walter de la Mare (1873–1956), whose combined influence secured her a civil list pension in 1923. She committed suicide in 1928 by drinking Lysol after the death of her closest sister, Anne. Because of its naturalistic form, her work is frequently linked with the early 20th-century Georgian school, despite her exclusion from representative anthologies of this poetic movement. However, her immunity from the stylistic innovations of modernism, as well as from the sexual and political freedoms of the 20th century, coupled with her thematic concerns with female self-repression, lost childhood and the past has led critics to regard her as a late Victorian in spirit. She published only two volumes of poetry and her reputation rests on twenty-eight poems, most of which were written before 1916. Her work is characterized by a complex use of the ▷ dramatic monologue, in poems such as 'The Farmer's Bride', 'In Nunhead Cemetery', 'The Quiet House' and 'Madeleine in Church', to explore gender relations, frustrated and obsessive sexuality, loss and extreme psychological isolation. In the 1920s both Hardy and Virginia Woolf (1882–1941) regarded her as the greatest living woman poet.
**Bib:** Leighton, A., *Victorian Women Poets: Writing Against the Heart*; Fitzgerald, P., *Charlotte Mew and Her Friends*.

### Meynell, Alice (1847–1922)

Poet and essayist, born in Barnes, London, and educated at home by her father. She converted to ▷ Catholicism in 1868, a faith shared by her concert-pianist mother. Her first volume of verse, *Preludes*, was published in 1875, attracting praise from ▷ George Eliot and from the author and editor Wilfred Meynell, whom she married in 1877. Further volumes followed, including *Poems* (1893); *Other Poems* (1896); *Later Poems* (1902); *Poems on the War* (1916) and *Last Poems* (1923). Meynell's lyrical and mystical poetry gained her a high reputation, particularly among writers, and after ▷ Tennyson's death she was proposed as Poet Laureate. She had eight children, and supported the family by writing for periodicals and newspapers, including *The National Observer* and *The Pall Mall Gazette*. Her essays were collected under various titles, which include *The Rhythm of Life* (1893), *The Colour of Life* (1896) and *The Spirit of Place* (1899). She also wrote translations, produced editions and wrote biographies of Holman Hunt (1893) and ▷ Ruskin (1900). She was active in the ▷ women's suffrage movement in the early years of the 20th century.
**Bib:** Michalik, K., *Meynell: Her Life and Works*; Badeni, J., *Life*.

### Middlemarch, A Study of Provincial Life (1871–2)

A novel by ▷ George Eliot, considered by many to be her finest work. It is set in the years immediately preceding the 1832 ▷ Reform Bill, a time of unrest, agitation and intense political discussion, but its ideas are more relevent to the mid-Victorian period when it was written. The material was originally intended for two novels, one centred on Dorothea Brooke and the other a study of provincial life in the town of Middlemarch, based on Coventry. Unity is achieved by the fusion of the two senses of 'provincial': the geographical sense of 'situated outside the capital' and the cultural one of 'ignorant of the central current of ideas'. Dorothea, the daughter of a country gentleman, aspires to a life of high spiritual conduct; she is, however, isolated geographically, socially and intellectually, and she finds no scope for her ambitions. In consequence she is led to an infatuation with Mr Casaubon, an elderly parson-scholar whose life's work is the writing of his *Key to all Mythologies*, in which he expects to demonstrate the centrality of the Christian scriptures. Unfortunately his work is rendered futile by his ignorance of the leading (German) scholarship in his field, and his egoism and narrowness of human experience prevent him from appreciating the quality of Dorothea's ardour and potentiality. He dies having failed in his ambition.

The disillusionment and failure of their

marriage runs parallel to that of Tertius Lydgate, a young doctor engaged in radical research, and the materialistic Rosamund Vincy. Unlike Casaubon, Lydgate is alert to the intellectual centre of his thought (Paris) and he has chosen to live in a provincial town only because he supposes that by so doing he can escape the social involvements and professional rivalries of the metropolis. Rosamund is the daughter of a Middlemarch manufacturer who has the typically provincial ambition to raise his family to the level of metropolitan fashion, and she is attracted to Lydgate only because he has aristocratic relations. She has no understanding of his intellectual promise and does nothing but frustrate it. Moreover, Lydgate's arrogance in viewing women as ornamental reflections of himself blinds him to Rosamund's real personality. Lydgate's career is virtually ruined when he becomes involved in a scandal concerning Bulstrode, a banker and bigoted ▷ Dissenter.

Dorothea's youthful desire is similarly thwarted, but at the end of the novel she seems to find happiness with Will Ladislaw, a young relative of her husband's who differs from the other characters by being essentially cosmopolitan in his background and outlook. Another centre of judgement is the Garth family, who acknowledge their provinciality and, by avoiding illusions, achieve balanced insights and clear directions for their energies in ways that are less provincial than those of their superiors. A minor character, but central to George Eliot's valuations, is the free-thinking parson Farebrother, condemned to a life of self-sacrifice by external causes. He is neither bitter nor unctuous, and is also capable of great sympathy for others. Through the portrayal of these characters, and others such as Cadwallader, Chettam and Brooke, Eliot analyses the social and political upheavals of the early 19th century and exposes the sexual prejudice that permeated the society of the day. The limitations imposed upon women's lives are highlighted in the case of Dorothea, while the dangers of contemporary ideologies of femininity are explored in Rosamund. The detailed and thorough analysis of gender in the novel has not prevented some critics from arguing that at the heart of Eliot's vision is a conservatism that emphasizes the need for individuals to curb their own desires in the face of social duty.

▷ Realism.

**Bib:** Peck, J., (ed) *Middlemarch: Casebook*; Brady, K., *George Eliot*.

### Mill, John Stuart (1806–73)

Writer on economics, politics, psychology, logic and ethics. He did not invent the word ▷ Utilitarian, but was the first to apply it to the reform movement which had been started by his father's friend ▷ Jeremy Bentham and of which his father, James Mill, was one of the leaders. The movement derived from 18th-century rationalism and the group was known as 'the philosophical radicals' because of the intellectual thoroughness with which they reasoned out their political and social standpoints. James Mill educated his son strenuously from a very early age but the education, wide as it was, ignored the imaginative and emotional needs of his son's character. J.S. Mill describes in his *Autobiography* (1873) how this neglect produced in him a spiritual crisis when he was twenty-one, after he had already made a brilliant start to his career. He discovered that he was emotionally indifferent to the ends for which he was working. He recovered partly through his discovery of the poetry of William Wordsworth (1770–1850), and the crisis enabled him to develop a far more sympathetic and balanced outlook on human needs than had been possessed by his father or Bentham.

Mill's literary output was very large and his influence on his time was great, though much of his writing (for instance his psychology, which he based on 18th-century associationism) has now been superseded by subsequent thinking.

### Mill on the Floss, The (1860)

A novel by ▷ George Eliot, set in the Midlands. Its central characters are Maggie Tulliver and her brother Tom – children of the miller of Dorlcote Mill on the River Floss. She is headstrong, intelligent and richly imaginative beyond the understanding of her family – particularly that of Tom, a boy of limited intelligence and sympathies to whom she is devoted. The novel is divided into seven parts; the first three lead up to Mr Tulliver's bankruptcy and form a rich and comic study of English country life in the mid-19th century with deep insights into the psychology of the rural middle class. The last three deal with the tragic love of Maggie for Philip Wakeham, the disabled son of the lawyer through whom Mr Tulliver has been ruined, the compromising of her reputation by the educated and agreeable Stephen Guest and her rejection by and alienation from her brother. In a ▷ melodramatic denouement Maggie rescues Tom from the flooded mill and they are reconciled before they drown. Although much is left unresolved, it is a powerful novel, particularly in terms of Eliot's representation of Maggie's psychological turmoil. In the provincial environment in which she grows up Maggie is prevented from following her desires and is forced to internalize all her intellectual and spiritual energies. Many women, including Simone de Beauvoir (1908–86), have identified with Eliot's semi-autobiographical portrayal of Maggie.

#### Modern Love (1862)

A series of sixteen-line poems resembling sonnets, by ▷ George Meredith. The poems tell the story of the breakdown of a marriage ending in the suicide of the wife. The tone is strongly emotional and the attitude to the emotions is self-scrutinizing; in these ways Meredith's *Modern Love* suggests comparison with the ▷ dramatic monologues of ▷ Robert Browning and ▷ Alfred Tennyson, for example Browning's *Any Wife to Any Husband* and Tennyson's ▷ *Maud*.

#### Molesworth, Mary Louisa (1839–1921)

Novelist and writer of ▷ children's literature. Born Mary Stewart in Rotterdam, she also wrote under the ▷ pseudonym Ennis Graham. She was educated at home by her mother in Manchester where they moved in 1841. In 1861 she married Major Reginald Molesworth and told stories to her own seven children, writing for and about them from a child's viewpoint and portraying a disciplined but loving world. In 1878 she separated from her husband who had undergone a personality change as a result of a head wound in the ▷ Crimean War, and from then on wrote to support her family. Her first three novels – *Lover and Husband* (1870), *She Was Young and He Was Old* (1872) and *Cicely* (1874) – were all concerned with the problem of women and marriage. She was advised to write for children by Sir Noel Paton, an illustrator, and concentrated on this market for the rest of her life. Works for children include: *Carrots* (1876); *The Cuckoo Clock* (1877), which is perhaps her most famous and popular; *The Adventures of Herr Baby* (1881); and *The Carved Lions* (1895), which describes her own childhood. Others include *The Tapestry Room* (1879) and *Two Little Waifs* (1883). Molesworth's stories are mostly lively blends of magic and ▷ realism, featuring female characters in central roles.
**Bib:** Avery, G., *Nineteenth-Century Children*; Lancelyn Green, R., *Tellers of Tales*.

#### Moodie, Susanna (1803–85)

The youngest of the literary Strickland sisters, born in Suffolk, England, Susanna Moodie lived near Southwold until her emigration to Canada in 1832. Her sisters, Agnes and Elizabeth, wrote *Lives of the Queens of England* and other biographies; her other sister, Catherine Parr Traill (1802–1899), wrote many natural history books. Moodie published early, contributing her stories, poems and sketches to various annuals. Susanna and Agnes collaborated on a poetry volume called *Patriotic Songs* (1830), and Susanna published her own *Enthusiasm; and Other Poems* in 1831, the same year she married John Wedderburn Dunbar Moodie. A year later the couple emigrated to Upper Canada (Ontario). In *Flora Lyndsay; or, Passages in an Eventful Life* (1854) Moodie offers a fictionalized version of the arduous journey, concluding with the trip up the St Lawrence River. Her best known works are *Roughing it in the Bush; or, Life in Canada* (1852) and *Life in the Clearings Versus the Bush* (1853), considered autobiographical but written using strong elements of fiction. Susanna Moodie as writer is effectively able to distance herself from Susanna Moodie as narrator. Both books detail the harshness of trying to wrest a living out of the uncleared wilderness. In essence, the Moodies were ill-equipped to deal with the demands of pioneer life, failed at farming, and moved to the town of Belleville in 1840, where Dunbar Moodie was appointed sheriff.

Despite her isolation, Susanna Moodie did not curtail her literary aspirations. She wrote serialized fiction for *The Literary Garland*, which was published in Montreal. In 1847 to 1848, the Moodies together edited *The Victoria Magazine* in Belleville. Susanna also wrote a number of sentimental novels, much less interesting than her Canadian material: *Mark Hurdlestone; or, the Gold Worshipper* (1853), *Matrimonial Speculations* (1854), *Geoffrey Moncton; or, the Faithless Guardian* (1855) and *The World Before Them* (1868). Although Moodie has been the recipient of much critical vitriol for her desire to warn potential settlers of what awaited them in Canada, her story is remarkable for its courageous endurance in the face of hardship. After her husband's death in 1869 she lived mostly with her family in Toronto.
**Bib:** Dahl, E.H., *'Mid Forests Wild': A Study of the Concept of Wilderness in the Writings of Susanna Moodie, J.W.D. Moodie, Catherine Parr Traill and Samuel Strickland*; Fowler, M., *The Embroidered Tent: Five Gentlewomen in early Canada*; Morris, A., *The Gentle Pioneers: Five*

*Nineteenth-Century Canadians*; Murray, H., in *A Mazing Space*; Shields, C., *Voice and Vision*; Thomas, Clara, in *The Clear Spirit*.

## Moonstone, The (1868)

A novel by ▷ Wilkie Collins. It is one of the earliest stories of detection and concerns the mysterious disappearance of a valuable diamond, formerly sacred to the Moon-god in one of the Indian temples. The novel is told in the first person by various participants in the events; it is plotted with skill, psychological ingenuity and a typically Victorian delight in characterization. Sergeant Cuff, the first detective in English fiction, appears in it.

▷ Detective fiction.

## Moore, George (1852–1933)

Irish novelist. He combined an aestheticism in tune with the ▷ aesthetic movement at the end of the 19th century, and the Celtic revivalism that went with a part of it, with a ▷ naturalism which showed the influence of late 19th-century French literature, especially from the novelist ▷ Zola. His most famous novels are: *A Mummer's Wife* (1885); ▷ *Esther Waters* (1894); *Evelyn Innes* (1898); *Sister Theresa* (1901); *The Brook Kerith* (1916); *Héloïse and Abélard* (1921). He was equally well known for his autobiographical studies: *Confessions of a Young Man* (1888); *Avowals* (1919, 1926); *Hail and Farewell* (1911–14) and *Conversations in Ebury Street* (1924). His carefully worked style was more admired in his own day than it is now.

▷ Irish literature in English.
**Bib:** Korg, J., in *Victorian Fiction* (ed. L. Stevenson); Brown, M.J., *Moore: a Reconsideration*; Sechler, R.P., *George Moore: 'a Disciple of Walter Pater'*; Yeats, W.B., in *Dramatis Personae*; Hough, G., in *Image and Experience*.

## Morning Chronicle

A London ▷ Whig ▷ newspaper founded in 1769; its contributors included dramatist Richard Brinsley Sheridan (1751–1816), critic Charles Lamb (1775–1834), James Mill, ▷ John Stuart Mill, ▷ Dickens, and ▷ Thackeray. It came to an end in 1862.

## Morning Herald, The

A London ▷ newspaper, 1780–1869. It had a large circulation, and published police cases, illustrated by the famous artist ▷ George Cruikshank, illustrator of ▷ Dickens's novel ▷ *Oliver Twist*.

## Morris, William (1834–96)

Poet, socialist thinker, designer and printer. He was one of the leading artists of his day, associated with, though not a member of, the ▷ Pre-Raphaelite Brotherhood, which sought to recover the cultural unity of ▷ medieval society. It is as a designer of textiles and wallpapers that he is most admired today. His aim was to counteract the industrial squalor of Victorian England, and to correct the major social injustice by which the proletariat were cut off from beauty of any sort by the nature of their environment: 'I don't want art for a few, any more than education for a few, or freedom for a few.' Paradoxically his campaign against aesthetic barbarism went with rejection of the machine and insistence on handwork, which cut him off from the economic realities of his age.

This withdrawal from social and political complexities is in keeping with his poetry, which expresses withdrawal into the romances of the Middle Ages (*Defence of Guinevere*, 1858; *Earthly Paradise*, 1868–70); into ancient Greek epic (*Life and Death of Jason*, 1867; translation of Virgil's *Aeneid*, 1875, and of Homer's *Odyssey*, 1887); and into Icelandic epic (*Sigurd the Volsung*, 1876). His verse (the majority of it translation) was voluminous, fluent, decorative and musical in the Spenserian tradition current in the Victorian period.

Nonetheless, his socialism was a reality. He was one of the founders of the Socialist League (1884) and edited its monthly periodical *Commonweal*, until in 1890 the anarchist wing of the movement drove him out. His *News from Nowhere* (1891 – previously contributed to *Commonweal*) is a prose ▷ 'utopia' describing England at a future date after the establishment of socialism. It is one of the most read of his works today. Another work of socialist inspiration, in mixed prose and verse, is *A Dream of John Ball* (1888).

Morris had some influence on the young W.B. Yeats (1865–1939), who remarked 'The dream-world of Morris was as much the antithesis of daily life as with other men of genius, but he was never conscious of the antithesis and so knew nothing of intellectual suffering' (*Autobiographies*, 1955).

▷ Arts and Crafts Movement.
**Bib:** Henderson, P., *Life*, Mackail, J.W., *Life*; Hough, G., *The Last Romantics*; Jackson, H., *Morris: Craftsman-Socialist*: Thompson, E.P., *Morris: Romantic to Revolutionary*; Lewis, C.S., in *Rehabilitations*. Thompson, P., *The Work of William Morris*; Kirchoff, F., *William Morris: The Construction of a Male Self: 1856–1872*;

Harvey, C., *William Morris: Design and Enterprise in Victorian Culture.*

## Morrison, Arthur (1863–1945)

Novelist and ▷ short story writer. Born in Poplar, Morrison worked as a journalist, contributing tales of East End life to ▷ *Macmillan's Magazine* (published as *Tales of Mean Streets*, 1894). His subsequent novels *A Child of the Jago* (1896) and *The Hole in the Wall* (1902) are also ▷ naturalistic accounts of slum life. Morrison also wrote ▷ detective fiction (*The Dorrington Deed Box*, 1897, in the manner of ▷ Conan Doyle), and later became a distinguished Orientalist.

## *Mothers and Daughters: A Tale of the Year 1830* (1831)

A novel by ▷ Catherine Gore, belonging to the 'silver-fork' school of ▷ fashionable fiction, like Gore's earlier work *Women as They Are* (1830). The central characters are Lady Maria Willingham and her two daughters, Claudia and Eleanor. The action revolves around the women's schemes for attracting aristocratic or wealthy men, and goes into great detail about the fashions of the day and the social milieu of the wealthy and privileged.

## Mudie, Charles Edward (1818–90)

Son of a bookseller, Mudie founded Mudie's Circulating Library, which loaned books to the public for a fee. Beginning in Bloomsbury, he expanded to Oxford Street, where the business ran for many years. Along with other ▷ circulating libraries, Mudie's exercised a noticeable moral ▷ censorship in the selection of books.

## 'My Last Duchess'

A poem by ▷ Robert Browning and one of his most powerful and successful ▷ dramatic monologues. It was first published in *Dramatic Lyrics* (1842). Ostensibly the poem describes an incident in the life of Alfonso II, Duke of Ferrara during the 16th century, but its interest lies mainly in the complex psychological portrait of the Duke that unfolds during its course. In an attempt to impress the envoy of a Count whose daughter he intends to marry with his knowledge of art and love of beautiful things, Alfonso draws back the curtain on a strikingly lifelike portrait of his first wife. As he describes her it becomes clear that he was jealously obsessed with the duchess and in order to possess her exclusively he arranged for her portrait to be painted and then for her murder.

# N

### Naden, Constance (1858–89)

Poet, painter and journalist. She was educated at the Birmingham Midland Institute and the Mason Science College where she studied the philosophy of ▷ Herbert Spencer. She wrote articles for the *Journal of Science* and lectured on scientific subjects. ▷ Darwinian theories of evolution also influenced her writing, which is distinctly ▷ atheist but nevertheless humorous. Her pamphlet *What is Religion? A Vindication of Freethought* anticipates a time when religious values will be superseded by scientific ones. Poems such as 'Evolutional Erotics' dispense with notions of 'romantic love' in favour of more Darwinian methods of selection and others confront the difficult choice between love and work as it affects women. Her overriding themes, however, concern the challenge to religious faith posed by Darwinian evolutionary theories as in poems such as 'The New Orthodoxy' and 'Poet and Botanist'.

In 1887 she travelled to Palestine, Egypt and India and retained an active interest in the medical needs of Indian women. In this she was encouraged by pioneer female doctor Elizabeth Garrett Anderson, and she was a loyal supporter of the new Garrett Anderson hospital for women in London. Literary acquaintances included ▷ Michael Field and ▷ Edith Cooper. She died at the age of thirty-one, after a major operation, of an infection possibly contracted in India. She was mourned by both the scientific and the literary communinity, and was highly praised as a woman poet by ▷ Gladstone in the ▷ *Spectator*.

**Bib:** Leighton, A. and Reynolds, M., *An Anthology of Victorian Women Poets*.

### Naturalism

In literature, a school of thought especially associated with the novelist ▷ Emile Zola. It was a development of ▷ realism. The naturalists believed that imaginative literature (especially the novel) should be based on scientific knowledge, and that imaginative writers should be scientifically objective and exploratory in their approach to their work. This means that environment should be exactly treated, and that character should be related to physiological heredity. Influential in France and Germany, the movement counts for little in Britain; the novelists ▷ George Gissing and ▷ Arnold Bennett (1867–1931) show traces of its influence in the treatment of environment in relation to character, as does ▷ Thomas Hardy.

▷ French influence on Victorian literature.

### Nesbit, Edith (1858–1924)

Nesbit was born in London and educated in France and Germany as well as England. Through her elder sister, Mary, she meet the ▷ Rossettis, ▷ Swinburne and ▷ William Morris, and published her first poem in *The Sunday Magazine* in 1876. She married the journalist Hubert Bland in 1880, and both became founder members of the ▷ Fabian Society in 1884. Hubert was a notorious womanizer, but Edith allowed his illegitimate offspring to live in the household along with her own four children (▷ H.G. Wells satirized the couple's unconventional lifestyle in his *Experiment in Autobiography*). Financial difficulties forced Nesbit to abandon poetry and write popular fiction and books for children – her first stories about the Bastable family appeared in 1898. Three 'Bastable' novels quickly followed: *The Story of the Treasure Seekers* (1899), *The Wouldbegoods* (1901) and *The New Treasure Seekers* (1904). Her blend of ▷ realism and magic proved highly popular, and her other famous children's novels include *Five Children and It* (1902); *The Phoenix and the Carpet* (1904); *The Railway Children* (1906) and *The Enchanted Castle* (1907). Her other published work includes early collections of poetry, political verse such as *Ballads and Lyrics of Socialism* (1908), a study of childhood, *Wings and the Child* (1913) and several ghost stories. Her last novel, *Lark*, appeared in 1922.

▷ Children's literature.

**Bib:** Moore, D.K., *Life*, Briggs, J., *A Woman of Passion*.

### Newcomes, The (1853–5)

A novel by ▷ William Makepeace Thackeray; it was published in instalments. The characters are drawn from the middle and upper classes, and the book is a study of the vices and virtues of such mid-19th-century society. The vices are shown in the worldly cynicism of Lady Kew who seeks a fashionable marriage for her grand-daughter Ethel Newcome; in the mean snobbery of Ethel's brother Barnes, who frustrates her marriage with his cousin Clive Newcome; in the hypocrisy, intrigue and viciousness of Clive's eventual mother-in-law Mrs Mackenzie, and in the philistinism and arrogance of the social world as a whole. The virtues are less successfully presented. Clive Newcome's father, Colonel Newcome, is the honourable, single-minded soldier who loses his fortune and is subjected to the tyranny of Mrs Mackenzie. Thackeray was inclined to see decency as overwhelmed by materialism.

▷ Bohemian.

**Bib:** McMaster, R.D., *Thackeray's Cultural Frame of Reference: Allusion in The Newcomes.*

## Newgate

In the Middle Ages, the principal west gate of the City of London. The gate-house was a prison from the 12th century, enlarged in the 15th century and burnt down in the ▷ Gordon Riots in 1780. Its destruction is described in ▷ Dickens's novel ▷ *Barnaby Rudge*. It was rebuilt and finally demolished in 1902, when the present Central Criminal Court (Old Bailey) was built on its site.

▷ Newgate novel.

## Newgate novel

Strictly speaking, a novel in which the characters and/or elements of plot are taken from *The Newgate Calendars*, which were records of notorious crimes, named after Newgate Prison in London, and published at various dates between 1773 and 1826. Examples are *Rookwood* (1834) by ▷ William Harrison Ainsworth and *Paul Clifford* (1830) by ▷ Bulwer-Lytton. The term is applied more loosely to novels about criminals, such as ▷ *Oliver Twist* (1837) by ▷ Charles Dickens. Newgate novels provoked a furious debate in the 1830s and 40s, because they often showed some sympathy for criminals and suggested that social conditions contributed to crime. They were attacked as morally corrupting by some critics, including the novelist ▷ Thackeray, who satirized the form in his novel ▷ *Barry Lyndon* (1844).

## *New Grub Street* (1891)

A novel by ▷ George Gissing. The title refers to Grub Street, which was inhabited in the 18th century by journalists of a low order, who wrote to gain a living without seriousness of intention or artistic standards. The living they earned was generally a mean one, but since 1875 the new periodicals and newspapers had found a way to achieve massive circulations by printing material which had an immediate appeal although its intrinsic quality was trivial or merely sensational. This commercialization of journalism had spread to the production of books. Gissing's novel is about the difficulties of the serious literary artist faced by successful competition from the now very well rewarded commercial writer without scruples, either moral or artistic. The serious writer in the book is Edwin Reardon (a self-portrait) and his successful competitor is Jasper Milvain. Commercial success is also illustrated by Whelpdale, editor of the

magazine *Chit-Chat* (based on the actual magazine *Titbits* founded in 1881) which never publishes articles longer than two inches in length. At the other extreme is the novelist Biffen, who has the artistic fastidiousness of the French novelist ▷ Flaubert and writes the same kind of book. Biffen and Reardon both end in failure but Gissing's novel was fairly popular, which perhaps argues against the extreme pessimism of his thesis.

▷ Newspapers.

## Newman, John Henry (1801–90)

Writer on religion and education. From 1833 to 1842 he was one of the most influential and controversial leaders of the Church of England, but in 1845 he was received into the Roman ▷ Catholic Church. As a Catholic convert he was even more influential, and he was made a Cardinal in 1879.

His first period of activity (1833–42) was as leader of the Tractarian Movement – more or less identical with the ▷ Oxford Movement, whose aim was to defend the Church of England against encroachments by the state on the one hand, and against adulteration of its doctrines by the Broad Church tendencies on the other. The Church of England was founded in the 16th century on a central position between the Catholicism of Rome and the whole-hearted ▷ Protestantism of Martin Luther (1483–1546) and John Calvin (1509–1604). This had always been both its strength and its weakness; it was able to accommodate a variety of believers, but it was inclined to lose itself in vagueness and become subservient to the state. Newman's *Tracts for the Times* tried to secure a firm basis for Anglican doctrine and discipline, as against supporters of the Broad Church party (such as ▷ Thomas Arnold) who cared less for doctrine than for social ethics. Newman's tracts led him steadily towards Roman Catholicism, however, until his *Tract XC* went so far as to say that the Anglican 39 Articles – which all clergy had to accept – were not incompatible with essential Roman Catholic beliefs, but only with distortions and exaggerations of them.

As a Roman Catholic, Newman's first valuable literary work was *The Scope and Nature of University Education* (1852), a collection of lectures to the new Catholic University of Dublin, of which he became Rector in 1854. These were combined with further lectures delivered in 1859 to make *The Idea of a University Defined* (1873). His spiritual ▷ autobiography, defending the sincerity of his Catholic beliefs against the accusations by the Broad Churchman, ▷ Charles Kingsley, came out with the title ▷ *Apologia Pro Vita Sua* (*Defence of his Life*) in 1864. It was not only very persuasive in convincing the public of the genuineness of his faith; it was also an eloquent and lucid presentation of the nature of religious belief at a time when much religious thinking in English was muddled, superficial and entangled in irrelevant controversies with scientific ▷ agnostics such as ▷ T.H. Huxley. His *Grammar of Assent* (1870) was a more strictly philosophical account of religious belief.

Newman also wrote some minor poetry, including the famous hymn *Lead Kindly Light*, and the ▷ dramatic monologue *The Dream of Gerontius*, better known for the music set to it by Elgar. He also wrote two religious novels, *Loss and Gain* (1848) and *Callista* (1856).

As a writer he is famous for the lucidity and grace of his style. His wide influence, still very powerful, arose from his ability to understand the tragic extremity of the emotional and intellectual bewilderment of his contemporaries, while refusing to compromise his beliefs.

**Bib:** Harold, C.F., *Newman: an Expository and Critical Study of his Mind, Thought and Art.*

### New Monthly Magazine

It started in 1814 and had editors of considerable literary note such as the poets Thomas Campbell (1777–1844) and Thomas Hood (1799–1845), the novelists ▷ Harrison Ainsworth and ▷ Bulwer-Lytton, and the essayist Theodore Hook. It gave considerable space to criticism. It closed in 1884.

### Newspapers

The first attempt to reach a mass circulation was made by journalist and political leader William Cobbett (1762–1835) with his periodical the *Weekly Political Register* (started 1802). In 1808 Leigh Hunt's weekly *Examiner*, directed towards a more educated public, though with less remarkable literary merit, began to rival Cobbett's paper as a medium of radical comment and criticism.

Of daily papers founded in the 18th century and continuing through the Victorian period, the *Morning Post* (started 1772), which survived until 1936 and ▷ *The Times* (started 1785), today perhaps the most prestigious daily, with a relatively small circulation, were the longest lived. Other important dailies with shorter lives were the ▷ *Morning Chronicle* (1769–1862), and the ▷ *Morning Herald* (1780–1869). Both reached peak

circulations of about 6000. To reach the very large circulations they do today, newspapers had to await the abolition of stamp duty – a tax on newspapers – in 1855. The Stamp Tax was started in 1712. It was a way of restricting circulations by raising the price of newspapers. The abolition of the tax, together with the advent of cheap paper and a greater potential readership thanks to universal literacy, led to a new kind of newspaper at the end of the 19th century. Alfred and Harold Harmsworth founded the *Daily Mail* in 1896; by 1901 it was selling a million copies. Other popular newspapers followed it with steadily increasing circulations. There was a strong tradition of weekly journalism in the 18th and 19th centuries. The oldest of the influential weeklies is the ▷ *Spectator*, which was founded in 1828.

Cobbett, like Daniel Defoe (1660–1731) before him, assumed that the main function of his journalism was to enlighten his readers. In the 1890s, however, the popular press emerged, with a desire to entertain as strong as that to inform, and with profitability as the major concern. During the last decades of the 19th century developments in printing, technology and mass increase in literacy went hand in hand. These bought into existence the popular press in the daily, weekly and monthly manifestations. They also bought into existence a new type of writer, often lower middle class in origin. The classic document on this and its effect on writing is ▷ George Gissing's ▷ *New Grub Street*. These new writers included ▷ H.G. Wells and Arnold Bennett (1867–1931) and for the first time popular literature shared a common territory and content with literature. The urban working-class life suddenly existed in literature in its own right. New magazines, ▷ reviews and periodicals exploded into existence.

### 'New Woman, The'

A term said to have been coined by novelist ▷ Sarah Grand in 1894 and popularized by journalists and literary reviewers. It was used in a general and often ill-defined way to describe the modern ▷ feminist figure who was emerging in the press and in novels (though to a lesser extent in real life) and who caused a considerable shock to conventional opinion by the radicalism of her ideas. Although there was never any identifiable single movement with which she was associated, the New Woman was thought to embody all that was most advanced in feminist ideology. Broadly, her beliefs included

rejection of ▷ marriage, a more honest and direct approach to female sexuality, and a demand for the reorganization of society so as to give women economic and personal independence. The 'New Woman fiction' enjoyed considerable notoriety, several novels and ▷ short stories of its kind becoming best-sellers. These included Sarah Grand's ▷ *The Heavenly Twins* (1893), ▷ George Egerton's ▷ *Keynotes* (1893), ▷ Grant Allen's *The Woman Who Did* (1895), and ▷ Mona Caird's *The Daughters of Danaus* (1894), and featured emancipated women with ideas well in advance of their time who are tragically thwarted by the restrictions placed by conventional society on their behaviour. In the eyes of society the New Woman was seen as liberated and bold, a rebel against the sexual ideology of the 19th century, a supporter of ▷ women's suffrage and advocate of women's rights. Several established novelists were accused of embodying New Women figures in their novels during the 1890s including ▷ Thomas Hardy in ▷ *Jude the Obscure* (1894–5) and ▷ George Gissing in *The Odd Women* (1893). The New Woman as a popular stereotype did not outlast the Victorian age and early 20th-century feminism concentrated its energies more on the suffrage movement than on the New Woman's ideals of personal integrity and sexual freedom.
**Bib:** Cunningham, G., *The 'New Woman' and the Fiction of the 1890's*; Boumelha, P., *Thomas Hardy: Sexual Identity and Narrative Form*.

### Nicholas Nickleby (1838–9)
A novel by ▷ Charles Dickens; like his other novels, it was first published in serial parts. Nicholas, his sister Kate and their mother are left penniless, and struggle for a living under the oppressive guardianship of Ralph Nickleby, an avaricious financier, the dead Mr Nickleby's brother. Morally, the tale is in black and white; Nicholas stands for ardent and youthful virtue, Ralph for meanness and cruelty. Nicholas is sent to teach at Dotheboys Hall, an iniquitous school run by Wackford Squeers to whom Nicholas gives a vigourous thrashing. Kate is apprenticed to Madame Mantalini, a dressmaker, where she is exposed to the vicous advances of Ralph's associate, Sir Mulberry Hawk. Nicholas beats him too. Ralph's evil intentions are eventually exposed by his eccentric but right-minded clerk, Newman Noggs, and the Nickleby family are befriended by the Cheeryble brothers. The novel is in Dickens's early, episodic and melodramatic style but many of the episodes are presented with great vividness and

comedy. It was dramatized, with huge success, by the Royal Shakespeare Company in 1980.
▷ Education.

### Nietzche, Frederick Wilhelm (1844–1900)
German philosopher. He challenged the concepts of 'the good, the true, and the beautiful' as, in their existing form of abstract values, a decadent system at the mercy of the common man's will to level distinctions of all kinds. He set his hope on the will to power of a new race of men who would assert their own spiritual identities. Among his more famous works are a book on the philosopher Schopenhauer and the composer Wagner, whom he regarded as his own teachers: *Unzeitgemässe Betrachtungen* ('Thoughts out of Season'; 1876); *Also sprach Zarathustra* ('Thus spake Zarathustra'; 1891).

Nietzsche was one of the important progenitors of Existentialism, and he had a considerable influence on some of the major English writers in the first quarter of this century. His ideas inspired ▷ George Bernard Shaw in the latter's belief in the Superman-hero as the spearhead of progress, eg his conception of Joan of Arc in his play *Saint Joan*. D.H. Lawrence (1885–1930) followed Nietzsche's spirit in his affirmation of spontaneous living from deep sources of energy in the individual – human 'disquality' (see *Women in Love*, ch. 8) as opposed to democratic egalitarianism. The Irish poet W.B. Yeats (1865–1939) also affirmed a natural aristocracy of the human spirit, and saw in Nietzsche a continuation of the message of the poet William Blake (1757–1827), who preached the transcendence of the human 'identity' over the 'self', which is defined and limited by the material environment. After 1930 Nietzsche's influence declined because he was seen as a prophet of the more vicious forms of fascism. However, in recent criticism Nietzsche's work has been re-evaluated by post-structuralist theory, especially with regard to his discussion of metaphor and metonymy and the privileging of a rhetorical reading of philosophical texts.
▷ German influence on Victorian literature; Atheism.

### Nineteenth Century, The
A monthly review founded in 1877 by J.T. Knowles, its first editor. It was renamed *The Nineteenth Century and After* in 1900, and *The Twentieth Century* in 1950. It was distinguished for bringing together leading antagonists of opposing views. Contributors included ▷ Ruskin, ▷ Gladstone, ▷ T.H. Huxley,

▷ Beatrice Webb, ▷ William Morris,
▷ 'Ouida' and ▷ Oscar Wilde.

**Nineties' Poets**
The group of poets centred around the
▷ Rhymer's Club in the 1890s, including
Lionel Johnson (1867–1902), ▷ Ernest
Dowson and ▷ Arthur Symons. The
Rhymer's Club met at the Cheshire Cheese
tavern near Fleet Street, immortalized by
W.B. Yeats (1865–1939) in *The Trembling of
the Veil* and 'The Grey Rock,' and published
two volumes of its members' verse in 1891
and 1894. Nineties poetry was part of the
*fin-de-siècle* ▷ Aesthetic movement. Strongly
influenced by ▷ French culture and
particularly French ▷ Symbolist poetry, it
was also a development of the work and ideas
of ▷ Algernon Swinburne, ▷ Walter Pater
and the ▷ Pre-Raphaelite Brotherhood.
The confessional and ▷ decadent quality
of their work, together with the incidence
of untimely death in their lives, led Yeats
to label them 'The Tragic Generation' in
his *Autobiographies*. They were important in
their influence on poets like Yeats and Ezra
Pound (1885–1912). Much of their work was
published in the journals ▷ *Yellow Book* and
*The Savoy* (which Symons edited).
**Bib:** Stanford, D., *Poets of the Nineties*;
Thornton, R.K.R., *Poetry of the 'Nineties*.

**Nonsense literature**
This covers several kinds of literature, which
have in common that they all in some way
deliberately defy logic or common sense, or
both. In English folk literature, many nursery
rhymes come into the category.
    The most important kind, however, is
undoubtedly in ▷ children's literature,
especially the poems of ▷ Edward Lear
and the *Alice* stories by ▷ Lewis Carroll,
both of which are to be taken seriously as
literature. Both writers are Victorian and
this perhaps accounts for their imaginative
depth; they wrote in a period of intense
mental restlessness before the time of
Sigmund Freud (1856–1939) and thus they
gave themselves wholly to their fantasies,
undisturbed by the idea that they might be
betraying secrets of their own nature. Modern
writers, eg James Joyce in his *Finnegans Wake*
(1939), will as fearlessly reveal their depths,
but it will not be to children. Another reason
why nonsense literature reached its peak in
the Victorian period is perhaps that this was
almost the earliest period when intelligent
minds considered that children were worth
writing for merely in order to amuse them,

and not to elevate their minds. Plenty of
20th-century writers have thought children
worth amusing but the child-public is now
a recognized one, whereas Lear and Carroll
wrote for a few young friends; they were thus
as much concerned with their own interest
and amusement as with that of their audience.

*North and South* (1854–5)
A novel by ▷ Elizabeth Gaskell, published
serially in ▷ Charles Dickens's periodical
▷ *Household Words*. *North and South* explores
the contrast between the rural south and the
industrial north of England, as the heroine,
Margaret Hale, moves from Hampshire
to Lancashire. During a dispute between
workers and employers, she encounters
Mrs Thornton and her son John, an inflexible
and unsympathetic manufacturer. Margaret
finds Thornton's attitudes repellent at first,
but gradually the couple move closer together
and are finally united. Margaret comes to
appreciate and respect both the mill owner
and his workers, while Thornton, through
Margaret's influence, adopts a more humane
attitude towards his employees. Like Gaskell's
▷ *Mary Barton*, *North and South* was an
important ▷ 'social problem' novel of the
mid-Victorian period, but the work achieves
an added richness through its exploration of
religious doubt and its use of industrial unrest
as a symbolic register of sexual awareness.
Recent feminist critics have argued that
it promotes the spread of maternal values
outside the sphere of the home and into the
commercial world.

**Northcliffe, Alfred Harmsworth, Viscount
(1865–1922)**
One of the principal founders of the 'popular
press' with its very large circulation, and in
particular of the *Daily Mail* (1896).
    ▷ Newspapers.

**Norton, Caroline (1808–77)**
Poet, novelist, dramatist and campaigner.
She was the granddaughter of the dramatist
Richard Sheridan (1751–1816), and married
George Norton in 1827. The marriage
was disastrous, and in 1836 her husband
brought an action for adultery against Lord
Melbourne, who had frequented Caroline
Norton's literary salon. The divorce case
collapsed for lack of evidence, but Norton's
sexual reputation was severely damaged. She
then began a long struggle to gain access to
and custody of her children, publishing *A
Plain Letter to the Lord Chancellor on the Infant
Custody Bill* (1839) under the ▷ pseudonym

Pearce Stevenson. Her efforts resulted in a change in the law in 1839. She later campaigned for the property rights of divorced women in *English Laws for Women in the 19th Century* (1854). She cannot be described as a ▷ feminist, however, since she believed in male superiority and sought legal change only on the basis that individual cases existed in which men had failed in their responsibilities. Norton's novels, which were admired in her day, include *The Wife and Woman's Reward* (1835); *Stuart of Dunleath* (1851); *Lost and Saved* (1863). Poetry includes *The Sorrows of Rosalie* (1829); *The Undying One* (1830) and *The Dream* (1840).

▷ Marriage; Divorce.
**Bib**: Ackland, A., *Life*: Perkins, J.G., *Life*.

## Novel of manners

This term is often used to designate a particular genre within 19th-century ▷ realism exemplified in the work of such authors as Jane Austen (1775–1817), ▷ Balzac, ▷ Turgenev, ▷ Trollope, ▷ Thackeray and ▷ Henry James. The novels characteristically analyse the individual and the social by bringing together representatives of two different social groups in such a way as to highlight the other's behaviour code by contrast. The plot mechanism usually hinges on love relationships between these representatives (who may stand for town and country; north and south; the *nouveau riche* and the aristocracy or, in Henry James's case, the United States and Europe) and whether the differences in their code of manners can be resolved by marriage. The mode is therefore an excellent vehicle for dissecting the marital economy, relations between the sexes and the social determination of love. It was perceived by hostile critics, including the ▷ naturalist writers of 1870 onwards, as overly genteel. The US novelist Frank Norris characterized the style as 'the tragedy of the broken teacup'. This is a misapprehension however, as, in the hands of its major exponents, larger aspects of the human condition such as love, sex, class and war are not so much avoided as refracted through social behaviour codes in a subtle, heavily nuanced and psychologically complex fashion. The genre continued in the 20th century with novels such as E.M. Forster's *A Passage to India* (1924) and is negotiated in Virginia Woolf's *To the Lighthouse* (1927) and *Mrs Dalloway* (1925).

**O**

### Odd Women, The (1893)

A novel by ▷ George Gissing which deals with many of the issues found in the ▷ 'New Woman' novels of the 1890s. Three 'odd' or 'surplus' women – spinsters – are left penniless by their improvident father, and the story concerns the limited choices each is forced to make. Monica Madden is pretty enough to marry for economic security rather than love, while her sisters Alice and Virginia become worn out and dispirited working in the only available jobs of teacher and ▷ governess, supported by the vain belief that they will start a school one day. Rhoda Nunn and Mary Barfoot are placed in direct contrast to them. Energetic, resourceful and committed to women's independence and emancipation, they run a business school to train women for work in commerce. Their plans are disrupted by a mutual affection which grows up between Rhoda and Everard Barfoot, Mary's cousin, and Rhoda has to reconcile love with her desire for independence. Gissing's Rhoda foreshadows ▷ Thomas Hardy's Sue Bridehead in ▷ *Jude the Obscure.*

▷ *The Bostonians*; Lesbianism; Women's Movement.

### Old Curiosity Shop, The (1840-1)

A novel by ▷ Charles Dickens; it was serialized as part of ▷ *Master Humphrey's Clock* in 1840-1 (published in book form in 1848).

The Curiosity Shop (a shop which sells second-hand goods of ornamental or rarity value) is kept by the grandfather of little Nell, Trent. The old man has been impoverished by the extravagances of his son-in-law and those of Fred Trent, Nell's brother. He is forced to borrow money from Quilp, a grotesque and malevolent dwarf, who believes the old man to be a miser with a hidden store of wealth. Quilp gets possession of the shop, and Nell and her grandfather take to wandering about the countryside. Eventually Nell dies, too late to be saved by her grandfather's brother, who has returned from abroad and finds them after a long search. Quilp is drowned while attempting to escape arrest. Other characters include Sampson Brass, Quilp's unscrupulous lawyer, his sister Sally and 'the Marchioness', a child whom the Brasses keep as a servant in vile conditions.

The novel shows Dickens's extraordinary vitality of imagination and also exemplifies the vulgarity which was part of his vitality. This vulgarity tended to display itself in melodrama and in sentimentality, here exhibited in the characters of Quilp and Little Nell respectively. The death of Little Nell is often regarded as Dickens's most notorious sentimental indulgence.

### Old Vic Theatre, The

Situated in Waterloo Road, this is one of London's most famous theatres. Built in 1816-18, during the 19th century it drew on the local working-class population for its audiences, with productions of popular ▷ melodramas. In 1880 it was converted into a temperance amusement-hall. From 1881 to 1883 it was managed by the Shakesperean actor and director William Poel.

### Oliphant, Margaret (1828–97)

▷ Scottish novelist, biographer and critic, born in Wallyford, Midlothian; also known as M.O.W. She married her cousin Francis Oliphant in 1852, but in 1859 he died of consumption, leaving Margaret with two children and expecting a third. She supported her family (and that of her widowed brother and his three children) by writing prolifically, becoming the author of over 100 works. She wrote fiction, biography and reviews, her best-known novels today being the ▷ *Chronicles of Carlingford* series (1863–76). Her first work, *Passages in the Life of Mrs Margaret Maitland* (1849) was well-received, and this was followed by the ▷ historical novel *Caleb Field* (1851) and *Merkland* (1851). *The Athelings* (1857) was a huge success, and is the best of Oliphant's many domestic ▷ romances. In 1862, her biography of Edward Irving appeared, and in 1863 the first of the *Chronicles, Salem Chapel*. The other four novels in the series were *The Rector and the Doctor's Family* (1863); *The Perpetual Curate* (1864); *Miss Marjoribanks* (1866) and *Phoebe Junior* (1876). Another group of books, *Stories of the Seen and Unseen*, dealt with matters of death and the soul, and include *A Beleaguered City* (1880) and *A Little Pilgrim in the Unseen* (1882). Also in 1882, her much admired *Literary History of England* appeared, and, in 1897–8, *Annals of a Publishing House*, which commemorated her long association with ▷ *Blackwood's Magazine*, to which she was a frequent contributor. Oliphant's best writing is sharply humorous and vivid in description, and she has been compared to ▷ George Eliot and ▷ Trollope, but the financial pressure to keep producing inevitably affected her work, not least since she was compelled to write scores of popular romances. Her posthumously published ▷ autobiography (1899) reveals the strain she was under,

and records her struggle to meet financial obligations.
**Bib**: Coghill, H. (ed.), *Margaret Oliphant: the Autobiography and Letters*; Williams, M., *A Critical Biography*; Colby, V. and R., *The Equivocal Virtue: Margaret Oliphant and the Victorian Literary Market Place*; Cunningham, V., *Everywhere Spoken Against: Dissent in the Victorian Novel*.

### Oliver Twist (1837–9)
A novel by ▷ Charles Dickens, published in instalments in 1837–9. Oliver is a child of unknown parents, born in a ▷ workhouse where he leads a miserable existence under the tyranny of Bumble, a beadle, ie a parish council official. He runs away to London and becomes mixed up in a gang of thieves led by Fagin and including the brutal burglar, Bill Sikes, Nancy his whore and a young pickpocket called the 'Artful Dodger'. He is temporarily rescued by the benevolent Mr Brownlow but a mysterious character called Monks, who has an interest in keeping Oliver's parentage a secret, induces the gang to kidnap him. He is finally rescued through the action of Nancy, who in consequence is brutally murdered by Sikes.

The novel shows the mixture of sentimentality and ▷ melodrama characteristic of early Dickens but in Bumble especially he exhibits keen social satire, and the London underworld is presented vividly. It was written at a time when a number of novelists (eg the ▷ 'Newgate School', especially ▷ Harrison Ainsworth) had written romances about crime, but Dickens dissociated it from these in the preface to the 3rd edition, and was realistic enough to startle the educated public into a new consciousness of the unprivileged and the criminal level of society, and to show how lack of compassion in the more privileged helped to make poverty a nursery of crime.
▷ Jews in Victorian literature.

### On Heroes, Hero-Worship and the Heroic in History (1841)
Frequently abridged to *On Heroes and Hero-Worship*, this book by ▷ Thomas Carlyle was cited by the liberal press of the time as evidence of his anti-democratic views. It is actually a study of the way in which the 'heroic' as a phenomenon evolves and changes throughout history. Originating as a series of lectures the book moves from the pagan god Odin through Italian poet Dante (1265–1321), religious leaders John Knox (1505–72) and Martin Luther (1483–1546), Scottish poet Robert Burns (1756–96),

Critic Samuel Johnson (1709–84), thinker Jean-Jacques Rousseau (1712–78), the prophet Mahomet and others, ending with Napoleon Bonaparte (1769–1821), and discusses each man's ability to discern new truths which, for Carlyle, is characteristic of a true hero. True heroism is the ability to act on these 'truths', to modify them and to discover new ones that will supersede them. Carlyle's heroism therefore appears progressive in its capacity for perpetual renewal and in its tolerance.
**Bib**: Rosenberg, J.D., *Carlyle and the Burden of History*.

### On Liberty (1859)
A political essay by ▷ John Stuart Mill, in which he discusses how far and in what ways the state is entitled to interfere with the liberty of individuals. He concludes that in general this interference should be restricted to the protection of other individuals, and of individuals collectively considered as society. Mill was mainly alarmed lest a new tyranny should arise from democratic majorities who might be indifferent to minority rights. The novelist ▷ Thomas Hardy numbered the essay among his 'cures for despair'.

### Ordeal of Richard Feverel, The (1859)
A novel by ▷ George Meredith. Sir Austin Feverel prides himself on the 'system' which he has devised for the upbringing and education of his motherless son, Richard; he is, however, a self-satisfied egotist who lacks disinterested understanding of his son's character. The 'system' breaks down in Richard's adolescence, when the boy falls in love with Lucy Desborough, a girl of lower social background than Sir Austin's ideal for his son's bride. They are secretly married but Sir Austin manages to separate them by egotistically exploiting Richard's love for him. Richard becomes involved with a beautiful woman of loose morals; he begins this new relationship with characteristically romantic and idealistic motives of redeeming her but he partly falls under her spell. Lord Mountfalcon, who is interested in permanently separating Lucy and Richard, is chiefly responsible for Richard's betrayal of her, and in remorse for his infidelity Richard fights a duel with him and is wounded. Lucy has meanwhile become reconciled with Sir Austin but the shock of the duel kills her. The novel – Meredith's first important one – exemplifies his combination of romantic intensity with psychological analysis.

***Origin of Species, The***
  ▷ Darwin, Charles.

**Orphans**
In mid-Victorian fiction, orphans frequently appear as central characters. In an age when the reading public responded to sentiment, the representation of orphans was sometimes used by writers as a catalyst for pathos. This was often the case with ▷ Elizabeth Gaskell, for example, whose novel ▷ *Ruth* creates sympathy for the ▷ 'fallen woman' by stressing initially the heroine's lack of parental guidance. Alternatively the effects of disinheritance and exclusion were illustrated through an orphan, as ▷ Emily Brontë demonstrates with Heathcliff in ▷ *Wuthering Heights*. Authors seeking to challenge the conventions of society often created orphaned central characters in order to speak from a marginalized position, to view society from 'outside'. The heroine of ▷ Charlotte Brontë's ▷ *Jane Eyre* is an example, although Jane, like many other fictional orphans, eventually discovers familial connections and financial support, thereby gaining both security and power. The necessary independence of orphans could also give rise to the theme of individualism and self-help which ran through the literature of the age, registering an unacknowledged complicity with the values of the middle classes. This paradoxical position is exemplified by the heroine of ▷ Elizabeth Barrett Browning's ▷ *Aurora Leigh*, who both resists as a woman the constraints imposed upon her by society and simultaneously advocates the conservative ideology that has oppressed her.
  ▷ *Professor, The.*

**'Ouida' (1839–1908)**
The ▷ pseudonym of Marie Louise de la Ramée. 'Ouida' began to write in the 1860s, contributing tales of high society life to *Bentley's Miscellany*. Flamboyant, extravagant and egotistical herself, 'Ouida's' novels are ▷ sensational ▷ romances set amidst exotic surroundings, featuring much passion and intrigue within privileged social circles. 'Ouida' aspired to the aristocracy herself and increasingly feared its pollution by middle-class vulgarity (though she was middle class herself). In *Moths* (1880), she describes the social hierarchy being eaten away by parasites and hypocrites. Other novels include: *Chandos* (1866); *Under Two Flags* (1867); *Pascarel* (1873); *Two Little Wooden Shoes* (1874) and *Princess Napraxine* (1884). *Views and Opinions* (1895) and *Critical Studies* (1900)

are collections of vituperative articles against
  ▷ women's suffrage, cruelty to animals, publishers, and the *nouveaux riches*.
  ▷ Women's Movement.
**Bib:** Ffrench, Y., *Ouida: A Study in Ostentation*, Bigland, E., *Ouida the Passionate Victorian*.

***Our Mutual Friend* (1864–5)**
The last complete novel by ▷ Charles Dickens, published serially 1864–5.
  The principal plot starts from the will of a deceased refuse-collector, Old Harmon, who bequeaths his fortune to his son, John Harmon, on condition that he marries a certain girl, Bella Wilfer. Young Harmon wishes to discover what she is like before he discloses himself. He intends to adopt a disguise but his identity is obscured beyond his intention when circumstances point to his death by murder. Since he is believed dead, the father's property goes instead to Mr Boffin, old Harmon's foreman. Boffin adopts Bella, and young Harmon, disguising himself as John Rokesmith, becomes engaged as Boffin's secretary. Bella becomes spoilt by wealth and contemptuously rejects Rokesmith-Harmon as a lover; she is, however, reformed by Boffin, who pretends himself to undergo complete debasement of character through his accession of wealth and thus gives Bella, who has been devoted to him, a violent distaste for the evils of money. Rokesmith's true identity as young Harmon is at length brought to light. With this main plot goes a minor story of Silas Wegg's attempt to blackmail Boffin. In addition there is a parallel main plot concerning the rival lovers of Lizzie Hexam, daughter of a Thames boatman; one of her lovers is the aristocratic young barrister, Eugene Wrayburn, and the other the embittered schoolmaster of low social origins, Bradley Headstone. Headstone tries to murder Wrayburn and nearly succeeds, but he is drowned in a struggle with Rogue Riderhood, another waterman who is also a blackmailer. Wrayburn, physically wrecked, marries Lizzie for whom he at last comes to have a real need. The two main plots are linked through the waterside characters who are connected with young Harmon's supposed murder at the beginning of the book. The novel extends through the Wrayburn-Lizzie story into upper-middle-class circles which include the arrogant Podsnaps, the Veneerings who attempt to climb into wealthy society and fall out of it again, the fraudulent social adventurers Mr and Mrs Lammle, the mean and ruthless financier Fledgeby. Through Fledgeby on the one side and Lizzie on the

other, the lower social circles include Riah, the benevolent Jew, and Jenny Wren, the bitter-sweet doll's dressmaker. The book is thus given an unusually wide variety of character and social environment, even for Dickens, and it is pervaded by a rich symbolism arising from the use made of the River Thames and the dust-heaps out of which the Harmon fortunes have been made. The motive of special social reform, more characteristic of early Dickens (eg ▷ *Oliver Twist*, 1838) is evident in the episode of Betty Higden, the poor woman who dies by the roadside sooner than enter a workhouse.

▷ Jews in Victorian literature.

## Owen, Robert (1771–1858)

Social reformer, and a leading socialist thinker in the early 19th century. He became part-owner of the New Lanark Cotton Mills in 1800, and found that its workers were living in the degraded and nearly desperate conditions common in the earlier phase of the Industrial Revolution. He set about improving their housing and working conditions, and established infant schools. His reforms were a success, but his expenditure on them caused resentment among his partners, and in 1813 he established a new firm, with ▷ Jeremy Bentham as one of his partners. In the same year he published a volume of essays, *A New View of Society*, in which he sought to prove that the human character is entirely created by its environment. In 1817, in a report to the House of Commons, Owen pointed out that the existing social misery was caused by men competing unsuccessfully with machines, and he recommended the establishment of socialist working communities in the country; they were to vary from 500 to 3000 in size, and were to be partly industrial. His views were received favourably by, among other people, the Duke of Kent, the father of ▷ Queen Victoria, but Owen spoilt his case with public opinion in general by mixing his proposals with anti-religious propaganda. Nonetheless two experiments were attempted in 1825, one in England and one in the US; both failed in under two years. Owen now became the leader of a socialist-secular movement, through which he sought to replace the emphasis on political reform by emphasis on economic action. His influence led to the

Grand National Consolidated Trades Union in 1834 (▷ Trade Union), but this also failed owing to bad organization. The word 'socialism' originated through discussions centred on the Association of all Classes of all Nations, which Owen founded in 1835. The only permanent success among Owen's experiments was his establishment of the Cooperative Movement, which nowadays is affiliated to the ▷ Labour Party.

## Oxford Movement (Tractarian Movement)

A religious movement within the Church of England; it had its origin and main centre in Oxford and ran from 1833, when it began with a sermon by the Anglican priest, theologian and poet Keble, until 1845 when its most eloquent leader, ▷ John Newman, entered the Roman ▷ Catholic Church. Some of the leaders of the Church of England realized (especially after the Act of Catholic Emancipation, 1829) that the Church was by its constitution largely at the mercy of the state, and was in danger of becoming in essentials a department of the state. The Oxford Movement preached that the Church had an independent, spiritual status, was in direct descent from the medieval Catholic Church, and represented a 'middle way' between post-Reformation Catholicism and ▷ Protestantism. The movement's propaganda was conducted through ▷ tracts, many of them by John Newman, and culminated in *Tract XC* which asserted that the Thirty-Nine Articles, on which Anglican doctrine is based, are compatible with Roman Catholic doctrine. The tracts divided Anglican opinion severely, and Newman's secession to the Church of Rome, followed by the secession of other High Anglican clergy, brought the movement into discredit with the majority of Anglican opinion. Edward Pusey, Professor of Hebrew at Oxford, was the leader of the Oxford Movement, which was in consequence often called Puseyite. An indirect result of the movement was to focus attention on the medieval background of the Church, and to encourage that reification of the Middle Ages which emerged in much Victorian literature, in the artistic movement known as ▷ Pre-Raphaelitism and in Victorian neo-▷ Gothic architecture.

# P

**Pageant, and Other Poems, A (1881)**
A collection of poems by ▷ Christina
Rossetti, including the sonnet sequence
'Monna Innominata' and the important poems
'The Thread of Life' and 'An Old World
Thicket', in which Rossetti explores her poetic
and religious identity. Other noteworthy lyrics
include 'An Immurata Sister', spoken from
the perspective of a nun who seeks release
from worldly (and gender-specific) constraints,
and 'A Life's Parallels', an enigmatic poem
addressing the mystery of death.

**Pair of Blue Eyes, A (1873)**
▷ Thomas Hardy's third and much
underrated novel, often unfairly overshadowed
by ▷ Tess of the d'Urbervilles (1891) which,
in many ways, it anticipates. Echoing the
circumstances of Hardy's courtship of his first
wife Emma Gifford it deals with the story, and
consequences, of the abortive love affair and
elopement of Elfride Swancourt, an isolated
rector's daughter living in Endlestowe on the
North Cornish coast, and a young architect
from London, Stephen Smith. Stephen's lowly
class origins are the reason for the Reverend
Swancourt's opposition the marriage, and
the couple elope on an impulse, only for
Elfride to lose heart and return home on the
next train. However, she has been seen in a
compromising situation by Mrs Jethway who
believes that Elfride's light-hearted flirtation
with her son caused her death. Stephen goes
off to India to make his fortune and promises
to return to claim Elfride. As a result of her
father's marriage to a wealthy widow, and her
attempts at novel writing, Elfride meets and
falls in love with the curiously fastidious Henry
Knight and breaks off her engagement with
Smith. Terrified that Knight might discover
her previous relationship with Smith, Elfride
is haunted by Mrs Jethway, who threatens
to betray her. Finally confessing to the
elopement she is immediately rejected by
Knight whose cruel judgement of her leaves
her heartbroken. Knight meets Smith, his
former friend and protégé, and both men
betray their love for Elfride hurrying down
to Cornwall to reclaim her, unaware that
the train on which they are travelling is also
carrying Elfride's copse back to Endlestow.
Her marriage to the wealthy Lord Luxellian
has not prevented her decline and she has
died in childbirth. ▷ Tennyson, ▷ Coventry
Patmore and Marcel Proust (1871–1922) were
wildly enthusiastic about the novel which is
now the subject of critical re-evaluation. The
scene on the Cliff Without a Name is one of
Hardy's most magnificent depictions of man's

relationship to an indifferent Nature, and is
deeply influenced by evolutionary theory.
▷ Darwin, Charles.

**'Palace of Art, The' (1832)**
Poem by ▷ Alfred Tennyson published
in *Poems* (1832). It is an allegory of the
aesthetic soul that vainly shrinks from the
encroachment of 'uncertain shapes', the
lengthening shadows of a dark reality. It is
evidence in Tennyson of the struggle between
a personal 'art for art's sake' philosophy and
art linked to the interests of 19th-century
society. It is a reaction to the anti-romantic
bias of the Victorian period that produced
a sociological aesthetic, and considers the
question of whether art should function as
an escape from or a means of considering
broader cultural and intellectual problems.
▷ Aestheticism.

**Palliser Novels, The (1864–80)**
A sequence of novels by ▷ Anthony Trollope
which is composed of *Can You Forgive Her?*
(1864–65), *Phineas Finn* (1867–9), *The Eustace
Diamonds* (1871–3), *Phineas Redux* (1873–4),
*The Prime Minister* (1875–6) and *The Duke's
Children* (1879–80). Trollope described them
as 'a series of semi-political tales'.

**Parnell, Charles Stewart (1846–91)**
Irish political leader. He entered Parliament
in 1875, and led the Home Rule party in its
fight for Irish self-government. He converted
▷ Gladstone and the ▷ Liberal Party to the
support of Home Rule, but was politically
ruined by becoming involved in a scandal
with the wife of Captain O'Shea in 1890. His
success was the more remarkable because he
was a ▷ Protestant; the scandal finally turned
the ▷ Catholic Church in Ireland against
him. His downfall caused a deep split among
the Irish nationalists.

**Past and Present (1843)**
An example of ▷ Thomas Carlyle's
immensely influential social criticism
in which the 'past' is epitomized by a
medieval chronicle of the monastery of Bury
St Edmunds, describing everyday life and
recording the procedure for electing a new
abbot. In this document Carlyle finds evidence
of all that he saw as missing from Victorian
society: spiritual power, organic community
and personal responsibility. Carlyle used
the fashion for ▷ medievalism, current at
the time, in order to make a diagnosis of
the contemporary world. The 'present' was

typified by a sensational news item which told of the murder of three children by their parents in order to defraud a burial society of £3 8s due on the death of each child. Using classical allusions such as the myth of King Midas, and Dante's myth of Ugolino who was driven by starvation to eat his own children, Carlyle mounted an attack on industrial England, which had the power to make money but could only produce starvation. The present is also portrayed in the form of a morality play with representative characters such as Plugson of Undershot, an unscrupulous industrialist, and Pandarus Dogsdraught, a corrupt politician. ▷ Charles Dickens was to develop this technique in his own novels. ▷ Matthew Arnold was also influenced by the style of *Past and Present* which put a number of useful terms into currency such as 'mammonism', 'dilettantism', 'windbag', 'cash-nexus' and 'captains of industry'.

### Pater, Walter Horatio (1839–94)

Scholar, essayist and critic. He was elected to a fellowship at Brasenose College, Oxford, in 1864. He was connected with the ▷ Pre-Raphaelite group, shared their idealistic worship of beauty and became an important influence in the cult of art which led to the ▷ aesthetic movement at the end of the century. His most important work was *Studies in the History of the Renaissance* (1873), a collection of essays on Italian painters and writers from the 14th to 16th centuries; the Conclusion to these essays, in which he advocates a fusion of psychic, moral and sensuous ecstasy, became a kind of manifesto of the aesthetic movement. His next most famous work is the philosophic romance ▷ *Marius the Epicurean* (1885). Other works: *Imaginary Portraits* (1887); *Appreciations with an Essay on Style* (1889); *Plato and Platonism* (1893); *The Child in the House* (1894); *Greek Studies* and *Miscellaneous Studies* (1895); an unfinished romance, *Gaston de Latour* (1896). Pater wrote with immense care for stylistic beauty, which became for him an end in itself. Bib: Levey, M., *The Case of Walter Pater*; Monsman, G., *Walter Pater*; Brake, L. and Small, I. (eds.), *Pater in the 90s*.

### Pathetic fallacy

A term invented by the critic ▷ John Ruskin in 1856 (*Modern Painters*, Vol. III, Pt. iv, Ch. 12) to denote the tendency common especially among poets to ascribe human emotions or qualities to inanimate objects, eg 'an angry sea'. Ruskin describes it by dividing writers

into four classes: those who do not use it merely because they are insensitive; superior writers in whom it is a mark of sensitivity; writers who are better still and do not need it because they 'feel strongly, think strongly, and see truly'; and writers of the best sort who use it because in some instances they 'see in a sort untruly, because what they see is inconceivably above them'. In general, he considers that the pathetic fallacy is justified when the feeling it expresses is a true one.

### Patmore, Coventry Kersey Dighton (1823–96)

Poet. He contributed to the ▷ Pre-Raphaelite periodical *The Germ*; in 1864 he became a ▷ Catholic. The two books by which he is most remembered are ▷ *The Angel in the House* (comprising *The Betrothed*, 1854; *The Espousals*, 1856; *Faithful for Ever*, 1860; *The Victories of Love*, 1862) and *The Unknown Eros* (1877). The former is about his first marriage and celebrates married love; the latter, consisting of forty-two irregular odes, is on a similar theme but more mystical. Both poems are examples of the type of philosophy in verse characteristic of William Wordsworth's famous *Prelude* (1850). Patmore had independent ideas on poetic technique, and has been considered by some critics to bear resemblance to the 17th-century Metaphysical poets. As much as for his own poetry, he is known today for being the friend and correspondent of the poet ▷ Gerard Manley Hopkins, whose work, however, he seems not to have properly appreciated. Other works include: *Amelia* (1878), which was his own favourite among his poems; the critical essays *English Metrical Law* (1878); *Principle in Art* (1879); *Religio Poetae* (1893); the religious meditations *Rod, Root and Flower* (1895). Bib: Patmore, D., *Life*; Oliver, E.J., *Life*; Page, F., *Patmore: a Study in Poetry*; Reid, J.C., *The Mind and Art of Coventry Patmore*; Hopkins, G.M., (ed. Abbott, C.C.) *Further Letters*.

### Payn, James (1830–98)

Novelist. Educated at Eton and Cambridge, Payn launched his literary career by contributing to ▷ Dickens's ▷ *Household Words*. His highly popular novels tapped into the vogue for the ▷ sensation novel of the 1860s and 1870s, melodramatically dealing with scheming relatives, disputes over wills and strange disppearances; of these, the best known are *Lost Sir Massingberd* (1864) and *By Proxy* (1878). Between 1883 and 1896 Payn edited the ▷ *Cornhill Magazine*.

**Peel, Sir Robert (1788–1850)**
British Prime Minister 1834–5 and 1841–56, responsible for repealing the ▷ Corn Laws in 1846, thereby freeing imports. Earlier in his career he was persuaded by the rising crime statistics that legal reform should be coupled with better crime prevention. In 1829, as Home Secretary, he carried through the Metropolitan Police Act that was responsible for the first disciplined police force for the Greater London area. Blue-coated, with top hats and truncheons, Peel's police helped to protect London from the riots that occurred in Bristol and elsewhere during the ▷ Reform Bill agitation in the early 1830s. From this point on the police force was gradually established throughout the whole country. 'Bobby', meaning policeman, derives from his name.

*Pendennis, The History of*
A novel by ▷ William Makepeace Thackeray, published serially 1848–50. It is about worldly upper-class society in London and the fortunes of a young man, Arthur Pendennis, whose 'bad angels' are his cynical, materialistic uncle, Major Pendennis, and the pretty but selfish Blanche Amory whom he nearly marries. Blanche's father, an escaped convict who is thought to be dead but is in fact – as Major Pendennis knows – still alive, haunts the book in the guise of Colonel Altamont. Arthur's 'good angels' are his widowed mother, Helen; Laura Bell, whom he eventually marries and whom his mother has adopted; and George Warrington, a friend with whom he shares rooms. The good influences are, however, less imaginatively presented than the bad ones, and the distinctiveness of the novel depends on its amusing portrayal of the vulgarity, intrigue, and materialism of London society and the journalistic and literary world of Fleet Street.

**Pfeiffer, Emily (1827–90)**
Welsh poet and polemical writer, born in Montgomeryshire. Pfeiffer wrote ten volumes of poetry, including *Gerard's Monument* (1873); *Poems* (1876); *Sonnets and Songs* (1880); *The Rhyme of the Lady of the Rock* (1884) and *Flowers of the Night* (1889). Her work is informed by a Victorian ▷ feminist perspective, is sympathetic to marginalized women and addresses subjects such as ▷ marriage, rape, ▷ education, sexuality and work. Pfeiffer also wrote political essays including *Flying Leaves from East and West* (1885), written after a tour of Asia and America, and *Women and Work*

(1887), where she protests against the limited vocational opportunities available to women. She died in 1890, leaving £2000 for higher education for women, which was used to build accommodation for female students at University College, Cardiff.
▷ Anglo-Welsh literature.
**Bib:** Hickok, K., *Representations of Women: 19th Century British Women's Poetry.*

**Phiz (Browne, Hablot Knight) (1815–82)**
Illustrator. He was the principal illustrator for the novels of ▷ Charles Dickens (especially ▷ *David Copperfield*, ▷ *The Pickwick Papers*, ▷ *Dombey and Son*, ▷ *Martin Chuzzlewit*, ▷ *Bleak House*). He also illustrated the works of other Victorian novelists, notably ▷ Harrison Ainsworth and ▷ Charles Lever.

*Pickwick Papers, The (1836–7)*
The first novel by ▷ Charles Dickens, published serially 1836–7. The story is the adventures of Mr Pickwick and his friends Tupman, Snodgrass and Winkle, who go on a journey of observation of men and manners on behalf of the Pickwick Club, of which Mr Pickwick is the founder and the chairman. The episodes are predominantly comic and Mr Pickwick seems at first to be intended as a mere figure of fun, destined always to be made a fool of owing to his extreme innocence of the ways of the world. Fairly early on, however, he acquires a servant, Sam Weller. Sam is the ideal servant; he is practical, good-humoured, resourceful and devoted. Pickwick now begins to be endowed with a new dignity; still very innocent, he is no longer a mere figure of fun, for he is also shown to have positive moral qualities, such as a determination to stand by the values of truth and justice. He becomes, in fact, a kind of 19th-century English middle-class Don Quixote with Sam Weller as a Sancho Panza, without any of the ridiculousness of Sancho, but with a great deal of comedy derived from his highly developed and typically Cockney sense of humour. At first there is a story but no plot; about half-way through, however, a semblance of a plot develops with Mrs Bardell's conspiracy to obtain £750 from Mr Pickwick for breach of promise of marriage. Assisted by a firm of unscrupulous lawyers, she is at first successful and Mr Pickwick goes to prison. This is the beginning of Dickens's constant preoccupation with prison and with the parasitic qualities of the legal profession. Various episodes illustrate the kinds of social viciousness which Dickens was to enjoy ridiculing or dramatizing – the

cheerful roguery of Mr Jingle; the hypocrisy of the 'shepherd', Mr Stiggins; the demagogic Mr Potts in the parliamentary election at Eatanswill, etc. By contrast, Mr Wardle represents the opulent philanthropy and cordial 'religion of Christmas' which were also to figure in Dickens's novels to the end but especially in the earlier ones. In the outcome, Mr Pickwick and Sam Weller emerge as a kind of ideal alliance between the middle and working classes – complete sincerity and integrity in moral guidance on Pickwick's part, total devotion and most useful practical capacity on Weller's side.

### Picture of Dorian Gray, The (1890)
A novel by ▷ Oscar Wilde which updates ▷ Goethe's Faust legend. Tempted by the selfish sybarite Henry Wotton, Dorian trades his soul for eternal youth and beauty while his portrait, painted by Basil Hallward, who appeals to the better side of his nature, bears the ravages of time and Dorian's decadent living. It was meant as an examination of the consequences of regarding sensual indulgence and moral indifference as aesthetic ends in themselves. Another version of the *doppelgänger*, it has much in common with ▷ Stevenson's ▷ *The Strange Case of Dr Jekyll and Mr Hyde*.
   ▷ Aestheticism.

### 'Pied Piper of Hamelin, The' (1845)
A poem by ▷ Robert Browning. It retells an ancient legend: a piper promises to rid the town of Hamelin in Germany of its plague of rats in return for a thousand guilders from the Council. The rats follow the music of his pipe as far as the river Weser, where they are drowned. The Council, however, refuse to pay the piper, whereupon he similarly plays the children out of town and into the side of a mountain which opens to receive them. The origin of the legend may be the Children's Crusade of 1212, when thousands of young people were persuaded to join an expedition to the Holy Land, and many of them perished on the journey.

### Pinero, Sir Arthur Wing (1855–1934)
Dramatist. His earliest plays were farces, but in 1889 *The Profligate* showed a great advance in seriousness over earlier plays in the century, when the English theatre had been practically bankrupt of contemporary drama of interest. At about this time, largely owing to the influence of ▷ Ibsen, drama was being revised radically in Europe. Pinero's *The Second Mrs Tanqueray* (1893) was at the time

of its production a conspicuous contribution to the new movement; it was translated into French, German and Italian, and attracted the leading European actress of the age, Eleonora Duse. Pinero followed this success with other plays which sustained his reputation in Britain at least, such as *Trelawny of the 'Wells'* (1898) and *The Gay Lord Quex* (1899). He was, in fact, a prolific writer, publishing thirty-nine plays between 1891 and 1930. His plays are now seldom produced and little studied: in wit and dramatic ingenuity he was soon excelled by ▷ George Bernard Shaw. Like Tom Robertson (1829–71) before him, his brilliance was like that of a candle in the dark: he was conspicuous in contrast to the dullness that preceded him.
Bib: Dunkel, W.D., *Life*; Boas, F.S., *From Richardson to Pinero*; Lazenby, W., *Pinero*.

### Plays Pleasant and Unpleasant (1898)
A collection of seven plays by ▷ George Bernard Shaw. The four 'pleasant' plays are comedies with serious themes (the character of the true soldier, what constitutes moral strength, the nature of greatness, etc) but nothing likely to dismay or shock the conventional moral sense of the audiences of the day. These are: ▷ *Arms and the Man*, ▷ *Candida, The Man of Destiny, You Never Can Tell*. The three 'unpleasant' plays dealt with social topics (sexual morality and the ownership of slum property) such as were generally felt to be unsuitable for presentation in the theatre. These are: *Widowers' Houses, The Philanderer, Mrs Warren's Profession*.

### Poe, Edgar Allan (1809–49)
▷ Detective fiction.

### Poel, William (1852–1934)
Actor, director and Shakespeare scholar. He founded the Elizabethan Stage Society in 1894. Poel's influential productions of the plays of Shakespeare and his contemporaries rejected the traditional techniques of stage realism dominant at the end of the 19th century. Characteristic of his productions was an attempt to recreate Elizabethan stage conditions by performing on a bare apron stage. He also pursued a policy, not always successfully, of restoring full uncut texts for production. Though it is now accepted that he overstressed the notion of the 'bare' Elizabethan stage, he was, with Harley Granville Barker (1877–1946), a great influence on the development of Shakespeare productions in this century.
   ▷ Old Vic Theatre.

**Bib:** Speaight, R., *William Poel and the Elizabethan Revival*.

### Poems (1844)

A collection of poetry by ▷ Elizabeth Barrett Browning, published after six years of invalidism during which Barrett (as she was then) focused her energies on poetic experiment. *Poems* (1844) is notable for its formal innovation (half-rhymes, metrical irregularity, compound words) and for the range of voices that surface in the collection. There is a mystical, opium-inspired voice in poems such as 'The House of Clouds' and 'A Vision of Poets'; a sentimental voice, found in the popular ▷ ballads and in poems such as 'To Flush, My Dog'. A concern with social class is evident in 'The Cry of the Children', a strategically sentimental protest poem about the working conditions of children. 'A Drama of Exile' reviews the Fall 'with a peculiar reference to Eve's alloted grief', while 'L.E.L.'s Last Question' and the pair of sonnets 'A Desire' and 'A Recognition' are poetic tributes to Letitia Landon (1802–38) and ▷ George Sand respectively. The collection established Barrett as a major Victorian poet.

### Poems by Currer, Ellis and Acton Bell (1846)

The first published work by the ▷ Brontë sisters, which included poems by Charlotte (Currer), Emily (Ellis) and Anne (Acton). Charlotte organized the publication after 'discovering' Emily's poetry, which she considered 'not at all like the poetry women generally write'. The collection sold only two copies, but received a few favourable notices.
    ▷ Pseudonyms.

### Political parties

The English political scene has been dominated by political parties since the mid-17th century. It was not till the 19th century that political parties became highly organized. From 1783 to 1830 the Tories were in power – their position strengthened by a number of issues which divided the nation. Chief among these was the French Revolution (1789–94), which influenced the Whigs (▷ Whigs and Tories) in the direction of political reform and the Tories in the direction of resistance to change. Another was the ▷ Industrial Revolution, which was rapidly expanding an urban middle class which lacked political rights owing to the anachronistic parliamentary electoral system. Finally, new social problems arose from the growth of a large urban proletariat. The ▷ Reform Bill of 1832 was a Whig victory and greatly increased the power of the urban middle class.
    1832 onwards saw the evolution of the modern political parties: ▷ Liberals, Conservatives and finally ▷ Labour. The parties became more self-conscious and closely organized; Whigs came to call themselves Liberals, and Tories changed their name to Conservatives. Until 1840 the division was between the agricultural interest (Conservative) and the industrial interest (Liberal), and the old religious divisions survived, so that the Conservatives were the guardians of the Church of England, and the more decidedly ▷ Protestant sects – now called Nonconformists (▷ Religious groups) – voted Liberal. In the second half of the 19th century the upper classes both of towns and countryside tended to vote Conservative, and the Liberals depended increasingly on the urban working-class vote. However, the Liberals, by their traditions, could never become a predominantly working-class party; hence the foundation of the Labour Party in 1900. The chief issue over which the Liberals and Conservatives fought in the mid-19th century was ▷ free trade against protection (by import taxes) of English agriculture. Later the Tories became the imperialist party, resisting Irish and South African Dutch nationalism – issues on which the Liberals took a less rigid view.
**Bib:** Parry, J., *The Rise and Fall of Liberal Government in Victorian England*.

### Poor Law (1834)

One of a series of laws giving public relief to those among the poor who could not earn their own living and were not supported by others. In the late 18th century local magistrates employed the 'Speenhamland System' under which workers who received wages below what was regarded as a subsistence level were provided with an allowance fixed and enforced in relation to the price of bread. This system of parish subsidy relieved employers of the necessity to provide a living wage for their work people and dramatically increased the burden of the poor rate on the small independent parishioner. The new Poor Law passed in 1834 was responsible for grouping parishes into unions under Boards of Guardians, elected by the ratepayers, who were responsible for administering the rules for Poor Law administration. The institution of the Poor Law was stimulated by the philosophy that pauperism among the able-bodied worker was evidence of a moral failing, and it provided no relief for such a claimant except for the misery of the ▷ workhouse. These were made as disagreeable as possible in order to deter the lazy and work-shy and to stimulate workers to seek regular employment rather than charity. In consequence the workhouses were harsh and unpopular places in which the sexes were strictly segregated and families separated. Their regime was particularly hard on children, old people and invalids. The Poor Law itself was justly regarded as an odious tyranny by both the rural and urban working class. The growth of humanitarian feeling in the 19th century helped to mitigate the harshness of the law in practice, but it was not replaced until 1925.

*Portrait of a Lady, The* (1881)
A novel by ▷ Henry James. The heroine, Isabel Archer, is brought from the US to England by her aunt, Mrs Touchett, the wife of a retired American banker. Isabel has the candour and freedom conspicuous among American girls of the period; she also has beauty, intelligence, and a spirit of adventure and responsiveness to life. She refuses offers of marriage from both Lord Warburton, a 'prince' of the English aristocracy, and Caspar Goodwood, a 'prince' of American industry. In the meantime her cousin, Ralph Touchett, has fallen in love with her, but he is slowly dying of consumption and dare not become her suitor. Instead, he tries to play the 'fairy godmother' by persuading his father to leave her the money which would have been due to himself. His action has two unfortunate results: it awakens Isabel's New England Puritan conscience through the sense of responsibility which the possession of wealth entails, and it attracts the rapacious Madame Merle, whose guilty secret is that she is looking for a rich stepmother for her daughter by her former lover, Gilbert Osmond. Osmond (like Madame Merle herself) is an artistic but cold-blooded and totally self-centred expatriate American. Isabel in her humility is easily made to feel her own cultural inferiority to the exquisite exterior qualities of Osmond, whom she sees as the prince she has been looking for – a man deprived of noble potentialities by the unjust circumstance of his poverty. She marries him, only to discover his hollowness, and that her marriage is imprisonment in the ogre's castle.

The novel, sometimes regarded as James's masterpiece, shows his conception of the relationship of the US and European consciousnesses; the Americans have

integrity, the will to live, and good will towards humanity, but they lack richness of tradition and are restricted by the limitations of the New England puritan inhibitions; the Europeans (especially some of the American expatriates) have rich cultural awareness but this commonly corrupts their integrity, and instead of good will they have immense rapacity. On the other hand the best kind of US expatriate (Ralph Touchett) combines the best of both worlds.
▷ Novel of manners.
**Bib:** Kirby, D. (ed.) *An Introduction to the Varieties of Criticism: The Portrait of A Lady.*

**Positivism**
▷ Comte, Auguste.

**Pre-Raphaelite Brotherhood**
A movement of painters and poets which began just before 1850; it was more important in painting than in poetry, but one of its leading members, ▷ Dante Gabriel Rossetti, was equally famous in both arts. The essence of the movement was opposition to technical skill without inspiration. This made it anti-Victorian, inasmuch as industrial techniques (illustrated by the ▷ Great Exhibition of 1851) were producing vast quantities of work which were products of engineering. Technical skill without inspiration was deemed to be an aspect of the neo-classical art of the 18th century, against which the ▷ Romantics had already protested, and behind neo-classicism lay the 16th-century Renaissance of Greek and Roman art, and the paintings of the Italian artist Raphael (1483–1520), who had produced religious pictures of extraordinary perfection in technique but (in the opinion of the Pre-Raphaelites) with an almost cynical disregard of spiritual feeling. This tenderness of the spirit had existed in ▷ medieval art; hence the Brotherhood, by no means hostile to highly polished technique, cultivated the artistic spirit of the Middle Ages. The principal painters of the Brotherhood were Rossetti, John Millais and Holman Hunt; its poets were Rossetti and his sister ▷ Christina Rossetti, and, a little later, ▷ William Morris.

The movement drew for its poetical inspiration on the ardour of the Romantic poet John Keats (1795–1821), who had also cultivated the Middle Ages, and it greatly revered the contemporary poet ▷ Alfred Tennyson, whose art owed much to Keats. But Pre-Raphaelitism was not merely an aesthetic movement; a great influence upon it was the work of the art critic ▷ John

Ruskin, who had a strong social conscience about the duty of art to society, and especially of the duty of redeeming the squalid life of the urban working classes. Less close to the movement, but still in harmony with it, was the poet critic ▷ Matthew Arnold, with his attack on the philistinism of the middle classes and the barbarism of the upper classes. Finally, the ground of Pre-Raphaelitism had been prepared by the ▷ Oxford Movement in the Church of England; this had rejected the interfering state, and by its cultivation of ritual in religious worship asserted that it had brought beauty back into religion.

However, Keats had not been dismayed by the world of his time so much as by the inevitability of desperate suffering as part of the human lot in every age. Arnold and Tennyson, in their poetry, were dismayed by the surface hideousness and the apparently irremediable injustices of their society. They had tended to write a 'poetry of withdrawal', creating an inner world of unassailable dreams (Tennyson) or a transcendent fortress of lofty feeling (Arnold). The Pre-Raphaelites followed this example. The poetry of D.G. Rossetti and of Morris is a 'literary' art, ie it depends on the proved poetic stimulus of a special 'poetic' language and imagery which was alien to the ordinary man of the age, and had no relationship to the economically productive genius of the age itself. (The intensely pious Christina Rossetti had a more authentic, religious inspiration, but even in her work the feeling is subjectively personal as compared to the work of a 17th-century religious poet such as George Herbert, 1593–1633, whom in some respects she resembled.) Thus, whatever the social consciences of Rossetti and Morris, they tended to take poetry to be an autonomous activity, largely independent of the political and social issues of the time. The poet ▷ Algernon Swinburne had the courage to take this autonomy seriously; with him, 'art for art's sake' was born, and the aesthetic movement (▷ Aestheticism). The only poetry which was moving strongly in another direction was that of ▷ Gerard Manley Hopkins from 1865 to 1889, and he was regarded as unpublishable. Another poet, W.B. Yeats (1865–1939), owed much to the Pre-Raphaelites and especially to Morris, but the bitter realities of Irish politics made him, in the next century, one of the leaders of the reaction against the whole direction of art as the worship of Beauty. This reaction has lasted to the present day. The Pre-Raphaelites had their own periodical ▷ The Germ; it first appeared in January 1850, and ran for only four numbers.

**Bib:** Stanford, D. (ed.), *Pre-Raphaelite Writing*; Pearce, L., *Woman, Image, Text: Readings in Pre-Raphaelite Art and Literature.*

## Presbyterianism

A ▷ Protestant doctrine of church organization devised by John Calvin (1509–1604) and other Reformers during the 16th-century Protestant Reformation. The word 'Presbyter' comes from a Greek word meaning 'elder', and Presbyterianism is a system of church government by councils of elders. It became dominant in Scotland under the leadership of John Knox (1505–72) and had wide support in England between about 1570 and 1648 when Oliver Cromwell (1599–1658) alienated the Presbyterian puritans and terminated the Presbyterian establishment because of their support for King Charles I. Briefly re-established after Cromwell's death it seceded extensively to ▷ Unitarianism during the 18th century. It was revived by Scottish settlers in England who began organizing their own congregations. In 1847 some Scottish and English Presbyterian congregations merged to form the United Presbyterian Church. The Presbyterian Church of England was formed in 1876 from a further amalgamation of the United Presbyterian Church and other such congregations. ▷ Thomas Carlyle was raised in Scotland as strict Presbyterian within the Burgher sect (which attempted to cling to a belief in an extreme Protestant theocracy throughout Cromwell's governance). His parents intended him to become a minister in the Burgher church, but he renounced his calling in 1817. By 1820 the sect had ceased to exist as an independent body.

## Primrose League

A Conservative political society founded in memory of ▷ Benjamin Disraeli, Lord Beaconsfield, whose favourite flower was said to be the primrose. The society was founded in 1883 and achieved large membership; it was one of the earliest successful attempts at permanent organization of public opinion in support of a ▷ political party.

## Prince's Progress, and Other Poems, The (1866)

The second published collection of poetry by ▷ Christina Rossetti, including the quest narrative 'The Prince's Progress', 'The Iniquity of the Fathers Upon the Children' (a narrative poem spoken from the perspective of an illegitimate child) and 'L.E.L.', a lyric dedicated to the poet Letitita Landon (1802–38). The simple diction and controlled poetic form which characterizes the collection reflects Rossetti's developing aesthetic of personal and artistic renunciation.

### Princess, The (1850)

Poem by ▷ Alfred Tennyson, originally titled *The Princess, A Medley* (1847), enlarged and revised in 1850. Despite bad reviews, *The Princess* was immensely popular and sold well on publication. Like ▷ Elizabeth Barrett Browning's ▷ *Aurora Leigh*, it was a key text in the so-called ▷ 'woman question' debate, displaced on to a pseudo-medieval scene. The tale of Princess Ida, champion of women's rights who rejects ▷ marriage and sets up a women-only university, is collectively told by a group of friends entertaining themselves. Ida was betrothed in infancy to the Prince, who narrates the tale of how he defies 'the inscription on the gate, LET NO MAN ENTER IN ON PAIN OF DEATH'. He and two friends dress as women and infiltrate the university. The men's identities are discovered by the women, and the university is attacked by the prince's father, who demands that they be released unharmed. In the ensuing battle between Ida's father and the Prince's, the three young men fall. Ida calls for the women to nurse them, and the women's university is turned into a hospital. When the Prince recovers he proposes a progressive marriage of equality to Ida, to which she yields:

> *My bride*
> *My wife, my life. O we will walk this world,*
> *Locked in all exercise of nobel end . . .*

▷ Education of women; Feminism; Medievalism.
**Bib:** Killham, J., *Tennyson and 'The Princess'*.

### Prisons

In the 11th and 12th centuries dungeons (underground cells) in castles were the prisons of those who displeased powerful barons or the king, and for long afterwards the Tower of London – fortress, palace and prison – was used for important political prisoners. In London there were the royal prisons of ▷ Newgate, the ▷ Marshalsea and the ▷ Fleet, which all lasted until Victorian times. In the 16th century houses of correction were set up for the incarceration of vagrants, who were regarded as a menace to the peace; these were modelled on the first to be established at Bridewell, London, in 1552, and were called 'Bridewells' after it. They were at first intended as ▷ 'workhouses' for the unemployed, but they became prisons in all but name. Prisoners were also kept in prison ships or 'hulks'.

Conditions in the prisons were very bad until the 19th century. Three principal reasons for this were:

**1** Prisons were not considered to be the responsibility of the authorities but of the gaolers; there was thus no supervision or maintenance of even the lowest standards of decency and hygiene, or of other aspects of living conditions.

**2** The gaolers were not regarded as officials, but as though they kept lodging-houses as tenants of the local or central authorities; they were paid no salaries, and drew their incomes from the prisoners who had to pay for privileges, and from whom the gaolers often extorted money by abominable treatment.

**3** Public attention to the necessity of a secure but humane prison system was delayed by the practice of 'transporting' criminals convicted of the more serious crimes to North American colonies or, after 1783, to Australia; transportation only ceased in the 1840s.

John Howard in the 18th century and Elizabeth Fry in the 19th were the leaders of the movement of reform in the prison system, which only made real advances after 1850. ▷ Jeremy Bentham was also influential in making prison organization more efficient and rational. The best known of all the writers who publicized the need for reform was ▷ Charles Dickens; he repeatedly used prison themes and episodes in his novels.

▷ *Great Expectations*.
**Bib:** Foucault, M., *Discipline and Punish*.

### Procter, Adelaide Anne (1825–64)

Poet and ▷ feminist, also wrote under the ▷ pseudonym Mary Berwick. She was born in London, the daughter of the poet Barry Cornwall. In 1853 she began to contribute poetry to ▷ *Household Words* and found an admirer in ▷ Charles Dickens, who wrote a foreword to her *Complete Works* (1905). A collected two-volume edition, *Legends and Lyrics* (1858 and 1861) includes her most popular verse, much of which is sentimental. Procter was a dedicated feminist and helped to found the Society for Promoting the Employment of Women. The proceeds from *Chaplet of Verses* (1862) went to a homeless women's refuge. Procter also edited an anthology of miscellaneous verse, *Victoria Regia*, which was published by Emily Faithful's Victoria Press in 1861.

▷ Women's Movement; Feminist
publishing.

### Professor, The (1857)

A novel by ▷ Charlotte Brontë, written in
1846 but not published until after the author's
death. In many ways it is an early version of
▷ *Villette*, although it is not as sophisticated.
The central character, William Crimsworth,
is an ▷ orphan who leaves England to seek
his fortune in Brussels. He falls in love with
Frances Henri, an Anglo-Swiss pupil-teacher,
and eventually marries her. Their relationship
is analogous to that of Lucy Snowe and Paul
Emmanuel in *Villette*, although it is not drawn
with as much complexity.

### Protestantism

Protestantism probably originated in the late
medieval period as an attempt to reform
▷ Roman Catholicism. The term was given
to those who protested against the Emperor
Charles V's condemnation of the reformers
in Germany at the Diet of Speyer in 1529.
It is now used to describe all varieties of
Christian belief which broke away from
Roman Catholicism during the Reformation in
the 16th century, or for religious communities
not in agreement with it. Protestants in Britain
include Anglicans, Presbyterians, Methodists
and Baptists.

The earliest form of Protestantism was
based on a rejection of the medieval Catholic
belief that the intercession of a clerical and
sacramental system was necessary in order to
restore men and women to God. Protestants
regarded the relationship between God and
mankind as more immediate and free. In
the 19th century Protestantism was deeply
influenced by the evangelical movement which
emphasized doctrines directly concerned
with the life, works and person of Jesus
Christ as described in the Gospels. Its
popularity in Britain was established by John
Wesley (1703–91), who was the leader of
the Methodist movement, and it was aided
by new techniques in revivalism. During
the 19th century the Protestant churches
entered their greatest period of expansion
and a new hymnody developed around the
movement. It eventually became the majority
faith in England and English-speaking
America and the great 19th-century Protestant
missionary movement carried it throughout
the British Empire and beyond. Many social
thinkers, economists and historians have
sensed a link between Calvinism (one of the
most disciplined and militant branches of
Protestantism) and the rise of ▷ capitalism.

The so-called 'Protestant work ethic' was
based on the doctrine that men and women
could be 'called' to do God's work just as well
at a machine or in an office as in a convent
or monastery and the movement gave rise
to a new seriousness regarding work in the
Victorian period. It was also instrumental
in the development of social services in the
rapidly expanding urban areas of Britain,
particularly in the area of nursing, temperance
work, care of the elderly and in the provision
of hospitals, orphanages, Sunday schools and
boys' and men's clubs in the city slums. The
Protestant movement provided much of the
impetus behind the extension of education to
the young and to working adults. The English
Baptist Charles H. Spurgeon (1834–92)
helped to establish Protestantism among the
educated poor of London, whereas William
Booth (1829–1912), a former Methodist
preacher, and his wife Catherine worked in
the more deprived areas using brass bands
and dancing to attract the men on the street
corners. Their evangelical movement became
known as the Salvation Army which became a
worldwide organization by the end of the 19th
century.

The development of Protestantism
was deeply influenced by the ▷ Oxford
Movement, founded by ▷ John Henry
Newman in 1833, which took the unique step
towards independence from the Protestant
tradition by emphasizing its Catholic elements.
Newman became a Roman Catholic in
1845 but the survivors of the Movement
transformed the worship, organization and
teaching of the Church of England. One of
the effects of this transformation was the
revival of nunneries from 1840 onwards and
of monasteries from 1860.

Religious belief, in particular Christianity,
was threatened by scientific and historical
advances (which called into question the
veracity of the Bible), and the growing
estrangement from religion of the urban
proletariat. In addition earlier forms of
socialism were fiercely ▷ atheistical, seeing
the Church as a bastion of that order of
society that must be overthrown in order to
obtain justice for the working man (▷ Karl
Marx). The 'Christian Socialist' Movement,
with its belief in social and economic justice,
grew up in response to this situation and
helped to draw the attention of Christians
to their social responsibilities. The Christian
Socialists included the novelist and clergyman
▷ Charles Kingsley, whose books display a
deep sympathy with and understanding of the
conditions of ordinary working people's lives.

The burning issue for Protestantism in the 19th century was how to reconcile a fundamental belief in the Bible as God's word with the recognition that the study and exposition of the Bible must be free from the compulsion to defend all its details as historical truth. In this way Protestantism was able to demonstrate an open-mindedness in the face of evolutionary theories and other scientific and anthropological advances. Biblical criticism was first embarked upon in the German universities where the emphasis was on the literary technique and sources of the Bible. The German Protestant philosopher, theologian and biographer David Friedrich Strauss (1808–74) claimed in *Das Leben Jesu Kritisch Bearbeitet* (1835–6; *The Life of Jesus, Critically Examined*, 1846) that the supernatural elements in the Gospels were a myth arising between the time of Christ and the period during which they were written. ▷ George Eliot translated Strauss in 1846 and the experience contributed to her loss of faith. Throughout the century, others such as the Cambridge scholar Joseph Barber Lightfoot (1828–1930) revolutionized the area of Bible study by placing the Bible in its historical setting and changing the previously accepted chronology of the Old Testament and the dating of the New Testament.

## Pseudonyms

Many women writers have adopted pseudonyms for a variety of reasons, the most common being to avoid discrimination on the basis of their gender. This is especially true in those cases where women have adopted male pseudonyms in a bid to have their writing judged on its literary merit rather than according to sexual prejudice. In 19th-century Britain the emergence of the pseudonym occurred during the 1840s when female novelists were becoming a recognizable professional group. The ▷ Brontë sisters first published under the androgynous pseudonyms Currer, Ellis and Acton Bell. Charlotte Brontë later admitted that 'a vague impression that authoresses are liable to be looked on with prejudice' had influenced the decision. ▷ George Eliot pleaded with Charles Gray not to expose her identity after she published an article in the ▷ *Westminster Review* in 1855. 'The article appears to have produced a strong impression,' wrote Eliot, 'and that impression would be a little counteracted if the author were known to be a *woman*.' Other examples might include the French writer ▷ George Sand (who had an enormous influence on Eliot), ▷ John Oliver Hobbes

and ▷ George Egerton: the pseudonyms of Aurora Dupin, Pearl Craigie and Mary Chavelita Dunne respectively, and ▷ Augusta Webster, whose first volumes of poetry were published under the name Cecil Home. ▷ Eliza Lynn Linton chose to write her ▷ autobiography under the name Christopher Kirkland. The collaborative poets Katherine Bradley and Edith Cooper wrote under the pseudonym ▷ Michael Field and entreated ▷ Robert Browning to guard the secret of their controversial dual authorship (which seemed to strike at the very notion of the sanctity of the writer), and most importantly their gender: 'We have many things to say that the world will not tolerate from a woman's lips,' declared Katherine Bradley. Edith Somerville and Violet Martin also wrote collaboratively, but their pseudonym, ▷ Somerville and Ross, was designed only to protect their identities as women. At the same time the market for women's literature was a lucrative one and some male authors such as ▷ William Sharp (Fiona Macleod) were not above changing sex – in name only – in order to exploit it. Women poets and novelists in the 19th century often favoured the use of enigmatic pseudonyms such as 'Speranza' (▷ Jane Wilde) and ▷ 'Ouida' (Marie Louise de la Ramée).

Many contributors to reviews and periodicals, such as the novelist ▷ Thackeray ('Charles James Yellowplush', 'Michael Angelo Titmarsh' and 'George Savage Fitz-Boodle'), disguised their names to conceal their ubiquity. At the same time the use of a *nom de plume* sometimes implied a second identity and allowed a writer to experiment with a variety of subject matter. ▷ Dickens published his first book ▷ *Sketches by Boz* using a pseudonym derived from his own infant attempts to pronounce the name 'Moses'.

## Public schools

Some public schools date from the 19th century, but those with the most prestige are usually much older: Winchester (founded 1382); Westminster (1560); Eton (1440); Harrow (1571); ▷ Rugby (1567). Until the 19th century ▷ education was largely restricted to study of the ▷ classics – ancient Greek and Latin language and literature – and the classics tended to attract those who wanted to enter the Church and the learned professions. From the 18th century, however, public schools began to be aristocratic educational institutions as it became increasingly regarded as indispensable to a

▷ 'gentleman' that he should possess a firm knowledge of classical culture.

In the 19th century the middle classes increased enormously in wealth and numbers and many of them aspired to be or regarded themselves as 'gentlemen' and required a 'gentleman's education' for their sons (▷ *Great Expectations*). At the same time ▷ Dissenting Academies declined and public school education broadened; ▷ Thomas Arnold as headmaster of Rugby (1828–42) imbued the school with a strong religious and moral feeling, suited to the traditions of the middle classes, in which Puritanism was a large element; and the country needed a large governing class for its rapidly growing empire. These facts contributed to the extension of public school education to much of the middle class. The inspiration of Thomas Arnold tended to make the public schools somewhat narrow; leadership and fair-mindedness were promoted at the expense of wide culture and intellectual flexibility. When Arnold's son, the poet and critic ▷ Matthew Arnold, described the English upper classes as 'barbarians', he was thinking of the products of the public schools (▷ *Culture and Anarchy*).

▷ Imperialism.

## Pun

A play on words depending upon a similarity of sound and a disparity of meaning. In the 19th century it was revived by humorous writers and writers for children, such as Thomas Hood (1799–1845), ▷ Edward Lear and ▷ Lewis Carroll (▷ Children's literature). Although their use of the pun was ostensibly comic, its effect in their writings is often unexpectedly poignant or even profound, especially in Carroll's *Alice* books. Puns continued to be despised by the adult world of reason, but they could freely and revealingly be used in what was regarded as the childish world of ▷ nonsense and fantasy.

## Punch

A weekly comic periodical, founded in 1841. Thomas Hood (1799–1845) and ▷ Thackeray were early members of its staff, and it employed a number of distinguished illustrators in the 19th century including Leech, Tenniel, Keene, and George Du Maurier (1834–96). From 1849 for a century it kept the same cover picture – of Punch of the puppet-shows. It was at first a radical paper, but as it became more and more an upper-class 'institution', so in politics, tone and taste it began to represent an influential but increasingly narrow section of the upper middle class. It has published the work of many famous cartoonists, including, in recent years, Ronald Searle, Michael Heath, Bill Tidy and Gerald Scarfe. The magazine was closed in 1993.

**Quid Pro Quo, or, the Day of the Dupes (1843)**

A play by ▷ Catherine Gore, which won a £500 prize for an 'English comedy'. The plot concerns social climbing, class division, and the political machinations of county folk. Although it was admired by the judges of the competition, it was a box-office failure, unpopular with both audiences and critics. It was Gore's last play.

# R

### Reade, Charles (1814–84)

The seventh of eleven children, Reade was born in Oxfordshire and educated largely at home; he excelled in sports and was self-motivated in study. In 1831 he went to Oxford and in 1843 was called to the Bar, but preferred music and the theatre. In 1845 he was made Dean of Arts at Magdalen College, Oxford, where he upset some members by wearing a green coat with brass buttons. In 1846 he tried medicine in Edinburgh, and in 1847 obtained a DCL and began to deal in violins. In 1851 he was made vice-president of his college, and began a long and prolific career as writer and dramatist. He met the actress Mrs Seymour in 1854 and they lived together until her death in 1879, after which he wrote little, turning to religion. He was a philanthropic man, helping the poor, distressed gentlefolk, lunatics, and waifs and strays; both impulsive and impatient, he was generous, boisterous and kept dogs, horses and other animals. He remained a theatre manager to 1882.

His writing career began with a stage version of Tobias Smollett's *Peregrine Pickle* (1751) in 1851. He co-wrote and produced *Masks and Faces* in 1852, turning it into the novel *Peg Woffington* the following year, when the 'reforming' novel about prisons, *Christie Johnstone*, also appeared. *It is Never Too Late to Mend*, in similar vein, followed in 1856, as well as the play *Gold!*; the novel was later dramatized and the play rewritten as the novel *Foul Play* (1869). He wrote short stories, pieces of journalism and plays at the same time. In 1858 he published *The Autobiography of a Thief* and *Jack of all Trades*, and in 1859 *Love Me Little, Love Me Long*. *The Cloister and the Hearth* was published in 1861. *Hard Cash* (1863) tackled the disgrace of lunatic asylums and in 1866 *Griffith Gaunt* triggered scandal and litigation by its frank attitude to sexual problems.

From this time on, Reade was a controversial and litigious figure. *Put Yourself in His Place* (1870) attacked enforced ▷ trade union membership; *The Simpleton* (1873) gave rise to a libel action and a quarrel with ▷ Anthony Trollope. Other novels and plays include *The Wandering Heir* (1873) and *A Woman Hater* (1877). Reade was both famous and successful, being regarded as the natural successor to ▷ Charles Dickens, and by ▷ Henry James and ▷ Swindburne as superior to ▷ George Eliot. He commented on himself, 'I am a painstaking man, and I owe my success to it.' His writing is now considered overburdened with detail, ▷ melodramatic and superficial in characterization. His most successful work was *The Cloister and the Hearth*.

**Bib**: Elwin, M., *Charles Reade: A Biography*; Burns, W., *Charles Reade: A Study in Victorian Authorship*; Hughes, W., *The Maniac in the Cellar: Sensation Novels of the 1860s*.

### Realism

A term, first used in France, for literary and visual forms which aim for the accurate reproduction of the world as it is. There is a long tradition of philosophical realism concerning the relationship of individual phenomena to abstract categories, and the relationship of ideas to the real world. Literary realism emerged in the late 18th and 19th centuries concomitantly with the rise of the novel and coterminous with industrial ▷ capitalism. In general, it means the use of the imagination to represent things as common sense supposes them to be. It does not only apply to 19th-century literature; Daniel Defoe (1660–1731) is commonly called a realist because of his factual description and narration. 19th-century realism in literature arose, however, from a reaction against 19th-century ▷ Romanticism, and is related to ▷ naturalism; for a discussion of late 20th-century critiques of realism as a vehicle of ideology, see Catherine Belsey, *Critical Practice*. ▷ George Eliot's ▷ *Middlemarch* (1871–2), with its carefully observed representation of the forces which structure society, is a notable example of English 19th-century realism. Many realist novelists chose to depict the lives and sufferings of the lower classes in texts that combine fiction with documentary. ▷ Elizabeth Gaskell's ▷ *Mary Barton* (1848) is a good example of this.

19th-century novels are often described, from a 20th-century perspective, as classic realist texts, a term devised by the film critic Colin McCabe in 1974 to describe *Middlemarch*. Classic realism, according to McCabe, who reverses the terms of Lukács's socialist realist attack on modernism, works by a sleight of hand, to hide the constructedness of the world; the world of the novel is presented to the reader as if it were a direct mirroring or reflection of the real world, rather than an ideologically saturated interpretation of the real. The term most often used to describe the strategy of the realist text is transparency. The illusion of transparency created by realism is contrasted with modernist writing which supposedly foregrounds its textuality.

Naturalism is a late 19th-century form of

realism, associated with the French novelist ▷ Emile Zola. It emerged out of an attempt to marry literary and scientific discourses, and demanded a scientific and empirical objectivity from writers, whose novels were supposed to be laboratory experiments to show how character is determined by environment. In practice, naturalism remained focused on the world as external material appearance, and imposed a rigid set of normalizing causal narratives. ▷ Thomas Hardy's ▷ *Tess of the d'Urbervilles* (1891) and ▷ *Jude the Obscure* (1895), ▷ George Gissing's ▷ *New Grub Street* (1891) and ▷ George Moore's ▷ *Esther Waters* (1894) are all influenced by naturalism. It is important to distinguish between different forms of realism – for example, classic realism, naturalism, socialist realism – and to recognize that they pre-suppose different kinds of relationship between the literary text and the world.

Dominant 20th-century critiques of realism regard it as a naturalization of ideological positions, presenting them as if they were commonsense perceptions or views. Latterly it has been argued that the polarization of realism and modernism, and the rejection of realism, has been too absolute. More work is being done on the many varieties of realism, and work on reading and fantasy suggests that earlier views of how the classic realist text operated assumed too simplistic a model of reading practices and modes of reception. ▷ Stendhal.
**Bib:** Levine, G., *The Realistic Imagination.*

### *Red Pottage* (1899)
A novel by ▷ Mary Cholmondeley. It centres on the lives of two women, Hester Gresley and Rachel West. Hester is a writer who lives with her bigoted clergyman brother and his narrow-minded wife. Her efforts at literary achievement are defeated when her brother burns the only copy of her novel, claiming it is immoral. The story of Hester's friend, Rachel, is a more conventional ▷ romance. The novel caused a minor sensation, being simultaneously denounced by clergymen and celebrated as a brilliant satire by journalists. Recent feminist readings have emphasized the strength of the relationship between Hester and Rachel, and praised the novel's defence of women's friendship.
**Bib:** Showalter, E., *A Literature of Their Own.*

### Reform Bills, Parliamentary
In English history, a succession of laws passed in the 19th and 20th centuries for the reform of the system of election of Members

of Parliament. The system has always been based on towns and rural districts, grouped into constituencies, each electing one or (until recently) sometimes more than one candidate as Member. The most important Reform Bill was the first, passed through Parliament in 1832, because it reduced the electoral confusion into a rational system. Most constituencies had remained unchanged since the Middle Ages; in consequence, some towns had grown to great size with inadequate representation in Parliament, or none at all, while others were represented by more than one Member although they had sunk into insignificance or even, in a few cases, had ceased to exist. This meant great power for the landed aristocracy, and great deprivation of power for the large and growing middle class. Some boroughs ('towns' – but often mere villages) were called 'pocket boroughs' because they were virtually owned by one landlord, who had them 'in his pocket', ie caused them to elect the Members of his choice; others were called 'rotten boroughs' because few inhabitants possessed the right to vote, and they were easily and habitually bribed. The law of 1832 redistributed Members of Parliament to correspond to the great centres of population, but limited the franchise (right to vote) to those who possessed a certain level of income, which ensured that electors belonged at least to the middle class.

The Reform Bill of 1867 extended the franchise to all male members of the working class in the towns, and that of 1884 to the rural working class. The delay in extending the franchise to the working class was bound up with the absence of any official state system of ▷ education; this was introduced in 1870. The town working classes received the vote before the rural ones owing to their greater experience in organization gained through ▷ trade unions and the running of Nonconformist (▷ religious groups) chapels.

The vote was now possessed by all men over twenty-one (with a few exceptions, such as lunatics, criminals, and peers who had seats in the House of Lords) but not by women. Women over thirty were enfranchised in 1918 thanks to the campaigning by suffragette movements (▷ women's suffrage) and the services performed by women in World War I. Women over twenty-one received the vote in 1928. The same laws enabled women to stand for Parliament. A 1969 Act lowered the voting age for both men and women to eighteen.

Much of the intimidation and corruption of voters was a consequence of votes being made openly; secret voting or 'voting by ballot', was introduced in 1872.

## Regional novel

A novel set in a real locality, accurately described. Regional novels became popular in Britain during the 19th century and many women writers used the form. ▷ George Eliot, ▷ Elizabeth Gaskell and the ▷ Brontë sisters are notable examples; lesser-known writers include ▷ Isabella Banks, nicknamed 'the Lancashire novelist' as a result of her detailed local description.

▷ Realism; Hardy, Thomas.

## Religious groups

Under the protectorship of the Puritan Oliver Cromwell (1599–1658), the Church of England ceased to exist as a state religious organization, but in 1660 the monarchy and the Church of England were restored, and Puritans were excluded from the Church, from political rights and from attendance at the universities of Oxford and Cambridge. From this time, the Puritans set up their own churches. They were released from their political restraints in 1828 and, during the 19th century it became more usual to call them Nonconformists or Free Churchmen. This term did not apply to Scotland, where the established Church was ▷ Presbyterian rather than the episcopalian Church of England. Within the Church, religious differences remained and were the basis of the newly emerging political parties, the ▷ Whigs being more in sympathy with the Puritans and the ▷ Tories being closer to, though never identified with, the Roman ▷ Catholics.

During the 18th century the apathy into which the Church of England had fallen was shaken by the religious revival led by John Wesley (1703–91), who worked mainly among the poorer classes. Although Wesley was forced to form a separate Methodist Church, his example inspired the ▷ Evangelical Movement within the Church of England, which by the 19th century was an important force towards social reform. A different sort of revival was led by a group of Anglicans at Oxford University, of whom ▷ John Henry Newman was the most active. This movement, inspired by a sermon by John Keble in 1833, and led by E.B. Pusey, Professor of Hebrew at Oxford, was dedicated to restoring High Church principles to the Church of England, and the resulting ▷ Oxford (or Tractarian) Movement affirmed the spiritual independence of the Church and its continuity

with the medieval (▷ medievalism) Catholic Church (▷ tracts). This was the beginning of Anglo-Catholicism, which was strongly criticized by bishops and clergy who were anti-Rome; Pusey was suspended from his post as university preacher at Oxford, accused of heresy. ▷ Charlotte Brontë's novel ▷ *Shirley* contains references to Anglo-Catholic practices. Newman and others eventually converted to Roman Catholicism, and the Oxford Movement lost in him its main inspiration. He left behind him, however, divisions of opinion within the Church that exist today: the High Church is composed of Anglicans who are essentially Catholic in belief, though they reject the authority of the Pope; they can be said to be decendants from Henry VIII's Reformation (1534–9). The Low Church feels itself to be ▷ Protestant, and can be said to favour the Reformation of Edward VI (1547–53). A third group prominent in the 19th century but not in existence now, was the Broad Church; it developed from the Evangelical Movement and was especially active in social and political reform. These have all existed under the common organization of the Church.

## Return of the Native, The (1878)

A novel by ▷ Thomas Hardy. Its setting is Egdon Heath, a wild tract of country in Dorset, in the south-west of England. The atmosphere of the Heath prevails over the whole book; as an environment, it repels some characters and absorbs others; those who are absorbed achieve a sombre integration with it but those who are repelled and rebel suffer disaster. The central character – 'the Native' – is Clym Yeobright, a Paris diamond merchant who has returned to the Heath in revulsion from the futility of his urban life and occupation. He intends to become a schoolmaster and marries the restless, self-seeking Eustacia Vye who is unfaithful to him; her affair with the unscrupulous Damon Wildeve leads to the death of both. Other charactes include Thomasin Yeobright whom Wildeve marries, to her misfortune and the grief of Diggory Venn, the travelling sheep-dyer (or 'reddleman') who represents a primitive sincerity and truthfulness, and Mrs Yeobright, Clym's mother, whom Eustacia estranges from her son. Clym becomes a furze-cutter on the Heath and eventually a travelling preacher. The novel is an example of Hardy's preoccupation with the relationship of characters with natural environment but it suffers from a weak conception of the central character, Clym.

## Reviews and periodicals

The English periodical press arose gradually from the controversial religious and political pamphleteering of the late 16th and 17th centuries. It became established as a recognized institution early in the 18th century, and it was also in the 18th century that the review, which expresses opinion, became distinguished from the newspaper, which gives priority to information on current events. The great age for the periodical press was, however, 1800–1914; this was the period when the quarterlies and the monthlies had their widest influence, and the weeklies their largest circulation proportionately to the size of the reading public. The word 'magazine', originally meaning 'storehouse', has also denoted, since the 18th century, a periodical containing miscellaneous material, eg the *Gentleman's Magazine* (founded 1731): 'a Monthly Collection to store up, as in a Magazine, the most remarkable pieces on the subjects above-mentioned' (introduction to the first number). In the 18th and early 19th centuries magazines differed from other serious periodicals (eg the ▷ *Edinburgh Review* and the *Quarterly Review*) only in having greater variety of content and being open to imaginative writing. Distinguished magazines of this kind include ▷ *Blackwood's* and the second *London Magazine* (1820–29). Later in the 19th century, magazines became predominantly popular periodicals devoted principally to fiction.
Bib: *Wellesley Index to Periodicals.*
▷ *All the Year Round; Athenaeum, The; Cornhill Magazine, The; Punch*; Newspapers.

## Reynolds, G.W.M. (George William MacArthur) (1814–79)

Novelist and journalist. A political radical, ▷ Chartist sympathizer and republican, Reynolds built up a substantial niche for himself in publishing and the newspaper business by writing specifically for the growing urban working-class readership: in 1846, he founded the penny weekly magazine *Reynolds's Miscellany* and in 1850 launched *Reynold's Weekly Newspaper* (which ran until 1967). One of the most successful purveyors of the so-called 'penny-dreadful' fiction (sensational stories issued in 1d serial form), he initiated the series *The Mysteries of London* (1846–50, based on Eugene Sue's *Les Mystères de Paris*, 1842–3), the Regency romance *The Mysteries of the Court of London* (1849–56), and various of the many ▷ Dickens plagiarisms and continuations that poured out in the 1840s, including *Pickwick Abroad* (1839),

*Pickwick Married* (1841) and *Master Timothy's Book-Case* (1842).
Bib: James, L., *Fiction for the Working Man*; Sutherland, J., *The Longman Companion to Victorian Fiction.*

## Rhymer's Club, The

Founded in 1891 at the Cheshire Cheese tavern near Fleet Street, it consisted of a group of poets including W.B. Yeats (1865–1939), ▷ Ernest Dowson, Lionel Johnson (1867–1902), ▷ John Davidson, Ernest Rhys, Richard Le Gallienne (1866–1947), ▷ Arthur Symons, ▷ Aubrey Beardsley and occasionally ▷ Oscar Wilde. Discussions centred on their own lyrics, which they read aloud, and poetry in general. They issued two anthologies (1892, 1894) of verse which exhibited many of the characteristics of the ▷ Decadent and ▷ Aesthetic movements.
▷ Nineties' Poets.
Bib: Yeats, W.B., *Four Years: 1887–1891*; Hough, G., *The Last Romantics.*

## Richard Feverel

▷ *Ordeal of Richard Feverel, The.*

## Risorgimento

Italian for 'resurrection'. The name given to the movement for the unification of Italy in the mid-19th century, led by Victor Emmanuel, king of Sardinia, his Prime Minister Cavour, the agitator Mazzini, and the soldier Garibaldi. In 1847 Cavour founded a newspaper called 'Risorgimento'. The movement appealed to English sympathies, which were strongly liberal at that time; references to it are common in mid-19th-century literature.

## Ritchie, Lady (Anne Thackeray) (1837–1919)

Novelist, ▷ short story writer and essayist, the daughter of ▷ William Makepeace Thackeray and aunt of Virginia Woolf (1882–1941). Almost all the literary celebrities of the day were known to the family, including ▷ Dickens, ▷ Tennyson, ▷ Robert and ▷ Elizabeth (Barrett) Browning, ▷ Charlotte Brontë and ▷ George Eliot. Ritchie wrote five novels: *The Story of Elizabeth* (1863); *The Village on the Cliff* (1867); *Old Kensington* (1873); *Miss Angel* (1875) and *Mrs Dymond* (1885). Her non-fiction includes *Toilers and Spinsters* (1874), which called attention to the plight of single, unemployed women, and *A Book of Sibyls* (1883), a collection of essays on women writers. Other works include *Records of Tennyson, Ruskin and Browning* (1892), and

*Alfred Tennyson and his Friends* (1893). The *Letters of Anne Thackeray Ritchie* was published in 1924. The character of Mrs Hilbery in Virginia Woolf's *Night and Day* is based on Ritchie, and she was well-known to the Bloomsbury Group.
**Bib:** Gerin, W., *Life*; Woolf, V., 'The enchanted organ: Anne Thackeray Ritchie' in *Collected Essays*, Vol. 4.

**Robertson, T. W. (1820–71)**
Dramatist. Plays include *Society* (1865), *Ours* (1866), *Caste* (1868). *M. P.* (1870). He is memorable chiefly for restoring to the drama some degree of relevance to contemporary social life at a time when contemporary plays had very little serious interest. His best-known play is the social comedy *Caste*.
**Bib:** Nicoll, A., in *A History of Late Nineteenth Century Drama 1850–1900*; Rowell. G., *The Victorian Theatre*.

**Robins, Elizabeth (1862–1952)**
Actress and novelist whose play *Votes for Women* was performed at the Court Theatre in 1907. In this she introduces an innovatory crowd scene of a suffragette rally at Trafalgar Square; the rest of the play is written within the conventions of society drama. She worked mainly in London and belonged to the group of Ibsenites encouraging the development of an English drama of ideas. She performed in the first productions of several of ▷ Ibsen's plays during the 1890s, including *Pillars of Society* (1889). *A Doll's House* and *Hedda Gabler* (both 1891).
▷ Women's Suffrage.
**Bib:** Robins, E., *Ibsen and the Actress*; Robins, E., *Both Sides of the Curtain*.

**Romance fiction**
In Victorian Britain it was commonly assumed that romance and the novel were inextricably entwined. This association was significant for women writers particularly, since affairs of the heart were seen as the woman's domain. To write about love, therefore, was considered 'natural', in a way that writing about politics was not. Almost every 19th-century woman writer, from Jane Austen (1775–1817) onwards, worked within the conventions of romantic fiction to a greater or lesser degree. Commentators and critics, eager to separate and categorize the writing of women, praised their 'special' ability to portray love and linked this to an essential feminine nature. Behind such praise lay prejudice, however, for a focus on love was also viewed as a limitation.

Women writers, it was argued, were unable to venture into abstract and 'universal' values. Women were, and ought to be, confined within the domestic and emotional in literature as well as life. Female writers who wished to express anything other than what women were 'supposed' to write about often adopted male ▷ pseudonyms. This restrictive ideology was increasingly undermined as the century wore on, but romantic novels remained as popular with women readers as they are today.
▷ 'Silly Novels by Lady Novelists'; 'Woman Question, The'; Blind, Mathilde; Broughton, Rhoda.

**Romanticism: Influence on Victorian literature**
The most prominent poets of the 'Romantic Movement' (1789–1824) were: William Blake (1757–1827), the pioneer of the movement; William Wordsworth (1770–1850), who developed the notion of pantheistic 'natural piety'; Lord Byron (1788–1824); John Keats (1795–1822) and Samuel Taylor Coleridge (1772–1834). The abstract noun 'Romanticism' did not enter the language until the mid-19th century, by which time all but Wordworth were dead. By this time readers began to see these poets as forming a single 'movement' and their work was simplified according to this categorization. Romanticism came to stand for an emotional reaction against the rational classicism of 18th-century Augustanism. Romanticism championed individual feeling over reason and social convention, and was characterized by a pervading fascination with dreams and the unconscious, an elevation of the power of the imagination and a new attitude towards the role of mankind in nature.

The early deaths of Keats, Shelley and Byron, coupled with the decline of Wordsworth and Coleridge, created a natural hiatus in the development of the styles, forms and critical standards of Romanticism. At the same time, however, Wordsworth's influence continued throughout the early years of Victoria's reign and he succeeded Robert Southey (1774–1843) as Poet Laureat in 1843.
▷ Charles Darwin and ▷ John Stuart Mill were great admirers of Wordsworth's verse as was ▷ Thomas Hardy who, in 1868, cited Wordsworth's 'Resolution and Independence' as a 'Cure for Despair'. The philosophies and political theories of Coleridge influenced both Mill and ▷ Disraeli although ▷ Thomas Carlyle rejected them for their philosophical aloofness and metaphysics, claiming that art

should be ▷ 'realistic' and possess a sense of sociological purpose. Carlyle and Mill both rejected Byron, who was greatly enjoyed by ▷ Tennyson and ▷ Ruskin. By 1850 Byron was being criticized for his subjectivity, his rhetoric and, more importantly, a perceived scorn of 'struggling humanity'. Keats's escapism found little favour with the major Victorian writers; neither did his doctrine of 'art for art's sake', although the ▷ Aesthetic Movement of the 1880s revived these ideas in direct opposition to high Victorian optimism and didacticism. Tennyson swiftly moved from his early enthusiasm for Keats to embrace a sense of doubt and despair found most eloquently in the work of ▷ Matthew Arnold. Shelley's idealism and impracticality were criticized by Tennyson, ▷ Kingsley and, of course, Carlyle but ▷ Robert Browning was converted to Radical politics and vegetarianism by reading Shelley's work and adapted Shelley's confessional style to his own ▷ dramatic monologues.

It was the birth and development of ▷ Benthamism and ▷ Utilitarian thought that led to the questioning of Romanticism and its literature. At the same time there was a movement towards the democratization of literature which became the province of the middle rather than the aristocratic classes. Growing awareness of what came to be known as ▷ 'the Condition of England', coupled with the social unrest of the ▷ Hungry Forties, led to a call for art to be centred on social and political issues. Art was seen to have a capacity to make people aware of social problems and a duty to change things for the better. The artist's first duty was to communicate, and his or her message should be one of social significance. Keats the aesthete and escapist was toppled by Carlyle the prophet and seer. Interestingly, both were born in the same year. Carlyle not only mistruted German metaphysics but he objected strongly to the notion of the artist as a divinely inspired being whose talent displayed itself in eccentricity and contempt for established social conventions.

However, the worst excesses of Romanticism were assiduously cultivated by the ▷ 'Spasmodic' poets who specialized in agitated, highly-strung and emotional verse. The Spasmodics also continued the tradition of the book-length poem which even the original Romantic poets found hard to sustain. Melodrama, insane passion and sensation – all characteristics of the ▷ Gothic novel – surfaced in the ▷ Sensation writing of the 1860s, and ▷ Dante Gabriel Rossetti

and the ▷ Pre-Raphaelites clung to the exuberance and lyric emotion favoured by Keats and Shelley. ▷ Emily Brontë's ▷ *Wuthering Heights* retains traces of the Romantic theory of the imagination developed by Coleridge and ▷ Elizabeth Barrett Browning's early work is characterized by a strong sense of the poet's mission and the holiness of the subjective impulse. Tennyson's ▷ *Maud* displays traces of the morbidity and subjectivity of the Romantic movement and it has been seen as a dramatization of the conflict within Tennyson and his fellow writers between the inclinations of Romanticism and the demands of Victorianism. Tennyson's work is characterized by a pervading struggle between a belief in 'art for art's sake' and a more pervading sociological aesthetic.

**Bib:** Ball, P.M. *The Central Self: A Study in Romantic and Victorian Imagination*; Christ, C.T., *Victorian and Modern Poetics*; Fletcher, L., *Romantic Mythologies*; Thomas, P., *The Post-Romantics*; Hough, G., *The Last Romantics*.

### Romola (1863)

A historical novel by ▷ George Eliot, serialized in ▷ *Cornhill Magazine* (1862–3). It is set in late-15th-century Florence at the time of the predominance of the reforming monk ▷ Savonarola. Romola is a high-minded girl who marries a self-indulgent and unscrupulous Greek, Tito Melma. Repelled by her husband and disillusioned by the course of Savonarola's career, she eventually finds her salvation in self-denial. In writing the novel, George Eliot was putting forward the principle that it is as important to actualize the society in which the characters move as to give reality to the characters themselves. The novel has been praised for the thoroughness of research which established the Florentine scene; on the other hand, by comparison with the later novels (▷ *Middlemarch* and ▷ *Daniel Deronda*) set in England, modern readers feel that medieval Florence did not touch the author in the sense that she participated imaginatively in its life, with the result that of all her novels, *Romola* is probably the least read.

▷ Historical novels.

### Rossetti, Christina (1830–94)

Poet, younger sister of ▷ Dante Gabriel and William Michael Rossetti. Her father, Gabriele, was an Italian patriot who came to England in 1824, her mother Frances Polidori was half-English and a former ▷ governess. Italian influence, particularly that of Dante, is noticeable in much of Rossetti's work. She was educated largely at home, her first poetry being published privately when she was twelve. Five poems appeared under the ▷ pseudonym Ellen Alleyne in the ▷ Pre-Raphaelite Brotherhood's journal *The Germ* (1850). She broke off an engagement to the painter James Collinson when he joined the ▷ Catholic Church in 1850, for she was a devout High Anglican, much influenced by the ▷ Oxford Movement. Although she was high-spirited as a child, she became increasingly reclusive and was plagued by illness, contracting Grave's disease in 1873.

Rossetti's best-known poem today is the sensual and complex ▷ 'Goblin Market', published with other poems in 1862. ▷ *The Prince's Progress, and Other Poems* appeared in 1866; ▷ *Sing Song, A Nursery Rhyme Book* in 1872 and ▷ *A Pageant, and Other Poems* in 1881. She also wrote religious prose works such as *Seek and Find* (1879); *Called to be Saints* (1881); and *The Face of the Deep* (1892). Her poetry often dwells on loss, renunciation and death, yet she is not limited to these subjects. The work ranges from fantasy verses to lyrics, ▷ ballads, ▷ nonsense poems, devotional verse and sonnets, including the 'Monna Innominata' series (1881). The 'simple surface' of the poetry often conceals the complications beneath: Rossetti's best work engages profoundly with epistemological, spiritual and psychic concerns. Her work has suffered from reductive interpretations, but she is increasingly being reconsidered as a major Victorian poet.
**Bib:** Crump, R. (ed.), *The Complete Poems of Christina Rossetti* (3 vols); Kent, D.A. (ed.), *The Achievement of Christina Rossetti*; Rosenblum, D., *Christina Rossetti: The Poetry of Endurance*; Harrison, A., *Christina Rossetti in Context*; Jones, K., *Learning not to be First: The Life of Christina Rossetti*.

### Rossetti, Dante Gabriel (1828–82)

Poet and painter; the son of an Italian political refugee and a half-English mother. In 1848 he started the ▷ Pre-Raphaelite Brotherhood with a number of fellow-painters, but the inspiration of his painting, as of his poetry, was essentially literary. The poetry is a continuation of the English ▷ Romantic movement, particularly the work of John Keats (1795–1821), inasmuch as its central impulse is the sensuous response to beauty. Another main inspiration for Rossetti and the Pre-Raphaelites was the direct appeal of detail in ▷ medieval painting. Rossetti also inherited, however, the feeling for the mysteriousness

of the Middle Ages which both he and Keats shared with the taste for 'Gothic' which was an aspect of Romanticism at the beginning of the century. In addition, he inherited some of the feeling for ▷ aestheticism in sanctity which had been part of the ▷ Oxford Movement in the Church of England during the 1830s and 40s. The triumph of English industrialism, with its admiration for technology, tended to disregard values which were not practical ones. Thus poets like Rossetti were tempted to use their poetry as a dream world of refuge from external squalor and commercial struggle and this led to a self-regarding nostalgia. This meant that fields of inspiration such as the Middle Ages and religion are not so much expressed in their own vitality as used as a defence against other, objectionable realities; Rossetti is accused of being 'religiose' rather than 'religious', and of having falsified the past. On the other hand, Rossetti's poetry, within these limitations, is sumptuous and melodious. He was at first much better known for his paintings, but his poem 'The Blessed Damozel' was published in the Pre-Raphaelite journal ▷ *The Germ* in 1850. Later came his translations from Dante, *The Early Italian Poets* (1861); *Poems by D.G. Rossetti* (1870); and *Ballads and Sonnets* (1881), including a sonnet sequence, *The House of Life*, which was expanded from a version in the 1870 volume, and is sometimes called his masterpiece.
**Bib:** Doughty, O., *A Victorian Romantic*; Winwar, F., *Poor Splendid Wings*; Holman Hunt, W., *Pre-Raphaelitism and the Pre-Raphaelite Brotherhood*; Boas, H.O.B., *Rossetti and his Poetry*; Cary, E.L., *The Rossettis*; Pater, W., in *Appreciations*; Hough, G., in *The Last Romantics*; Rees, J., *The Poetry of Dante Gabriel Rossetti*.

### Rubaiyat of Omar Khayyam, The

Verses by Omar Khayyam, a Persian scholar and poet who died in 1123. He was an outstanding mathematician and astronomer, but is still more famous for his verse epigrams written in 'rubai', ie four lines, the first, second and fourth of which have the same rhyme while the third is usually rhymeless. The rubai had been invented for the epitomizing of subtle thoughts on Islamic belief, but Omar used them to satirize religious bigotry with a free-thinking irony. This has caused him to be referred to as 'the Voltaire of the East'.

The English poet ▷ Edward FitzGerald published a translation of the Rubaiyat in 1859 (75 verses); he enlarged this to 110

verses in a new edition in 1868, and issued
other versions (101 verses) in 1872 and 1879.
FitzGerald emphasizes the pleasure-loving
aspect of the Persian poet, and the poem was
extremely popular in Victorian England both
for its musicality and for its expression of a
liberated way of life which contrasted with the
narrow and bigoted codes of mid-Victorian
respectability. The poet Robert Graves
(1895–1985) also published a translation of
the Rubaiyat.

## Rugby School

One of the most famous of the English
▷ public schools. It was founded in 1567, but
its importance begins with the headmastership
of ▷ Thomas Arnold (father of the poet
and critic ▷ Matthew Arnold) from 1828 to
1842. Hitherto, the ancient public schools
had imparted ▷ education (chiefly in the
Greek and Latin languages and literatures)
but without any consistent moral instruction.
Rugby became a pioneer of 'character-
building', which came to be regarded as the
most typical quality of the English 'public
school tradition'. The virtues were supposed
to be those of physical and moral discipline,
leadership and fair-mindedness. A large
number of public schools were founded in
the second half of the 19th century, and they
were modelled on Arnold's ideals. Since the
large Empire of which Britain was the centre
required an extensive class of administrators,
these ideals were eminently useful in
producing them. A once popular novel, *Tom
Brown's Schooldays* (1857) by ▷ Thomas
Hughes, describes life at Rugby under
Arnold.

There is a tradition that the game of rugby
football was invented at Rugby in 1823.

## 'Runaway Slave at Pilgrim's Point, The' (1850)

A poem by ▷ Elizabeth Barrett Browning.
The speaker of the poem is a black woman
slave who relates how she was torn from her
lover and then raped by a white slave-owner.
She bears a child, whom she murders and
buries in a forest. The rage, grief and pain
of the woman is chillingly conveyed in the
first person narrative. The speaker cannot
bear to see 'the *master's* look' on the child's
face, yet is driven to frenzied distraction after
the murder. Reconciliation is offered for the
mother and child only 'In the death-dark
where we may kiss and agree'. Barrett
Browning's impassioned protest against
slavery made a considerable impact upon her
contemporaries; it is still a powerful read.

## Ruskin, John (1810–1900)

Writer on art and on its relationship with
society. His central inspiration was that great
art is moral and the corollary that the working
men of industrial England were spiritually
impoverished. Like the ▷ Pre-Raphaelites
(he was a patron of ▷ D.G. Rossetti, their
leader), he found the contrast to the England
of his day in the freedom of individual
response to environment among the medieval
artists, and he expressed this view in the
famous chapter called 'The Nature of Gothic'
in *The Stones of Venice*. In the field of design,
Ruskin, like ▷ William Morris, advocated
a return to handicrafts and to medieval
conditions of production.

The latter part of his life was much
concerned with attacks on the social
philosophies of political economists, such
as ▷ John Stuart Mill, to whom he did less
than justice, and in endeavours to awaken
the working classes to the nature of their
combined artistic and moral impoverishment.
He wrote his artistic books in a style of
elaborate but precise and delicate eloquence
but his social gospel had more concentrated
and direct fervour. His puritanical mother
(he was an only child) had given him a
concentrated education in the Bible and
though his religious views as an adult were not
explicit, his conception of art as fundamentally
spiritual arose out of the intensity of his
early religious training. Though a supporter
of the Pre-Raphaelites, Ruskin did not
lean like them towards 'art for art's sake'
but towards 'art for the spiritual health of
man'. In his campaign against the mediocre
aspects of industrial culture, he was a disciple
and admirer of ▷ Thomas Carlyle but he
extended Carlyle's vision of greatness and
has proved to be a writer of more permanent
interest.

His principal works are: *Modern Painters*
(1843–60) in which he champions Turner,
one of the greatest of English painters and at
the time one of the most controversial; *The
Seven Lamps of Architecture* (1849) leading
to *The Stones of Venice* (1851–3) in which he
makes his discovery of 'the Nature of Gothic';
this took him towards problems about the
nature of civilized society in *The Political
Economy of Art* (1857), *The Two Paths* (1859)
and, one of his most famous books, ▷ *Unto
This Last* (1862). *Sesame and Lilies* (1865),
*Ethics of the Dust* (1866), *The Crown of Wild
Olive* (1866) are essays in criticism on the age,
and *Fors Clavigera* (1871–84) is composed of
96 letters to an educated artisan in which he
shows himself distrustful of liberal democracy.

*Praeterita* (1885–9) is one of the celebrated ▷ autobiographies in English, although it is fragmentary and incomplete. Its most famous section is the first, in which Ruskin describes his unusual, in some ways unnatural, yet fertilizing childhood.

▷ Gothic architecture; Medievalism.
**Bib:** Selections by Quennell, P.; Clark, K.; Rosenberg, J.D.; Leon, D., *Life*; Evans, J., *Life*; Ladd, H., *The Victorian Morality of Art*; Rosenberg, J.D., *The Darkening Glass*; Wilenski, R.H., *John Ruskin*; Lippincott, B., *Victorian Critics of Democracy*.

**Russian influence on Victorian literature**
The international importance of Russian literature belongs chiefly to its achievements in the 19th century. Until the middle of the 19th century, the influence was chiefly from Britain upon Russia: Laurence Sterne (1713–68), Walter Scott (1771–1832), Lord Byron (1788–1824) and, later, ▷ Charles Dickens all made an important impression on Russian writers. Since about 1850, however, the balance of influence has been in the opposite direction, although Russian literature has chiefly been known in translation, which has limited extensive public knowledge to prose works, especially the novels. These have been widely read, especially in the famous translations by Constance Garnett, who translated the works of Leo Tolstoy (1828–1910), Fyodor Dostoevsky (1821–81), ▷ Turgenev, Anton Chekhov (1860–1904) and Nikolai Gogol (1809–52) in the decades before and after 1900.

Tolstoy and Turgenev were the first Russian novelists to receive wide acclaim in Britain and Tolstoy is still considered the supreme novelist. His reputation in Britain owed much to ▷ Matthew Arnold, whose essay in praise of Tolstoy appeared in 1887, and is included in ▷ *Essays in Criticism, Second Series*, 1888. His tribute is the more noticeable because he otherwise ignored novelists in his criticism, and it made its mark because he was the most influential critic of his day. However, other critics contributed their admiration for the Russians in the last quarter of the 19th century. This interest was awakened by the feeling that the Russians, besides the French, were the only nation to produce a range of major novelists comparable to those writing in English and that, unlike the French, they shared with the British and North Americans a moral concern with human nature in society. There was also the feeling that the Russian novelists went beyond the British and North Americans, excelling

in their rendering of religious experience, though the full force of this was not felt until Constance Garnett produced her translation of Dostoevsky's *Brothers Karamazov* in 1912.

In the US, interest in Russian writing seems to have gone deeper, because of a feeling that these two great continental nations shared comparable experiences in the disorderly variety of their rapid growth. It was not merely this, however, that made the Anglo-American novelist ▷ Henry James a lifelong admirer of Turgenev. Turgenev was already well known in England from the middle of the century when he became the friend of ▷ George Eliot. These two novelists were the predominant influences on James's own work. He admired both for the depth of their moral insights but he admired Turgenev for what he saw as his superior artistic strictness in handling the elusive novel form. Turgenev thus combined for James the virtues of the French novelists with those of the English novelist he most admired. Gilbert Phelps, in *The Russian Novel in English Fiction* (1956), traces Turgenev's influence in some of the detail of James's novels and suggests his further influence on ▷ George Gissing, ▷ George Moore, ▷ Arnold Bennett, John Galsworthy (1867–1933) and ▷ George Bernard Shaw.

*Ruth* (1853)
A novel by ▷ Elizabeth Gaskell. Ruth Hilton, an ▷ orphan, is seduced by wealthy and self-interested Mr Bellingham and abandoned after a brief affair. She is taken in by the Dissenting minister, Mr Benson, and his sister, and assumes the identity of Mrs Denbigh, a widow, so that she and her illegitimate son will be accepted in society. Ruth finds employment as a ▷ governess to the Bradshaw family, and later re-encounters her seducer, who is now the local MP, re-named Mr Donne. He offers to marry her, but she refuses, having determined to seek redemption for her sin. Later, her true identity is discovered, and Mr Bradshaw casts her out (Donne is not known to be the seducer). After many futile attempts to find employment she offers her services as a sick-nurse during a typhus epidemic, and through her devoted work becomes revered in the eyes of the community. Her last unselfish act is to nurse delirious Mr Donne through his fever, after which she catches typhoid and dies a martyr's death. The novel was burned by members of Gaskell's congregation and criticized both for its sympathetic treatment of the ▷ 'fallen woman' and for its

unrealistically saintly portrayal of Ruth, who is throughout a picture of innocence, humility and Christian submissiveness. Flawed as it is by religiosity and narrative contrivance, *Ruth* nevertheless reveals the ideological contradictions of Christian and Victorian attitudes towards women.

**Rutherford, Mark**
 ▷ White, William Hale.

# S

### Sadler's Wells

Originally a health resort in north London, on account of its mineral spring. A theatre was built there in the 18th century and in the 19th century this became – like the ▷ Old Vic in south London – famous for its productions of Shakespeare. Since 1931 it has been used principally for ballet and opera. Both theatres are in once unfashionable parts of London, and their policy of appealing to poorer and less educated people caused them to become the starting-point for a National Theatre in the 20th century.

### Saintsbury, George Edward Bateman (1845–1933)

Literary historian and critic. His works include: *A Short History of French Literature* (1882); *A Short History of English Literature* (1898); *A History of Criticism* (1900–4); *A History of English Prosody* (1906–21); *The History of English Criticism* (1911); *A History of the French Novel* (1917–19). He also wrote studies of John Dryden (1631–1700), Walter Scott (1771–1832) and ▷ Matthew Arnold. His treatment of literary study was historical; that is to say, principles of evaluation or critical theory were for him secondary to coherent narration.

### Salome (1891)

A play by ▷ Oscar Wilde centred on the destructive love of Salome for John the Baptist. It was written first in French and translated by Lord Alfred Douglas, whose edition appeared in 1893 illustrated by ▷ Aubrey Beardsley. Although the play went into rehearsal in 1893 it was banned by the Lord Chamberlain for representing a biblical subject, and was not performed in Britain until 1931. It was first staged in Paris in 1896 with Sarah Bernhardt in the leading role: by that time Wilde was in prison for 'homosexual acts'. Salome has been called the 'Goddess of Decadence', the symbolic incarnation of undying lust. Wilde imagined her dressed in green 'like a curious poisonous lizard', contrasting strongly with the yellow costumes of the other characters. ▷ New Women writers such as ▷ George Egerton appropriated the image of Salome to represent sexual desire.

### Sand, George (1804–76)

French Romantic novelist and the best known French woman writer of the 19th century. Her influence on Victorian writers and the Victorian reading public was enormous and her work was a formative influence on the Victorian consciousness. Sand was born Aurore Dupin and brought up at her paternal grandmother's country property at Nohant. After a convent education in Paris she returned to Nohant where her independent spirit was encouraged. She read Jean-Jacques Rousseau (1712–78), Byron (1788–1824), Shakespeare and Vicomte de Chateaubriand (1768–1848), the greatest French writer of his generation and the father of French Romanticism. She married the baron Dudevant with whom she had two children, but in 1831 was living with a young writer Jules Sandeau whose surname she adapted as her pen-name. She subsequently enjoyed a stream of extra-marital affairs, the most famous of which were with the poet Alfred de Musset (1810–57), recorded in her novel *Elle et Lui* (1859), and with composers Franz Liszt (1811–86) and Frédéric Chopin (1810–49). She played an active role during the political upheavals of 1848, but disassociated herself from radical ▷ feminist attempts to get her elected to the National Assembly, as she was a reformist rather than a revolutionary at heart. She enjoyed a period of bourgeois respectability towards the end of her life and died peacefully at Nohant in 1876.

The ▷ *Athenaeum* mentioned her work in February 1833 with a mixture of moral outrage and admiration and from that point on she was widely read and reviewed in England, and very much a talking point in middle-class drawing rooms. Her main impact was made with works written during the first twenty years of her career when her doctrines were *avant garde* and challenging. In works such as *Indiana* (1832), *Valentine* (1833), *Léila* (1833) and *Jacques* (1834) she described ▷ marriage as 'one of the most barbaric institutions [society] has ever invented'. Her views were bold and outspoken, especially on the subject of relationships between the sexes and she was widely credited with having introduced passion as a major theme in the novel.

The 'second' phase of Sand's writing coincided with her increased enthusiasm for humanitarianism, socialism and Christianity. During this period she produced novels in which her desire to see humanity regenerate itself through a combination of social change and adherence to the teachings of Christ is very apparent. These include *Spiridion* (1838), *Les Sept Cordes de la Lyre* (1839), *Consuelo* (1842–3) and *La Comtesse de Rudolstadt* (1843–4). They were followed by a series of pastoral and/or socialist novels – *La Mare au Diable* (1846), *La Péché de M. Antoine* (1847),

*La Petite Fadette* (1849), *François le Champi* (1850) and *Les Maitres Sonneurs* (1853) – for which their author is most famous, and which reveal her tendency to idealize working-class rural life. In the mid-1850s she produced her less successful novels and her twenty-volume ▷ autobiography *Histoire de ma Vie* (trans. 1855).

▷ Matthew Arnold went on a pilgrimage to the middle of France in order to meet her and ▷ Clough drew inspiration for a poem from her novel *Jeanne*. For ▷ Jane Carlyle, ▷ George Eliot, Geraldine Endsor, the ▷ Brontës, and ▷ Elizabeth Barrett Browning, George Sand was the model of a dedicated professional writer who held her own with men, asking for no allowance to be made for her sex. Elizabeth Barret found her novels intense and liberating in their testimony to the irresistible power of human passion. The Brontës valued her resistance to received doctrines which forbade women equality, frankness and the right to a similar intensity of love to that enjoyed by men. ▷ Kingsley and ▷ Samuel Smiles also admired her work and ▷ George Lewes claimed she and Jane Austen (1775–1817) were the two touchstones for feminine literary greatness. Arnold and Clough identified with her idealism, her revolt against contemporary social norms, her delight in natural scenery and her faith in humanity. ▷ Thomas Carlyle, however, coined the term 'George Sandism' to describe tolerance of immorality, romantic effusiveness, lack of common sense, high flown sentiments and an obsession with love. ▷ Thomas Hardy and ▷ Henry James were deeply impressed with her work and James was singing her praises well into the 20th century.

▷ French influence on Victorian literature.
**Bib:** Thomson, P., *George Sand and the Victorians*; Blount, P.G., *George Sand and the Victorian World*; Cate, C., *George Sand: A Biography*; Crecelius, K.J., *Family Romances: George Sand's Early Novels*.

**Sartor Resartus: The Life and Opinions of Herr Teufelsdröckh**
A disguised spiritual ▷ autobiography by ▷ Thomas Carlyle. It was serialized (1833–4) in *Fraser's Magazine* and published in book form in Boston, USA, in 1836 and in Britain in 1838. Carlyle was under the influence of the German ▷ Romantics, eg Jean Paul Richter. The title is Latin for 'the tailor re-patched': Carlyle offers the fable that human beliefs and institutions are like clothes and need renewing. Against the poet Byron's (1788–1824) attitude of doubt, isolation and

suffering, Carlyle calls for the affirmativeness of the German poet ▷ Goethe; heroic qualities such as sacrifice and devotion to duty must redeem the inner man and, through men, the directionless age in which Carlyle felt himself to be living – the age of flux and the decay of unquestioning religious faith. Besides the drive of ▷ German influence, Carlyle felt the force of the old-fashioned Scottish Calvinism such as had animated his father. The three crucial chapters are 'The Everlasting No', 'Centre of Indifference' and 'The Everlasting Yea'. Despite the difficulty he had in getting the book published in Britain, it marks the beginning of his exposition of the creed of heroism, which made Carlyle an inspiring figure in commerce-dominated mid-19th-century Britain.

**Saturday Review**
It was founded in 1855 and noted for the brilliance of its contributors and the severity of its criticism. Later it took a greater interest in literature and included contributions from ▷ Thomas Hardy, ▷ Max Beerbohm, ▷ Arthur Symons and ▷ H.G. Wells. ▷ George Bernard Shaw was drama critic from 1895 to 1898.

**Scenes of Clerical Life (1857)**
Three tales by ▷ George Eliot, and her earliest work in fiction: *The Sad Fortunes of the Rev. Amos Barton; Mr Gilfil's Love-Story*; and *Janet's Repentance*. The hero of each is a clergyman. They were published first in ▷ *Blackwood's Magazine* in 1857 and collected as *Scenes of Clerical Life* in 1858.

**'Scholar Gipsy, The'**
A poem by ▷ Matthew Arnold, first published in 1853. He took the subject from a legend reported by Joseph Glanvill in *The Vanity of Dogmatizing* (1661). The Scholar of the legend renounced the anxiety of seeking a career through his scholarship, and took to wandering with the gipsies, dedicating himself to learning their lore. Arnold regards him as an immortal figure, and uses him as the type of a man who has happily escaped the anguish of the 19th-century intellectual's loss of faith and controlling convictions. The poem is not always considered to be Arnold's best, but it is one of his most famous, since it expresses the distress and doubt that is widely evident in mid-Victorian writing. It is written in twenty-five ten-line stanzas resembling those of John Keats's (1795–1821) Odes. It is

like the Odes too in its sensuous evocation of natural surroundings, though Arnold's tone is often nostalgic and insular. In 1867 Arnold published a companion-piece to 'The Scholar Gipsy' entitled *Thyrsis*, an elegy to his friend ▷ Clough, who died in 1861.

### Schreiner, Olive (Emilie Albertina) (1855–1920)

Daughter of a ▷ Methodist missionary of German descent and an English mother, Olive Schreiner was born in Basutoland, in South Africa, the sixth of twelve children. Self-educated, she became governess to a Boer family at the age of fifteen and began to write. She came to England in 1881 to seek a publisher and in 1884 met ▷ Havelock Ellis with whom she developed a close friendship. Ten years later she returned to South Africa and married the politician Samuel Cronwright who became her literary assistant and later literary executor. They took trips to England and travelled around Africa together. Her first and most acclaimed work is *The Story of an African Farm* (1883), which was published under the ▷ pseudonym Ralph Iron. Its unorthodox religious views and ▷ feminist standpoint caused a considerable stir. She wrote most after her return to South Africa: *Trooper Peter Halket of Mashonaland* (1897), *From Man to Man* (1926) and *Undine* (1929), all with feminist themes, and short stories, *Dreams* (1891), *Real Life* (1893) and *Stories, Dreams and Allegories* (1920). She also wrote *Woman and Labour* (1911). See also: *Letters* (1924).

Bib: Schreiner, S. C. C., *The Life of Olive Schreiner*; First, R. and Scott, A., *Olive Schreiner: A Biography*.

### Science fiction

The term 'science fiction' was coined in the mid-19th century, though it was 're-invented' and given wider currency in the late 1920s by a US magazine editor, Hugo Gernsback, who popularized stories which pre-eminently derived from ▷ H.G. Wells and ▷ Jules Verne. Science fiction, which is a product of and response to an era of rapid scientific and technological development, has often been concerned to promote new ways of seeing appropriate to the times. For example, in the Victorian period, the human consequences of industrialization and the implications of ▷ Darwinian evolutionary theory were explored in science fiction. Critics hostile to the science fiction genre have complained that its presentation of human character compares unfavourably with that of ▷ realist fiction, whereas others have argued that characterization in science fiction represents a response to a world dehumanized by technology, or a radically different viewpoint from which the question 'What constitutes the human?' can be asked.

Mary Shelley's *Frankenstein* (1817), centrally concerned with this question of defining the human, may be regarded as a significant root work of science fiction but it was H.G. Wells who established the genre in the 1890s. Works such as *The Time Machine* (1895), *The Invisible Man* (1897), *The War of the Worlds* (1898) and *The First Men in the Moon* (1901) share with *Frankenstein* an unsettling pessimism deriving from a perception of the destructive and alienating uses to which technological development might be put. Wells established an influential British tradition of bleak Darwinism, emanating from an imperial culture already in decline. Wells's *The Time Machine* provides a model for a range of subsequent science fiction. It introduces, in almost comic pseudo-scientific discourse, a technological means of travel through time; it facilitates sociological criticism and prediction through the use of ▷ utopian and dystopian discourses; it treats the theme of confrontation with the alien, of the last man on earth, of the entropic death of the world; it provides new contexts for old myths; and it defamiliarizes the cosy certitudes of the late Victorian male world in which it starts. *The War of the Worlds*, repeatedly adapted and imitated in the 20th century, may be regarded as the genesis of the bulk of science fiction treatments of interplanetary war or invasion by the alien. Many of Wells's contemporaries in the science fiction genre were sons of clergymen converted to free thought by the discrediting of traditional religious views by science, which revealed that the earth was but a tiny atom in a vast impersonal universe and that the history of mankind was a brief moment even in comparison with the history of the earth. These writers included ▷ Charles Grant Allen. Wells called his science fiction novels 'scientific romances', and the relation between ▷ romance, particularly Gothic romance, and science fiction has often been remarked on by definers of the form.

### Scott, Hugh Stowell (1862–1903)

Writer of adventure ▷ romances, which he published under the name 'Henry Seton Merriman'. Most of them have rapid, exciting plots and exotic settings, which Scott researched on his extensive travels. The son of a shipowner in Newcastle-upon-Tyne,

Scott abandoned a business career early on to pursue writing and travelling; it has been suggested that he worked for the British intelligence services, and some of his work is strongly pro- ▷ imperialist. His novels include: *The Slave of the Lamp* (1892); *With Edged Tools* (1894); *The Grey Lady* (1895); *In Kedar's Tents* (1897); *The Isle of Unrest* (1900); *Barlasch of the Guard* (1902); *The Last Hope* (1904).

## Scottish literature in English

This belongs above all to the Lowland; it is a distinctive branch of literature in the English language. The Lowland Scottish form of English originally had a close resemblance to that spoken in the north of England. Racially, liguistically and culturally, Lowland Scottish ties with England were close, despite the constant wars between the two countries in the late 13th and mid-16th centuries. By contrast, until the 18th-century destruction of Highland culture, the Lowlanders had little more than the political bond of a common sovereign with their Gaelic-speaking fellow-countrymen of the north. While it is not true to say that Scottish literature is a branch of English literature, the two literatures have been closely related. Robert Burns (1759–96) was perhaps the first famous Scottish poet after the 16th century, but by the 18th century the tide of English influence had moved strongly into Scotland; Walter Scott (1771–1832) collected Scottish ▷ ballads, and produced a few fine examples in the ballad tradition, but his longer poems belong to the history of English verse narrative, though their subject was often Scottish history and legend. Gaelic literature of the Highlands had what is said to be a 'golden age' in the later 18th century, just at the time when Gaelic culture was being destroyed by the English and the Lowland Scots for political reasons.

The Scottish prose writers of the Victorian period were mainly anglicized in their prose expression. The most famous of these was ▷ Thomas Carlyle who was one of the major literary influences of the 19th century. He was raised as a strict ▷ Presbyterian within the Burgher sect, who retained a strong allegiance to the ▷ Presbyterian Covenant ratified by the Scottish Parliament in 1644, during the time of Oliver Cromwell's victories over the monarchy. However, by the time Carlyle was twenty-five the sect had ceased to exist as an independent body, as its peculiar religious and political beliefs had become untenable. Although Carlyle renounced the ministry in 1817 his sectarian upbringing gave him a peculiar slant on history and he continued to place great faith in the values he had inherited. Apart from Walter Scott other writers participated in the adventurous narrative, such as Edinburgh-born ▷ Robert Louis Stevenson (1850–94) and ▷ R.M. Ballantyne (1825–94), well-known for their escapist fantasies often read as ▷ children's fiction, although Stevenson's work is the subject of some re-evaluation. Other Scottish novelists include George Macdonald (1824–1905), Lucy Walford (1845–1915), 'Sarah Tytler' (Henrietta Keddie (?1826–1914), and ▷ Margaret Oliphant. Oliphant produced a number of novels dealing with Scottish life. The Evangelical novelist ▷ Catherine Sinclair (1800–64) wrote books on Sheltand and Scotland as well as fiercely anti- ▷ Catholic didactic novels such as *Beatrice; or, the Unknown Relatives* (1852).

The 'Kailyard' or 'Cabbage Patch' school describes a group of Scottish writers including Ian Maclaren (who first coined the phrase in his collection of stories *Beside the Bonnie Briar Bush*, 1894), ▷ J.M. Barrie, and S.R. Crockett (1860–1914), who wrote *The Stickit Minister* (1893). It refers to a type of writing, often in the vernacular, dealing with village life, which has a tendency to over-sentimentality. It was extremely popular during the last decade of the 19th century.

▷ Blind, Mathilde; Buchanan, Robert; Sharp, William.

## Sensation, Novel of

A genre that emerged in Britain from about 1860, influenced by Gothic literature and characterized by extravagant, passionate and sometimes horrific events. It is often considered the precursor of the modern thriller. Sensation novels were extremely popular with the reading public and formed a large part of the stock of ▷ circulating libraries. Examples of the genre include ▷ Mary Braddon's ▷ *Lady Audley's Secret* (1862); ▷ Mrs Henry Wood's ▷ *East Lynne* (1861) and ▷ Rhoda Broughton's ▷ *Cometh Up as a Flower* (1867). In *A Literature of Their Own* (1977), Elaine Showalter argues that sensation novels form a significant part of the tradition of 19th-century women's writing. Novelists such as Mary Braddon subverted the stereotype of the 'blonde angel'; others brought a wide range of suppressed female emotions to the surface of their texts and constructed powerful fantasies of escape and protest.

▷ Collins, Wilkie; Corelli, Marie.
**Bib:** Hughes, W., *The Maniac in the Cellar: Sensation Novels of the 1860s*.

**Sewell, Anna (1820–78)**
Famous for the one book she wrote, *Black Beauty* (1877), whose success was largely posthumous. Sewell was paid only £20 for the book, which was published just before her death. The story, of a black mare's unhappy adventures, ending happily, has remained a children's classic.
  ▷ Children's literature.
**Bib**: Chitty, S., *Life*.

**Sewell, Elizabeth (1815–1906)**
Novelist and polemical writer. She was born in Newport on the Isle of Wight and went to school in Bath until recalled home at the age of fifteen. She began to write partly to help the family finances, publishing her first work, *Amy Herbert*, in 1844. A keen supporter of the ▷ Oxford Movement, her novels are deeply religious and moral, yet their focus on women's lives has aroused recent feminist interest. Works include: *Laneton Parsonage* (1846); *Margaret Percival* (1847); *Katherine Ashton* (1854); and *Ursula* (1858). Sewell also wrote devotional works, including *Thoughts for Holy Week* (1857) and *A History of the Early Church* (1861), as well as an *Autobiography* (1907).
**Bib**: Foster, S., *Victorian Women's Fiction: Marriage, Freedom and the Individual*; Showalter, E., *A Literature of Their Own*.

**Shaftesbury, Lord (Anthony Ashley Cooper, 7th Earl of Shaftesbury, 1801–85)**
Statesman and philanthropist. His politics were right wing, but he devoted his career to improving the condition of the working classes. It was largely owing to him that the Ten Hours Bill, restricting hours of work in ▷ factories, became law in 1847, and in the same decade his efforts led to improvement in the mines. After 1846, he gave his attention to the London slums; clearance of the squalid district of Seven Dials led to the building of Shaftesbury Avenue, called after him; the statue of Eros in Piccadilly Circus also commemorates him. Shaftesbury was an adherent of the religious revival known as the ▷ Evangelical Movement, working against the ▷ Utilitarian theories of the political economists (Adam Smith, ▷ Jeremy Bentham, ▷ Thomas Malthus) in the shaping of the industrial changes and urban expansion of the mid-19th century.
  ▷ Anti-industrialism.

**Shalott**
  ▷ *Lady of Shalott, The*.

**Sharp, William (1855–1905)**
Scottish novelist and poet, who published much of his better work in the 1890s under the name 'Fiona Macleod', supposedly his cousin, an alter ego whose real existence he always maintained (she appeared in *Who's Who*) and may even have believed in. The novels of Fiona Macleod are mystical, nostalgic tales of Celtic peasant life, such as *Pharais: A Romance of the Isles* (1894), *The Mountain Lover* (1895), *The Sin Eater* (1895) and *Green Fire* (1896). Sharp also wrote novels under his own name, including the epistolary novel *A Fellowe and his Wife* (1892), jointly authored with the US writer Blanche Willis Howard. After early, uncongenial work as a clerk, Sharp had begun his literary career in the 1880s as a journalist, and by writing commissioned biographies and poetry, but in the 1890s spent much of his time travelling. The dual personality provoked a nervous crisis in 1897.
  ▷ Scottish literature in English.

**Shaw, George Bernard (1856–1950)**
Dramatist, critic, social thinker. His family belonged to the Irish Protestant gentry. His father was an unsuccessful businessman; his mother was a musician of talent. Apart from the musical education he received from her, he was practically self-educated. He came to London in 1876, and set to work as a novelist. The novel proved not to be his medium, but his efforts in the form were an apprenticeship for dramatic writing in which he excelled. He wrote five novels in all: the best known are *Cashel Byron's Profession* (pub. 1885–6) and *The Admirable Bashville* (pub. 1901). In 1884 he joined the newly formed socialist ▷ Fabian Society, of which he became a leading member; he edited *Fabian Essays* (1887) which was influential in forming socialist opinion in Britain. Between 1885 and 1898 he wrote much criticism for a number of papers; he was probably the most astute music and dramatic critic of his time.
  His career as a dramatist began in 1892 and lasted substantially until 1939, though he wrote his last play when he was over 90. Through ▷ William Archer, the translator, he had come to know the work of the Norwegian dramatist ▷ Henrik Ibsen and was profoundly impressed especially by Ibsen's plays of social criticism such as *A Doll's House*. In 1891 came his study *The Quintessence of Ibsenism*, and then he embarked on plays of social purpose on his own account. Shaw's art is, however, very different from Ibsen's; whereas for Ibsen the characters are always more important than the

ideas in a play, and the characters engage in convincing talk, in Shaw's plays it is the ideas that really matter, and his characters don't talk – they make speeches. The speeches are composed in the operatic tradition of Mozart; Shaw once said that it was Mozart who taught him to write. As a dramatic critic and a student of Ibsen, he had learnt stage-craft thoroughly, and he knew how to achieve theatrical effect, to which his unique talent for wit, surprise, and paradox strongly contributed. In regard to ideas, he was concerned to shock his audiences out of their unthinking acceptance of social conventions, but he was careful (unlike Ibsen) never to scandalize them beyond their willingness to listen. Apart from socialism, his leading doctrine (derived partly from the French philosopher Bergson and partly from the German philosopher ▷ Nietzsche) was his belief in the 'Life Force' – that the progress of humanity depends in every generation on the evolution of geniuses, who comprise the spearheads of advance but inevitably arouse the hostility of their contemporaries. He was the first dramatist to realize that the reading public for plays was now larger than the theatre-going public; accordingly he published his own plays with long prefaces, which are commonly as famous as the plays themselves, and with elaborate stage directions intended not only for stage producers but for readers accustomed to the kind of detail provided by novels.

His most famous plays are probably: *Man and Superman* (1903); *Major Barbara* (1905); *Pygmalion* (1912); *Heartbreak House* (1917); *Back to Methuselah* (1921); *Saint Joan* (1924). Other plays: in ▷ *Plays Pleasant and Unpleasant* (1898) – *Widowers' Houses* (first staged 1892); *The Philanderer; Mrs Warren's Profession;* ▷ *Arms and the Man;* ▷ *Candida; The Man of Destiny; You Never Can Tell.* In *Plays for Puritans* (1901) – *The Devil's Disciple; Caesar and Cleopatra; Captain Brassbound's Conversion.* Other plays before 1914: *John Bull's Other Island; How He Lied to Her Husband; Press Cuttings; The Doctor's Dilemma; Getting Married; The Showing up of Blanco Posnet; Misalliance; Fanny's First Play; Androcles and the Lion; Overruled; Great Catherine.* After 1918: *The Apple Cart; In Good King Charles's Golden Days.*

Among Shaw's extensive political writings are his attack on the British government, *Common Sense about the War* (1914) and *The Intelligent Woman's Guide to Socialism and Capitalism* (1928).

▷ Irish literature in English.

**Bib:** Pearson, H., *Life;* Henderson, A., *Life;* Chesterton, G.K., *George Bernard Shaw;* Bentley, E., *George Bernard Shaw;* Meisel, M., *Shaw and the Nineteenth Century;* Morgan, M., *The Shavian Playground.*

### Shirley (1849)

A novel by ▷ Charlotte Brontë. It is set in Yorkshire at the time of the Napoleonic wars and is concerned, like several novels of the 1840s, with labour relations. Robert Gerard Moore is a half-English, half-Belgian mill owner who introduces the latest labour-saving machinery to the workplace, ignoring the protests of his employees. They turn against him and attempt to destroy the mill and to take his life. In an effort to raise funds Robert proposes to the spirited Shirley Keeldar, an heiress. She refuses him and eventually marries Robert's brother, Louis, a tutor in her family. Robert marries Caroline Helstone, his cousin. The novel protests against the limited opportunities available to women, demonstrated particularly in the life of Caroline, confined in her uncle's rectory and prohibited even from working as a ▷ governess. In the character of Shirley, Brontë claimed she was drawing a portrait of her sister ▷ Emily Brontë, 'had she been placed in health and prosperity'.

▷ Historical novel; 'Woman Question, The'; Social Problem novel.

### Shorthouse, Joseph Henry (1834–1903)

Novelist, whose *John Inglesant* (1880), a historical and philosophical ▷ romance set in England and Italy during the 17th century, was initially rejected by publishers but later became a ▷ best-seller and acquired something of a cult following. Shorthouse was brought up as a Quaker but converted to the Church of England, and religious loyalties and conversion play a large part in the novel. Shorthouse worked in business despite poor health; his other literary works were relatively minor historical romances, such as *The Countless Eve* (1888) and two novels set in the present: *Sir Percival* (1886) and *Blanche Lady Falaise* (1891).

▷ Historical novel.

### Short story

This very early type of fiction was first taken seriously in the 19th century as an independent literary form, making different demands on the writer and the reader from those of longer works of fiction such as the novel. Three writers originated the art of the short story: the US writer, Edgar Allan Poe

(1809–49), who defined it as a genre in a review of Nathaniel Hawthorne's *Twice-Told Tales* in 1842; the Frenchman, Poe's disciple, Guy de Maupassant (1850–93); and the Russian, Anton Chekhov (1860–1904). These writers evolved the qualities especially associated with the short story: close texture, unity of mood, suggestive idiom and economy of means. Such qualities associate the short story with the verse poem, and we find that in English the verse story anticipated the prose story in works such as the tales of George Crabbe (1754–1832), and ▷ Arthur Hugh Clough's *Mari Magno* (1862). However, no relationship can be established between the verse of such writers and the prose of ▷ Rudyard Kipling, with Maupassant behind him, or that of Katherine Mansfield (1888–1923), who was strongly influenced by Anton Chekhov. These two wrote little else in prose except stories (Kipling wrote two novels), but the greatest masters of the short story form, like ▷ Henry James, were predominantly novelists.

One of the earliest English short stories of the 19th century is Sir Walter Scott's 'The Two Drovers' (1827), which is 5000 words long and may well have been the inspiration for French novelist Prosper Mérimée's 'Mateo Falcone'. However, the short story was slow to develop in England compared to the United States, France and Russia. This was due to the unchallenged supremacy of the novel as the dominant literary form. ▷ Charles Dickens wrote a number of relatively short pieces such as ▷ *A Christmas Carol* (1843) and *The Chimes* (1844) as well as other brief prose narratives, most of which appeared in his own magazines ▷ *Household Words* and ▷ *All the Year Round*. These were probably intended as 'fillers' between the initial serial parts of his own novels. ▷ *Sketches by Boz* is probably closest to the modern short story. In 1858, ▷ George Eliot published three short stories called ▷ *Scenes From Clerical Life*. ▷ R.L. Stevenson published his first short story 'A Lodging House For the Night', set in the 15th century, in 1877. He went on to produce some of the finest ▷ horror stories of the period. One of his best stories is 'The Beach at Falesá' (1891).

In addition to his plays, poetry and essays ▷ Oscar Wilde also wrote several short stories, often for children, which became favourites in Britain and the US. The pioneer feminist writer ▷ George Egerton became famous for her stories about unhappy wives trapped in empty marriages. She published mainly in the ▷ *Yellow Book*, and her first volume ▷ *Keynotes* (1893) carried a monogram designed by ▷ Aubrey Beardsley. It was followed in 1894 by *Discords*.

Henry James produced 110 short stories, despite being frustrated by the conventional length of 8000 words. Works like ▷ *Daisy Miller* and *Miss Ganton of Poughkeepsie* are among his most famous, although James preferred to call them *nouvelles*. It is difficult to make a clear distinction between the short story and the *nouvelle* (novella or long story); it is difficult also to say at what point a *nouvelle* stops short of being a novel; on the whole the *nouvelle* seems to share with the short story as generally understood a unity of mood which is not so likely to be found in a true novel, however short. All the masters of the short story mentioned here were also masters of the *nouvelle*, but not necessarily (eg Chekhov) of the novel form.

▷ Joseph Sheridan Le Fanu was a master of the short story form, producing some of the most powerful tales of terror and the supernatural. His best single collection is *In A Glass Darkly* (1872). Rudyard Kipling's *Plain Tales From the Hills* (1888), set in the Anglo-India of the late 19th century, gave the form prestige, enabling writers of fiction to take it seriously. ▷ Thomas Hardy published four collections of short stories: *Wessex Tales* (1888), ▷ *A Group of Noble Dames* (1891), *Life's Little Ironies* (1894) and later *A Changed Man and Other Tales* (1913).

Towards the end of the 19th century developments in printing and technology coupled with a mass increase in literacy helped to usher in the era of the popular press, bringing with it a generation of new writers – often lower middle class in origins – including ▷ H.G. Wells and Arnold Bennett (1867–1931). This, coupled with the influence of ▷ realism and ▷ naturalism, meant that for the first time popular writing and literature shared a common territory and content. Urban working-class life became a dominant theme in literature. Arnold Bennett's 'A Letter Home' was first published in the *Yellow Book*. Bennett was influenced by ▷ Gustave Flaubert, and Guy de Maupassant, who by the end of his life in 1893 was probably the most famous short story writer in the world. Other stories of urban working classes included ▷ Arthur Morrison's *Tales of Mean Streets* (1894), which dealt with low life in the East End of London. Outlets for the genre were found in new magazines and periodicals such as *The Strand Magazine* (1891) which published writers such as ▷ Arthur Conan Doyle – who perfected the format of the detective story – ▷ H.G. Wells, W.W. Jacobs and P.G. Wodehouse (1881–1975).

▷ French influence on Victorian literature; Newspapers; Reviews and Periodicals.
**Bib:** Allen, W., *The Short Story in English*; Orel, H., *Victorian Short Stories: An Anthology*; Bates, H.E., *The Modern Short Story*; O'Faolain, S., *The Short Story*.

**Sick Man of Europe, The**
In the second half of the 19th century, a way of referring to Turkey, regarding that country as one which was too large to ignore, yet too weak to be able to control its own conquered territories, so that it had become a subject of chronic international crisis. The phrase was originated by Tsar Nicholas of Russia in conversation with the British ambassador.

▷ Crimean War.

**'Signs of the Times' (1829)**
A highly influential and analytical essay by the historian and social critic ▷ Thomas Carlyle which originated as an anonymous article in the *Edinburgh Review*. In it Carlyle claims that the mechanical age and its reverence for moribund institutions has led to a lack of spirituality among men and women. Carlyle proposed heroic individualism as the solution to the problem. It was a specific attack on ▷ Utilitarianism, which it condemned as a 'mechanical' rather than a 'dynamic' system of thought. The essay influenced a number of Victorian writers, in particular ▷ Charles Dickens, who dedicated his novel ▷ *Hard Times* (1854) to Carlyle.

▷ Anti-industrialism.

**Silas Marner (1861)**
A novel by ▷ George Eliot. Silas Marner is a weaver who has been driven out of his religious community as a result of a false charge of theft. He loses his religious faith and moves to a Midland village, Raveloe, where he re-establishes his trade, but maintains a self-imposed exile from the community. He lives only for money, hoarding his gold until it is stolen from his cottage by Dunstan Cass, son of the local squire. Dunstan then disappears, leaving Silas in despair. A transformation in Silas's life occurs following the mysterious arrival of a young child who finds her way into his cottage. Silas, initially, sees the child as a substitute for his lost wealth, and adopts her. But the relationship soon draws him from his miserly ways and he and the child, whom he calls Eppie, become devoted to one another. It is later revealed that Eppie is the

daughter of Dunstan's brother, Godfrey, and Molly Farran, a working-class woman whom Godfrey had married, but refused publicly to acknowledge. Molly and her child had been forced to live in squalor and wretchedness, and Molly eventually dies, abandoned, in a ditch. When Eppie is almost grown up, Godfrey finally acknowledges his paternity, but Eppie refuses to leave the man who has cared for her. She refuses, also, to be seduced by Godfrey's wealth, and remains loyal to the working-class values of her closest friends. In *Silas Marner*, Eliot is critical of the rigid system of patriarchal law and its associated ethics of individualism, and argues for an alternative morality based upon more malleable and socially responsible codes.

**'Silly Novels by Lady Novelists' (1856)**
An article by ▷ George Eliot, printed in the ▷ *Westminster Review*. With scathing ridicule, Eliot attacks the unreality of many women's novels, criticizing their false portrayals of character and sexual relationships, their romantic wish-fulfilment and ludicrous representations of female learning. Eliot argues that the effect of such 'Silly Novels' is to make female aspirations appear risible and to undermine female achievement. '[R]otten and trashy books' depreciate 'the sacredness of the writer's art' and obscure a genuine women's tradition. 'For there is a distinctive women's writing,' Eliot asserts, '"a precious specialty", lying quite apart from masculine aptitude and experience.'

**'Silver-fork' School, The**
▷ Fashionable Novel, The

**Sinclair Catherine (1800–64)**
Scottish novelist and writer of ▷ children's literature. She was born in Edinburgh and lived there for most of her life, concerning herself with philanthropic work in the city. Her famous novel for children is ▷ *Holiday House* (1839), while her adult novels include *Jane Bouverie or, Prosperity and Adversity* (1846, reissued as *Jane Bouverie or, How She Became an Old Maid*, in 1855). Most of Sinclair's writings are moralistic and religious, and she published in 1852, *A Letter on the Principles of the Christian Faith*.

▷ Scottish Literature in English.

**Sing Song, A Nursery Rhyme Book (1872)**
A collection of ▷ nonsense verse and nursery rhymes by ▷ Christina Rossetti. Written for children, the poems explore the imaginative

possibilities of language, emphasizing sound, repetition and word play. Notable lyrics include 'Who has seen the wind?' and 'How many seconds in a minute?'. *Sing Song* has been compared to William Blake's *Songs of Innocence and Experience* (1789 and 1794)
▷ Children's literature.

### Sketches by Boz (1836)

Early journalism by ▷ Charles Dickens. The sketches, 'Illustrative of Everyday Life and Everyday People', were begun in 1833, published in various magazines, and collected into book form in 1836.
▷ Short story.

### Smiles, Samuel (1812–1904)

Journalist: philosopher of 'self-help'. Born at Haddington in Scotland, one of eleven children, his early life was a struggle, dominated by the vigour of his widowed mother. He graduated in medicine at Edinburgh University in 1832, and began practising as a doctor in his home village. Competition was severe however, and he exchanged medicine for journalism, becoming editor of the *Leeds Times*. He also became secretary to railway companies, and in this capacity he made acquaintance with George Stephenson (1781–1848), inventor of the steam railway engine. His *Life of Stephenson* was published in 1857, and was followed by the lives of other famous 19th-century engineers: *James Brindley* (1864); *Boulton and Watt* (1865); *Telford* (1867). But the book that made him famous was *Self-Help* (1859); it sold 20,000 copies in the first year and was translated into at least seventeen languages. He followed it by similar books, all demonstrating the worldly advantages of certain moral virtues: *Character* (1871); *Thrift* (1875); *Duty* (1880). The success of these books was due to their optimism, and to the simple, practical expression of his ideas. His international prestige is illustrated by his reception of the Order of St Sava from the King of Servia in 1897. Smiles represents the vigorous and hopeful aspect of the Industrial Revolution, as it affected ordinary people, in contrast to the sceptical view of it taken by many other writers.

### Snobs, The Book of (1848)

A collection of satirical sketches by the novelist ▷ William Makepeace Thackeray, first published in the periodical ▷ *Punch* in 1846–7 as *The Snobs of England by one of themselves*. The title is based on a Cambridge student paper, *The Snob*, to which he contributed as an undergraduate in 1829.
▷ Jews in Victorian literature.

### Social Problem novel (Condition of England novel)

A type of novel which came to prominence in the 1840s (known as the ▷ 'Hungry Forties' because of starvation among the urban working classes). These novels addressed the social and economic problems arising from the Industrial Revolution, including urban poverty, unemployment and industrial conflict, and attempted to promote reform. Notable examples are ▷ *Mary Barton* (1848) and ▷ *North and South* (1854–5) by ▷ Mrs Gaskell, ▷ *Coningsby* (1844) by ▷ Disraeli and ▷ *Alton Locke* (1950) by ▷ Charles Kingsley. The phrase 'condition of England' was coined by ▷ Carlyle in his work *Chartism* (1839) (▷ Chartist movement).
**Bib:** Winn, S.A. and Alexander, L.M. (eds.), *The Slaughter-House of Mammon: An Anthology of Victorian Social Protest Literature*.

### Somerville and Ross (Edith Anne Oenone Somerville, 1858–1949, and Violet Florence Martin, 1862–1915)

Collaborative novelists and second cousins, both of them belonging to the wealthy Anglo-Irish ascendancy. Edith Somerville grew up at the family seat in County Cork, and went on to study art in Düsseldorf, Paris and London. Violet Martin was born in West Galway. Somerville exhibited as an artist from 1920–38 but began her literary career in 1889, three years after meeting her cousin. Their first collaborative book was *An Irish Cousin* (1889), which charts the decline of the Irish land-owning classes. They were very successful and popular for their portrayal of the humour of the indigenous Irish at the expense of their landed masters. Their comic masterpiece, *Some Experiences of an Irish RM* (1908), details the experiences of a resident magistrate in Ireland in the form of a series of ▷ short stories. This was followed by more tales of Irish life in *A Patrick's Day Hunt* (1902), *All on the Irish Shore* (1903) and *Further Experiences of an Irish RM* (1908). They also published ▷ travel books including *Through Connemara in a Governess Cart* (1892) and *In the Vine Country* (1893), which described their travels in France. *Beggars on Horseback* (1895) recounts a riding tour of North Wales. Their novels include *The Real Charlotte* (1894), which overturns the

stereotype of the 'good' and beautiful woman, *The Silver Fox* (1898) and *Dan Russell the Fox* (1911), which was the last collaboration before the death of Martin. Somerville continued to publish novels under their ▷ pseudonym right up until 1938, believing that she retained a spirit connection with Martin. Somerville became the first female Master of Fox Hounds in 1903 and both women worked for the ▷ women's suffrage cause in Ireland, although they distanced themselves from the militant activity and anti-Home Rule stance of the English suffragists. Towards the end of her life Somerville was awarded the Gregory Medal for her contribution to ▷ Irish literature.
▷ Lesbianism.
**Bib:** Cronin, J., *The Lives of 'Somerville and Ross'*; Robinson, H., *A Critical Study of Somerville and Ross*; Keane, M. (ed.), *Selected Letters of Somerville and Ross*.

**Sonnet**
A short poem of fourteen lines and a rhyme scheme restricted by one or other of a variety of principles. The most famous pattern is the Petrarchan sonnet, named after its masterly use by the Italian poet Petrarch (1304–74). This divides naturally into an eight-line stanza (octave) rhyming *abba abba*, and a six-line stanza in which two or three rhymes may occur; the two stanzas provide also for contrast in attitude to the theme. The subject matter is commonly love, but after the 16th century it becomes, at least in England, much more varied. The sonnet enjoyed a revival during the first thirty years of the 19th century in the work of the ▷ Romantic poets and continued to be popular after 1830, notably in the work of ▷ Christina Rossetti, ▷ Dante Gabriel Rossetti and ▷ Elizabeth Barrett Browning (▷ *Sonnets from the Portuguese*, 1847). ▷ G.M. Hopkins experimented very boldly in what he claimed to be sonnets, though they are often scarcely recognizable as such.

**Sonnets from the Portuguese (1850)**
A sequence of forty-four sonnets by ▷ Elizabeth Barrett Browning, written during her courtship with ▷ Robert Browning in 1845–6. In the course of the *Sonnets* Barrett Browning writes about love from a series of different perspectives, at times positioning her lover as a muse, at other times expressing her willingness to be his inspirational figure. She disrupts the conventions of amatory poetry in her treatment of the lovers' relationship, substituting a fluid and shifting relation for

the gendered fixture characteristic of courtly love-poetry. The *Sonnets* were not originally intended for publication, and it was only on Robert Browning's insistence that they were included in Barrett Browning's *Poems* of 1850. Although they attracted little critical attention during the 19th century, they are now considered a major achievement.

**'Spasmodic' school of poetry**
The 'Spasmodic' poets espoused a crude ▷ Romanticism which revered the poet as a divinely inspired being whose eccentricities should be humoured and encouraged, especially in the realm of accepted social conventions, and whose observations were projected through the lens of a melancholy solipsism. It was their bursts of ranting emotion, often ill-disguised as spontaneous feeling, that earned them their sobriquet. Pioneered by ▷ Philip James Bailey in his dramatic poem *Festus* (1839) and indulged by Alexander Smith (1830–67) in *A Life Drama* (1853), the style reached its height in ▷ Sydney Dobell's *Balder* (1854), the excesses of which led the literary critic and satirist ▷ William Aytoun to coin the term 'Spasmodic' in his brilliant parody *Firmilian, or The Student of Badajoz: A Spasmodic Tragedy by T. Percy Jones* (1854). *Firmilian* mimicked the extravagant imagery of Smith and Dobell and burlesqued their plots, even managing a sideswipe at their champion, the critic ▷ George Gilfillan. Others of the 'Spasmodic' school included John Stanyan Bigg (1826–65), Ebenezer Jones and Gerald Marston. It is possible to detect the influence of the 'Spasmodics' on ▷ Emily Brontë, Elizabeth Barrett Browning and ▷ Tennyson. After *Firmillian* the 'Spasmodic' tragedy disappeared from serious verse and much of its energy may have been channelled into the ▷ sensation novels of the 1860s.

**Spectator, The**
The name of two periodicals, the first appearing daily (1711–12 and 1714), and the second a weekly founded in 1828 and still continuing. The earlier is the more famous of the two, owing to the contributions of its famous editors, Joseph Addison (1672–1719) and Richard Steele (1672–1729); it had an important influence on the manners and culture of the time. The later *Spectator* has also had a distinguished history, however; it began as a radical journal, but is now the leading intellectual weekly periodical of the right.
▷ Reviews and periodicals.

### Spencer, Herbert (1820–1903)

Philosopher. He was representative of an
important aspect of the Victorian period
in his faith in evolutionary theory and his
trust in scientific progress. He is most
notably associated with the phrase 'Social
Darwinism', which can be roughly glossed
as extreme *laissez-faire* economics endowed
with a supposed biological sanction. Basing
his ideas on the evolutionary theories of the
French scientist ▷ Lamarck (1744–1829), a
forerunner of ▷ Darwin, Spencer concluded
that everything was in the process of
development, interaction, change, growth
and progress. In this way, the laws of science,
nature and evolution could only be beneficial.
Spencer regarded society as an organism
which was evolving from a simple primitive
state to a complex heterogeneous form
according to the designs of an unknown and
unknowable absolute force. The same theory
was applied to the development of knowledge
from an undifferentiated mass into the
various separate sciences. Spencer's scientific
determinism was extremely popular in the
latter half of the 19th century. He formulated
his ideas independently of Darwin and was
responsible for coining the phrase 'survival
of the fittest' which he used as early as
1852. In that year Spencer heard ▷ Thomas
Huxley's paper on oceanic hydrozoa and
used some facts from it in his 'Theory of
Population deduced from the General Law
of Animal Fertility'. He also helped to put
the word 'evolution' into common parlance
in the 1850s. Some of his more influential
books were *Social Statics* (1850), in which he
developed his idea of progress as inevitable
rather than accidental, and *Education:
Intellectual, Moral and Physical* (1861) in which
he claimed that science (including social
science, psychology, economics, sociology and
political theory) was the only discipline worth
studying. The best-selling *The Man Versus the
State* (1884) proclaimed the popular notion
that individual freedom depended on the
absence of all forms of interference including
government intervention. In 1857 Spencer
decided on a massive system of philosophy,
beginning with the humble biological origins
and ending with the highest ethical principles,
that was to be his life's work. The ten
volumes of his *System of Synthetic Philosophy*
took him nearly forty years to produce and
included *First Principles* (1862), and volumes
on biology, psychology, morality and sociology.
It was completed in 1896. At the height of
his popularity he influenced ▷ George Eliot
(with whom he was romantically linked for a

time) who applied his *Principles of Psychology*
to the detailed creation of her characters.
The character of Casaubon in ▷ *Middlemarch*
is based on Spencer. Others he influenced
included T.H. Huxley, ▷ John Stuart Mill,
and ▷ Beatrice Webb.
**Bib:** Peel, J.D.Y., *Herbert Spencer: The
Evolution of a Sociologist*; Low-Beer, A., (ed.)
*Spencer*; Wiltshire, D., *The Social and Political
Thought of Herbert Spencer*.

### Spoonerism

Derived from the name of the Rev. W.A.
Spooner (1844–1930) of New College,
Oxford, who was reputed to have made such
errors when speaking. The term describes
the transposition of the initial letters of two
or more words as in 'You have hissed the
Mystery lectures' (OED). The technical term
for this is metathesis.

### Sprung Rhythm

A term used by the poet ▷ Gerard Manley
Hopkins to denote the method by which
his verse is to be scanned. In his time most
English verse was written in running rhythm,
ie metres with regular stresses in the line:

> Tonight the winds begin to rise
> And roar from yonder dropping day
> (Tennyson – *In Memoriam*)

Hopkins wished to free English verse from
this rhythm, so as to bring verse into closer
accord with common speech, to emancipate
rhythm from the linear unit, and to achieve
a freer range of emphasis. His theory of
Sprung Rhythm (contained in the Preface to
his *Poems*) is complicated, perhaps because
he felt he had to justify himself to rather
academic metricists like his friend ▷ Robert
Bridges. In fact he was reviving the rhythm
of Old English alliterative verse (he cites
Langland's 14th-century narrative poem *Piers
Plowman* as being in sprung rhythm) and
folk poetry, including many ▷ ballads and
nursery rhymes. In sprung rhythm the number
of stresses in each line is regular, but they
do not occur at regular intervals, nor do the
lines have a uniform number of syllables. The
rhythm also drives through the stanza, and
is not basically linear. The following is an
example:

> Summer ends now: now, barbarous
> in beauty,
>   the stooks rise
> Around: up above, what wind-walks! what
> lovely behaviour

*Of silk-sack clouds! has wilder,*
  *wilful wavier*
*Meal-drift moulded ever and melted across*
  *skies!*
            (Hopkins – *Hurrahing in Harvest*).

### Spurgeon, Charles Haddon (1834–92)

An extremely popular Baptist preacher,
for whom the Metropolitan Tabernacle,
Newington, London, was built to hold
audiences of 6,000. His sermons were in the
old Puritan tradition, with strong appeals to
the emotions and the conscience, but also
varied by a bold and unusual kind of humour.
In doctrine he was thoroughly traditional, and
eventually he left the Baptists because of his
distrust of the new biblical criticism.

### Steel, Mrs Flora Annie (1847–1929)

Novelist. Brought up in London and
Scotland, she married at twenty and lived
for some twenty-one years in the Punjab,
India, where her husband was a civil servant.
She worked extensively for the health and
education of Indian women, founding a
school for Indian girls and working as a
school inspector. She started writing after
returning to England in 1889, and most
of her fiction is set in India: *On the Face of
the Waters* (1896), about the Indian mutiny;
*Wide Awake Stories* (1884), tales set in the
Punjab; *Hosts of the Lord* (1900), about Indian
religions; and *The Curse of Eve* (1929), which
advocates birth control. She was involved
with the ▷ women's suffrage movement and
wrote an ▷ autobiography, *The Garden of
Fidelity* (1929).
**Bib:** Powell, V., *Flora Annie Steel: Novelist
of India.*
  ▷ Colonialism.

### Stendhal (pseudonym of Henri Beyle) (1788–1842)

French writer, known for his novels *Armance*
(1822), *La Chartreuse de Parme* (1839), *Le
Rouge et le Noir* (1830) and *Lucien Leuwen*
(unfinished and published posthumously in
1894). Considered the first of the French
▷ realists, Stendhal is renowned for his
exact depiction of milieu and for his close
attention to psychological verisimilitude
and motivation. However, his realism is
neither a simple fidelity to detail nor does
it underwrite the values and representations
which aristocratic and bourgeois society makes
of itself. Stendhal does depict the conflict of
social verisimilitudes with narrative inventions
which contravene such verisimilitudes; so the
mainspring of *Le Rouge et le Noir* is the socially

unacceptable love of the aristocratic Mathilde
and the commoner Julien, while *Armance*
raises the 'shocking' issue of ▷ homosexuality
before its Byronic conclusion. On the author's
side, irony is his means of refusing to endorse
such values. Irony here is not a purely
corrosive negativity. It discreetly raises the
issue of the ethics of representation itself,
moving outwards from the hero and society to
ask whether the novel can hold together that
encounter of social and individual forces it
narrates.

Stendhal's interests were wide and he
was the author of travel books, journalism
and controversial literary pamphlets (*Racine
et Shakespeare*, 1823 and 1825, in which he
declared his support for the ▷ Romantics).
Three volumes of autobiographical writings
were published after his death: his *Journal*
(1888), *La Vie de Henry Brulard* (1890) and
*Souvenirs d'égotisme* (1892).
  ▷ French influence on Victorian literature.

### Stephen, Sir Leslie (1832–1904)

Critic and biographer. He began his career
as a tutor at Trinity Hall, Cambridge, and
university rules demanded that he should
be in orders as an Anglican clergyman. His
philosophical studies led him to the religious
scepticism so frequent among intellectuals
of the middle and later 19th century, and he
renounced his orders in 1875. From 1866 he
contributed critical essays to the ▷ *Cornhill
Magazine* and political ones for the *Nation*;
he also wrote for the ▷ *Saturday Review* and
helped to found the *Pall Mall Gazette* (1865).
In 1871 he became editor of the *Cornhill*; the
eleven years of his editorship made it one
of the most distinguished literary reviews
of the later 19th century. His critical essays
were published in book form in *Hours in a
Library* (1874–9). He wrote philosophical
essays, defining his agnostic position: *Essays
on Free Thinking and Plain Speaking* (1873). He
contributed a number of biographies to the
*English Men of Letters* series: *Johnson* (1878);
*Pope* (1880); *Swift* (1882); *George Eliot* (1902),
and *Hobbes* (1904). His most distinguished
work is firstly his editorship of the *Dictionary
of National Biography*, started in 1882, to which
he contributed many of the articles, and his
book on *The English Utilitarians* (1900). His
last book was *English Literature and Society in
the Eighteenth Century* (1904).

Today, Stephen is one of the most
respected among critics of the later 19th
century; the rigour and sincerity of his
thinking make him a link between the
Victorians and 18th-century rationalist

traditions of thought which continued into
the 19th century in the ▷ Utilitarian school
of thinkers. He has twice been used as the
basis of character in the masterpieces of
distinguished novelists: Vernon Whitford in
▷ *The Egoist* by ▷ Meredith, and Mr Ramsay
in *To the Lighthouse* (1927) by Virginia Woolf
(1882–1941), his daughter by his second wife.
His first wife had been a daughter of the
novelist ▷ Thackeray.

   ▷ Agnosticism; Reviews and periodicals.
**Bib:** Lives by F.W. Maitland; Noel Annan.

**Stevenson, Robert Louis Balfour (1850–94)**
Novelist, essayist, poet. The son of an
engineer, he intended to take up the same
profession, for which he showed early talent,
but bad health prevented this. Partly because
of his health and partly for love of travel, he
spent much of his life abroad and some of his
best writing is in essays of travel, eg *An Inland
Voyage* (1878) and *Travels with a Donkey in
the Cevennes* (1879). His most famous works,
however, are the fantasy, so often used as
an emblem of divided personality, ▷ *The
Strange Case of Dr Jekyll and Mr Hyde* (1886)
and his adventure story ▷ *Treasure Island*
(1883). Still well known are his Scottish
historical romances, in the tradition of Walter
Scott (1771–1832): *Kidnapped* (1886), ▷ *The
Master of Ballantrae* (1889), and *Catriona*
(1893); it has been said that *Weir of Hermiston*,
also in this style but left unfinished, would
have been his masterpiece. Other works of
fiction: *New Arabian Nights* (1882); *Prime Otto*
(1885); *The Black Arrow* (1888); *The Wrong
Box* (1889); *The Wrecker* (1892); *Island Nights
Entertainments* (1893); *The Ebb Tide* (1894);
*St Ives*, also left unfinished at his death.
Essays: *Virginibus Puerisque* (1881); *Familiar
Studies of Men and Books* (1882); *Vailima
Letters* (1895). His *A Child's Garden of Verses*
(1885) was for long considered a minor
children's classic (▷ Children's literature),
and he published other poetry in *Underwoods*
(1887). Stevenson was strongly influenced by
French ideas of literary style and to a lesser
extent by ▷ aestheticism. He has had a
wide popular readership which has perhaps
denied him critical attention: critics have
detected a darker side to his writing beneath
the swashbuckling, and dualism is a theme in
evidence.
**Bib:** Balfour, G., *Life*; Daiches, D., *Robert
Louis Stevenson*; Elwin, M., *The Strange Case
of Stevenson*; Furnas, J.C., *Voyage to Windward*
(life); Eigner, E.M., *Robert Louis Stevenson and
Romantic Tradition*; Calder, J. (ed.), *Stevenson
and Victorian Scotland*.

**Stoker, Bram (1847–1912)**
Irish novelist and ▷ short story writer, now
remembered principally for the universally
known, much parodied and frequently filmed
▷ *Dracula* (1897), which was influenced by
▷ J. S. Le Fanu's vampire novel *Carmilla*
(1872). Stoker spent most of his career as
secretary and business manager to the actor
Henry Irving; he wrote many ▷ horror
stories, other novels of the supernatural,
such as *The Lady of the Shroud* (1909),
and adventure novels such as *The Snake's
Pass* (1890).

   ▷ Irish literature in English.

***Strange Case of Dr Jekyll and Mr Hyde,
The* (1886)**
A novel by ▷ Robert Louis Stevenson which,
along with ▷ *Treasure Island*, is probably his
best known work. The story of Dr Jekyll, who
discovers a drug that reduces him periodically
to an embodiment of his purely evil impulses
– Mr Hyde – is told to the reader through a
series of disparate narratives. It has attracted
much commentary in recent times, being
read as a case study of male sexual hysteria, a
fable of late 19th-century homosexual panic,
a variant on the *doppelgänger* myth and a
pre-Freudian study of ego and libido.
**Bib:** Showalter, E., *Sexual Anarchy*.

**Stretton, Hesba (Sarah) (1832–1911)**
Novelist and writer of ▷ children's literature.
She contributed to ▷ Dickens's periodicals,
▷ *Household Words* and ▷ *All the Year
Round*, and had much work published by the
Religious Tract Society. An ▷ Evangelical
Christian, she wrote a large number of novels
with religious messages, which were extremely
popular. *Jessica's First Prayer* (1867) made her
internationally famous and was translated into
several languages. Her works include *Little
Meg's Children* (1868), *Alone in London* (1869)
and *Pilgrim Street* (1872).

**Surtees, Robert Smith (1805–64)**
Novelist. In 1832 he helped to found the *New
Sporting Magazine*, which he edited for five
years and to which he contributed sketches
collected in 1838 under the title of *Jorrocks's
Jaunts and Jollities*. It was this book which
suggested to the publishers, Chapman and
Hall, the idea that ▷ Charles Dickens might
write a similar series of sketches about a
Nimrod Club of amateur sportsmen. Dickens
adapted this idea to the Pickwick Club and
thus started ▷ *The Pickwick Papers*, issued
in twenty parts in 1836–7 and published in
book form in 1837. Surtees's most famous

fox-hunting novel is probably *Handley Cross* (1843), still regarded as a minor classic. He published eight novels in all.
**Bib:** Cooper, L., *R.S. Surtees*; Welcome, J., *The Sporting World of R.S. Surtees*.

**Swinburne, Algernon Charles (1837–1909)**
Poet and critic. His family background was aristocratic: his father was an admiral and his grandfather a baronet. He was educated at Eton and at Balliol College, Oxford. The style of his poetry is very distinctive, and his literary sympathies were wide. Swinburne led a dissolute, wild life (his predilection for flagellation is infamous), and produced poetry which shocked those who read it carefully, and intoxicated his youthful contemporaries, especially ▷ Thomas Hardy and the ▷ Pre-Raphaelites. He read eclectically, absorbing ▷ classical literature, the Elizabethans, the US poet Walt Whitman, William Blake (1757–1827), the Marquis de Sade (1740–1814) and ▷ Baudelaire. In his first dramas *The Queen Mother* and *Rosamond* (1860), he was, like most English 19th-century verse dramatists, in the Elizabethan tradition, but his more famous ▷ *Atalanta in Calydon* (1865) as well as his much later *Erectheus* (1876) were in the style of the ancient Greek tragedy of Sophocles. The eroticism of his lyrics in *Poems and Ballads* (1866) owed something to the Latin poet Catullus, and more to Pre-Raphaelite poetry of his own day, chiefly that of ▷ Dante Gabriel Rossetti. In this book he is rebelling against the moral repressiveness of the dominant middle-class attitude to sex; in the *Song of Italy* (1867) and *Songs before Sunrise* (1871) he is siding with Italian political revolt against oppression, in the spirit of the French 19th-century poet Victor Hugo (1802–85). *Chastelard* (1865) and *Bothwell* (1874) are the first two plays, again in Elizabethan style, on Mary Queen of Scots, and were completed by *Mary Stuart* in 1881. A second series of *Poems and Ballads* in 1878 contains tributes to the contemporary French poets, Baudelaire and Théophile Gautier and translations of the medieval French poet François Villon. *Songs of the Springtides* and *Studies in Song* (1880) show the strong inspiration he drew from the sea, and the Arthurian legend *Tristram of Lyonesse* (1881) is a romance of the Middle Ages (▷ medievalism) comparable to those of ▷ William Morris and ▷ Alfred Tennyson, amongst other mid-Victorians. In *Marino Falieri* (1887) he produced a drama on a theme drawn from medieval Venice already used by the poet Byron (*Marino Falieri*, 1821);

it was published with another drama, *Locrine*. His later works are: the dramas *The Sisters* (in prose, 1892) and *Rosamund, Queen of the Lombards* (1899); poems – *Poems and Ballads*, 3rd series (1889); *Astrophel* (1894), *A Tale of Balen* (1896), *A Channel Passage* (1904), *The Duke of Gandia* (1908).

Swinburne was thus a poet who drew on a wide range of influences and interests, and was prolific in output. Against the prejudices of his time, which declared that poets should be morally serviceable, he asserted the right to pursue the poetic vocation to express beauty, but this in itself isolated him from contemporary English culture, especially the novel, which emphasized the search for deeper moral experience. Swinburne's influence was strong on his younger contemporaries of the ▷ aesthetic movement.

In his criticism, Swinburne is notable for studies of dramatists who were contemporaries of Shakespeare as well as of Shakespeare himself: *Study of Shakespeare* (1880); *The Age of Shakespeare* (1990). He also wrote a study of William Blake (1868), *A Note on Charlotte Brontë* (1877), *A Study of Victor Hugo* (1886), amongst other criticism.

Swinburne also wrote novels, which are very little known; they have been praised by the distinguished US critic Edmund Wilson in *The Bit between my Teeth*. One of them, *Love's Cross-Currents*, was published in 1905. They show the influence of the Marquis de Sade.
**Bib:** Gosse, E., *Life*; Lafourcade, G., *La Jeunesse de Swinburne*, literary biography (in English); Chew, S.C., *Swinburne* (critical study); Nicolson, H., *Swinburne*; Welby, T.E., *A Study of Swinburne*; Winwar, P., *The Rossettis and their Circle*; Eliot, T.S., 'Swinburne as a Poet' in *Selected Essays*; Hyder, C.K., *Critical Heritage*.

**Sybil, or The Two Nations (1845)**
A novel by ▷ Benjamin Disraeli. The 'two nations' are the rich and the poor. The country is shown to be governed by the rich in the interests of the rich – ie the landlords and the employers. Sybil is the daughter of Gerard, a ▷ Chartist leader; she is loved by an enlightened young aristocrat, Charles Egremont, younger brother of an oppressive landlord, Lord Marney. Disraeli gives romantic historical background to his theme by causing Sybil to belong to the same family as the last abbot of Marney, whose lands Lord Marney's ancestors had seized at the time of the dissolution of the monasteries under Henry VIII (1509–47). The poor nation is likewise identified with the Anglo-Saxons,

despoiled of their land by the Norman conquerors of the 11th century. This novel, like ▷ *Coningsby* (1844), is part of Disraeli's campaign to renew the Tory (▷ Whig and Tory) party through the Young England movement by inspiring it with a true and disinterested ideology. The novel combines a rather comic element of operatic Romanticism with shrewd observation and social satire.
    ▷ Social Problem novels.

### Sylvia's Lovers (1863)
An ▷ historical novel by ▷ Elizabeth Gaskell, set in the whaling port of Monkshaven during the Napoleonic wars. The plot revolves around the activities of press-gangs who capture men and force them to work on naval warships. Daniel Robson, Sylvia's father, is hanged after leading an attack on the press-gang's headquarters. Her lover, Charley Kinraid, is seized by the gang, but he sends a note pledging his love and faithfulness via Sylvia's cousin, Philip Hepburn. Philip conceals the message as he loves Sylvia himself, and she later agrees to marry him, believing Charley to be dead. Years later Charley returns, Philip's treachery is revealed, and Sylvia swears lifelong enmity to her husband. The novel explores gender relations through the marriage of Sylvia and Philip and analyses the interaction of public and private events in its focus on aggression, revenge and rivalry.

### Symbolism
A name primarily associated with a school of French poets writing in the second half of the 19th century. The movement grew out of the work of ▷ Baudelaire (1821–67) and is above all associated with Paul Verlaine (1844–96), Arthur Rimbaud (1854–91) and Stephane Mallarmé (1842–98). In addition to Baudelaire, the US writer Edgar Allan Poe (1809–49) and the German music-dramatist Richard Wagner (1813–83) contributed to the shaping of Symbolism. It constituted a development from ▷ Romanticism inasmuch as it was poetry of the feelings as opposed to the reason, but it was a reaction against it in that it was more intellectual in its conception of the way poetry operates. This intellectualism did not imply that the content of poetry should be one of what is ordinarily called ideas: Mallarmé's affirmation was that 'Poetry is not made with ideas; it is made with words'. This looks forward to much 20th-century thought in all the arts, requiring that the artist should above all have respect for the medium in which he has chosen to work; it also anticipates T.S.

Eliot's (1888–1965) praise of the English 17th-century Metaphysical poets that 'they were, at best, engaged in the task of trying to find the verbal equivalent for states of mind and feeling'. Since 'states of mind and feeling' are ultimately mysterious and elusive, the Symbolists emphasized the suggestiveness of poetic language, but though this emphasis on suggestiveness makes much of their poetry obscure, their care for the organization and operation of language kept it from vagueness, in the sense in which the poetry of their English contemporary, the late Romantic ▷ Algernon Swinburne, is very commonly vague. Swinburne is also much concerned with the poetic medium of words, but in such a way that his verse subdues the reader into a state of passive receptivity, whereas the French Symbolists evoke active participation; Swinburne relies for his effect on stimulating emotions already latent in the reader, whereas the Symbolists incite extension of these emotions. T.S. Eliot's essay on Swinburne (in *Selected Essays*) is a help in elucidating the distinction.
    The French Symbolists are particularly important in English literature for their decisive influence on the two most important poets writing in English in the first half of the 20th century: T.S. Eliot and W.B. Yeats (1865–1939). Eliot's understanding of them was much the more intimate and profound, but ▷ A. Symons's *The Symbolist Movement in Literature* (1899) acted on them both.

### Symons, Arthur (William) (1865–1945)
Poet, critic and leading light of the ▷ Decadent movement in the 1890s. His friends included ▷ Ernest Dowson, Lionel Johnson and ▷ Oscar Wilde, with whom he socialized at the ▷ Rhymer's Club. He contributed to the ▷ *Yellow Book* and became editor of ▷ *The Savoy* in 1896. His volumes of poetry include *Days and Nights* (1889), *Silhouettes* (1892), *London Nights* (1895) and *Images of Good and Evil* (1899). He introduced ▷ French ▷ Symbolism to English readers in his influential study *The Symbolist Movement in Literature* (1899) and also translated Baudelaire's *Les Fleurs Du Mal* (originally published 1857) and Zola's *L'Assommoir* (originally published 1878). His other critical studies include *An Introduction to the Study of Robert Browning* (1886), *William Blake* (1907), *Charles Baudelaire* (1920) and *Studies in Elizabethan Drama* (1920). He particularly influenced the work of W.B. Yeats (1865–1939).

**Tale of Two Cities, A (1859)**
A novel by ▷ Charles Dickens. The cities
are London and Paris, and the tale is a
▷ romance of the French Revolution
(1789–94). The hero is a young French
nobleman, Charles Darnay, who has
renounced his status as nephew of the
Marquis de St Evrémonde from hatred of
the pre-revolutionary aristocratic oppression,
exemplified by his uncle. He marries the
daughter of Dr Manette, who at the beginning
of the novel has just been released from
the Paris prison of the Bastille, where he
was confined eighteen years before by the
secret influence of the Marquis. Darnay,
owing to his aristocratic descent, nearly falls
victim to the Terror (a period in the French
Revolution when many people were executed
without trial), but he is saved by the dissolute
Englishman, Sydney Carton, who redeems
himself by sacrificing his life for Darnay;
this is made possible because Carton and
Darnay exactly resemble each other, so that
the former is able to substitute himself for the
latter. The novel is notable for its scenes of
revolutionary violence, for which Dickens was
indebted to ▷ Thomas Carlyle's *History of the
French Revolution* (1837). The revolutionaries
Monsieur and Madame Defarge, and the
English body-snatcher Jerry Cruncher, who
makes a living by stealing corpses and selling
them for medical dissection, are memorable
characters.
    ▷ Historical novels.

**Tate Gallery, The**
A public gallery for modern paintings and
sculpture on the north bank of the Thames
in London. It was established by a sugar
merchant, Sir Henry Tate, and opened
in 1897.

**Taylor, Harriet (1807–58)**
Writer, philosopher and poet and leading
light of the early ▷ feminist movement.
Her friends included ▷ Harriet Martineau,
▷ Sarah Flower Adams and later ▷ John
Stuart Mill, whom she eventually married
after an extended friendship. It was Taylor
who influenced Mill's views on female
emancipation and the political education
of the working classes; all his work from
1840 onwards including *The Principles of
Political Economy* (1848) and ▷ *On Liberty*
(1859) was written in collaboration with her.
She is best remembered for her eloquent
essay 'The Enfranchisement of Women'
published in the ▷ *Westminster Review*
in 1851.

Bib: Hayek, F.A., *John Stuart Mill and
Harriet Taylor.*

**Taylor, Jane (1783–1824) and Ann
(1782–1866)**
Authors of popular children's books in verse:
*Original Poems for Infant Minds* (1804), *Rhymes
for the Nursery* (1806), in which appears
'Twinkle twinkle, little Star' (parodied by
▷ Lewis Carroll in *Alice in Wonderland*, 1865),
and *Hymns for Infant Minds* (1810).
    ▷ Children's literature.

**Taylor, Tom (1817–80)**
Dramatist, editor and critic, Taylor was born
in Sunderland the son of a self-educated
farmer turned brewer. He attended Glasgow
University and was made a fellow of Trinity
College, Cambridge. He became a professor
of English literature at University College,
London from 1845–7 and also practised
briefly as a barrister before taking up a
position in the Health Department where he
remained for twenty years. From 1874 until
his death in 1880 he was editor of ▷ *Punch*
magazine. He was also an enthusiastic
amateur actor. In addition he wrote 80 plays,
leading articles for ▷ newspapers such as
▷ *The Morning Chronicle* and *The Daily News*
and was an art critic for ▷ *The Times* and
*The Graphic* as well as contributing regularly
to *Punch*. He was the resident dramatist
at the Olympic Theatre (1853–60) and the
Haymarket (1857–70). His dramatic styles
included farce, pantomine, historical verse
drama and comedy, but he excelled in
▷ melodramas such as *Plot and Passion* (with
John Lang, 1853) and *The Ticket-of-Leave
Man* (1863). His comic plays, including *Masks
and Faces* (with ▷ Charles Reade, 1852),
*To Oblige Benson* (1854), *The Overland Route*
(1860) and *New Men and Old Acres* (with A.W.
Dubourg, 1869), also contain a degree of
social perception. In addition to tempering
melodrama with ▷ realism, Taylor's *The
Ticket-of-Leave Man* (1863) focuses on the
rehabilitation of ex-criminals and presents an
accurate picture of lower middle-class culture.
Others, including *Birth* (1870), rework his
favourite themes of class-prejudice and the
conflict between industrialists and the landed
aristocracy.
Bib: Tolles, W., *Tom Taylor and the Victorian
Drama*; Banham, M. (ed.), *Plays by Tom
Taylor.*

**Tenant of Wildfell Hall, The (1848)**
A novel by ▷ Anne Brontë, first published
under the ▷ pseudonym Acton Bell. The

tenant of the title is Helen Graham, who has recently moved into the neighbourhood with her son, Arthur. The narrator, Gilbert Markham, falls in love with her, but is puzzled by her relationship with her landlord, Lawrence. Markham ignores the village rumours until he overhears Helen and Lawrence in intimate conversation, after which he assaults Lawrence. Helen reveals the story of her past in a lengthy journal which tells of her unfortunate marriage to Arthur Huntingdon, who, after a short period of happiness with Helen, slipped back into a life of drunkenness and infidelity. It is revealed that Helen has left Arthur to seek refuge with Lawrence, who is in fact her brother. She later returns to Arthur to nurse him through a fatal illness. After his death, Markham and Helen are able to pursue their relationship, and finally agree to marry. The novel was received as a morbid story, especially since it came from a woman's pen. Anne Brontë's comment in the Preface to the 1850 edition highlights the double standards imposed on women writers: 'I am at a loss to conceive how a man should permit himself to write anything that would be *really disgraceful* to a woman, or why a woman should be censured for writing anything that would be proper and becoming for a man.'

### Tennyson, Alfred (1809–92)

Poet, usually known, after he was made a baron in 1884, as Alfred, Lord Tennyson. Fourth of twelve children (two others of whom, Frederick and Charles, were also poets) of a Church of England clergyman. The family was long established among Lincolnshire landowners, but the poet's father had been disinherited by his grandfather, and Alfred's childhood and youth were spent in comparative poverty; he was partly educated by his father but later he went to Trinity College, Cambridge. Tennyson's family background does not conform to the 20th-century ideal of the family in the 19th century. His father was a violent alcoholic rector, his mother was distressed and wretched, two of his brothers became insane and a third was also an alcoholic. Images of mental illness, doubt and conflict thus naturally fracture Tennyson's work, especially the most interesting and intense poems. His earliest work (*Poems by Two Brothers*, in which his brother collaborated) is unimportant, and he did not begin to win fame until the 1840s. Thereafter he achieved popularity unequalled by any other English poet in his own lifetime. In 1850 he was

made Poet Laureate (in succession to William Wordsworth, 1770–1850) and in 1884 he was made a Baron – the only English poet ever to have been ennobled purely for his poetry. This popularity arose from two facts: he had, on the one hand, exquisite poetic skill; he was, on the other hand, in his mental and emotional outlook, very representative of his age. He had a characteristically Victorian insular patriotism; he was both exhilarated and disturbed, like so many of his contemporaries, by the social and industrial changes of the age, and he was distressed by the shaking of traditional religious beliefs by the scientists – in his youth, the geologist ▷ Charles Lyell (*The Principles of Geology*, 1830–33), and in his middle age, the biologist ▷ Charles Darwin (*The Origin of Species*, 1859). He countered this threat from the intellect by an emotional, sometimes sentimental, idealism which was extremely acceptable to the middle-class reading public. His idiom was that of the ▷ Romantics – Wordsworth, Shelley (1792–1822), and especially Keats (1795–1821) – but his formal technique was as meticulous as that of the 18th century poets; the combination was both beguiling and reassuring. Physically and in his dress, he was imposing and romantic, and with this appearance he typified the poet for the nation.

The first three books of his sole authorship (1830, 1832, 1842) include much of what is now considered his best, most disturbing and challenging work – eg *Mariana*, ▷ *The Lady of Shalott, Ulysses*, ▷ *Morte d'Arthur*, ▷ *The Lotos-Eaters*. In 1833 his great friend, Arthur Hallam, died, and the great grief of this loss produced the series of elegies which are usually considered to be his masterpiece – ▷ *In Memoriam* A.H.H., eventually published in 1850. Queen Victoria declared that she valued it next to the Bible; however, it was the mixture of picturesque Romanticism and acceptable idealism in ▷ *The Princess* (1850) which greatly extended Tennyson's popularity with the general public. In 1852 he produced the most impressive of his public poems, *Ode on the Death of the Duke of Wellington*, and in 1854, the most popular of English patriotic poems, the ▷ *Charge of the Light Brigade*. ▷ *Maud* (1854) is one of the most singular of his works, evoking mentally deranged states, and written at the time of the Crimean War.

Other works: his immensely popular cycle of tales, ▷ *Idylls of the King* (1859–72); dialect poems, eg *The Northern Farmer* (1864); narrative, in the tradition of Wordsworth, ▷ 'Enoch Arden' (1864); ▷ ballads, notably *The Revenge* (1880), and a number of verse

dramas, of which the most successful is
*Becket* (1884).

Taste in the early 20th century on
the whole turned against his poetry; the
accusation of one of his earliest critics,
▷ John Stuart Mill, (reviewing the 1832
volume) that Tennyson's poetry is deficient in
power of thought anticipated modern opinion,
which has been until recently, attuned to
T.S. Eliot (1888–1965) and the 17th-century
Metaphysical poets. It was still admitted that
he had an extraordinary ear for cadence and
rhythm, but it was implied that this virtue
did not compensate for the mediocrity of
his intelligence. However, this tribute to his
'fine ear' amounted to acknowledgement that
Tennyson was a fine artist. His first three
books and *In Memoriam* contain poems in
which some of the deeper emotional conflicts
of his time are beautifully articulated. In
recent years readings of Victorian poetry have
freed themselves from modernist valuations,
and Tennyson's work has been re-read with
interest for its strong acknowledgement
and analysis of problematic areas of psychic
and social existence; questions of mental
health, the role of women, war and economic
conditions.

**Bib:** Sinfield, A., *Alfred Tennyson*; Nicholson,
H., *Tennyson: Aspects of his Life, Character and
Poetry*; Palmer, D.J. (ed.), *Tennyson*; Killham,
J., *Tennyson and The Princess*; Killham, J. (ed.),
*Essays on Tennyson*; Ricks, C., *Tennyson*; Ricks,
C. (ed.), *Poems*.

### Tess of the D'Urbervilles, A Pure Woman (1891)

A novel by ▷ Thomas Hardy. The heroine
is Tess Durbeyfield, daughter of a poor
west-country peasant who learns that he
may be a descendant of the aristocratic
D'Urbervilles. The novel is about her tragic
predicament between her brutal seducer, Alec
Stoke D'Urberville, and her husband Angel
Clare. Both Alec and Angel are intruders
into Tess's environment; Alec (who has no
proper title to his aristocratic surname) is the
son of a north-country businessman who has
bought his way into the class of gentry; Angel
is the son of a conventional clergyman and
has dissociated himself from his background
by acquiring vague liberal ideas. When
Tess confesses to him her seduction, his
old-fashioned prejudices overcome him and
he casts her off, repenting when it is too
late. Forsaken by her husband, Tess is faced
by renewed assaults from Alec, whom she
eventually murders. After a period of hiding
with Angel, Tess is tried, condemned and

executed for murder. The finest passages of
the book are the episodes set in the peaceful
environment of Talbothays Dairy Farm, where
Tess meets Alec, and the grim surroundings
of Flintcomb Ash, where she works when
Angel has forsaken her. Tess is represented
as the victim of cruel chance – an example
of Hardy's belief that the world is governed
by ironical fate – but as usual in his work it is
the intruders who are the instruments of the
destructive force.

### Thackeray, William Makepeace (1811–63)

Novelist. He had a conventional upper-
class education at a ▷ public school –
Charterhouse – and Cambridge University,
which he left in 1830 without taking a
degree. For the next sixteen years he worked
as a comic illustrator and journalist, writing
satirically humorous studies of London
manners in *The Yellowplush Correspondence*
(▷ *Fraser's Magazine* 1837–8), and *Snob
Papers* (▷ *Punch* 1846–7) – later published
as ▷ *The Book of Snobs*; parodies of the
contemporary fashion for the criminal-hero
(*Catherine*, 1839, and ▷ *Barry Lyndon*, 1844);
humorous travel books (*The Paris Sketch-Book*
and *The Irish Sketch-Book*, 1840 and 1843),
tales of humour and pathos (*The Great
Hoggarty Diamond*, 1841).

His first major novel, ▷ *Vanity Fair*,
came out in the year 1848 (it was published
serially, as were most of his novels, and the
date given is that of completion); it was a
social panorama of the English upper-middle
classes, satirizing their heartlessness and
pretentiousness at the height of their
prosperity; it was followed by novels in a
similar field: ▷ *Pendennis* (1850), and ▷ *The
Newcomes* (1853–5). ▷ *Henry Esmond* (1852)
is an historical novel set in the reign of Queen
Anne (1702–14) and represents Thackeray's
strong taste for the 18th century; *The
Virginians* (1859) is its sequel in 18th-century
England and North America. The same
taste for 18th-century England is expressed
in his historical lectures, *The Four Georges*,
published in 1860. In 1855 he published his
comic-romantic ▷ children's story, *The Rose
and the Ring*. In 1860 he became editor of the
famous ▷ *Cornhill Magazine*, and contributed
to it ▷ *The Adventures of Philip* (1861–2),
his essays *Roundabout Papers* and the novel,
unfinished at his death, *Denis Duval*.

Thackeray was once considered the great
counterpart to ▷ Charles Dickens in the mid-
Victorian novel (the years 1850–70). Dickens
conveyed a panorama of the lower half of
society and Thackeray of the upper half; both

were great humorists, with a strong bent for satire and a capacity for social indignation. Thackeray is now chiefly remembered for *Vanity Fair*. His imaginative intensity is seen to be less than that of Dickens and the sentimentality with which he counterbalanced his satire is the more conspicuous. Like Dickens, he opposed the ▷ utilitarianism of his age by an appeal to spontaneous affection and he tried to counterbalance it by an appeal to 18th-century proportion and elegance, but he also felt impulses of ▷ Romanticism, which in Dickens are far more uninhibited.
**Bib:** Ray, G.N., *Life*; Tillotson, G., *Thackeray the Novelist*; Stevenson, L., *The Showman of Vanity Fair*; Stevenson, L., ed. in *Great Victorians*; Studies by J. Dodd, L. Ennis, J.Y. T. Greig and G.N. Ray; Tillotson, G., and Hawes, D. (eds.), *The Critical Heritage*; Carey, J., *Thackeray: Prodigal Genius*; Shillingsburg, P.L., *Pegasus in Harness: Victorian Publishing and W.M. Thackeray*.

### Thompson, Francis (1859–1907)
Poet. He gave up the study of medicine in Manchester to seek his fortunes in London, where he nearly starved. He published his *Poems* in 1893. Thompson was a ▷ Catholic; the most famous of his poems (included in the above volume) was the intensely religious *Hound of Heaven*. Its bold, extravagant style recalls the work of the 17th-century Catholic poet ▷ Richard Crashaw (?1612–49), one of the English Metaphysicals. On the other hand, Thompson was more in the tradition of his immediate predecessors in his employment of sensuous, ornate ▷ symbolism; in this he resembles the ▷ Pre-Raphaelites of the mid-19th century, and another Catholic poet – one of the first of his admirers – ▷ Coventry Patmore. In this respect, a comparison of the *Hound of Heaven* with ▷ *The Wreck of the Deutschland* (1875) by yet another Catholic, ▷ Gerard Manley Hopkins, is instructive; Hopkins shows equal emotional intensity with much more of the intellectual rigour of the 17th-century poets. Thompson's other volumes were *Sister Songs* (1895) and *New Poems* (1897). His prose work includes his *Essays on Shelley* (1909).
**Bib:** Lives by Meynell, E., Meynell, V., and Thompson, P. van K.; critical study by Reid, J.C.

### Thomson, James (1834–82)
Poet. He was the son of a sailor in the merchant navy, and of a deeply religious woman who belonged to one of the narrower ▷ Protestant sects. He was an army schoolmaster, 1850–62, during which period he had a tragic love affair, and made friends with Charles Bradlaugh, who became a well-known ▷ atheist radical. Thomson is chiefly known for a long, sombre, atheistic poem, *The City of Dreadful Night* (1880), which expressed in the most uncompromising terms the darkest aspect of the loss of religious belief common among Victorian intellectuals. He was also capable of gaiety (*Vane's Story and Other Poems*, 1881). A Voice from the Nile and other Poems was published posthumously in 1884. He commonly wrote under the initials B.V. (Bysshe, from Percy Bysshe Shelley, and Vanolis, anagram for the German poet, Novalis).
**Bib:** Dobell, B., *The Laureate of Pessimism*; Walker, E.B., *James Thomson*.

### Through the Looking-Glass and What Alice Found There
▷ Carroll, Lewis.

### Times, The
British newspaper. It was founded in 1785 as *The Daily Universal Register*, and took its present name in 1788. In the 19th century it took the lead in contriving new methods of collecting news (notably through the employment of foreign correspondents), and its succession of distinguished editors and contributors gave it an outstanding status among British ▷ newspapers. Though always in private ownership, it has always claimed to be an independent newspaper rather than a party one. The literary style of one of its staff writers caused it to be nicknamed 'The Thunderer' in the 19th century; the novelist ▷ Anthony Trollope consequently refers to it as *The Jupiter* in his novels, since this king of the gods was known as the Thunderer by the ancient Romans. *The Times* publishes *The Times Literary Supplement*, *The Times Education Supplement*, *The Times Higher Education Supplement* and *The Sunday Times* weekly. Its outlook is traditional and often Conservative in political terms.

### Tolpuddle Martyrs
In 1834 six farm labourers from Tolpuddle in Dorset were transported to Australia for swearing men into a ▷ trade union lodge. The men were respectable – five were Wesleyans – and were returned home after three years of the seven-year sentence. But the lack of ▷ Whig support revealed the limits of common interest between the middle and working classes. The event nourished the

▷ Chartist movement and the men were seen as martyrs to the cause of unskilled-labour trade unions.

**Tom Brown's Schoolday's**
▷ Rugby School; Hughes, Thomas

**Tory**
▷ Whig and Tory

**Tract**
An essay or treatise, usually short but published singly and usually on a religious subject. The most famous in English are the *Tracts for the Times* (1833–41) by a group of devout Anglicans, Hurrell, Froude, Pusey, Keble, and ▷ Newman. Their purpose was to increase the spiritual dignity and independence of the Church of England by the revival of doctrines stressed in the 17th century but since then largely neglected, with the consequence, as the authors believed, that the Church was losing its spiritual identity and was exposing itself more and more to secular ▷ utilitarianism and domination by the state. Newman's was the predominating spirit in the group; he started the series, and he wrote *Tract XC*, which caused scandal by emphasizing the closeness of the Anglican to the older ▷ Catholic tradition, and thus ended it.
▷ Oxford Movement.

**Tractarian Movement**
▷ Oxford Movement; Tract

**Trade unions**
Britain's trade unions are among the oldest in the world. The impulse to start trade union associations arose from the early development in England of ▷ capitalist industrialism and the congregation of workers in ▷ factories in the later 18th century. At first workers associated chiefly in small ways for such purposes as mutual insurance against unemployment in what were known as 'friendly societies'. Nonetheless, the societies were regarded with suspicion by the government, who saw them initially as in 'restraint of trade' and later as possible centres of revolution, especially after the French Revolution of 1789–94. Consequently, Parliament passed the Combination Acts of 1799 and 1800, which declared unions to be criminal conspiracies against the public and forbade their formation. These laws were repealed in 1824, and thereafter the activity of forming associations amongst employees

was a lawful one, but this did not include striking. In 1834 six labourers from the village of Tolpuddle in Dorsetshire (▷ The Tolpuddle Martyrs) were tried on a charge of administering false oaths and transported to a penal colony in Australia for seven years. In the same year the socialist reformer ▷ Robert Owen attempted to organize local trade clubs into a national movement, the Grand National Consolidated Trade Union, but with little lasting success. For thirty years industrial relationships remained stormy, but until 1890 working-class energies were taken up with other movements such as the ▷ Chartist Movement and the Anti-Corn Law League (▷ Corn Laws, Repeal of the).

A respectable kind of trade unionism was initiated by the Amalgamated Society of Engineers who established the pattern for the 'new model' unions in 1851. Their main function was to limit the number of apprenticeships in order to raise the premium of skilled labour and to act as 'friendly societies', providing mutual assistance in case of sickness or to aid emigration. During the same period a number of leaders of the craft unions formed the so-called *Junta* and, in addition to engaging in political activity, joined ▷ Marx's International Workingmen's Association (the First International), despite an imperfect grasp of the principles of Marxist socialism.

In the 1860s a number of outrages in the industrial north of England alerted public suspicion of trade unions and the government appointed an inquiry into their activities which was so reassuring that unionism began to prosper. In 1868 the Trades Union Congress (TUC) was started, thus initiating a new phase in which trade unionism once again had a national body capable of organizing the interests of industrial workers. From 1870 to the 1980s trade unionism developed (since when its power has declined), becoming for a time one of the most powerful factors of national life. Two laws gave the movement new legal security; that of 1871 legalized action through strikes, and that of 1876 gave unions the right to exist as corporations, able to own property and to defend their rights corporatively (ie, not as mere collections of individuals) in courts of law. After 1871 unions of agricultural workers, seamen, gas workers, general and municipal workers, and dock workers were organized. This period of union activity culminated in the successful dock worker's strike of 1889. Nationwide collective bargaining, an eight-hour day and a legal minimum wage became dominant issues.

The movement became influenced by socialist ideas and the working class formed political organizations such as the Independent Labour Party which helped to initiate the formation of the ▷ Labour Party shortly after the turn of the century.

Contemporary authors tended to regard the infant trade union movement with fear and suspicion, especially during the aftermath of the Chartist movement of 1837–48. In ▷ Elizabeth Gaskell's ▷ *Mary Barton* (1848) trade unions are seen as necessary and beneficial when dispensing mutual aid but dangerous when indulging in subversive activity such as channelling the despair and anger of basically 'good' men like John Barton into acts of violence and murder. ▷ Charles Dickens likewise betrays a conviction of the incompatibility of working-class decency and militant action in ▷ *Hard Times* (1854) where the operatives of Coketown are shown being led astray by the sonorous and extravagant rhetoric of the trade union delegate Slackbridge.

### Travel and transport

In 1840, England had 22,000 miles of good roads, maintained by 8000 turnpikes; it also had a magnificent canal system for industrial use. In 1843 it had in addition 2000 miles of railway, which increased to 5000 miles by 1848, and was to exceed 23,000 by the end of the century. The first steam railway had been opened in 1825, a distance of eleven miles. Thus, no sooner had the 18th-century system of transport reached perfection than it was superseded by the 19th-century one. The great canal system decayed and the road system lost most of its long-distance traffic. Railways could move passengers and goods more economically, in far greater quantities, at hitherto unimagined speeds, and perhaps not even the car has caused such marked changes in the economic and social life of Britain. They were the more marked, of course, because of the swiftness of the spread of railways. Steam made much slower progress at sea: in 1847, steamships represented only 116,000 tons out of a total of three million tons of British merchant shipping. Not until the end of the century did steamships completely supersede sailing ships on long voyages.

The effect of railways was to bring all the regions of the country into close relation with one another and to make extensive travel possible for all the social classes for the first time. They had, in fact, an effect on single countries comparable to that which

air travel has had on the entire world in the 20th century. The formerly enclosed, regional cultures lost their self-sufficiency, so that British civilization in the 20th century has become much more uniform than it once was. The railways were breakers of social barriers, too: they were a comparatively democratic mode of travel. Hitherto only the rich and leisured had been able to afford the money and time to travel extensively, but now the poor could manage it too; and trains mixed the social classes, despite the provision of first, second and third class coaches. Perhaps the most important effect of all was that railways greatly increased the movement of population from the countryside into the towns, although this had already begun in the 18th century. Many industrial towns in the north owned their rapid enlargement to railways, so that railways are one of the most important explanations for England becoming the first thoroughly urbanized country in the world.

Railways naturally extended the habit of foreign travel from the upper to the middle class, which visited foreign countries in the second half of the 19th century in far greater numbers than ever before. In the 1840s, encouraged by George Hudson, the 'railway king, the general public speculated wildly in railway companies, many of which were bogus or unsuccessful. ▷ Thackeray's *Diary of James de la Pluche, Esq.* chronicles this.

But humbler kinds of travel also became common in the 19th century for the first time, for reasons that had nothing to do with the invention of the steam engine. Until the later 18th century, Britain was too rural for people to have much curiosity about the countryside, and travel for pleasure was chiefly limited to friendly visits and journeys to pleasure resorts such as Bath and – when sea bathing became fashionable in the reign of George III (1760–1820) – the seaside towns such as Brighton.

In every century from the 16th there were individuals who had the curiosity to make surveys of the entire country – Leland and Camden in the 16th century, Fynes Morrison in the 17th, Daniel Defoe (1660–1731) in the 18th and William Cobbett (1762–1835) in the early 19th – but they were interested in economic and social facts, not landscape. However, the ▷ Romantic writers who were contemporary with Cobbett, including Walter Scott (1771–1832), Samuel Coleridge (1772–1834), William Wordsworth (1770–1850) and John Keats (1795–1821), awakened a new interest in scenery as part of their new kind of attention to nature, and they walked about the countryside merely for the pleasure it gave them. Such an activity would have been incomprehensible to a medieval man, but by the middle of the Victorian period it had become an accepted one. When the pedal cycle came into popular use at the end of the century, touring the countryside for its fresh air and natural beauty extended to women as well as men.

The first cars appeared on the roads of Britain in 1894, but it was not until after 1918 that they became widespread, and not until after 1945 that ownership of a car extended to all but those on the lowest income levels.

## Travel writing

With the discovery by Europeans of the coastlines of Australia and New Zealand, the main outlines of world geography became known in the West, and the interest both of explorers and their readers passed from accounts of great voyages, such as those undertaken by Captain James Cook, to the mysteries of the great undiscovered interiors of the continents. With this change in subject matter, a change also came over the style of travel literature. ▷ Sir Richard Burton's book about India, *Scinde or the Unhappy Valley* (1851), and his later books about his exploration of East and Central Africa (*First Footsteps in East Africa*, 1856; *The Lake Regions of Central Africa*, 1860) bear the stamp of the author's personal feelings and reactions. Partly, no doubt, this arose from the new importance attached to authorial personality due to ▷ Romanticism; also the contact with strange physical environments and peoples (in contrast to the emptiness and impersonality of the ocean) inevitably drew out authorial response. At all events, travel literature began to draw nearer to ▷ autobiography. Not only 'darkest Africa', but the Arabian peninsular fascinated writers. Burton was one of the first Englishmen to visit the holy city of Mecca, and wrote an account of it in *Pilgrimage to Al-Medinah and Mecca* (1855). Later Charles Doughty tried to restore the vividness of 16th-century language to 19th-century prose in his *Arabia Deserta* (1888), and T.E. Lawrence's *Seven Pillars of Wisdom* (1926) belongs to the same tradition of art made from travel in Arabia. ▷ George Borrow (1803–81) did not go so far for his material, but he went a stage further than these writers in combining travel literature and imaginative art, so that it is difficult to know whether or not to classify his books with the novel. They are full of personal encounters with individuals,

chiefly among the common people; he was particularly interested in the gypsies (*The Gypsies in Spain*, 1841; *Lavengro*, 1851; *Romany Rye*, 1857) and he was talented at conveying the intimate texture of the life of a country (*The Bible in Spain*, 1843; *Wild Wales*, 1862). James Kingslake's account of his travels in the lands of the Eastern Mediterranean, *Eothen* (1844), and Lafcadio Hearne's *Glimpses of Unfamiliar Japan* (1894) are two other examples of travel literature which owe their classic status as much to the author's art and personality as to their subject matter. Thus travel literature became a natural subsidiary form for the novelists; it is among the best writing of ▷ R.L. Stevenson.

Many 19th-century British women writers travelled abroad and recorded their experiences in published accounts. ▷ Anna Eliza Bray (1790–1883) and ▷ Frances Power Cobbe (1822–1904) were tourists primarily, and travelled mainly within Europe. Others, including ▷ Frances Trollope (1780–1863), Anna Jameson (1794–1860), ▷ Harriet Martineau (1802–76) and ▷ Barbara Bodichon (1827–91) visited North America and wrote about their experiences in the 'New World'. Bodichon also travelled to the Sahara with ▷ Matilda Betham-Edwards (1836–1919), who published a record of the trip. Another group of women, including ▷ Isabella Bird Bishop and ▷ Mary Kingsley were genuine 'explorers'. Bishop journeyed through China, Japan and India; Kingsley in West Africa. In recent years, feminist scholars have begun to examine travel writing in relation to gender and colonialism.

▷ Imperialism.

**Bib:** Foster, S., *Across New Worlds: 19th Century Women Travellers and Their Writings*.

## *Treasure Island* (1883)

A romance by the novelist ▷ Robert Louis Stevenson, perhaps his best known work. It is set in the 18th century and the plot concerns the search for hidden treasure buried in a desert island by an actual 18th-century pirate, Captain Kidd. The story contains the basic elements of a traditional English ▷ romance – treasure, pirates, adventure, a desert island – and belongs to a line of desert island literature descending from Defoe's *Robinson Crusoe* (1719).

## Tree, Sir Herbert Beerbohm (1853–1917)

English actor-manager famous for his productions at the Haymarket and Her Majesty's theatres, and for founding the Royal Academy of Dramatic Art. Productions at the Haymarket included ▷ Oscar Wilde's *A Woman of No Importance* (1893), Shakespeare's *The Merry Wives of Windsor* (1889) and *Hamlet* (1892). Most successful was an adaptation of a ▷ George Du Maurier novel, ▷ *Trilby* (1895), the proceeds from which enabled him to build Her Majesty's. The repertoire at Her Majesty's was dominated by Shakespeare and historical verse drama. His Shakespeare productions were illustrative of the fashion of the period for spectacular 'romantic realism'. Detailed ostentatious sets, busy stage action and sometimes bizarre stage additions were all characteristic of these productions, disparagingly referred to by designer Gordon Craig as 'beautiful copies of Irving' (▷ Henry Irving). Tree combined the qualities of the showman and pioneer. The Shakespeare festivals at Her Majesty's from 1905 to 1913 matched those being given by actor-manager Frank Benson at Stratford. He also championed the cause of ▷ Ibsen, by running matinée performances of *An Enemy of the People*.

**Bib:** Bingham, M., *The Great Lover.*

### Trilby (1892)

Novel, written and illustrated by ▷ George du Maurier. It tells the story of Trilby O'Ferrall, an artists' model in Paris with whom all the art students fall in love. She comes under the mesmeric influence of Svengali, a German-Polish musician who makes her famous. His spell is so strong that when he dies she loses her voice, fails and dies herself. The novel enjoyed enormous popularity and was dramatized in 1895. Trilby's soft felt hat with an indented crown is the original 'trilby'.

### Triple-decker/three decker

A novel published in three volumes. This was the dominant form of fiction during the period from the 1820s until 1894, and the novels were distributed primarily via the ▷ circulating libraries, such as ▷ Mudie's.

### Trollope, Anthony (1815–82)

Novelist. The unbusinesslike qualities of his father, a barrister who forsook the law and ruined himself in farming, caused his childhood to be poverty-stricken, although his mother ▷ Frances Trollope kept her family from the worst hardships by writing. Trollope himself was a prolific novelist, and though he worked seriously his *Autobiography* (1883) deeply offended the taste of the time by his frank statement that the writing of novels was a craft and a business, like making shoes, with

nothing exalted or inspired about it. He was a strong admirer of the novels of ▷ Thackeray and shared Thackeray's contempt for the commercial arrogance of the British upper-middle classes. On the other hand, unlike Thackeray, Trollope had also strong faith in the traditional virtues and values of the English gentry, and several of his novels are about how the gentry class opened its ranks (through marriage, and after a struggle) to the best elements of less-privileged classes. His first novel was published in 1847, but it was in 1855 that he published the first of his most famous series, the ▷ Barsetshire novels – ▷ *The Warden*. The series continued with *Barchester Towers* (1857); ▷ *Dr Thorne* (1858); *Framley Parsonage* (1864); *The Small House at Allington* (1864); ▷ *The Last Chronicle of Barset* (1867). It is in these books that he displays his very conservative values most winningly and convincingly; they present a world of very solidly portrayed church dignitaries and landed gentry and show a loving care for fully-rounded characterization. The world he shows with such conviction was perhaps already passing, and in presenting it Trollope does not forget the weaker side of its values nor the assaults and encroachments upon it of political adventurers and the more vulgar of the middle class. His later work became more political, for instance *Phineas Finn* (1869); ▷ *The Eustace Diamonds* (1873); *Phineas Redux* (1874); *The Way We Live Now* (1875); *The Prime Minister* (1876); *The Duke's Children* (1880). Some critics consider that this group of his novels is unduly neglected; the setting is commonly London, which Trollope thought a source of evil, and the tone is more critical of society. *The Way We Live Now* reflects his disillusionments most strongly; it includes a powerful portrait of a fraudulent tycoon in Melmotte, and is not so much political as a devastating social study.

Trollope lost favour after his death, but regained strong popularity in the mid-20th century. This was because this period of insecurity and war made Trollope's world of traditional values seem very reassuring. Yet critics seldom allow him rank equal to his contemporary ▷ George Eliot; he does not even pretend to insight as deep, or tragic vision, though he is often subtle and fond of pathos.

**Bib:** Sadleir, M., *Life*; Bowen, E., *Trollope: a new Judgement*; Cockshut, A.O.J., *Anthony Trollope: a Critical Study*; Gerould, W.G. and J.T., *Guide to Trollope*; Smalley, D. (ed.), *The Critical Heritage*; Wall, S., *Trollope and Character.*

## Trollope, Frances (1780–1863)

Born Frances Milton in Somerset, the daughter of a vicar, she married in 1809 and had six children, including the novelist ▷ Anthony Trollope. She began writing when she was over fifty to support the family in the face of her husband's financial disasters and published in all some 114 books on ▷ travel, and novels. Despite the financial success of her first book she worked extremely hard, from before dawn each day, writing and caring for her family. She visited North America for an extended period and lived in France, Austria and Italy (meeting the ▷ Brownings, ▷ Dickens and ▷ Walter Landor) for a few years. Her writing owed its popularity perhaps to her scathing views of Americans, also to its exuberant quality and her rather coarse, humorous women. *Domestic Manners of the Americans* (1832) brought her fame and popularity; *Paris and the Parisians* (1835), *Vienna and the Austrians* (1838) and *A Visit to Italy* (1842) were also successful. Her novels include *The Vicar of Wrexhill* (1837), portraying a mixture of vice and religion, *The Widow of Barnaby* (1838) and *The Life and Adventures of a Clever Woman* (1854).

**Bib:** Trollope, F.E., *Frances Trollope: Her Life and Literary Work from George III to Victoria*; Johnston, J., *The Life, Manners and Travels of Fanny Trollope: A Biography*.

## Turgenev, Ivan Sergeevich (1818–83)

Novelist and dramatist. Born in Orel, central Russia, educated at Moscow and St Petersburg Universities and Berlin. After a brief spell in the civil service he devoted himself to literature. In 1852 he was imprisoned for a month for his article on the death of Ukrainian writer Gogol (1809–52), and was subsequently banished to his estate. He left Russia in 1861 and, apart from a few visits, remained in self-imposed exile, largely in Baden Baden and Paris, where he died, although he continued to write of Russia and his own class, which he perhaps sensed was doomed. The novels have something of an autumnal character. He fell in love with the singer Pauline Garcia Viardot who did not give him an easy life, and this is also reflected in the novels in the theme of a strong woman and rather weak man. He knew ▷ Flaubert, ▷ George Sand and other French writers, and from 1847 visited England. He was widely read in English, admiring ▷ Shakespeare greatly; he knew and valued ▷ Charles Dickens and ▷ George Eliot, and was acquainted with ▷ William Thackeray, ▷ Anthony Trollope, ▷ Thomas Carlyle, ▷ Robert Browning, ▷ Alfred Tennyson, the ▷ Rossettis and others. He admired, met and influenced ▷ Henry James, and influenced many writers including ▷ George Moore, Joseph Conrad (1857–1924) and Virginia Woolf. He published a little poetry in 1838 but his first published prose was *A Hunter's Notes* (1847–51). He wrote a series of novels illuminating social and political issues: *Rudin* (1856), *A Nest of Gentlefolk* (1859), *On the Eve* (1860), *Fathers and Sons* (1862), *Smoke* (1867) and *Virgin Soil* (1877). His short stories include 'Asya' (1858), 'First Love' (1860) and 'Torrents of Spring' (1870); his most famous and critically acclaimed play is *A Month in the Country* (1850).

▷ Russian influence on Victorian literature.

## Turn of the Screw, The (1898)

A novella by ▷ Henry James, published in *The Two Magics*. It is a ghost story, about a governess given sole charge of two children, Miles and Flora, in a country house named Bly. She comes to believe that she has to contend with the evil, ghostly influence of two dead servants, Peter Quint and Miss Jessell, over the children, who are ostensibly angelic but invisibly corrupted. Flora is taken away to London by the housekeeper, but Miles, when confronted by the governess with her belief, dies in her arms. The possibility that the governess is an hysteric who hallucinates the ghosts and herself manipulates the children provides a second layer of meaning. This layer is, however, absent in Benjamin Britten's opera of the same title. James's story, which he described as 'a trap for the unwary', is a masterpiece of ambiguity throughout.

**Bib:** Kirby, D. (ed.), *An Introduction to the Varieties of Criticism: The Portrait of A Lady/The Turn of the Screw*.

## Turpin, Richard (Dick) (1706–39)

A famous English highwayman and thief, hanged at York for horse-stealing. He was greatly romanticized by the novelist ▷ Harrison Ainsworth in his novel *Rookwood* (1834), in which Turpin's famous ride from London to York on his mare, Black Bess, is described. The ride, like other romantic episodes told about him, is fictional.

# U

## Uncommercial Traveller, The

A collection of tales, sketches and essays, descriptive of places, society and manners, by ▷ Charles Dickens. They were published in ▷ *All the Year Round* and reissued in book form in 1861 and 1868.

## Under the Greenwood Tree (1872)

The first of the ▷ Wessex novels by ▷ Thomas Hardy. The story is a village love affair between a schoolmistress, Fancy Day, and Dick Dewy, son of a 'tranter' or carrier of goods. It includes the theme of the rivalry of the village orchestra, who have hitherto played the music in church services, with Fancy, who takes over from them by substituting the harmonium. The story is thus slight and idyllic compared to Hardy's later Wessex stories but it is written with delicacy and insight. The title is the first line of a song in Shakespeare's *As You Like It*.

## Unionist

A name used by politicians from 1886 to express opposition to Home Rule for Ireland, ie a separate Parliament for that country. The word at first united Conservatives with a number of Liberals who resisted the Home Rule policy of their leader, ▷ Gladstone. Later 'Unionist' became synonymous with 'Conservative', and it is still used by members of that party, though it officially accepts the existence of the Irish Republic.

## Unitarianism

A religious group that rejects the usual Christian doctrine of the Trinity, or three Persons in one God (the Father, the Son, and the Holy Ghost), in favour of a belief in the single being of God the Father. It originated in Britain in the 18th century and was in accord with the rationalistic approach to religion of that century. The first Unitarian church opened in London in 1774. The Unitarian Christianity preached by Joseph Priestley (1733–1804), a scientist and dissenting minister, was based on a number of convictions including the notion of Jesus as man with unique and miraculous powers; the all-powerful and all-knowing nature of God; the primacy of reason and morals; scientific determinism, materialism and political reform. Around 1840, the theologian and philosopher James Martineau (1805–1900) challenged Priestley's rationalism with a plea for deeper feeling and a more intuitive faith.

The Unitarians flourished at the end of the 19th and the begining of the 20th centuries, building a large number of new churches to house their increasingly large congregations. They were also renowned for their social idealism, and their concept of humanism emphasizes the human condition and scientific progress. Victorian Unitarians include ▷ Elizabeth Gaskell and her husband William, who was a Unitarian minister.

## Unto This Last (1860–2)

Four essays on political economy by ▷ John Ruskin. They were intended to be part of a larger treatise, but their publication in the ▷ *Cornhill Magazine* aroused so much hostility that the editor (▷ William Thackeray) discontinued them. The reason for the anger was that Ruskin (an art critic) was, as it seemed to the public, stepping out of his professional function in order to attack the predominant economic theory of trading relationships, which he was considered by the middle-class public unqualified to do. The middle classes were inclined to believe that the subject had been reduced to the clear elements of a science by the political economists and ▷ Utilitarian thinkers of the first half of the 19th century – men such as ▷ Jeremy Bentham, David Ricardo, (1772–1823), ▷ Malthus, James Mill (1773–1836) and ▷ John Stuart Mill. Ruskin pointed out that what was called 'political economy' was really 'commercial economy' and that it was untrue since it omitted facts of human nature, unjust since it unduly favoured the employing middle class and uncivilized since it omitted the cultural values that ought to underlie wealth. He found space to praise ▷ Charles Dickens's novel ▷ *Hard Times*, itself an attack on Utilitarianism. In spite of the hostility and scorn of Ruskin's contemporaries, much of his thinking in these essays has been accepted by later sociologists and economists. The Indian leader Mahatma Gandhi admitted a debt to *Unto This Last*, as did a number of the early leaders of the British ▷ Labour Party.

## Utilitarianism

A 19th-century political, economic and social doctrine which based all values on utility, ie the usefulness of anything, measured by the extent to which it promotes the material happiness of the greatest number of people. It is especially associated with ▷ Jeremy Bentham, at first a jurist concerned with legal reform and later a social philosopher. Followers of the movement are thus often called 'Benthamites' but Bentham's disciple ▷ John Stuart Mill used the term 'Utilitarians'. Owing to their habit of criticizing social concepts and institutions on strictly rational tests, the leaders of the movement were also known as Philosophical Radicals.

Utilitarianism dominated 19th-century social thinking, but it had all its roots in various forms of 18th-century rationalism. In moral philosophy David Hume (1711–76) had a strong influence on Bentham by his assumption that the supreme human virtue is benevolence, ie the disposition to increase the happiness of others. Psychologically, Bentham's principle that humans are governed by the impulses to seek pleasure and avoid pain derives from the associationism of David Hartley (1705–57). But Bentham and his associates believed that the virtue of benevolence, and human impulses towards pleasure, operate within social and economic laws which are scientifically demonstrable. Bentham accepted Adam Smith's reasoning in *The Wealth of Nations* (1776) that material prosperity is governed by economic laws of supply and demand, the beneficial operation of which is only hindered by governmental interference. ▷ Malthus, in his *Essay on the Principle of Population* (1798), maintained that it is mathematically demonstrable that population always tends to increase beyond the means of subsistence, and David Ricardo (1772–1823), a friend of Bentham's, applied Malthus's principle to wages, arguing that as the population increases wages will necessarily get lower, since the increase is more rapid than that of the wealth available to support the workers. Smith, Malthus and Ricardo were masters of what was called the science of political economy, and the inhuman fatalism with which they endowed it caused to be known as the ▷ dismal science. However, it was not dismal for the industrial middle class of employers, whose interests it suited; they were already 'utilitarians' by self-interest and thus willing converts to the theory.

Thus the operation of Utilitarianism in the 19th century was paradoxical. It liberated society from laws which were inefficient survivals from the past (the Elizabethan Poor Laws) but it replaced them by laws that often operated with cold inhumanity (eg the ▷ Poor Law of 1834). It reduced senseless government interference with society but its concern with efficiency encouraged a bureaucratic civil service. It liberated the employers but it was often unsympathetic to the interests of the employees. Its principle was benevolence but its faith in reason often made it indifferent to individual suffering. The inhumanity of the creed, and its

indifference to cultural values unless they could be shown to be materially useful, caused it to be vigorously attacked by leading writers between 1830 and 1870, including ▷ Thomas Carlyle, ▷ Charles Dickens, ▷ John Ruskin and ▷ Matthew Arnold. But perhaps its sanest and most lucid critic was John Stuart Mill; though himself a Utilitarian to the end of life, he saw the philosophical limitations of the movement and exposed them in his essays in 1838 on Bentham and on ▷ Samuel Taylor Coleridge (1772–1834) whom he admired as the father of the opposing tendency of thought. Mill's essay *Utilitarianism* (1863) emphasized that some kinds of pleasure are better than others – a distinction Bentham failed to make – and that the highest virtue in humanity is 'the desire to be in unity with our fellow creatures'. Mill was aware, as Bentham had not been, of the importance of the artistic imagination, in particular of poetry, in a civilization.

Our society is still in many ways utilitarian but as a systematic philosophy Utilitarianism did not outlast the 19th century. The last important figures connected with the movement are the philosophers ▷ Herbert Spencer and ▷ Leslie Stephen.

  ▷ *Unto This Last*.

## Utopian literature
Sir Thomas More's political and philosophical treatise *Utopia* (1516) introduced into the English language the word 'utopian' (imaginary and ideal), and was the inspiration for a succession of 'utopias' in English literature. The idea of inventing an imaginary country to be used as a 'model' by which to judge earthly societies originated, however, with More's master, the Greek philosopher Plato (?428–?348 BC), who did the same in his dialogues *Timaeus* and the *Republic*. ▷ William Morris's *News From Nowhere* (1890) is a noteworthy socialist utopia in which he describes a non-industrial society which has much in common with his own beloved medieval ideal (▷ medievalism). It lacks a central government, and legal, monetary and class systems. Much utopian literature from the 18th century onwards is satirical and intended to give a warning of vicious tendencies in society rather than to exemplify ideals. Such is the case with ▷ Samuel Butler's anti-utopias: the satirical novel ▷ *Erewhon* (1872) and its sequel *Erewhon Revisited* (1901) which characterize many aspects of Victorian society, including its hypocrisy and parental despotism.

In the late 19th and early 20th centuries

women writers produced a number of utopias in which the vision of an ideal world is set against the particular oppression of women. Examples include Catherine Spence's posthumously published *Handfasted* (written, 1879, published 1984) and the US writer Elizabeth Corbett's *New Amazonia: A Foretaste of the Future* (1899) (▷ Amazons). British feminist utopias of the period were concerned with furthering the cause of ▷ women's suffrage. 'Dystopia' was first used by ▷ John Stuart Mill to suggest an imagined state which was undesirable. However, every writer's utopian vision is subjective and the desirability of the ideal societies imagined is often open to question, as in Edward Bellamy's version of a socialist utopia, *Looking Backward: 2000–1887* (1888), in which every individual is forced to join an 'industrial army'. Morris's *News from Nowhere* was written in response to this version of an earthly paradise. ▷ Walter Besant's novel *The Revolt of Man* (1882) is an anti-feminist dystopia prompted by the debate surrounding the ▷ 'New Woman'.

**Bib:** Albinski, N., Bowman, *Women's Utopias in British and American Fiction*; Taylor, B. *Eve and the New Jerusalem*.

### Vanity Fair (1874–8)

A satirical ▷ historical novel by ▷ William Thackeray published in monthly issues. The title, borrowed from John Bunyan's *Pilgrim's Progress* (1678 and 1684), shows that Thackeray's subject matter is the worldly, materialistic society of his time. He shows his men of religion to be either hypocrites or deluded. ▷ Dissenters, the descendants of Bunyan, include old Osborne, the arrogant, sombre and unfeeling businessman; ▷ Evangelicalism is represented by the hypocritical Bute Crawley.

The novel is subtitled 'A Novel without a Hero' and there is in fact nothing heroic about the society that Thackeray presents. However, its heartlessness and snobbery are skilfully manipulated by the central character, Becky Sharp, an ingenious and vigorous adventuress of poor parentage. She begins her socially ambitious career with a friendship with Amelia Sedley, the soft-hearted, weakly sentimental heroine of the book. Becky tries to marry Jos Sedley, Amelia's brother, a foolish but rich 'nabob'. Frustrated in this, and reduced to being a ▷ governess, she then makes love to the mean and avaricious Sir Pitt Crawley, but makes the mistake of marrying his second son, Rawdon, a gallant but ignorant and dissolute man who, despite his incapacity, is later made Governor of the unhealthy Coventry Islands. Her marriage does not prevent her from pursuing her social ambitions still further by becoming the mistress of the aristocratic and degenerate Lord Steyne. Her ambitions are eventually defeated but she manages to end up as a respected member of society.

Amelia Sedley first marries the worthless young officer, George Osborne, who is killed at the battle of Waterloo. The only fine human values are characterized by his friend, Dobbin, an English ▷ gentleman in the moral rather than the social sense, who eventually becomes Amelia's second husband. The novel is an impressive, if negative, landscape of upper-class society in the first half of the 19th century; its best parts are those that concentrate on Becky Sharp and are written with a keen, sardonic humour. The novel is commonly regarded as Thackeray's most successful work.

### Verne, Jules (1828–1905)

French author of adventure stories and ▷ science fiction, notably *Voyage to the Centre of the Earth* (1864), *Twenty Thousand Leagues Under the Sea* (1869) and *Round the World in Eighty Days* (1873).

### Victoria, Queen (1837–1901)

Born in 1819, Victoria came to the throne at the age of seventeen and was the longest reigning monarch in British history. In addition to re-establishing the prestige of the monarchy, she became a monumental symbol for the nation during the 60 years of the greatest power and influence Britain had ever known. The British Empire (▷ Imperialism) grew and was consolidated, with her as its figurehead. Her effectiveness as such was recognized by her Prime Minister ▷ Benjamin Disraeli when he induced her to adopt the title Empress of India in 1877. Victoria's jubilees of 1887 and 1897 were great national occasions, on which the sovereign was identified with the nation as never before since the reign of Elizabeth I (1558–1603). Victoria was also seen as an exemplary wife and mother, having nine children with her husband ▷ Prince Albert of Saxe-Coburg-Gotha, whom she married in 1840 and to whom she was devoted. When he died in 1861 she entered a period of mourning that was to end only with her death. She was responsible for setting a standard for the domestic virtues of rectitude of personal conduct and devotion to her husband and family, virtues greatly esteemed by the middle classes at a time when these classes dominated national life. Needless to say she was a life-long opponent of 'women's rights'.

Victoria was well-read; her diaries record her reading of ▷ the Brontës, ▷ Elizabeth Gaskell and ▷ George Eliot, as well as many male writers. She was especially fond of the works of ▷ Tennyson, who became her Poet Laureate in 1850. The Queen wrote scores of letters, which are published in five volumes edited by Roger Fulford, and accumulated over 100 volumes of diaries and journals. Selections from her journals (subsequently destroyed) along with some edited correspondence, have been published in three volumes edited by A.C. Benson and Viscount Esher (1907). The only writings published during her lifetime were *Leaves from a Journal of Our Life in the Highlands* (1848–61) (1868) and *More Leaves* (1883), in which she records her travels in Scotland. **Bib:** Longford, E., *Victoria R.I.*

### Villanelle

Originally a rustic song; made into a regular form of courtly grace and sweet tunefulness by the French poet Passerat (d 1602). The form was not much used in England until the period 1880–1910, when a fashion developed – chiefly among minor poets – for all such graceful forms (the ballade, rondeau, triolet, etc.). It consists of five three-line stanzas and a final four-line one; the first and third lines of the first stanza recur, alternately, as refrains and make a concluding couplet to the last stanza.

### Villette (1853)

Novel by ▷ Charlotte Brontë. Like her earlier novel, ▷ *The Professor, Villette* is based on the author's experiences in Brussels, where she worked as a teacher. The narrator, Lucy Snowe, loses her family and means of financial support early in the novel, and leaves for Villette (the name Brontë chose for Brussels) to find employment with Mme Beck, initially as a nursery ▷ governess and later as a teacher in Mme Beck's school. Lucy's pupils are mostly vain, frivolous and shallow, unlike her in personality, but she succeeds in establishing authority. Much of the novel is devoted to the tempestuous relationship between Lucy and the professor M. Paul Emmanuel, Mme Beck's cousin. Ultimately M. Paul establishes Lucy in a school of her own before leaving on a business trip to the West Indies. The ending is ambiguous, for the reader is left to decide whether he returns to marry Lucy or is drowned on the way back to Belgium. The novel fuses Gothic elements with 19th-century ▷ realism, and the narrative strategy is unusual for its time. Recent feminist criticism has focused on the instability of the narrator's discourse and the gaps, ellipses and psychological projections which appear in *Villette*'s exploration of subjectivity.

**Bib:** Newton, J., 'Villette' in *Feminist Criticism and Social Change*, ed. Newton and Rosenfelt; Jacobus, M., 'The Buried Letter: Romanticism in *Villette*' in *Women Writing and Writing About Women*.

**Walford, Lucy (1845–1915)**
Scottish novelist, born in Portobello, near
Edinburgh. Her first work, *Mr Smith: A
part of His Life*, was published in 1874, and
resulted in Walford being presented to
▷ Queen Victoria, who had asked to meet the
book's author. Walford went on to write more
than thirty works, including *Pauline* (1877);
*Troublesome Daughters* (1880); *A Pinch of
Bubble* (1895); *A Dream's Fulfilment* (1902) and
*The Enlightenment of Olivia* (1907). She also
published two non-fictional works: *Recollections
of a Scottish Novelist* (1910) and *Memoirs of
Victorian London* (1912).

**Ward, Mrs Humphrey (1851–1920)**
Novelist, born Mary Augusta Arnold, the
granddaughter of ▷ Thomas Arnold. She was
born in Tasmania but moved with her family
back to England in 1856, where she was
educated in private boarding schools. In 1872
she married Thomas Humphrey Ward, an
Oxford don. She contributed to the *Dictionary
of Christian Biography* in 1877, and in 1881
moved to London and wrote for ▷ *The Times*,
*Pall Mall Gazette* and ▷ *Macmillan's Magazine*
as well as publishing a children's story, *Milly
and Olly* (1881). Her first novel for adults, and
her most famous, was *Robert Elsmere* (1888).
It is the story of a clergyman who loses his
faith through a study of the 'higher criticism'
of Bible texts (the novelist ▷ George Eliot
lost her faith in the same way). The purport
of the book is that the revitalization of
Christianity requires more attention to the
social obligations of the Church and the
abandonment of its supernatural – or at
least its miraculous – constituents of belief.
The novel was an immediate success, and
she wrote twenty-four more, including:
*The History of David Grieve* (1892); *Marcella*
(1894); *Sir George Tressady* (1896); *Helbeck of
Bannisdale* (1898); *Lady Rose's Daughter* (1903);
*The Marriage of William Ashe* (1905); *Diana
Mallory* (1908); *Delia Blanchflower* (1915)
and *Cousin Philip* (1919). Her novels deal
principally with social and religious themes,
often contrasting tradition with progress. She
was a leading intellectual figure and an active
philanthropist, yet although she campaigned
for higher ▷ education for women, she
strongly opposed the ▷ women's suffrage
movement. She generated support for an
'Appeal Against Female Suffrage', published
in 1889, and became the first President
of the Anti-Suffrage League in 1908. Like
many Victorians, she believed that women
should set a moral example, issuing firstly
from the home. Ward was also known to be

a severe critic of other women writers. Her
▷ autobiography, *A Writer's Recollections*, was
published in 1918.
**Bib:** Trevelyan, J.P., *The Life of Mrs Humphrey
Ward*; Jones, E.H., *Mrs Humphrey Ward*; Huw
Jones, E., *Mrs Ward*; Peterson, W.S., *Victorian
Heretic: Mrs Humphrey Ward's Robert Elsmere*.

**Warden, The (1855)**
A novel by ▷ Anthony Trollope, the first to
be a success with the public, and the first of
his ▷ Barsetshire series.
   The theme of the novel is the two aspects
of the problem of the reform of public abuses.
It shows how an office which brings to its
holder an income much in excess of his duties
may nonetheless be conducted usefully and
with integrity, so that to abolish the office may
be an act of personal injustice although the
abolition may be justifiable on public grounds.
   The novel is set in the cathedral city of
Barchester in Barsetshire. A clergyman, the
Reverend Septimus Harding, is Warden
of Hiram's Hospital, a long-established
charitable institution for maintaining twelve
poor old men in comfort. For this he draws
an income which in the course of time has
increased to £800 a year, although his actual
duties are almost non-existent. However,
he maintains with the old men affectionate
relationships which are inestimable financially.
The wardenship is attacked as a public
abuse by John Bold, a Barchester surgeon,
although Bold is in love with Harding's
daughter Eleanor. Bold is opposed (on the
wrong grounds) by the worldly churchman
Archdeacon Grantly, who is Harding's
son-in-law. Harding resigns his office as a
matter of conscience, but the Bishop refuses
to appoint a new Warden, and the old men
of the Hospital lose the chief solace of their
old age.

**Water Babies, The (1863)**
A moral fantasy for children, by ▷ Charles
Kingsley, subtitled *A Fairy Tale for a
Landbaby*. The little boy Tom is employed as
a chimney-sweep by the brutal Mr Grimes;
he falls into the river, gets turned into a water
baby and is carried down to the sea. He meets
a number of fabulous creatures and undergoes
ordeals which effect moral instruction. He
emerges purified, on equal terms with Ellie,
the little girl in whose house he once swept
the chimneys. Grimes is sent away to a
penance of sweeping out Etna. The book is
partly an attack on the exploitation of child
labour and on the brutalization of the poor,
and partly a fable about their moral education.

Some of the moralizing is offensive, socially and psychologically, to modern readers but the book remains a children's classic for the sake of the ingenuity of its fantasy.

▷ Child labour; Children's literature.

### Way of All Flesh, The (1903)

A novel by ▷ Samuel Butler, written 1873–5 and published after his death, in 1903. It is one of the few purely satirical works of distinction of the Victorian period; the satire is directed against the Victorian cult of the family as the sacred and blessed nucleus of society, and (as so often in ▷ Charles Dickens) the refuge from the harshness of the world. The arrogant, self-righteous, intolerant and stupid kind of Victorian parent is exemplified in the clergyman Theobald Pontifex, father of Ernest Pontifex. Victorian authoritarianism and repressiveness is also attacked in Theobald, seen as a religious humbug, and in Dr Skinner, headmaster of the ▷ public school that Ernest attends. The first fifty chapters of the book are autobiographical; Butler even includes actual letters in the text. The narrative is not told through Ernest (Butler as a boy) but in the first person through his friend the middle-aged Overton, who represents a more tolerant aspect of Butler; by this means, Butler conveys criticism of his intolerant younger self, in the person of Ernest. The book was much praised, especially by ▷ G.B. Shaw.

▷ Autobiography.

### Webb, Beatrice (1858–1943)

Sociologist. She was the daughter of Richard Potter, a railway director and friend of the philosopher ▷ Herbert Spencer, who exercised a guiding influence over her education. Her mother was a product of the 19th-century ▷ Utilitarian school of thought. She early developed a strong social conscience, which led her to choose as her career the almost unprecedented one of 'social investigator'. Victorian sensitiveness to social abuses was strong amongst the intelligentsia, but she realized that constructive action was hampered by lack of exact information: 'The primary task is to observe and dissect facts.' In order to do so, she took bold steps for a Victorian girl of the prosperous middle class, such as disguising herself as a working girl and taking employment under a tailor in the East End of London. She and her husband were among the early members of the ▷ Fabian Society, and among the founders of the ▷ Labour Party. Her autobiographies *My Apprenticeship* (1926) and *Our Partnership*

(1948) are in the tradition of ▷ John Stuart Mill's *Autobiography* (1873) in being essentially histories of the growth of opinions and ideas; *My Apprenticeship*, however, is very enlightening about social backgrounds in the 1880s, and a valuable addition to the Victorian novels, which, she said, were the only documents for the study of society available in her youth. She and her husband were among the founders of the weekly journal *New Statesman*, still a leading left-wing journal.

### Webster, Augusta (1837–94)

Poet, dramatist and essayist, who also wrote under the ▷ pseudonym Cecil Home. After marrying Thomas Webster at the age of twenty-six, she published her first collection of verse, *Blanche Lisle and Other Poems* (1860). A committed ▷ feminist, much of her work focuses on female subjects. ▷ *Dramatic Studies* (1866) includes poems about spinsterhood, ▷ marriage and motherhood; ▷ 'A Castaway' (1870) is concerned with prostitution; 'Circe' (1870) is a psychological portrait of the mythological figure; *A Housewife's Opinions* (1878) is a collection of essays on the lives of married women. Webster was at times criticized for her forthrightness and unabashed ▷ realism, but she was also favourably compared to ▷ Elizabeth Barrett Browning, ▷ Christina Rossetti and ▷ Jean Ingelow. Her unfinished sonnet sequence, *Mother and Daughter* (1895), was published posthumously, edited by William Michael Rossetti, Christina and ▷ Dante Gabriel's brother. Dramatic works include *The Auspicious Day* (1872); *Disguises* (1879) and *In a Day* (1882).

▷ Women's Movement.

**Bib:** Hickok, K., *Representations of Women: 19th Century British Women's Poetry*.

### Wells, H.G. (Herbert George) (1866–1946)

Novelist and journalist. He was brought up in the lower middle class, the son of a professional cricketer; in 1888 he took an excellent degree in science at London University. His social origins and his education explain much of his approach to life as a writer. The great novelist of the 19th-century lower middle classes is ▷ Dickens and some of H.G. Wells's best fiction is about the same field of society; novels such as *Kipps* (1905) and *The History of Mr Polly* (1910) are of this sort, and they have the kind of vigorous humour and sharp visualization that is characteristic of early Dickens. On the other hand, rising into the educated class at a time of rapid scientific and technical progress, he ignored the values of traditional culture and art, and became fascinated with the prospects that science offered, for good as well as for ill. This side of him produced a different kind of writing: Wells was one of the inventors of ▷ science fiction. *The Time Machine* (1895), *The Invisible Man* (1897), *The War of the Worlds* (1898) and *The First Men in the Moon* (1901) are examples of his fantasies. But his social experience and his interest in technology also drew him to writing fictional-sociological studies in which he surveyed and analysed, often with the same Dickensian humour, the society of his time; *Tono-Bungay* (1908) is perhaps the best of these. Other examples are *Ann Veronica* (1909) about the problems connected with newly emancipated women, *The New Machiavelli* (1911) about socialist thinking – Wells had joined the ▷ Fabians in 1903 – and *Mr Britling Sees It Through* (1916) about World War I seen from the point of view of the 'Home Front'. But the interest in science also made him a ▷ utopian optimist, and this point of view caused him to write such didactic works as *A Modern Utopia* (1905) and *New Worlds For Old* (1908). There was always a great deal of naivety in Wells's optimism, and later in his life he paid the penalty by reacting into excessive gloom, in *Mind at the End of its Tether* (1945). He declared that *The Open Conspiracy* (1928) contained the essence of his philosophy. He was never a deep thinker, however; his work lives by the vitality of his humour and by the urgency with which he pressed his ideas. This urgency necessarily made him a popularizer, and his most notable work of popularization was *The Outline of History* (1920).

In some ways Wells resembles his contemporary, the dramatist ▷ George Bernard Shaw; both were socialists, both felt the urgency to enlighten mankind as quickly as possible, and both cared more that their works should have immediate effect than that they should be works of art – Wells told the novelist ▷ Henry James that he would rather be called a journalist than an artist. Possibly the most penetrating remark on Wells was that addressed to him by the novelist Joseph Conrad (1857–1924): 'You don't really care for people, but you think they can be improved; I do, but I know they can't.'

**Bib:** Mackenzie, N. and J., *The Time Traveller: Life of H.G. Wells*; Bergonzi, B., *The Early H.G. Wells* and *H.G. Wells: Twentieth-Century Views*; Parrinder, P. (ed.), *H.G. Wells; the Critical Heritage*.

**Wessex**
The kingdom of the West Saxons from the 6th century till the reign of Alfred at the end of the 9th, after which it developed into the kingdom of England. The capital was the town of Winchester in Hampshire, and the area also included Dorset, Somerset, Wiltshire, and Berkshire. The name of Wessex was revived by the novelist and poet ▷ Thomas Hardy for his ▷ regional novels.
▷ Barnes, William.

***Westminster Review***
It was founded in 1823 as a vehicle for the Benthamite (▷ Jeremy Bentham) otherwise known as the ▷ Utilitarian school of thought, and at first kept severely to its principles. Its politics of ruthless, scientific institutional reform made it not only a strong opponent of the Tory *Quarterly Review* but put it well to the left of the ▷ *Edinburgh Review*. It appealed to a narrower public, and tended, in the Utilitarian manner, to regard the arts with disdain. In 1836 it combined with the now livelier Utilitarian *London Review* and continued as the *London and Westminster Review*, under the editorship of the distinguished Utilitarian ▷ John Stuart Mill. Mill wanted to broaden Utilitarian thinking, and writers who were not followers of the movement were brought in, such as ▷ Carlyle and the novelist ▷ George Eliot, who was assistant editor 1851–4. Later contributors varied as greatly as ▷ Walter Pater, father of the ▷ Aesthetic movement, and the positivist Frederic Harrison. It continued to advocate scientific progress, and by the end of the century it ceased to be literary.

***What Maisie Knew*** **(1897)**
A novel by ▷ Henry James. Its theme is the survival of innocence in a world of adult corruption, the influence of adults on a child, and her influence on them.

Maisie Farange is a small girl whose parents have divorced each other with equal guilt on both sides. The parents are heartless and indifferent to their daughter, except as a weapon against each other and in their farcical, though not wholly vain, struggles to maintain acceptable social appearances. Maisie is passed from one to the other, and each employs a governess to take responsibility for her welfare. Both parents marry again, and eventually relinquish Maisie herself. By the end of the book Maisie finds herself torn between two prospective 'step-parents', each formerly married to her real parents, divorced from them, and about to marry each other,

Maisie herself having been the occasion of
their coming together. Her 'stepfather', Sir
Claude, is charming and sweet-natured, but
weak and self-indulgent; her 'stepmother',
Mrs Beale, is genuinely fond of Maisie
(as Sir Claude is) but is basically selfish
and rapacious. In addition, the child has a
simple-minded, plain and elderly governess,
Mrs Wix, who is herself in love with Sir
Claude, and devoted to Maisie. The affection
of none of them, however, is single-minded,
as hers is for each one of them. The
pathos of the novel arises from the warm
responsiveness, deep need, and pure integrity
of Maisie, from whose point of view all the
events are seen. Its irony arises from the way
in which the child's need for and dependence
on adult care and love is transformed into
responsibility for the adults themselves, who
become dependent on her decisions. In the
end these decisions lead her to choose life
alone with Mrs Wix, who naively hopes to
imbue her with a 'moral sense', unaware
that beside Maisie's innocence her own
idea of a moral sense represents modified
corruption.

The novel is written in James's late,
compressed and dramatic style, and is one of
his masterpieces.

**Whig and Tory**
Political terms distinguishing the two
parties which were the forebears of the
present ▷ Liberal and Conservative parties
respectively. They were originally terms
of abuse, provoked by the attempt of Lord
Shaftesbury (1621–83) in 1679 to exclude
James, Duke of York (later James II), from
succession to the throne because he was a
▷ Catholic. Shaftesbury and his party were
called Whigs because their preference for
the ▷ Protestant religion over the law of
hereditary succession caused their opponents
to liken them to the Scottish ▷ Presbyterian
rebels of the time – called derisively 'whigs'
from the nickname given to Scottish drovers.
They retaliated by calling the supporters of
James 'tories', from the Irish term for robbers,
implying that they no more cared about
safeguarding the Protestant religion than did
the Irish Catholic rebels.

About 1830 the names Liberal and
Conservative began to replace Whig and Tory
in popular use, and these terms were officially
adopted some thirty years later. 'Tory'
survives, to some extent, as interchangeable
with Conservative (it is shorter for newspaper
headlines), but 'Whig' has been altogether
superseded.

**White, William Hale (1831–1913)**
Novelist who used the ▷ pseudonym Mark
Rutherford. His father was a ▷ Dissenter
and intended his son to be a Dissenting
clergyman. However, William White could
not reconcile his ideas and the religious
doctrines that he was required to believe,
and instead he had a civil service career in
the Admiralty. His three famous novels were
*The Autobiography of Mark Rutherford* (1881),
*Mark Rutherford's Deliverance* (1885) and *The
Revolution in Tanner's Lane* (1887). The first
two are ▷ autobiographical and concerned
with loss of faith. White makes Rutherford
more outwardly unfortunate than he was
himself, since he had a successful career both
as a writer and as a civil servant; the reason
seems to be that he makes his character
represent not only his own loss of Christian
faith but the sense of impoverishment that
accompanied it. In his study of John Bunyan
(1905), he makes the statement: 'Religion is
dead when imagination deserts it.' White's
own questioning of his belief started from
reading William Wordsworth (1770–1850)
in *Lyrical Ballads* (1798–1800) and the
subsequent feeling that nature stirred him as
'the God of the Church' could not. As studies
of spiritual loss and contention with it, the
Mark Rutherford novels have wide human
relevance. The third novel is concerned with
radical movements in the early 19th century
and shows White's political intelligence,
which comes out directly in his pamphlet
on the political franchise. His other novels
are *Miriam's Schooling* (1890), *Catherine
Furze* (1893) and *Clara Hopgood* (1896).
Other works: *Pages from a Journal* and *More
Pages from a Journal* (1900 and 1910); *Last
Pages* (1915).
    ▷ Agnosticism.
**Bib:** Maclean, C.M., *Life*; Stone, W., *Life*;
Stock, I., *William Hale White*; Lucas, J., *The
Literature of Change: Studies in the Nineteenth-
Century Provincial Novel* (chapter).

**Who's Who**
An annual biographical dictionary of eminent
contemporary men and women. First
published in 1849.

**Wilde, Jane Francesca (1826–96)**
Irish writer, born in Wexford, the daughter
of an archdeacon. In 1851, she married a
surgeon, Sir William Wilde, and was widowed
in 1871. She died in considerable poverty
in London in the year her son, ▷ Oscar
Wilde (1856–1900), was publicly tried and
disgraced on grounds of ▷ homosexuality.

Frequently using the ▷ pseudonym Speranza, she contributed regularly to *The Nation*, and published a collection, *Poems*, in 1864. Her writings about folklore and collections of Irish legends include: *Driftwood from Scandinavia* (1884), *Ancient Legends of Ireland* (1887) and *Ancient Cures* (1891). Her other books are *Men, Women and Books* (1891) and *Social Studies* (1893).

▷ Irish literature in English.

## Wilde, Oscar Fingal O'Flahertie Wills (1856–1900)

Dramatist, poet, novelist and essayist. He was the son of an eminent Irish surgeon and ▷ Jane Francesca Wilde. At Oxford University his style of life became notorious; he was a disciple of ▷ Pater, the Oxford father of ▷ aestheticism, and he carried the doctrine as far as to conduct his life as an aesthetic disciple – a direct challenge to the prevailing outlook of the society of his time, which was inclined to regard overt aestheticism with suspicion or disdain. In 1888 Wilde produced a volume of children's fairy tales very much in the melancholy and poetic style of the Danish writer ▷ Hans Christian Andersen – *The Happy Prince*. He followed this with two other volumes of stories, and then the novel, ▷ *The Picture of Dorian Grey* (1891), whose hero is an embodiment of the aesthetic way of life. More commonly known were his comedies, ▷ *Lady Windermere's Fan* (1892), *A Woman of No Importance* (1893), *An Ideal Husband* (1895), and above all the witty ▷ *Importance of Being Earnest* (1895). The plays are apparently light-hearted, but they contain strong elements of serious feeling in their attack on a society whose code is intolerant, but whose intolerance is hypocritical. In 1895, by a libel action against the Marquis of Queensberry, he exposed himself to a countercharge of immoral ▷ homosexual conduct, and spent two years in prison. In 1898 he published his ▷ *Ballad of Reading Gaol* about his prison experience, proving that he could write in the direct language of the ▷ ballad tradition, as well as in the artificial style of his *Collected Poems* (1892). His *De Profundis* (1905) is an eloquent statement of his grief after his downfall, but modern critics are equally as impressed by the intelligence of his social essays, such as *The Critic as Artist* (1891) and *The Soul of Man under Socialism* (1891). The paradox of Wilde is that, while for his contemporaries he represented degeneracy and weakness, there is plenty of evidence that he was a brave man of remarkable strength of character who made an emphatic protest against the vulgarity of his age and yet, artistically, was himself subject to vulgarity of an opposite kind.

**Bib:** Critical studies by Roditi, E., Ransome, A.; Lives by Ellman, R.; Lemmonier, L.; Ervine, St J.; Pearson, H.; Bentley, E.R., in *The Playwright as Thinker*; Beckson, K. (ed.), *The Critical Heritage*; Bird, A., *The Plays of Oscar Wilde*; Worth, K., *Oscar Wilde*.

## William IV (1830–37)

He was brother of his predecessor, George IV (1820–30), and uncle to his successor, ▷ Victoria. He was a well-meaning man of small ability, but the most popular member of a royal family which was otherwise very unpopular.

## Winter, John Strange (1856–1911)

▷ Pseudonym of novelist Henrietta Palmer (she also wrote as Violet Whyte). She was born in York, the daughter of a rector who came from a military family. Winter's writings show the army influence, often describing the lives of wives and children of military heroes. The pseudonym was adopted on the advice of her publishers, who considered that works such as *Cavalry Life* (1881) and *Regimental Legends* (1883) would be more credible if thought to have been written by a man. Winter's most successful work was *Bootle's Baby: A Story of the Scarlet Lancers* (1885), which was serialized in the *Graphic* and adapted for the stage, playing at the Globe theatre in London in 1889. Other works include *He Went for a Soldier* (1890), *A Soldier's Children* (1892), and *A Summer Jaunt* (1889). Winter also founded the *Golden Gates* magazine in 1891, was President of the Writer's Club (1892) and President of the Society of Women Journalists (1901–3).

## Wives and Daughters (1864–6)

A novel by ▷ Mrs Gaskell, published serially in the ▷ *Cornhill Magazine* and not completed at her death. It is a study of two families, the Gibsons and the Hamleys, in a small country town and the relationships of the parents and the children in each. The central character is Molly Gibson, whose liberal, frank, sincere and deeply responsible nature is painfully tested by the marriage of her widowed father (a country doctor) to a silly, vain widow. The widow brings with her, however, her own daughter, Cynthia, a girl with her mother's outward charm but without her silliness and with feelings guided more by her discerning intelligence than by spontaneous loyalties. Cynthia at sixteen has become engaged to a coarse but astute man, Mr Preston, who is a local land-agent. The two girls become involved with the two sons of Mr Hamley, the local squire. The elder boy, Osborne, is superficially brilliant and charming, and much overestimated by his father. The younger son, Roger, has much less showy qualities but a deeper nature and eventually wins the academic success expected of but not achieved by the elder, who makes an unfortunate marriage, is cast off by the father and dies young. The novel thus brings out the differences between superficial and deep natures, and the perils that result from consequent false estimates of character, made even by the intelligent.

## Wolstenholme-Elmy, Elizabeth (1834–1913)
Essayist and poet, who also wrote under the pseudonyms E. Ellis, Ellis Ethelmer, and 'Ignota'. ▷ Orphaned as a child and deprived of an adequate ▷ education, she became an ardent ▷ feminist and vigorous campaigner. She was Honorary Secretary to the Manchester ▷ Women's Suffrage Society (1865), Secretary to the Married Women's Property Committee (1867–82), a founding member of the Women's Franchise League (1899) and the founder of the Women's Emancipation Union (1891). She published a long feminist poem, ▷ *Woman Free* (1893); two sex education manuals (*The Human Flower*, 1894, and *Baby Buds*, 1895) and many pamphlets, including her last work, *Woman's Franchise: The Need of the Hour* (1907).
▷ Women's Movement.
**Bib:** Strachey, R., *The Cause.*

## Woman Free (1893)
A long poem by ▷ Elizabeth Wolstenholme-Elmy, concerned with women's subordination. The poem attacks the 'brainless bondage' to which women are subjected in ▷ marriage, and protests against male sexual aggression, claiming that women must be 'Free from all uninvited touch of man'. The poem also contains many notes which supplement the author's ▷ feminist perspective. The author writes: 'Anyone who has looked a little below the surface of women's lives can testify to the general unrest and nervous exhaustion or malaise among them, although each would probably refer her suffering to some cause peculiar to herself and her circumstances, never dreaming that she was the victim of an evil that gnaws at the very heart of society, making almost every woman the heroine of a silent tragedy.'
▷ Women's Movement.

## 'Woman Question, The'
From the 1830s onwards Victorian Britain was obsessively concerned with the 'Woman Question', as they called it. The arguments in this debate were complex and multivocal; the issue of woman's role in society was discussed in newspapers, magazines, and literary, philosophical, educational and medical journals; in Parliament, in church and in the home. No single cultural myth prevailed, and the idea of 'Woman', her 'mission', her 'sphere' and her 'influence' became a site of struggle where competing ideologies strove for dominance. Some commentators challenged the constraints placed upon middle-class women's lives and argued for greater vocational and educational opportunity; others argued passionately that women and men should operate in separate spheres of existence. Recent critical examination of the 'Woman Question' has explored the interrelationships between the Victorian preoccupation with history, national identity and Empire, and the widespread concern with the status and function of women (see Christina Crosby's *The Ends of History*, 1991). Numerous extracts from contemporary writings on the 'Woman Question' can be found in Helsinger et al. (eds) *The Woman Question: Society and Literature in Britain and America 1837–1883.*
▷ Education of women; Feminism; 'New Woman, The'; Linton, Eliza Lynn; Divorce.
**Bib:** Crosby, C., *The Ends of History: Victorians and 'The Woman Question'*; Rubenstein, D., *Before the Suffragettes: Women's Emancipation in the 1890s.*

## Woman's Friendship (1853)
A novel by ▷ Grace Aguilar, concerned with the importance of female bonding. The central character, Florence, becomes friendly with Lady Ida Villiers, a woman whose social status is considerably higher than her own. Florence is warned by her 'mother' (who turns out to be a foster-parent) that this friendship cannot be mutual because Lady Villier's class position prohibits it. Later, Florence's true parentage is revealed, and after a period of estrangement from one another Florence and Lady Villiers are re-united in friendship. Aguilar writes at the end of the book that although female bonding is 'in general scorned and scoffed at . . . [it] may be the invisible means of strengthening in virtue'.

## Woman Who Did, The (1895)
A novel by ▷ Grant Allen which openly engaged with the ▷ 'Woman Question' and

the issue of 'free union'. It was attacked, along with ▷ Thomas Hardy's ▷ *Jude the Obscure*, by ▷ Margaret Oliphant for being 'anti-marriage'. The heroine of the novel, Herminia, is martyred in the cause of free union, a fact which was seen to militate against Allen's message of 'free love' and feminine emancipation. The book and its author were convincingly attacked by Millicent Garrett Fawcett in ▷ *The Contemporary Review* in 1895. Allen's novel, which was a best-seller in its time, was mercilessly parodied in *The Woman Who Didn't* by 'Victoria Crosse' and *The Woman Who Wouldn't* by 'Lucas Cleeve'.

## Women's Movement, The

In 1800 the population of the British Isles was approximately 12 million. By 1900 it has risen to 38 million and, throughout this period, women were in excess of men by about 1–2 million. The stereotypical image of Victorian womanhood as passive, self-sacrificing and content with a purely domestic role (▷ 'The Angel in the House') was progressively challenged by scores of activist women who worked together in radical ▷ feminist circles to campaign for ▷ women's suffrage, better education (▷ education of women), reform of ▷ marriage and ▷ divorce and infant custody laws, and wider vocational opportunities. Women like ▷ Lucy Aiken, ▷ Mathilde Blind, ▷ Barbara Bodichon, ▷ Mona Caird, ▷ Sarah Grand, ▷ Harriet Martineau, ▷ Elizabeth Wolstenholme-Elmy and others were passionately concerned with the position of women in society, and published works which exposed the hypocrisies, and protested against the injustices, of Victorian patriarchy. Although Victorian feminism was largely a middle-class movement which did not engage with wider analyses of social structures, working-class women (especially in the cotton towns of the north of England) campaigned for the vote and a wide range of women's rights including equal pay, birth control, child allowances and the right to work. Women like Hannah Mitchell, Mary Cooper, Helen Silcock, Selina Cooper and Ada Nield Chew combined political activity with family commitments and arduous employment. Their contribution to the struggle for women's rights has been largely overshadowed by the militant suffrage campaign. This perspective on the Women's Movement was significantly altered by Jill Liddington and Jill Norris, and Sheila Rowbotham (see bibliography) in the late 1970s.

The rise of socialist feminism can be traced to the activities and ideals of the early utopian socialist ▷ Robert Owen, and was charted by Barbara Taylor (see bibliography) in 1983. Many middle-class feminists failed to challenge the dominant view that men and women were *essentially* different and created to occupy separate spheres of activity (women's sphere being largely dominated by motherhood) and campaigns around issues of sexuality generally aimed to curtail male sexuality rather than free female libido. Others recognized that woman's 'separate sphere' was largely the product of the exclusion of women from most remunerative occupations which put economic independence out of their reach. This meant that women were forced into economic dependency on men, and sexual subservience. They were denied an active participation in society because it was assumed that their proper place was in the home bearing children. Denying women the vote served to perpetuate the status quo.

Legislation such as the Contagious Diseases Acts of 1864, 1866 and 1869; the Infant Life Protection Act; and the Factory Acts of 1874 and 1878 all discriminated against women. The Contagious Diseases Act, designed to curb the spread of venereal disease in the military, mandated the examination and enforced hospitalization for up to nine months of prostitutes, or any woman suspected of prostitution, but left their male customers unmolested. These were repealed in 1886 largely due to the activity of Elizabeth Wolstenholme-Elmy and political activist and writer Josephine Butler. The Infant Life Protection Act was meant to protect those born out of wedlock, but it did so by policing mothers and nurses while doing nothing to enforce the father's financial responsibility. As far as married couples were concerned, the father had total control over his children and was permitted by law to deny his wife access even to her newly born baby if he so desired. This was changed by the campaign of ▷ Caroline Norton which led to the Infant Custody Act of 1839, allowing women to petition for custody of children under the age of seven and access to those under sixteen.

Norton and Barbara Lee Smith (later Bodichon) revolutionized the pernicious English marriage and divorce laws. Thanks to their activities the Married Women's Property Acts of 1870 and 1886 gave women rights over their own property and earnings, which had hitherto passed into the control of their husbands on marriage. The Factory Acts, which limited a woman's working day, were motivated by the conviction that women needed protection because they were weak and, more importantly, because they were potential mothers. These acts effectively curtailed the earning power of working-class women. Similar legislature was passed affecting women in the coal mines. As far as middle-class women were concerned, paid employment was regarded as the last desperate recourse of the spinster who had no man to provide for her. Women's education was largely focused on domestic and cultural training and was aimed at fitting women to suit the marriage market. Consequently, unmarried women had few prospects until the second half of the 19th century.

Improvements in the education of girls led to the extensive employment of ▷ governesses to teach the children of wealthy families but it was likely to be an unpleasant, underpaid and despised occupation, as novelists ▷ Anne and ▷ Charlotte Brontë found. Nursing was also open to women, but nurses had no training and were commonly a low class of woman like Betsey Prigg and Mrs Gamp in ▷ Charles Dickens's ▷ *Martin Chuzzlewit* until Florence Nightingale (1820–1910) reformed the profession (▷ Crimean War). The entry of women into the medical profession as doctors was initiated by Elizabeth Garrett Anderson (1836–1917), whose name was placed on the British Medical Register in 1859. The struggles of Anderson and Nightingale are documented by Ray Strachey (see bibliography). Women's access to other fields of employment was initiated by the Langham Place Group: a group of women interested primarily in advancing women's opportunities for education and employment. They included among their number Bessie Parkes, Mary Howitt, Barbara Leigh Smith, Jessie Boucherett and ▷ Frances Power Cobbe. ▷ George Gissing's novel ▷ *The Odd Women* is based on the activities of this group.

Parliamentary ▷ Reform Bills of the 19th century had no effect upon the status of women. The Bills of 1832, 1867 and 1884 progressively expanded the franchise so that by the end of the century all non-institutionalized male members of society had the right to vote. Despite the persistent campaigning for women's suffrage, the franchise was not achieved until 1918. The Victorian period was the heroic age for women in Britain. No other age before the 20th century has produced such a distinguished line of women writers. In addition there was the prison reformer Elizabeth Fry (1780–1845), the explorer ▷ Mary Kingsley, the sociologist ▷ Beatrice Webb and

pioneers in education such as Dorothea Beale (1831–1906) and Frances Buss (1827–94).
**Bib:** Liddington, J., Norris, J., *One Hand Tied Behind Us: The Rise of the Women's Suffrage Movement*; Rowbotham, S., *Hidden From History*; Taylor, B., *Eve and the New Jerusalem: Socialism and Feminism in the Nineteenth Century*; Walkowitz, J.R., '*We Are Not Beasts of the Field': Prostitution and the Campaign Against the Contagious Diseases Acts, 1869–1886*; Forster, M., *Significant Sisters: The Grassroots of Active Feminism 1889–1939*; Strachey, R., *The Cause: A Short History of the Women's Movement in Great Britain*; Lacey, C.A. (ed.), *Barbara Leigh Smith Bodichon and the Langham Place Group*.

## Women's suffrage

The first National Association for Women's Suffrage was formed in Manchester in 1865, and in 1866 a petition of 1500 signatures was presented to ▷ J.S. Mill, whose essay 'On the Subjection of Women' had been published that year. Signatories of the petition included ▷ Barbara Bodichon, ▷ Harriet Martineau and ▷ Matilda Betham-Edwards. Mill presented a motion to Parliament to include female suffrage in the 1867 ▷ Reform Bill, but he was defeated by 196 votes against 73. Throughout the rest of the 19th century women continued to campaign for the vote. Societies were formed in London, Edinburgh, Birmingham and Bristol in the late 1860s, and the first Women's Suffrage Bill was presented to Parliament by Jacob Bright in 1870. The first reading was carried by 124 votes to 91, but the government then opposed the Bill, and on the second vote it was defeated by 220 to 94. Although hopes were running high when a new government (led by ▷ Disraeli) came to power in 1874, no significant change of policy occurred. In 1880 ▷ Gladstone succeeded as Prime Minister, and the first women-only demonstration was held in Manchester's Free Trade Hall. The next major event was the new Parliamentary Reform Bill of 1884 – a crushing defeat for the suffragists since Gladstone made it clear that he was inexorably opposed to the inclusion of women in the Bill. It was defeated by 271 to 135. Among the MPs who voted against the Bill were 104 Liberals who had pledged support.

In 1889 ▷ Mrs Humphry Ward led an 'Appeal Against Female Suffrage', stating that 'The political ignorance of women is irreparable and is imposed by nature.' Although Ward had many notable supporters, the tide of public opinion was slowly beginning to turn. Another Women's

Suffrage Bill was presented in 1892, and was only defeated by twenty-three votes. In 1897 Millicent Fawcett became President of the new National Union of Women's Suffrage, and the campaign for the vote was boosted after the Boer War, which bridged the end of the 19th and the beginning of the 20th centuries.

The first decade of the 20th century marked a shift towards violent action as a means to secure the vote. Among the leading figures of the movement was Emmeline Pankhurst (1858–1928), who campaigned with her daughters Christabel and Sylvia. The arrest of Christabel and the Irish trade unionist Annie Kenney during their protest at a Liberal Party meeting in 1905 marked the turning point in the movement's strategies and public profile. Emmeline Pankhurst was first arrested in 1908, and consistently thereafter.

The suffrage movement ended in 1918 when votes were granted to women at the age of thirty. In 1928 Parliament decreed that women should have equal voting rights with men.

▷ Cobbe, Frances Power; Grand, Sarah; Lyall, Edna; Meynell, Alice; 'New Woman, The'; Ouida; Wolstenholme-Elmy, Elizabeth; 'Woman Question, The'; Yonge, Charlotte.
**Bib:** Pankhurst, S., *The Suffragette Movement*; Rubenstein, D., *Before the Suffragettes*.

### Wood, Mrs Henry (Ellen) (1814–87)
Novelist, who also wrote under the ▷ pseudonym Johnny Ludlow. She was born in Worcester, the daughter of a manufacturer. Wood's early short stories appeared in the *New Monthly Magazine* and her first novel, *Danesbury House*, was published in 1860. Her second, ▷ *East Lynne* (1861), was hugely successful, selling over 2.5 million copies by 1900. The conservatism of this book is also apparent in the rest of Wood's *oeuvre*, with *Mrs Halliburton's Troubles* (1862) and *A Life's Secret* (1867) exhibiting extreme hostility to working-class activism. She was prolific, writing over thirty novels and 300 short stories, as well as editing a periodical, *Argosy*. Most of her works are novels of ▷ sensation underscored by a rigid Victorian morality. They include *The Channings* (1862); *The Shadows of Ashlydyat* (1863); *Lady Adelaide's Oath* (1867) and *The Master of Greylands* (1873). Her last work was *Ashley and Other Stories* (1897). *A Life's Secret* (1867) portrayed a negative side of ▷ trade unionism and caused her publisher's office to be mobbed by a hostile crowd. The *Johnny Ludlow* series of stories (1868–9) drew on local and family

history from her early life, and lacked some of the melodramatic and sensational elements of many of her other novels.
**Bib:** Hughes, W., *The Maniac in the Cellar: Sensation Novels of the 1860s*.

### Woodlanders, The (1887)
A novel by ▷ Thomas Hardy. The setting is Dorset in the south-west of England and the human relationships are a kind of movement upwards, downwards and upwards again from the primitive rural base. The primitive peasant girl, Marty South, is in love with the young cider-maker, Giles Winterbourne, who is as simple in his background as she is herself but has great natural delicacy of feeling. Giles is himself in love with Grace Melbury, the daughter of a local timber merchant, who has had a 'lady's' education (▷ education of women). She has not been spoiled by this but her sensibilities have spoiled her for the primitive environment to which Giles belongs. Her parents marry her to the young doctor, Edred Fitzpiers, who, however, is enticed away by the great lady of the district, Felice Charmond. Grace takes refuge in the woods with Giles, who, though a sick man, abandons his cottage to her and lives in a hut nearby, where he dies. Grace and Marty South mourn together over his grave but Grace becomes reconciled to Fitzpiers and Marty is left to mourn alone. Neither Fitzpiers nor Mrs Charmond belongs to the rural background and their intrusion into it is disruptive of its values, embodied above all in Giles Winterbourne.

### Workhouses
Institutions to accommodate the destitute at public expense, and to provide them with work to ensure that they were socially useful. They were first established under the Poor Law of 1576; they increased in number, but by the 18th century the administration of them, the responsibility of the parish, had become seriously inefficient, and magistrates were more inclined to administer financial relief to the paupers in their homes. This 'outdoor relief – the 'Speenhamland System', so called from the parish in which it was first used – tended to be demoralizing to the working poor, who earned very little more than the workless paupers. The whole system was remodelled by the New ▷ Poor Law of 1834, by which workhouses were established regionally and administered by Boards of Guardians. The philosophy behind the Poor Law was that most destitution was due to laziness and vice, so that workhouses ought to

be practically penal institutions. Consequently, though they ceased to be places of brutality and vice as they had been in the 18th century, they became coldly inhuman, providing only the barest necessities of existence. Their inhumanity aroused ▷ Dickens to his indignantly satirical picture of them in ▷ *Oliver Twist*; in his last complete novel, ▷ *Our Mutual Friend*, Dickens returned to the theme by portraying the old woman, Betty Higden, as dying by the roadside sooner than enter a workhouse. Workhouses were indeed bitterly hated by the poor, and in the 20th century they were gradually eliminated by the institution of the Welfare State.

### 'Wreck of the Deutschland, The'

A poem by ▷ Gerard Manley Hopkins, written in 1875, but not printed until the first editions of his collected poems (edited by ▷ Robert Bridges) was published in 1918, apart from a short extract in Bridges's anthology *The Spirit of Men* (1918). Hopkins had ceased writing poetry when he entered the Jesuit Order in 1868. He broke his silence in consequence of being deeply moved at the news of the loss of the ship *Deutschland* at the mouth of the Thames in the winter of 1875, and of the drowning of five German nuns, who were passengers and exiles on account of Bismarck's anti-Catholic legislation (the Falk Laws).

It is the first of Hopkins's important poems to be written in what he called ▷ sprung rhythm, which he employed for most of his subsequent poetry; the lines have a regular count of rhythmic stresses but a varying count of syllables. This rhythm enabled Hopkins to combine the emphasis and syntax of the spoken language with the musical devices of the verse, and his use of it illustrates his

statement that the language of poetry is 'that of current speech heightened'. The technique was very foreign to 19th-century ideas of poetic decorum, and explains why the poem was not published until much later: Hopkins offered it to the Jesuit journal *The Month*, but the editor declared that he dared not publish it.

### *Wuthering Heights* (1847)

A novel by ▷ Emily Brontë, first published under the ▷ pseudonym Ellis Bell. The story is narrated by two characters, Lockwood and Nelly Dean, who recount the tale of Heathcliff and his involvement with the Earnshaw and Linton families. The arrival of the foundling Heathcliff disrupts the lives of Catherine Earnshaw and her brother, Hindley. Catherine and Heathcliff develop an intense bond, but Heathcliff overhears her saying to Nelly Dean that marrying him would degrade her. He then leaves Wuthering Heights, returning three years later, by which time Catherine has married Edgar Linton. In revenge, Heathcliff marries Edgar's sister, Isabella, mistreating and brutalizing Hindley and his son, Hareton. Catherine dies shortly after giving birth to a daughter, Cathy. After Edgar's death, Cathy is lured to the Heights and subjected to Heathcliff's terrible will. At the end of the novel, Heathcliff dies and Cathy and Hareton are united. *Wuthering Heights* has generated an enormous body of criticism, and has always been recognized as a novel of great power and originality. Recent interpretations have focused on the complex narrative structure, the novel's treatment of temporarility, its transgression of conventional sexual and moral codes, and its intense examination of the nature of desire.

▷ Orphans; Gothic novel; Romanticism.

### Yates, E.H. (1831–94)

Novelist, dramatist, journalist and editor. A prolific and versatile literary figure, who was drama critic of the *Daily News*, edited various journals before founding the society magazine *World*, was gossip columnist for the *Illustrated Times*, published numerous novels and plays, gave lecture tours and worked for the General Post Office into his forties. His career was profitable but controversial; in 1858 he was expelled from the Garrick Club for insulting ▷ Thackeray in *Town Talk* and in 1885 he was imprisoned for a libellous article in *World*. He was a friend and admirer of ▷ Dickens. His novels are sensational stories of intrigue and crime, including *Running the Gauntlet* (1865), *Land at Last* (1866) and *The Black Sheep* (1876)

▷ Sensation, novel of.

**Bib:** Sutherland, J., *The Longman Companion to Victorian Fiction*.

### Yellow Book

An illustrated quarterly review, 1894–7. It was a main organ of the arts during the period, and although it was especially the voice of the ▷ Aesthetic Movement, it also published writers who did not belong to this movement, eg ▷ Henry James.

▷ Nineties' Poets.

### Yellow peril

A phrase used at the end of the 19th century, expressing the fear that the Mongolian races might sweep across Asia and destroy the European ones. The fear is partly based on previous events, such as the invasion of the West by the Huns, and that of eastern Europe by the Tartars, and partly because of the rise of Japan and hostility to Europeans among the Chinese at the end of the 19th century.

### Yonge, Charlotte (1823–1901)

Editor, historian, biographer, translator and hugely successful novelist. She was born in Otterbourne, near Winchester, where she remained for the rest of her life, apart from visiting Paris briefly in 1869. In 1838 she came under the influence of John Keble and adopted the religious views associated with the ▷ Oxford Movement, which influence all her writing. Her most famous novel, ▷ *The Heir of Redclyffe*, was published in 1853. Other tales of contemporary life include *Heartsease* (1854); *The Daisy Chain* (1856); *The Clever Woman of the Family* (1865) and historical ▷ romances for children (*The Prince and the Page*, 1865, and *The Dove in the Eagle's Nest*, 1866). For forty years she edited the girls' magazine, *The Monthly Packet*.

Yonge was highly religious and conservative, opposed to ▷ women's suffrage and socialism, and a great defender of traditional Victorian standards and morals. The message of *The Clever Woman of the Family* is that women should not pursue intellectual subjects, but accept their inferiority to men.

▷ Women's Movement; Historical novels; Children's literature.

**Bib:** Battiscombe, G., *Charlotte Mary Yonge: An Uneventful Life*; Mare, M. and Percival, A.C., *Victorian Best-Seller: The World of Charlotte M. Yonge*.

# Z

**Zola, Emile Edouard Charles Antoine (1840–1902)**

French novelist. He carried the ▷ realism of ▷ Flaubert a stage further into the doctrine of ▷ naturalism. He believed that the biological sciences (notably the discoveries of ▷ Darwin) had changed the conditions under which the human character should be presented and interpreted, and that in future the novelist should present his characters in relation to the influences of heredity and environment. This he carried out in the succession of novels about the Rougon and Macquart families (1871–93) including *La Fortune des Rougon* (1871), *La Curée* (1874), *Le Ventre de Paris* (1874), *La Conquête de Plassans* (1875), *La Faute de l'Abbé Mouret* (1875), *Son Excellence Eugène Rougon* (1876), *L'Assommoir* (1878), *Nana* (1880), *Germinal* (1885), *La Terre* (1888), *La Débâcle* (1892) and *Docteur Pascal* (1893). Zola's influence was healthy in England inasmuch as his doctrine counteracted an English prejudice against the ugly, the 'indecent' and the horrible in art. He had English imitators, eg ▷ George Moore, and he influenced such realists as ▷ George Gissing and ▷ H.G. Wells.